Jesuit Saints and Blesseds

SPIRITUAL PROFILES

FOREWORD BY
Father General
Arturo Sosa, SJ

D1611543

HISTORICAL
INTRODUCTIONS BY
John W. O'Malley, SJ

EDITED BY
Jacques Fédry, SJ and
Marc Lindeijer, SJ

Library of Congress Control Number: 2023933531
ISBN: 978–1–947617–17–9
Copyright 2023 by the Jesuit Conference, Inc., United States.

"Compagnons de Jésus, pour aimer et server," © Éditions Vie chrétienne, 2020 - 47, rue de la Roquette 75011 Paris, France. www.viechretienne.fr

Cover Design: Keith Ake

Cover Photography: Mark Beane, © Copyright 2007, Loyola University Chicago.

Institute of Jesuit Sources
at the Institute for Advanced Jesuit Studies
Boston College
140 Commonwealth Avenue
Chestnut Hill, MA 02467, USA

Email: iajs@bc.edu
https://jesuitsources.bc.edu

Fees are subject to change

INSTITUTE FOR
ADVANCED JESUIT STUDIES
BOSTON COLLEGE

Jesuit Saints and Blesseds
Spiritual Profiles

Edited by Jacques Fédry, SJ and Marc Lindeijer, SJ

Jesuit Saints and Blesseds

SPIRITUAL PROFILES

Institute of Jesuit Sources
Boston College

Table of Contents

5

Foreword

In the Ignatian Year 2021-22, the Society of Jesus and the Church celebrated the centenaries of the conversion (1521) and canonization (1622) of Saint Ignatius. We know how important it was for him, in order to "see all things new in Christ," to read the Lives of the saints, which together with the *Life of Christ* were offered to him in Loyola. From this was born his initial desire to imitate them.

In the *Spiritual Exercises*, which he began to write in Manresa, the "saints of the heavenly court" appear to him at key moments of discernment and choice. Before those saints, too, Jesuits pronounce their vows. Moreover, Ignatius encourages retreatants, from the second week of the retreat, to read the Lives of the saints as something "greatly beneficial."

Aware of the importance that the Society of Jesus has given from the beginning to its saints and blessed, the editors of this book have opportunely chosen the celebration of the Ignatian Year to bring out a new edition of "spiritual profiles." The first edition, in various languages, was published in 1974 by the Liturgical Commission and the Office of the Postulator General of the Society, and edited by Paolo Molinari, SJ. Several generations, individually and in community, have been helped by it to rediscover our spiritual tradition. It has allowed us to acquire an interior knowledge of the many men and women who make up the Society's family of saints, whom we often know only superficially.

Since then, the Church has continued to canonize and beatify our companions, whose lives and heroic martyrdom should also be an encouragement to us. First of all, this is because the saints are the best way for us to understand the Gospel, translating and shaping it into accessible and stimulating examples of Christian life. As is often said, they are the ones who have best followed the path of the imitation of Christ, the same path that we are walking ourselves. Secondly, because they show us—Jesuits and non-Jesuits—with great realism and accuracy how the charism and the spirituality of Saint Ignatius have borne fruit in such varied and rich ways, and in so many places.

Each of us can have our favorite saint and feel more affinity with one or the other. But their great diversity reveals to us that in every circumstance and life situation in which the Society of Jesus has played its part, it has been possible to live in an extraordinary way the daily dedication to the mission entrusted to us. In all these cases, our saints and blessed have been recognized as models of union with Christ and as "men for others." In fact, before being canonized by the Church, their heroic way of life or their generous death has been attested to by witnesses and documents—solid proof that their example was important and meaningful to this or that place or time and, as such, fruitful and conducive to the good life.

Is there a specific and typical way of living holiness in an Ignatian way? Certainly! Given some basic evangelical characteristics, the *Constitutions* indicate a few elements when setting before us our ideal of life. I am referring to the so-called "solid and perfect virtues" acquired through self-denial, which is practiced by setting aside all "self-love, desire, and interest." And the virtues that Saint Ignatius prefers are humility, charity, obedience, and poverty. It is precisely on this last virtue that we will focus our attention in the Ignatian Year —poverty as the domain where we perceive the call to conversion.

Some of the spiritual profiles in this new edition depict non-Jesuits who shared our life and mission; moreover, several of these notices have been written by non-Jesuit experts. Others have been preserved from the first edition. Yet all of them show well "the most beautiful face of the Church," as Pope Francis said (*Gaudete et exsultate*, 9). That face is shaped by the examples of people who abandoned themselves to God and followed more closely and intensely the way of Jesus Christ. They are the beacon that illuminates and guides us in our mission with the inspired light of Saint Ignatius. Imitating our saints and blessed and imploring their intercession will help us to better develop our vocation.

Arturo Sosa, SJ
March 12, 2020
Canonization Day of Saint Ignatius of Loyola[1]

---

1. Translation Marc Lindeijer, SJ.

Introduction

*For in reading the life of Our Lord, and of the saints, he stopped
to think, reasoning within himself: "What if I should do this
which Saint Francis did? And this which Saint Dominic did?"*

Ignatius of Loyola, Test §7

Over five hundred years ago, in 1521, Ignatius was recovering from a shot
wound at his home at Loyola when his heart and mind were transformed by
reading the life of Christ and the lives of the saints. This book invites the reader to a similar experience: "What would it be like if I did what Saint Ignatius
did, and what the saints and blesseds of the Society of Jesus did, following
its founder?" Their lives can help us enter more deeply into the spirit of the
religious family to which the Jesuits are proud to belong, as well as the members of the various Ignatian religious congregations, the members of Chemin
Neuf, those of the Christian Life Communities (CLC), and many others. It is
also a powerful incentive. These older brothers in the Society show us how
the Spiritual Exercises shaped them and helped them orient their lives, beginning with Ignatius's two Parisian roommates, Peter Faber and Francis Xavier,
who became saints in his company. Just as Ignatius's Autobiography allows
us to enter into his spirit, the profiles of the Jesuit saints and blesseds nourish
our understanding of Ignatian spirituality.

The fifty feasts of saints and blesseds on the Jesuit liturgical calendar in
2020 seem to have a certain equilibrium: twenty-seven feasts of confessors
and twenty-three of martyrs. But in reality the numerical differences are much
greater, because the martyrs are counted in groups, sometimes small like
the five martyrs of Salcete, more often large, like the forty martyrs of Brazil
or the fifty-six martyrs of China. So many Jesuits and their lay collaborators
gave their lives to Christ in the "foreign missions," mainly in Japan, India,
South and North America. Others suffered death in Christian Europe in the
sixteenth and seventeenth centuries, during the violent phases of the Refor-

mation. More recently, others again fell victim to anti-religious persecution brought about by atheistic regimes, from the French Revolution to the civil wars in Spain, Mexico, and Albania.

Presenting all the martyrs was impossible. We had to choose among those that are best known or best represent the group, with a certain preference for small "bands" that show how the martyrs—Jesuits and non-Jesuits alike—worked together for the greater glory of God.

There is another intriguing disparity. After the abundance of Jesuit saints and blesseds in the second half of the sixteenth century, and again in the seventeenth, they seem to become scarce in the eighteenth century (despite the 23 Jesuit martyrs of the French Revolution) and in the first half of the nineteenth, that is, before and after the suppression of the Society of Jesus (1773–1814). Is this a sign of the order's decline in this period? Or were there other causes? We leave it to the historians to answer that question. Here, we will focus on the saints that were, not on those who might have been ...

The organization of the book is evident from the table of contents: the order of the profiles is partly chronological, partly "categorical." In this, we follow the new liturgical calendar of the Society of Jesus, which has grouped a number of saints and blesseds according to their shared charism, apostolate, or historical context. Also, we thought that those who would like to read this work from cover to cover might find it more convenient this way.

The "liturgical" reader, who would like to meditate on the life of a saint or blessed according to the feasts, can use as an index the liturgical calendar of the Society of Jesus, reproduced at the end of the book.

The subtitle of this book, *Spiritual Profiles*, is taken from a booklet published in 1974. Like the growth of a tree over fifty years, this new publication is both a continuity and a new extension. Continuity of a work well done, the initiative of Father General Pedro Arrupe, which was edited by the then postulator general Paolo Molinari, SJ and published for the use of Jesuits only. Nineteen of the biographies from this first publication have been reproduced here, that is, half of them, sometimes with slight revisions.

But it is also an extension. After forty-six years, the first work needed to be updated. Ten new biographies have been included, taken from the *Yearbook of the Society of Jesus*, which faithfully reports on the latest beatifications and canonizations by publishing articles, often written by Jesuits who worked for the cause of the saint concerned. We are very grateful to Pierre Bélanger, SJ and Caterina Talloru of the Public Relations Office of the general curia, who made these articles available to us, as well as to the Society's postulator general, Pascual Cebollada, SJ, and Valeria Torchio, who helped us in many ways.

For the other saints and blesseds, added to our liturgical calendar long ago or in recent times, we have looked for biographies elsewhere, in serious journals or on reliable websites, or we have asked current specialists for their contribution; tellingly, they are no longer only Jesuits. The enthusiasm with which they offered their help stimulated and touched us.

From the start, it has been our desire to illuminate the lives of the saints by putting them into their historical context. This has been made possible, more than we had dared to hope for, thanks to the contribution of the eminent Jesuit historian John W. O'Malley, SJ.

In keeping with Ignatian wisdom, which prefers depth to length, the profiles are relatively brief, suited to spiritual reading. Here and there, we have added a meditative text, taken from the writings of the saints or from papal homilies and letters of the superior general written on the occasion of a beatification or canonization. In some cases, we were able to add a prayer formulated by a saint or a blessed of the Society.

This collection is meant to appear in French, English, and Spanish. We would like to thank Fathers Walter Boehme, Philip Cooley, and Michael Kolb, who generously helped translating a number of biographies into English. We also mention with reverence Guy Verhaegen, SJ, who passed away in 2019. He translated and distributed the summary made by Thomas Rochford, SJ of Joseph Tylenda's classic *Jesuit Saints and Martyrs*, which served as our inspiration.

A special word of gratitude goes to Father General Arturo Sosa. When he kindly agreed to write the preface, no one thought that he would have to do so, confined in the general curia because of the COVID-19 pandemic. But, as more than one biography in this book shows us, Jesuits, including superior generals, have often been in the front line in times of epidemics.

Finally, our gratitude goes to the French CLC publisher Vie Chrétienne, in particular to its editor-in-chief Françoise Bordeyne, and to the Boston College Institute for Advanced Jesuit Studies and its director Casey Beaumier, SJ, for the great care given to this publication.

The history of the saints of the Society of Jesus is like a fire that spreads, from the days of Saint Ignatius to our time: may it ignite the heart of the reader!

Jacques Fédry, SJ and Marc Lindeijer, SJ
Brazzaville/Breda, July 31, 2021
Feast of Saint Ignatius of Loyola

To Be a Soldier of God under the Standard of the Cross, and to Serve God Alone in the Church under the Leadership of the Sovereign Pontiff

Whoever desires to serve as a soldier of God beneath the banner of the cross in our Society, which we desire to be designated by the name of Jesus, and to serve the Lord alone and the Church, his spouse, under the Roman pontiff, the vicar of Christ on earth, should, after a solemn vow of perpetual chastity, poverty, and obedience, keep what follows in mind. He is a member of a Society founded chiefly for this purpose: to strive especially for the defense and propagation of the faith and for the progress of souls in Christian life and doctrine, by means of public preaching, lectures, and any other ministration whatsoever of the Word of God, and further by means of the *Spiritual Exercises*, the education of children and unlettered persons and the spiritual consolation of Christ's faithful through hearing confessions and administering the other sacraments. Moreover, he should show himself ready to reconcile the estranged, compassionately assist and serve those in prisons or hospitals, and indeed to perform any other works of charity, according to what will seem expedient for the glory of God and the common good. Furthermore, all these works should be carried out altogether free of charge and without accepting any remuneration for the labor expended in all the aforementioned activities. Still further, let any such person take care, as long as he lives, first of all to keep before his eyes God and then the nature of this Institute, which is, so to speak, a pathway to God; and then let him strive with all his effort to achieve this end set before him by God—each one, however, according to the grace that the Holy Spirit has given to him and according to the particular grade of his own vocation.

The Formula of the Institute of the Society of Jesus, no. 1, approved by Pope Julius III in 1550

Part 1

THE ORIGINS (1540–56)

"Spain with its mountains, its rivers, its cities, its peoples and its islands. In the northern center we see Azpeitia and Pamplona, from where the pilgrim Ignatius of Loyola began his journey to Rome and the founding of the Society of Jesus."

Sebastian Münster, Cosmographey oder Beschreibung aller Länder (around 1550). First edition of the map of Spain, Portugal, and the Islands of Majorca and Minorca.

O n September 27, 1540, Pope Paul III issued the Bull *Regimini militantis ecclesiae* approving the Society of Jesus and empowering its members to minister in the Catholic Church. He thereby put this nascent religious order on the same juridical level as the Dominicans, Franciscans, and other orders. The very fact of being born in the mid-sixteenth century, however, helped create a spiritual and ministerial profile for the Society that was different in significant ways from that of the older religious families.

In the first place, a new political order took shape in Europe at that time. Spain finally united as one country with the marriage of Ferdinand of Aragon and Isabella of Castile, and Portugal's monarchs assumed greater authority over the country. France fully emerged from the devastations of the Hundred Years' War to become a wealthy, strong, and aggressive monarchy. England took shape under the Tudor dynasty at the end of the War of the Roses, and the Holy Roman Empire produced an emperor, Charles V, with resources seemingly sufficient to bring order to that fractious collection of political units.

That situation deeply affected the fortunes of the Society of Jesus, offering both opportunities and challenges. The Spanish and Portuguese, for instance, had taken command of the seas. They explored new lands, established colonies, and carried with them missionaries to evangelize the native people. Scholars call this phenomenon "the first globalization."

That reality made indelible inroads into the consciousness and concerns of the members of the Society of Jesus, as indicated by the fact that fully professed Jesuits pronounced a special "Fourth Vow" to be missionaries. We should not be surprised, therefore, that in the very year Paul III approved the order, Francis Xavier was, at the behest of the king of Portugal, already on his way to "the Indies."

"Indies" was a term used loosely to refer to almost everywhere outside Europe. For the Spanish, it meant the southern half of the Western hemisphere. Missionaries other than the Jesuits had been at work there since the time of Columbus. The Portuguese established claims to Brazil—the Jesuits arrived there in 1547—but also ventured into Southeast Asia as traders and colonizers.

India was where the Portuguese first arrived. They quickly managed to turn Goa into a colonial center, which missionaries began to use as a base whence they ministered to the indigenous peoples, many of whom were poor and illiterate. Xavier arrived there in 1542. The Portuguese also had their eyes on present-day Indonesia, and, most significantly, on Japan, where Xavier set foot in 1549. As an advanced civilization, Japan posed challenges for Jesuit missionaries, unlike those they met elsewhere.

In Europe itself, religious practice flourished. At every level of society, churches were full, priests and nuns abundant, pilgrimages and the cult of relics flourishing. Confraternities—pious voluntary associations, especially of laypersons—seemed ubiquitous. It was a religious age.

Nonetheless, critics at the time satirized its religious practices as mechanical, superficial, and sometimes superstitious—a piety without spiritual depth. They made easy fun of ignorant priests and greedy prelates. They took special aim at the venality of the papal court.

Dark though the situation may have been in some places and in some regards, it was in other places and in other regards bright and promising. The religious orders, for instance, had for over a century undertaken, at least intermittently, a program of self-reform. In Spain, Ferdinand and especially Isabella had promoted an effective reform of the Spanish clergy.

The demand for "reformed priests"—educated, virtuous, and devout—emerged as an ideal that had to be realized across the Church. People paid the Jesuits a welcome compliment when they referred to them as reformed priests. More broadly, the cry for reform of the Church "in head and members, in faith and mores" had become a mantra for serious Christians across Europe. It was a leitmotif of the Council of Trent, which met intermittently in three periods from 1545 to 1563.

Martin Luther and then other Protestant reformers raised the most strident and radical calls for reform. Peter Faber was the first of the Society of Jesus's original ten companions to live for a while in the Holy Roman Empire, where the Reformation broke out and at first seemed poised to conquer it. Even so, Ignatius did not reckon it as a special concern of the Society until the last year of his life.

It was not the Reformation but Renaissance humanism, a powerful literary, cultural, and educational movement, that had the more immediate impact on the Jesuits. By mid-century, it had burst out of its birthplace in Italy onto the full European stage. Its practitioners were by then well on the way to convincing upper-class Europeans that no one was truly educated unless educated according to their program. The program aimed at forming a certain kind of person—ethical, reflective, devoted to the common good, a person equipped with rhetorical skills to lead others along that good path.

The Jesuits almost immediately found that program marvelously consonant with the formational goals of their own ministry. The program was, moreover, consonant with the "war against ignorance and superstition" that engaged leaders of society everywhere in Europe. Few objectives were more characteristic of the sixteenth century.

By 1550, Ignatius had committed the Society to founding and staffing schools according to the humanist program. The schools produced upright laymen but also fostered vocations to the priesthood and religious life.

The humanists turned their attention to simplifying theology by focusing it on the basic mysteries of Creation and the Incarnation. In so doing, they created a distinctive and attractive model of piety that was altogether different from the model they widely satirized. Andrea Brenta, a preacher imbued with humanist ideals of piety, beautifully summarized it in a sermon in the Sistine Chapel before Pope Sixtus IV in 1483: "Our cult of God is spiritual. It consists in thinking honest thoughts, speaking helpful words, doing good deeds, and firming up a wealth of virtue that no accident of fortune can snatch away." Once again, the humanists sounded a note the Jesuits found congenial to their own piety.

Humanists turned their literary skills to sacred texts and were able in some instances to recover realities that the centuries had obscured. They recovered, for instance, the literal meaning of "apostolic life" (*vita apostolica*) to mean the life of itinerant preachers of the Gospel. They made clear that Saint Paul exemplified the apostolic life most perfectly and dramatically. Paul was just as much the exemplar of the ideal Christian missionary as he was teacher and theologian. No wonder that Jerome Nadal, Ignatius's peripatetic agent in the field and best interpreter, told the Jesuits, "Paul is our model in ministry."

Important for the Jesuits though the piety and educational ideals of the humanist movement were, the "Devotio Moderna" exercised an earlier and more palpable impact. The Devotio had developed in the Low Countries in the late fourteenth century. It flourished and had a pan-European impact. The monastery of Montserrat in Spain became an important center of it.

The most important product of the Devotio Moderna was the *Imitation of*

Christ, the spiritual classic that was a call to interiority. Ignatius discovered the book early in his conversion and recommended it to others from that point forward. The third of the *Imitation*'s four parts was entitled "The Book of Internal Consolation," which suggests the strong level of influence the book had on Jesuit spirituality.

Ludolph of Saxony's *Life of Christ* was another product of the Devotio that had widespread diffusion. An important feature in it was a method of prayer that consisted in an imaginative placing oneself in a biblical scene and interacting with the persons there. The method made the Bible passages personal and thus able to touch the soul in an intimate and affective way. It is only one instance of the broad influence of the Devotio Moderna on the early Society of Jesus.

Ignatius's inward journey took on new depth at Manresa, where he made notes regarding it, the nucleus out of which the *Spiritual Exercises* developed. It is difficult to exaggerate the originality of that book. Although it can at first glance seem to be a tissue of late-medieval devotional practices, it marshaled them into coherent yet flexible programs to enable persons to get in touch with themselves and with God acting in their lives. In the whole of Christian literature up to that time, nothing like it existed. Its seedbed was the spiritual yearning of the age in which Ignatius lived, but the *Exercises* became symbol and engine for deepening that yearning. It was the touchstone and first foundation for the spirituality of the Society of Jesus and therefore of the spirituality of the saints that God gave the Society.

John W. O'Malley, SJ

The Holy Name of Jesus

TITULAR FEAST OF THE SOCIETY OF JESUS

Solemnity on January 3

Eight days after Mary's child was born, he was incorporated into the People of God by the rite of circumcision, and, in accordance with God's will, he was given the name Jesus. It is this Holy Name that the Church celebrates on January 3, and the Society of Jesus has chosen this as the principal feast on its calendar.

It is the most important of its feasts because, while others remind us how the saints gave living witness of the spirit of their order, the feast of the Holy Name sums up the spirit itself: to have for our sole model and rule of life, and our only Lord, Jesus, the son of Mary.

They Wanted to Serve Jesus Christ

The choice of the title "Society of Jesus" marks an important stage in the history of the Jesuits. It took place at the end of a long period of preparation, in Paris and Venice, before any plan had been worked out to found a new religious order. After their collective oblation to God at Montmartre in 1534 and their priestly ordination at Venice in 1537, Ignatius and his companions divided into groups of two or three; some of them continued their studies while the others set out for Rome.

The future was very indeterminate. Although they did not yet know that they were to become a religious order, they were conscious of being, in the fullest sense of the word, a community. Then, at Vicenza, before separating, they chose a name: they would call themselves the Society of Jesus. They did not think of themselves as the Society of Ignatius or anybody else. Ten years later, recording their impressions, Juan Alfonso de Polanco was to observe that "there was no other leader or superior among them except Christ, and it was him alone they wanted to serve."[2] It was with this goal in view that they went to put themselves at the disposal of the pope.

This first decision was soon confirmed by the interior experience that Ignatius underwent on the road to Rome, especially in the vision subsequently established as having occurred at La Storta, just outside Rome. According to Diego Laínez, who, along with Peter Faber, accompanied him on the journey, Ignatius said that it seemed as if he saw Christ with the Cross on his shoulder and next to him the Eternal Father saying to him, "I want you to take this man as your servant." So Jesus took him and said, "I want you to be our servant."[3]

It was evidently this vision at La Storta that made Ignatius decide to establish irrevocably the name the companions had chosen during their deliberations at Vicenza. Laínez concludes his account by saying: "Having conceived a very great devotion for this most holy Name, Ignatius wished to call the congregation the 'Society of Jesus.'"[4]

The companions continued their deliberations in Rome and eventually decided to form a religious institute. The Formula of the Institute, in its opening line, asked the pope to give official recognition to the adopted name, "Society of Jesus."

Jesus, Companion on the Journey

Those are the historical data, but what did these men mean by using the name of Jesus to designate their group? At first sight, nothing special: after all, every Christian can claim fellowship with Christ. For them, however, and for their brethren today, the title carries clear echoes. It defines the way they have chosen.

It was Jesus who transformed what proved to be the most zealous of human lives: not only Peter, John, and Paul but also others like Francis of Assisi and Dominic. Setting out in the footsteps of those whose devotion to their master

---

2. *Fontes Narrativi* I, Mon. 7, no. 86 (Monumenta Ignatiana IV-I) (Rome 1943), 204.

3. *Fontes Narrativi* II, Scriptum 25 (Monumenta Ignatiana IV-II) (Madrid 1918), 74–75.

4. Ibid.

Giovanni Battista Gaulli, known as Baciccio, The Triumph of the Most Holy Name of Jesus (late 1670s), fresco in the Church of the Gesù, Rome (Italy).

was absolute, the companions of Ignatius thought to themselves: Why not us too?[5]

Jesus, designated by his own name rather than by the title of Christ; Jesus, true man, our divine companion along the road of life, sharing our hardships, our joys, our sorrows: we must contemplate him, we must "know, love, and follow" him (*Spir. Ex.*, 104) in order to know the way to the Kingdom, to find the words that impart God's message, and to have the attitude to life by which we can bear witness to him: poor because he was poor, ready to accept humiliations because he did so (*Spir. Ex.*, 167). In a word, the living Jesus is to be our rule of life.

Jesus is to direct our work. Our apostolate is not to be limited in advance, either in its forms or methods or scope. A listening heart, eyes raised towards the Lord to see where he is looking and whom he wishes to benefit from our work. "We must hold ourselves poised, like the pointer on a scale, ready to move towards what we feel to be more in conformity with the glory and praise of God our Lord and the salvation of our souls" (*Spir. Ex.*, 179).

Jesus is to be our guide and our master, and he is the soul of the community in which we serve him together; we must seek him, not in heated argument, but in communal deliberation; after the superior will make his will known to us, to protect us from the danger of following only our own inclinations under the guise of obedience.

We must recognize Jesus joyfully and unhesitatingly in his Church, giving him our personal service by putting ourselves at the disposal of the successor of Peter through whom alone every organization does its work as a member of the whole body of the Church.

On his way to Rome, Ignatius earnestly prayed to the Madonna to "put him with her Son." He was sure his prayer would be heard by God (*Autobiography*, 96). To be with Jesus the Son of God "in suffering and then in glory" (*Spir. Ex.*, 95) is something we cannot achieve by ourselves: only the Spirit of God can bring about this assimilation. Being a companion of Jesus is not just a juridical expression nor an undertaking in which we keep a certain degree

---

5. The newly converted Ignatius wanted to emulate the heroism of the saints (*Autobiography*, 7). No doubt he subsequently purified his earlier intention, but many others, like Ignatius, discovered in the witness of the saints how worthy Christ is of our service.

of independence and the prospect of great personal achievement. It is a way of living for the Gospel in constant dependence on the Spirit of God: it is our sharing in the mystery of the Incarnation.

The honor and service of God in the faithful following of the example set by Jesus himself have been the very life of the saints in our calendar: that is the path we must follow too.

José Feder, SJ

Saint Ignatius of Loyola (1491–1556)

FOUNDER OF THE SOCIETY OF JESUS

Solemnity on July 31

Ignatius of Loyola wished to disappear behind the work that God asked him to accomplish. To discover him, we must turn to the testimony of his first companions.

In the Twilight of the Middle Ages (1491–1522)

By birth and education, Ignatius was still a man of the Middle Ages. His universe was that of the romances of chivalry: to distinguish himself by doing great deeds for the love and service of a lady of high lineage. His faith was unwavering, but it was based more on a received heritage than on personal adherence. His education was that of a page: fencing, horsemanship, poetry, music. A tenacious legend presents him as a military man, converted at the age of thirty following a wound received during the siege of Pamplona. In truth, he was never a military man, but like all the nobles of his time, he was ready to take up arms in defense of his suzerain. This is what he did when the French attacked Navarre. He ran to defend the besieged Pamplona and locked himself up in the citadel, where he was the soul of the resistance. On May 20, 1521, he was wounded; the besieged surrendered. The French, as a tribute to his courage, treated his wounds and had him carried on a litter to Loyola. This feat of arms, the only one of his life, lasted only a few days. Previously, he signaled himself to the attention of the viceroy of Navarre in missions of a diplomatic nature. Sent to restore peace in the provinces in effervescence, he showed there great aptitudes to "deal with the men."

As a teenager in the service of two distinguished Spanish nobles—the minister of finance of Ferdinand and Isabella, then the viceroy of Navarre—he experienced a brilliant society. Spain had just completed its reconquest of the Moors with the capture of Granada. It opened itself to distant adventures with the discovery of America. Before the rest of Europe, it was already experiencing an intellectual and spiritual renaissance with Cardinal Cisneros' reform of university and Church. It was at the beginning of the sixteenth century, which would be its golden age, the one that would give to the Church, along with Ignatius, Francis Xavier, Peter of Alcántara, Teresa of Ávila, John of the Cross, Francis Borgia ...

Anchored in the Middle Ages and open to new horizons, the Spain where Ignatius grew up remained on its guard against the new ideas that were beginning to agitate Northern Europe: Erasmus, for example, remained suspect. And when Ignatius, during his long convalescence at Loyola, began to look inwardly at himself and to raise questions about his new life, it was as a man of the Middle Ages that he reacted. He saw himself as a knight of Christ, imitating the noble deeds of the saints, and his gaze spontaneously turned to Jerusalem, where he decided to make a pilgrimage.

He Left Alone and on Foot (1522–28)

The manner in which he made up his mind, however, was already that of a new man. He could have asked one of the great spiritual institutions of the Middle Ages to accept him and guide his convert's fervor. He thought of this for a moment, thinking of entering the Carthusian monastery in Burgos. The path he took was different, and this explains the difficulties he would have for a long time with the Inquisition (no fewer than eight trials in twelve years). He made his decision alone, following what he called the divine motions: the inspirations he received in prayer. And from then on, he would have no other course of action, waiting in prayer for God to make his will known to him, showing himself to be as resolute in its execution as he was patient and prudent in his decision. In this way of acting, he was already a man of the new times: the one who becomes the subject of his actions. Not that he was seduced by new ideas or revolted by the past, but he experienced the Spirit's guidance in this regard. In Loyola, then in Montserrat, in Manresa, and in Jerusalem, throughout this four-year peregrination, he recognized that God was speaking to him, calling him through the disparate movements of his spiritual sensitivity, enlightening him about his deepest desires. A God who expects a response from him. He did not dictate it; it was up to Ignatius to find it by preparing himself in advance for the divine will and by using all the riches of his intelligence and his heart to discern and accomplish it.

Setting out alone, with no other support or guide than the Spirit who led him, he went from stage to stage, not knowing where God was leading him, experiencing little by little the way of life that would become his and that of his companions. The first important stage was Montserrat, where he made a general confession of his past sins and gave his sword to Our Lady after a long night of prayer on the feast of the Annunciation. Having exchanged his clothes with a beggar, he left the monastery early in the morning. On his way to Jerusalem, he stopped in Manresa to write down in his notebook some points that seemed important to him. He stayed there for nine months in solitude, prayer, and penance. This was to be, he would later say, his first Church: the time when God, taking pity on his inexperience, led him by the hand like a child.

In fact, God led him to the desert to relive the experience of all his chosen ones: that of spiritual combat. Tried and tempted to the point of suicide, he persevered in the life of prayer and penance that he had set for himself, never doubting this God who was so far away. Filled with the highest mystical graces, he kept a cool head, asking himself only what God expects of him. He kept a record of all this, noting in his notebook what seemed useful for his personal conduct and perhaps for that of others, if God allowed him to do some good one day by helping souls, as he began to do in the few conversations he had with those who came to speak to him in his hermitage. This notebook, from which Ignatius would never part, would become the *Spiritual Exercises,* which he would use in Paris to win his first companions to the service of God.

When the time appeared ripe, he left Manresa, arriving in Jerusalem at the end of a pilgrimage, during which he sought to live in the most radical poverty, an expression of his total trust in God. Now, having reached his desired goal, he determined to brave everything to remain in Jerusalem at the service of the Holy Places. However, when the Franciscan provincial ordered him to leave in the name of the Church, he submitted without a word. God's will could not lead him to oppose the Church.

The Schoolboy of God (1528–38)

Back in Barcelona, matured by the graces and trials of those years of solitary journey, at the age of thirty-three, Ignatius made a decision that nothing in his past could have predicted: he returned to school. Not just for a few years, the time that would allow him to become a priest, but for ten years, in Alcala, in Salamanca, and finally in Paris. He, whom God had taken to his school, now put himself in the school of his own time, humbly, patiently, beginning with the basics, without worrying about the passage of time and what an adult of his caliber could accomplish on the world stage. The test turned out to be more radical than he had anticipated. In order to study to help souls, he would have to give up the life he had chosen and in which he had found great joy, that of following Christ as a poor pilgrim. So he did what the needy students did, he would work during the vacations in order to pay for his room and board during the year. Moreover, he came to recognize that studies take all of the man and that the spirit, tired by the courses and the school exercises, can no longer taste the spiritual joys that were familiar to him. He renounced them, convinced that the most important thing was to courageously do God's will. Undertaken for the sole service of God, studies became for him, in their very austerity, the best of devotions.

In Alcala, in Salamanca, he gathered around himself some companions to whom he tried to communicate his desire to study in order to help souls. The inquisitor suspected the group of unorthodoxy, the companions became discouraged, and Ignatius once again left for Paris alone. Made more discerning by this first community experience, Ignatius, in Paris, would put all his care into recognizing and forming those whom God wanted to call with him to his service. He would guide them, as he himself had been guided, in the experience of the *Spiritual Exercises*, thus giving them the possibility of discerning and maturing a commitment to follow Christ. Thus Peter Faber, Francis Xavier, and others became his companions and disciples.

On August 15, 1534, they met on the hill of Montmartre, at the Chapel of the Martyrs; Faber, who was a priest, celebrated Mass. Before taking communion, all seven of them pledged to live in celibacy and poverty and to make the pilgrimage to Jerusalem at the end of their studies. If this proved impossible, they would then put themselves at the disposal of the pope for any mission that he would like to entrust to them, among the faithful or the infidels.

Ignatius was forty-three years old; until then, he had been a solitary man on the paths of God. From now on, his life became inseparable from that of the companions he had hoped for and received from the hand of God. His biography, which was written in "I," will now be written in "we." The seven from Paris would remain faithful to him; it is together that they met in Venice in the hope of leaving for Jerusalem. As this proved impossible, they met in Rome to put themselves at the service of the pope.

Rome and the New Times (1538–40)

On the outskirts of Rome, Ignatius stopped for a moment in the chapel of La Storta to entrust his future to God. There he experienced a profound spiritual illumination that reminded him of those in Manresa. He sees himself associated with the mission of Jesus and hears the Father say to him: "In Rome, I will be favorable to you." From then on, he had no hesitation about the name of Companions of Jesus that they had given themselves in Venice to answer the questions they were asked, nor about the way of life that it meant for them.

He entered Rome, leaving Jerusalem behind. Jerusalem was still the Middle Ages, the pilgrimage and the crusade. Rome was the Renaissance and the reform of the Church: the new world. Denying nothing of the past that had carried his dreams and forged his desire to serve, he turned resolutely towards the future. What guided him, once again, was not a brilliant strategic intuition, but a sign from God, a motion from the Spirit.

What would they do in Rome? Ignatius didn't yet know. He was free, available, rooted in the love of the poor and humble Christ, convinced that there was nothing greater than helping souls to order their lives for the service of God.

At the end of these long years of preparation, events were beginning to unfold rapidly. In two years, the companions, still an informal and unknown group, suspected by the Inquisition—Ignatius would have to confront it one last time upon his arrival in Rome—would become a new religious order approved by the Church. In Rome, they set to work, caring for the sick in hospitals and preaching in the squares, as they had become accustomed to doing on their travels from Paris to Venice and then to Rome. Pope Paul III—who a few years later would convene the Council of Trent—received them and blessed them, entrusting them with missions in Rome, in Italy, and soon in India.

Were they to disperse and thereby remain faithful to their vow of availability? Did God, who had gathered them from different nations—there were now ten of them—have no other purpose for them than to lead them to the pope, or did he expect their group to seek recognition of the Church for the kind of life that he had led them to discover? In other words, should they keep only spiritual companionship among themselves or should they try to form a new religious order? They deliberated together, with Ignatius remaining at the heart of the group's discussions without steering it according to his views.

The question was not simple. The Church was not ready to admit new foundations; it had even rejected the idea in principle at the Fourth Lateran Council. However, the companions were aware that the vocation they had discovered together could not be lived under any of the existing rules. After having discussed it among themselves, and realizing that they had divergent opinions, they decided to entrust this question to God in prayer. They would meet again three months later to share what God had communicated to them. They were surprised to find that they were unanimous in their belief that God was calling them to form a religious order. Ignatius was asked by the group to write a draft proposal to present to the pope for approval. Upon reading it, Paul III is reported to have said, "The finger of God is here." He then entrusted it to the papal curia for examination. Against all odds and in less than a year, the text was approved without correction and became the founding bull of the Society in 1540.

A Man for the Mission (1541–56)

Did Ignatius think his role ended there? He had been a gatherer; now it was up to someone else to lead the group that had become a religious order. He refused to accept the vote of the companions who unanimously chose him as superior. He asked for a second vote with the same result, then for a period of reflection, and only accepted when his confessor made it clear that further opposition would be a lack of docility to the Holy Spirit. Xavier, at the request of the pope, had already taken the road to India; the others would very quickly disperse. Ignatius remained in Rome and never left. The pilgrim became a writer: from his work table, an incessant correspondence linked him to his companions in Europe, Asia, and soon in Africa and America. For them, he clarified the modalities of this way of proceeding to which God had called

Domenico Zampieri, known as Domenichino, Saint Ignatius of Loyola sees Christ and God the Father at La Storta (circa 1622).

them and which the Church had just recognized. For them too, he prepared the *Constitutions* that were to become the rule of life for companions.

He did this in his own way, in fidelity to the manner God had formed him. He reflected, surrounded himself with advice and authorized opinions, submitted his ideas to the scrutiny of experience, presented contentious points to God in prayer, and finally maked up his mind according to the promptings of the Spirit. He was not in a hurry to finish. When in 1551 he presented a first draft to the companions gathered in Rome, he humbly, perhaps too humbly, accepted the remarks and criticisms and patiently went back to work. Instead of adopting, as is the custom in similar texts, a thematic plan dealing successively with the different obligations of religious life, he chose a genetic plan that takes the Jesuit at his entry into the Society, and follows him in his formation to lead him to a life of an apostle in a religious body structured for the mission. This concrete and progressive way of seeing things, more pedagogical than normative, was very characteristic of his spirit.

The Society developed rapidly: the ten of 1540 would become a thousand by the death of Ignatius in 1556. This success worried him a little: he wondered if the spiritual demands of the mission were well understood. He then wrote a text for the superiors called to examine the candidates for the Society, in which he strongly recalled the traits that should mark this following of the poor and humble Christ.

The apostolic fields diversified. From the Indies, Xavier went as far as Japan and died exhausted off the coast of China in 1552, before he received Ignatius's letter calling him back to Rome to take stock of his mission. Jesuits left for Ethiopia with long instructions from Ignatius, both precise and open, for this famous kingdom of Priester John, about which almost nothing was known except that Christians were living there, separated from Rome. In Europe, the Society saw a field of action open up that Ignatius had not foreseen: the education of youth. He committed himself to this field without hesitation as soon as it appeared to him that the greater glory of God was at stake. He did not hesitate to adapt the lifestyle of his companions, which he had initially thought to be more itinerant, to better accommodate this new mode of action.

Both inside and outside the Society, he encountered opposition. The kind of life he proposed was so new, both common and daring. Some would like it to be more marked by traditional religious practices: long periods of prayer, services sung in the choir. Others found it difficult to accept the availability and self-denial that apostolic mobility implies and hesitated to leave those to whom they had given themselves to go where a more universal good called them. Even in the Vatican, with the election of Paul IV (1555), reticence arose that contrasted with the previous approval.

In the face of all this, Ignatius never ceased to defend what he called "our way of proceeding." Patient with people, especially with those who were his first companions, he was firm on principles. Neither the pleas of the Spaniards nor the requests of Borgia would make him retreat from the principle he had chosen as a rule for the companions: "In all that concerns prayer, meditation and study, as well as the material practice of fasts, vigils and various austerities or penances, there will be, it seems, no need to give them any other rule than that which will be dictated to them by their discerning charity. The only condition is that their confessor should always be kept informed, as well as the superior in case of doubt as to what should be done" (*Constitutions* no. 582). Likewise, he (Ignatius) who *himself* loved the offices and ceremonies would never consent to the imposition on Jesuits of reciting the office in choir. If he failed to countenance the possibility that a Jesuit would refuse the mission given to him, he insisted that the superiors be attentive to discern the desires and aptitudes of the religious entrusted to them.

Ignatius asked the fathers whom the pope appointed as theologians for the Council of Trent to go and stay in hospitals, at the service of the sick and the poor, so that it would be clear that all service to the Church must be lived in the spirit of the Gospel. If he did not hesitate to let his companions go far away, sometimes alone, he did everything possible to keep alive the bonds that the spiritual experience of the *Exercises* had created among them. He devoted an entire chapter of the *Constitutions* to describing an ingenious system of correspondence between the Jesuit and his superior, the Jesuit and his brothers, intended to maintain between them the bonds of a living charity.

The *Constitutions* of the Society would remain unfinished on Ignatius's table. Certainly the essentials were said, the different parts composed, but to the end experience remained the teacher of life, and Ignatius never ceased to reread, to correct, to modify according to what life taught him. One of his last concerns was to call his superiors to be the servants of a living tradition and not of a sacralized text. So, like those who give the *Exercises*, they should have rules and advice very much in mind in order to be able to adapt them to the various circumstances of the mission.

The Most Common Death (July 31, 1556)

The great things to be accomplished for the honor of God led him to his work table where the heat of the summer months also gave him no respite. His distant brothers are there present in his thoughts; for them, he does not stop. He tried to live to the end that "charity full of discernment" of which he spoke so often. A charity that is constantly concerned with translating the motions of the Spirit into daily decisions. For him, the absolute of love had no other place of expression than the banality of daily life. It is there that death would meet him, at the end of a day like any other.

Feeling more tired than usual, Ignatius asked his secretary to go to the Vatican to ask for the pope's blessing for the dying. The pope is Paul IV, at whose election Ignatius had shuddered. He knew that from him he had everything to fear, but he was the vicar of Christ, so he implored his blessing for himself and for the Society. When consulted, the house doctor did not detect anything alarming; the secretary, Father Juan Alfonso de Polanco, invoked the need to finish the mail that was to leave that evening for Portugal and the Indies. He would go to the Vatican tomorrow; Ignatius agreed and withdrew. In the night, he was heard to sigh: "My God!" In the morning, he was found dying; Father Polanco rushed to the Vatican: when he returned, Ignatius was dead. He had passed away calmly, silently, in the place where God had called him.

This life begun with the desire to do great things ended with the work of God accomplished. The one whom his companions affectionately called Father Ignatius left them without a sound, without a farewell message. Before he died, he destroyed the *Spiritual Diary* in which he wrote down the graces he had received in prayer each day, leaving only a few pages that shed light on the choice of the mode of poverty in the Society.

A few years earlier, he had agreed to dictate to Father Gonçalves da Câmara the account of how God had led him from Loyola to Rome. It is an autobiography, if you like, but even more so a founding account that roots the vocation of the companions in the spiritual journey of Ignatius. When they read it, they could no longer doubt that they were inspired by the Spirit himself. It was Ignatius who brought them together, but in this, as in everything else, he acted according to the Spirit. In retracing his pilgrim's route for them, he gave way to the One who led him: Christ our Lord.

He then gained the title that his companions spontaneously gave him: Father Master Ignatius. Was he not for them essentially this master who, with fatherly kindness, made them attentive to the action of the Spirit within them?

Michel Rondet, SJ[6]

Ignatius of Loyola was beatified by Paul V in 1609 and declared a saint by Gregory XV on March 12, 1622, with his companion Francis Xavier.

Take, Lord, and receive all my liberty, my memory, my understanding, and my entire will, all that I have and possess. Thou hast given all to me. To Thee, O Lord, I return it. All is Thine, dispose of it wholly according to Thy will. Give me Thy love and Thy grace, for this is sufficient for me.

Saint Ignatius of Loyola
Spiritual Exercises (234)

---

6. "Ignace de Loyola, cet inconnu", Garrigues 1991, nr. 31, pp. 2-8 (abridged)..

Saint Peter Faber (1506–46)

Memorial on August 2

Peter Faber was born in Savoy in 1506, in the village of Villaret; it was there that he grew up tending his parents' flocks. In 1525, he began his studies in Paris, where his roommates were Francis Xavier and Ignatius of Loyola, who named him as the first of all his companions. Ordained a priest in 1534, he was the first priest of the future Society and was one of the theologians sent by Ignatius to the Council of Trent. On the orders of Pope Paul III, he traveled on foot throughout France, Italy, and Germany, and worked effectively for the Catholic restoration. He died exhausted in Rome on August 1, 1546.

A Life on the Frontiers

Faber led a vagabond life, to the point where some got the impression that he was fickle. "It seems that he was born to stay nowhere," wrote one of his colleagues of him. After a few months spent in Rome, where he taught positive theology, an itinerant life took him to all the hot spots where the political and religious future of Europe was at stake. From June 1539 to September 1541, he was in Parma. After a year and a half, he was sent to Germany as an advisor to Dr. Pedro Ortiz, Charles V's representative at the Worms colloquium and the Diet of Regensburg (1541). Nine months later, he left for Spain, from where, after only six months, he was recalled to Germany for three months, before embarking for Portugal and Spain, where he spent two years (July 1544 to July 1546). Summoned to Rome to participate in the Council of Trent, he died of exhaustion at the age of forty, on August 1, 1546, after having crisscrossed Europe for seven years, traveling between fifteen thousand and twenty thousand kilometers on foot or on the back of a mule, and having made two sea crossings.

A simple apostolic worker, available for any mission entrusted to him, Faber tirelessly traveled the world of his time, opening promising worksites (apostolic initiatives) without ever having the satisfaction of reaping their fruits. Political, cultural, or geographical borders were of little importance to him. At every stage of his travels, he tried to bring the salvation of Jesus Christ, with no other home than the missions that were entrusted to him. These constant journeys involved painful ruptures. Thanks to a sympathetic dispositon, Peter adapted easily, making friends readily. Thus, with each new mission, he faced being uprooted as he was called elsewhere. He had to set out on uncertain journeys, with poor health, subject to episodes of fever that sometimes immobilized him for several months.

Sent to the frontiers, where two worlds clashed, the medieval and the Renaissance, where two conceptions of Christianity, Roman Catholicism and Lutheranism, and where Germanic and Latin culture collided, Peter regularly found himself confronted with a conception of the Church and of faith for which neither his education nor his sensitivity or his studies had prepared him. Only his burning love of Christ allowed him to adapt. Although he sometimes complained, he remained the available Jesuit whose vocation was to travel the world and to be present on the frontiers.

The Unity of a Life in Motion

What could have maintained the unity and coherence of this life in perpetual movement? Obedience certainly, even if it was not always easy for him. Peter set out because he was sent by the pope or by his superior. From then on, Italy, Germany, Flanders, Portugal, and Spain were only the unique and ever renewed place of his Jesuit commitment.

But there is more. While traveling through such diverse regions, Peter was operating within a higher environment, in a kind of spiritual geography that unified his life and saved it from dispersion. He approached every situation from above, following the downward movement of the Incarnation. Because every person and every event has its extension in heaven, Peter lived in a world where saints, angels (both good and bad), God, and Christ are in action. On his travels, he met the local saints and angelic protectors of the countries, regions, and cities he visited. These good spirits were faithful and effective companions on whom he could count; they smoothed his way, arranged fruitful encounters, prepared the hearts to which he would address himself, in a word, they facilitated his apostolate. These meetings with the inhabitants of heaven marked out his route with such precision that it is possible to draw up a celestial atlas of his travels!

Beyond the saints and angels, there was Christ incarnate, as he knew him through the *Exercises*. It was from this point of view that Faber approached the world, the life of the Church, daily tasks, ordinary and common encounters, unexpected situations, which were no longer perceived as simple occasions of service, but as the place of an active and beneficent presence. Every event, every encounter, every place, thus acquired a universal dimension in the image of the salvation brought by Christ. This breadth of vision nourished in him an astonishing spiritual freedom, which, combined with a gentle and benevolent nature, preserved him from any ideological narrowness, and forbade him any partisan and polemical approach. Peter thus escaped the dogmatic myopia that inspired many of the opponents of Lutheranism.

The approach proposed in the *Exercises* to contemplate the life of Christ characterized his understanding of the mystery of the Incarnation: to see, hear, smell, taste, and touch what the protagonists of the Gospel stories live, say, and do. As a result, the body became the providential instrument given by God to allow the spirit to concretize its inspirations in daily reality. This realistic and "carnal" understanding of the Incarnation influenced even his conception of the apostolate. He wanted pastors who, rather than writing scholarly books against heretics, would seek out souls by visiting them personally, seeing them with their own eyes, touching them with their own hands, hearing them with their own ears, arguing with deeds and blood.

Reforming through the Exercises

Like Ignatius, Faber was an authentic reformer. If for him the question of structures was less important than for Luther, he aimed at the reform of life (reforming lives), especially of those who held responsibilities and were capable of leading others. As soon as possible, he proposed to them to make the *Exercises*. This ministry was his favorite, and he devoted several hours a day to it, even at the height of his occupations. Ignatius claimed that of all the Jesuits who gave the *Exercises*, the first place unquestionably belonged to Master Peter Faber.

Gifted with a remarkable capacity for introspection and attention to inner movements, Peter was able to reach people in the depths of their individuality, where feelings and not ideas come into play. Never a prisoner of any ideology, he encountered them in those areas where they were living and feeling. The advice he gave was not based on the teaching of a doctrine, but on a more global experience, which also made use of affectivity. Feeling remains the key word in his spiritual anthropology. He understood it in the sense given to it by Ignatius in the *Exercises*: "It is not to know much that satisfies the soul, but to feel and taste things interiorly."

Whoever wants to reach a person where he is, to help him find his way in the confusion of ideas and morals, must accept to leaving the apparent security of a dogmatic attitude to move onto a frontier, on the borders of an unknown land. They find themselves exposed, in a zone where the established knowledge and the great theoretical principles do not necessarily apply spontaneously to a concrete situation. The mentor must then show discernment and have the courage to take a risk. Faber experienced this tension; he was a restless man, alien to ready-made solutions, haunted by the search for God's will.

A Ministry of Reconciliation

A man of dialogue, Faber was a guide in the exercise of a ministry of reconciliation. Served by a kind and gentle temperament, he undeniably had a personal charisma. As the first Jesuit directly confronted with the Reformation, he found himself on the front lines, where Lutherans and Roman Catholics clashed with violence and passion. For him, more than a doctrinal difficulty, it was an emotional incompatibility. Faced with the Reformation, he did not take refuge behind theological rigidity, as did many official theologians. Persuaded himself of the urgent need for a reform of the Church, a man of the field rather than of the laboratory, he preferred personal encounters, dialogue, and the accompaniment of people, even heretics. Seeking out points of contact, informing himself in order to better understand the motivations of his opponents, conversing with them, reading their works, he treated people with love, gentleness, and cordiality, avoiding controversy and anything that might exasperate them. Convinced that his compassion for heretics was the sign of a good spirit, he disapproved of the way they were condemned, and

Saint Peter Faber walks on the road, accompanied by angels. From heaven, the Holy Family and Saint Peter watch over him. Painting by Brother Frans Quartier, SJ (1874).

regularly prayed for the champions of the Reformation as well as for the pivotal cities where the future of the faith was at stake.

Shortly before his death, when asked by a colleague for advice on how to deal with heretics, Peter wrote: "The first thing is that whoever wishes to help the heretics of today must have great charity towards them and love them in truth, driving from his mind any consideration likely to cool the esteem that one may have for them ... This is achieved by conversing familiarly with them on matters that are common to us, avoiding any discussion in which one party might give the impression of prevailing over the other." Such words denote a way of proceeding that, even today, has lost none of its relevance.

Pierre Emonet, SJ

Peter Faber was beatified by Pope Pius IX in 1872. In December 2013, Pope Francis canonized him.

Do not put your trust therefore in those wicked spirits who represent all things in an unfavorable light as bound to have an unsuccessful outcome and who exaggerate the evil in what is turning out badly. Being evil themselves, they portray in their own likeness a situation they want and wish to make hopeless. Strive rather to become an instrument of the good spirit, for he it is who shows you what he wishes to bring about in a situation and in the circumstances and how he is ready, with your help, to change it.

Saint Peter Faber
Memoriale (158)

From a Homily of Pope Francis

To be a Jesuit means to be a person of incomplete thought, of open thought: because he thinks always looking to the horizon which is the ever greater glory of God, who ceaselessly surprises us. And this is the restlessness of our inner abyss. This holy and beautiful restlessness! We need to seek God in order to find him, and find him in order to seek him again and always. Only this restlessness gives peace to the heart of a Jesuit, a restlessness that is also apostolic, but which must not let us grow tired of proclaiming the kerygma, of evangelizing with courage. It is the restlessness that prepares us to receive the gift of apostolic fruitfulness. Without restlessness we are sterile.

It was this restlessness that Peter Faber had, a man of great aspirations, another Daniel. Yet his was also a restless, unsettled, spirit that was never satisfied. Under the guidance of Saint Ignatius he learned to unite his restless but also sweet—I would say exquisite—sensibility, with the ability to make decisions. He was a man with great aspirations; he was aware of his desires, he acknowledged them. Indeed for Faber, it is precisely when difficult things are proposed that the true spirit is revealed which moves one to action (cf. *Memoriale*, 301). An authentic faith always involves a profound desire to change the world. The Constitutions say that: "we help our neighbor by the desires we present to the Lord our God" (*Constitutions*, 638).

Peter Faber had the true and deep desire "to be expanded in God": he was completely centered in God, and because of this he could go, in a spirit of obedience, often on foot, throughout Europe and with charm dialogue with everyone and proclaim the Gospel. Faber was consumed by the intense desire to communicate the Lord. If we do not have his same desire, then we need to pause in prayer, and, with silent fervor, ask the Lord, through the intercession of our brother Peter, to return and attract us: that fascination with the Lord that led Peter to such apostolic "folly."

We are men in tension; we are also contradictory and inconsistent men, sinners, all of us. But we are men who want to journey under Jesus' gaze. We are small, we are sinners, but we want to fight under the banner of the Cross in the Society designated by the name of Jesus. We who are selfish want nonetheless to live life aspiring to great deeds. Let us renew then our oblation to the Eternal Lord of the universe so that by the help of his glorious Mother we may will, desire and live the mind of Christ who emptied himself.

Homily of January 3, 2014, given in the Gesù Church, Rome, at the Mass in thanksgiving for the canonization of Peter Faber.

Saint Francis Xavier (1506–52)

UNIVERSAL PATRON SAINT OF THE MISSIONS

Feast Day on December 3

A Man with a Heart of Fire

A saint is always intimidating, and Francis Xavier is more so than any other. This "giant of the mission" can even make us dizzy with his extraordinary existence: one hundred thousand kilometers in eleven years of incessant travel by land and sea, a tireless apostle, preaching, baptizing, and confessing to the point of fatigue, a "globetrotter of the Gospel" enduring dangers and privations in a heroic way, founding missions and colleges, dying alone at the gates of China at the age of forty-six ... What a great and inimitable life! And what if this greatness, this sanctity, hid another? Yes, behind the missionary epic of this exceptional figure, there is another holy story, that of the humble Xavier, with his passions, his disappointments, his limitations; that of the companion of Jesus, not converted once and for all, but seeking, sometimes groping, sometimes in clarity, to act according to what the Spirit gives him to "feel," living a spiritual battle that is rougher than the storms at sea. It is this Xavier, close, vulnerable, tried and tested, and yet confident, passionate about God and men, who gives us the true secret of his life and leads us in his wake.

A Man of the Renaissance

Born in 1506 in Navarre, Xavier died in 1552 on the island of Sancian, opposite Canton, during a period of intense cultural and religious upheaval. In the Church, it was the time of the Reforms, prepared by a long crisis of the papacy and the clergy, leaving the Christian people to themselves, not perceiving the new expectations of the laity.

49

In Europe, it was the opening up of the New World: horizons widened, stimulating adventurers of all kinds, merchants and missionaries at a time when conquest and evangelization went hand in hand. In this meeting of peoples and clash of cultures, Europe was both split asunder and remolded. Little by little, national consciences were awakening, national languages were gaining ground at the expense of Latin, and secular ideas were advancing among "enlightened" minds.

At the age of eighteen, Xavier found himself the youngest member of a noble family, having lost everything but his honor in the war when Navarre rebelled against Spain. With his fortune gone and his military future blocked, the only way forward was to study law and pursue an ecclesial career in Paris, where the university enjoyed a European reputation. Francis arrived there with the firm intention of making a name for himself, a fortune, and returning home with his head held high.

Francis indulged in the easy life of the student who works not too much but who succeeds quite well and whose career is assured. After graduating, he became a master of arts and enjoyed his time: sports, nightlife, flirting with new ideas; he was curious but cautious, surrounded by friends but not following them in all their excesses. With a few good assets in hand, Xavier forged ahead, building his life project step by step. On this well-laid out path, an encounter occurred that would turn everything upside down.

The Encounter with Ignatius or Converted Ambition

The unexpected was the four years of sharing lodgings with Ignatius and Peter Faber, the prolonged resistance of Francis to the influence of Ignatius, the decision of Faber to follow Ignatius, and the year-long face-to-face meeting between Xavier and Ignatius in 1533. Of all this, we have only one precious testimony, that of Juan Alfonso de Polanco, Ignatius's secretary in Rome, which speaks volumes: "I have heard our great molder of men, Ignatius, say that the roughest dough he ever handled was, in the beginning, this young Francis Xavier, of whom God nevertheless made more use than of any other subject of our time ...."

What could have touched Xavier to the point of making him change his mind? Xavier always spoke of Ignatius as a "father in the faith" in the sense of one who gave him birth to a new life. Ignatius was the "mediator," and even more so the friend who knew how to see beyond appearances, how to sense hidden thirsts, how to wait, but also how to speak out when necessary, and how to say blunt words, such as: "What good is it for a man to gain the whole world if he loses his soul?" (Mt 16:26). This is the word of scripture that appears most often in Xavier's letters. More secretly, it was the Other who lived in Ignatius that attracted Xavier, it was Christ encountered personally thanks to the witness Ignatius: "Francis could not resist the power of the Holy Spirit who spoke to him in his servant Ignatius."

The fruit of this encounter was the transformation of desire in the strongest sense of the word, the reorientation of all inner powers, of all natural and acquired gifts, in the service not of oneself or, more subtly, of the ideal image of oneself, but of the surpassing of oneself and one's interests for those of another. At this moment in his life, Xavier gave God the most beautiful and decisive gift, that of his freedom. The importance of the *Exercises* conducted with Ignatius after his conversion is worth mentioning. The ambitious man used everything, including God, to succeed; the convert accepts being led to other heights, those of service, of humble and gratuitous love.

Xavier discovered that he was loved, saved from a trap, that of vanities. He had only one desire, to make known to others the name and love of God who changed his life.

A Motto: "More"

Xavier was a man who, in his rare hours of sleep—he prayed often and at length at night—had dreams. He recalled two of them that allow us to enter into his intimacy.

On the roads of Italy, he woke his companion Jacques Lainez one night: "Jesus, how utterly distraught I am! Do you know what I was dreaming? I was carrying an Indian on my back, and it was so heavy that I could not carry it" (five years before the call to Rome!).

On the eve of embarking for Goa, he said to Simão Rodrigues: "Do you remember, my brother Simão, that night in the hospital in Rome, when I woke you up with my repeated cry: More! More! When you asked me the reason for my cry, I told you not to worry about it. Now you must know that I saw myself in very great toil and peril for the service of God our Lord; and yet his grace sustained me and animated me to such an extent that I could not help asking

Saint Francis Xavier personifies the phrase of Saint Paul: "But we preach a crucified Messiah" (1 Cor. 1:23). Engraving by Gérard Edelinck (circa 1670) after a drawing by Jérôme Fourley, published by François de Poilly.

for more. I hope that the hour is coming when what was shown to me before-hand will be realized."

From the moment he chose to follow Ignatius in his apostolic project, the life of Xavier was a succession of calls, of departures toward, further, more. Geographically, he would be called to Lisbon, Goa, South India, the Moluccan Islands, Japan, China. Culturally, he would be called to adapt to the different environments, to the customs, to the languages that he wanted to learn but that he only touched, always dependent on translators. How can we not think of Paul saying: "Free from all, I have made myself all things to all; I have made myself a Jew with the Jews, a Gentile with the Gentiles" (1 Cor. 9:19–20), when we see him working on deck with the sailors, sharing the threatened life of the pearl fishermen, talking trade with the merchants, becoming an outcast with the outcasts and a scholar with the scholars? All the echoes report his power of empathy, his human warmth, his contagious joy, which did not prevent him from being uncompromising when the interests of the Kingdom were at stake.

Furthermore, spiritually, he would be called to the way of self-denial, of trust, and of consenting passivity: "I have placed all my trust in God," he writes in a thousand ways. Xavier's confidence was certainly stimulated by undeniable apostolic successes, but it was also greatly tested, exposed to dis-couragement, solitude, and all sorts of difficulties coming from others, from the elements or from himself.

In fact, he was thwarted in his most cherished projects, he was slowed down by his compatriots, and constantly hampered by language problems: "I am like a statue in the midst of the Japanese." But this poverty, which sometimes went as far as impotence, would become in him the space of grace. "The ser-vant is not above his master." Francis experienced what it means to commune with the sufferings of Christ, to participate in his resurrection. He confided: "There is a great difference between the one who trusts in God while having all the necessities and the one who trusts in God without having anything and depriving himself of the necessities, in order to imitate Christ more closely" (letters of June 22, 1549 and November 5, 1549).

The more he advanced, the more he discovered his limits, the disproportion between the work to be accomplished and his poor strength, especially when the Evil One was involved, and the more he relied on God alone. "I ask you, therefore, to put all your foundations in God, for all things, and not to trust in your power, in your knowledge, or in human opinion." It was in this crucible that the saint abandoned himself, allowing himself to be molded in the hands of God, and that the true adventure of Francis Xavier appeared: not so much the evangelization of new lands by the apostle as the seizure of the apostle by God, henceforth moved and inspired by him to the point that his action became that of God.

Francis in Asia was a man who was increasingly free, deeply committed, and yet free from success and failure, sure that the last word was God's. What was Francis Xavier's secret?

The Spiritual Urgency of the Mission

Francis was aware that he was sent by Christ, a sinner among sinners, to those who were in danger of spiritual death. As a sixteenth-century man, he was haunted by the question of salvation. This was not a metaphysical question for him, but an emergency, a matter of life and death. He knew from which deadly trap the Lord had drawn him, the trap of pride and false assurances. He knew that the Tempter, the "Enemy," continues his deadly battle in the midst of the world, and that souls are at stake in this spiritual drama, very "concrete" souls, those of Anjiro the Japanese, of Anthony the Chinese, of Pirate the Portuguese, of Gomez the Jesuit. "What we intend to do in these countries is to attract people to the knowledge of their Creator, Redeemer, and Savior Jesus Christ our Lord ... We intend to explain and manifest the truth, no matter how many contradictions we are confronted with, because God obliges us to love the salvation of our neighbors more than our own physical lives" (Letter of November 5, 1549).

This clear certainty, some would say simplistic, that there is no other Name by which we are saved than that of Jesus Christ "Way, Truth, Life," made him judge other beliefs in an expeditious manner most of the time. Buddhism, Hinduism, Confucianism, Islam, there was nothing to hope for from these pagan religions that had turned away from the true God. Xavier left with simple ideas for a complex Orient. Some after him would have a different approach.

However, in his own way, Xavier practiced a form of inculturation of the Gospel: foundation of colleges for native students, translation of the catechism and the liturgy into the language of the country, missions entrusted to laypeople, sung prayers, perhaps even gestures, interest in popular religion, attempts to meet with the learned, and so on. A characteristic of Xavier's mission was its emphasis on a Church of the laity.

The Strength of the Ecclesial Anchorage

Xavier was a man alone but not isolated, lost at the end of the world but united by his heart, prayer, obedience, docility to the Spirit and his spiritual family—"If I forget you, Society of Jesus, may my right hand dry up"—and more broadly to the great church in heaven and on earth. He believed in the communion of saints, in the circulation of the energies of love in a living body where everything is held together. All these living beings, angels, saints of the Church, brothers of the Society already in heaven or dispersed far away, Mary, Joseph, he mobilized them as actors with him. He could go all the further in daring and freedom of decision as he was "anchored" in dependence and in the common mission.

Xavier needed others. He said so and lived it by asking for advice, counsel, prayers and information; his letters show a constant concern for news from Europe and from his brothers. He surrounded himself with collaborators from the start.

As for the bond between Xavier and Ignatius, it can be said that it became more and more profound as the years went by. Xavier could not hide his emotion when he reads the end of some of Ignatius's letters: "All yours, without ever being able to forget you, Iñigo." Ignatius at the center, immobile in Rome, Xavier at the outposts, pilgrim of the Gospel, complemented each other like the point and the circle; the Church perceived this when it canonized them together in 1622. We know from a letter that arrived in India six months after Xavier's death that Ignatius wanted to recall him to Rome.

The Sympathetic Power of His Heart

Here is what he wrote in 1549 to a confrere who had remained in India: "Men pay attention only to speeches that go to the very depths of their conscience. You must reveal men to themselves if you want to captivate them ... In order to express their thoughts well, it is necessary for you to know them; and to know them, there is only one way, which is to live in their society, to study them, to deepen them, to penetrate them. These are the living books that you must read."

Everything is there: Xavier loved his fellow human beings and this love was transmitted, and as he loved them in the strength and tenderness of God, he worked wonders. He surely had the charism to open hearts through his enthusiasm, his generosity in the gift of himself, his freedom available to all, his joy, of the children he put on his side for the mission to the parents.

Is he really a saint for us today? Whether from the outside or from the inside, his life was inimitable, his holiness inaccessible. Saint Francis Xavier is fire, and one does not approach fire without burning a little. But it is a fire that has been kindled on ordinary wood, like ours. May it lead us to the hearth of love, to the heart of Christ who gives us the secret of his life: *"I have come to light a fire on earth; I want it to spread and to burn"* (Lk. 12:49).

Dominique Paillard, SFX[7]

Francis Xavier was beatified by Paul V in 1619 and canonized on March 12, 1622, along with Ignatius, by Pope Gregory XV. In 1927, he was proclaimed patron of all Catholic missions by Pius XI.

---

7. See her article on www.communaute-sfx.catholique.fr (abridged).

Prayer of Saint Francis Xavier
(translated by Gerard Manley Hopkins)

O God, I love thee, I love thee—
Not out of hope of heaven for me
Nor fearing not to love and be
In the everlasting burning.

Thou, thou, my Jesus, after me
Didst reach thine arms out dying,
For my sake sufferedst nails and lance,
Mocked and marred countenance,
Sorrows passing number,
Sweat, and care and cumber,
Yea, and death, and this for me.
And thou couldst see me sinning:

Then I, why should I not love thee,
Jesus, so much in love with me?
Not for heaven's sake; not to be
Out of hell by loving thee;
Not for any gains I see;
But just the way that thou didst me
I do love and will love thee:

What must I love thee, Lord, for then?
For being my King and God. Amen.

From a Letter of Saint Francis Xavier to Saint Ignatius of Loyola

Multitudes out here fail to become Christians only because there is nobody prepared to undertake the holy task of instructing them. I have often felt strongly moved to go to the universities of Europe, especially Paris, crying out like a madman, and say to those in the Sorbonne who have more learning than good will to employ it advantageously: "How many souls are missing heaven and going to hell through your negligence?"

If only, while they studied their humanities, they would also study the account that God will demand for the talent he has given them, many might feel the need to engage in spiritual exercises, so as to discover God's will in their hearts and to embrace it rather than their own inclinations, saying: "Lord, here I am. What would you have me to do? Send me where you will, if necessary even to India."

Liturgy of the Hours, Second Reading for December 3

Part 2

THE EXPANDING SOCIETY (1556–1640)

The Far East, 1604 copy of the Map of the Myriad Countries of the World, printed in China at the request of Emperor Wanli, produced by Matteo Ricci, SJ, and his Chinese collaborators, Mandarin Zhong Wentao and translator Li Zhizao.

I n 1640, the Jesuits celebrated their centenary. They looked back on those hundred years with gratitude to God for what he had wrought through the Society. The Flemish province produced a volume, *Imago primi saeculi*, a retrospective account of the previous hundred years. Although the volume was not devoid of self-congratulation, its elegant frontispiece made the appropriate point by quoting Psalm 115: "Not to us, Lord, not to us, but to thy name give glory."

During those hundred years, the Society grew almost exponentially. Its membership consisted of three categories, each of which constituted about a third of the number of Jesuits at any given time. Jesuits were either priests, scholastics (young Jesuits in training for the priesthood), or "temporal coadjutors" (members not destined for the priesthood who contributed to the Society through their professional skills).

The Society attracted more than its share of talented and devout young men. Special among them were two who died in their youth relatively soon after joining the Society. They gained a reputation for sanctity and were later canonized—Stanislaus Kostka and Aloysius Gonzaga. The cult of Stanislaus and Aloysius as patrons of youth, much promoted by Jesuits in their colleges and churches, took a strong hold in Catholic culture soon after their deaths and remained so for centuries.

The temporal coadjutors (also known as brothers) were a large, crucial, and often overlooked segment of the Society. Depending on their background, they performed a number of different services, ranging, for instance, from cook and tailor to architect and renowned artist, such as Andrea Pozzo in Italy and Giuseppe Castiglione in China. Among the exemplary coadjutors from this period were the saintly porter Alphonsus Rodríguez, and the former soldier Dominic Collins, who would die a martyr's death.

The Society now plied its ministries in a world that had changed significantly from what it was even in the lifetime of Ignatius. In 1555, Emperor Charles V had to abdicate after losing his long struggle against Lutheran military forces. The resulting Peace of Augsburg stipulated that local rulers could determine the religion of their subjects. This was the first step in the division of the continent into Catholic states and Protestant states.

Which states would be which did not crystalize, however, until after decades of war, polemic, and brutal persecutions. The Jesuits came to realize their responsibility for areas where the controversies raged. The turning point in their attitude occurred in the fateful year of 1555. Jerome Nadal went to Germany for the first time, acting as a papal theologian for the negotiations at Augsburg. He was shocked by the shambles in which he found Catholicism there. He sounded the alarm in the Jesuit headquarters in Rome, and, with that, the Society took up the challenge there and in other parts of northern Europe.

In German-speaking lands, Peter Canisius emerged as the most important Catholic figure in the crucial second half of the sixteenth century. He also exerted considerable influence in Poland, where religious allegiance hung in the balance all through the century. France suffered thirty years of intermittent religious wars until the Catholic cause triumphed towards the end of the century. The British Isles, except for Ireland, were a lost cause for Catholicism, as was Scandinavia.

For its labors in these areas, the Society paid a huge price in its martyrs. The list is long—Edmund Campion in England, Jacques Salès and William Saultemouche in France, the three martyrs of Košice in Slovakia, and a number of others. In 1570, the Society suffered its greatest single loss when the Huguenot corsair, Jacques de Sores (Sourie), intercepted a ship carrying forty missionaries to Brazil. When Sores discovered that the passengers were Jesuits, he ordered them executed and their bodies thrown into the sea.

This bellicose situation had repercussions on theology. The irenic culture of the Renaissance gave way to apologetics and polemics. Even the peaceable Robert Bellarmine entered the fray, though in a serene and measured tone. Preaching, especially in lands where the struggle was the most bitter, adopted the same pattern, which prevailed in full force until 1648, the end of the Thirty Years' War, the last of the so-called wars of religion.

Meanwhile, the Council of Trent, which had had a troubled eighteen-year history, finally concluded in 1563. Although the council opened with hope of reconciliation with the Lutherans, it met obstacle after obstacle in trying to achieve that objective and finally abandoned it to turn its attention to shoring up Catholicism.

The council reaffirmed major doctrines that were under attack and legislated desperately needed reforms of the Church, most of which had a directly pastoral purpose. Two Jesuits—Diego Laínez and Alfonso Salmerón—had the rare distinction of participating in all three periods of the council. Once the council was completed, it became a rallying point for Catholics that gave them new energy and a sense of cohesion.

In this situation, the Jesuits continued to develop pastoral strategies to strengthen the faith and devotion of Catholics and to reconvert Protestants. Later historians labeled the Society a Counter-Reformation order. The label, although not without merit, gives a lopsided view of the Society and of its ministries in this period. In many places and in many regards, the Counter-Reformation had little or no impact on how the Jesuits worked for "the good of souls."

They showed, for instance, great ingenuity in developing new ministries or refashioning old ones. Of the traditional ministries, the most important was preaching the Word of God. The Jesuits were untiring in this ministry and created new occasions of public worship in which to exercise it, such as novenas and the "Forty Hours" Eucharistic adoration.

In their churches, they accompanied preaching with "sacred lectures." The best equivalent today for such lectures is adult education. The lectures took place in the body of the church and were held one, two, or three afternoons a week. They dealt for several weeks with a specific subject such as the Epistle to the Romans, the Seven Works of Mercy, or the Gifts of the Holy Spirit. Members of the congregation came armed with writing materials, which reveals the instructional character of this ministry.

The most significant new ministry the Jesuits created was of course preaching and directing retreats according to the programs of the *Spiritual Exercises*. The Jesuits opened their first retreat house in Alcalá in Spain in 1553. Others followed, but even more popular were adaptations of the *Exercises* preached to groups according to the directives of the Eighteenth Annotation.

Loosely related to such retreats were the "missions" the Jesuits undertook in areas remote from cities and larger towns. The Jesuits were the first to exploit the full potential of this ministry by developing elaborate programs of sermons, catechetical instruction, confessions, processions, and other public ceremonies. The missions lasted anywhere from a week to a month and often entailed a team of two or more Jesuits. They became an important and characteristic ministry of the Society and continued to be such into the twentieth century. Bernardine Realino in Italy and John Francis Regis in France were so untiring and sometimes heroic in their dedication to this ministry that the former was asked to be the city's patron on his deathbed and the latter is known as the apostle of the region in which he labored.

The missions brought the Jesuits into direct contact with the lower socio-economic strata of society, but they were not the only situation that did so. From the very beginning, the Jesuits undertook a wide range of social ministries such has hospital and prison chaplaincies. Ignatius himself was responsible for one of the Jesuits' most creative social ministries, the founding of halfway houses for prostitutes. The houses were refuges where the women could safely retire for a number of months until benefactors found them honest employment, usually as domestics, or provided them with dowries so that they could marry or enter a convent.

By the time Ignatius died, schools had become the premier ministry of the Society and the ministry that absorbed most of its manpower. Highly regarded and much sought after, they proliferated across Western Europe. By 1640, they had developed into a massive network. There were, for instance, some ninety in German-speaking lands, seventy in France, and thirty-six in the small area of the two Belgian provinces (Spanish Netherlands).

Although the schools were primarily concerned with the formation of their students, they served as centers for the other ministries of the Society, and they trained the Jesuits who labored in them. During holidays and the long summer vacation, Jesuit teachers generally took to the road for ministry, especially for directing retreats and engaging in the missions to the countryside.

The schools, whose students were young laymen destined for non-clerical careers, required the Jesuits, unlike other clerics at the time, to become skilled in secular subjects such as poetry, drama, and natural philosophy, which included mathematics, optics, astronomy, and similar subjects. The Jesuits became poets, dramatists, cartographers, astronomers, hydraulic engineers, botanists, and even pharmacists—skills that served them well on the overseas missions.

In both Europe and on the missions, music began to play an important role in Jesuit ministries. In Spain, for instance, the Jesuits learned early how to set catechism lessons to simple tunes, a great aid in memorization and especially appropriation. In Brazil, José de Anchieta made use of this method as well as his skills as dramatist and poet.

The sung catechism became almost a trademark of Jesuit popular ministries. Moreover, students in the schools had to be taught singing and dancing if they were to take their role in society, which meant their Jesuit teachers had to know those arts. In the overseas missions, the Jesuits made use of music to help in their work of evangelization. In that regard, Anchieta was not an exception. When he and the others first arrived in Brazil, they discovered the amazing musical talent of the native Brazilians, and so immediately began to capitalize on it.

The Jesuits thus never forgot they had been founded as a missionary order. Overseas missions remained all through the Society's history a highest priority. Once the French in the early seventeenth century undertook the foundation of a colony in present-day Canada, the Jesuits became among the first missionaries there. Even so, they were most active in lands under the aegis of either the Spanish or the Portuguese crowns.

To the extent possible, Jesuits in mission lands made use of the same ministries as they did in Europe. By 1640, for instance, they operated thirteen schools in Mexico, eleven in Peru, and nine in the province of Goa. Yet, conditions did not always allow for simply reproducing ministries that worked in Europe. In evangelizing the indigenous peoples of North and South America, for instance, the Jesuits had first to create dictionaries and grammars of their languages so that they could even begin to communicate with them. Despite the Jesuits' best efforts, the native peoples often feared and resented them. The result was sometimes ugly in the extreme and resulted in martyrdom.

The overseas missions thus required an extraordinary measure of courage, flexibility, and accommodation on the part of the Jesuits. In that regard, two of their undertakings stand out. Both of them later caused the Society tragic difficulties.

The first was the radical cultural accommodation that the Jesuits first put into effect in Japan and then later in China and India. This strategy meant the Jesuits had to divest themselves as much as possible of their European ways and adopt those of the country in which they found themselves. It was a strategy that in Japan worked remarkably well until persecutions broke out in the early seventeenth century and utterly obliterated the mission. In China, however, the experiment went well for a century, even though critics, especially from other religious orders, questioned its legitimacy. The Jesuits' skill in astronomy, cartography, and mathematics gained them favor in the imperial court in Beijing and thus ensured that they and other missionaries would not be expelled or persecuted.

The second was the establishment of permanent settlements in parts of Spanish America for the Guaraní and to some extent for the Moxos, the two most docile peoples. The Jesuits had several aims in creating these "reductions," as they were called, but crucial among them was protecting the indigenous people from the Spanish and Portuguese slave traders who roamed the jungles in search of them. These peaceful settlements also provided the Jesuits with ideal circumstances for evangelizing the natives and for teaching them skills so that they might support themselves and pay the onerous taxes imposed on them by the government.

The experiment was a resounding success. By the mid-eighteenth century, the Jesuits had founded thirty reductions with a total population of some 110,000 natives. Although two or three Jesuits oversaw a given settlement, which might have as many as ten thousand inhabitants, the natives essentially governed themselves. The reductions became renowned for the quality of the products they produced and sold, among which musical instruments were particularly prized.

In 1640, therefore, the Society had reason to celebrate its accomplishments. Setbacks and frustrations abounded, as the number of Jesuit martyrs during this period testify, but they did not essentially affect the overall success of the Society. As the next century moved along, however, the skies eventually turned dark for the Society of Jesus.

John W. O'Malley, SJ

Saint Francis Borgia (1510–72)

GENERAL OF THE SOCIETY IN EXPANSION

Memorial on October 3

When the duke of Gandía, ex-viceroy of Catalonia, one of the closest confidantes of Emperor Charles V, wrote to Saint Ignatius saying that he had decided to become a Jesuit, he was advised to keep this decision secret because, as Father Ignatius said, "the world has no ears to hear this explosion."

In the mind of the emperor, the Society of Jesus was a new order, as yet little known and even criticized by many. But Francis Borgia, once he became a widower, sought to follow that path of humility traced by these new apostles of his century. When he was still in Barcelona as viceroy, he had been given notice of the papal approval of this kind of life. He knew the reputation for sanctity of the founder from the mouths of friends whom Ignatius of Loyola had left there. He had begun a relation of spiritual direction with Antonio Araoz and Peter Faber, and even, it is said, communicated with Father Ignatius.

Later it was he, as duke of Gandía, who founded a college of the Society, soon converted to a university, in his city. He was thirty-six when in 1546 he himself decided to become a Jesuit, while he was making the *Spiritual Exercises* in Gandía under the direction of the rector of the college. In February 1548, he made his solemn profession, although with the pope's permission to hold on for three years to allow for the disposing of his fortune in favor of his children. His case is exceptional, but the founder of the Society had foreseen it.

An Unparalleled Moral Authority

Father Ignatius called him to Rome on the occasion of the Holy Year of 1550. Borgia would have to give his opinion on the *Constitutions* of the Society of Jesus, already prepared for presentation to the professed members of the Society, to whom he belonged. He stayed in the Roman house for three months, dressed as duke and accompanied by his youngest son, the object of admiration of many Roman nobles and ecclesiastical dignitaries, who had offered him lodging more in accord with his state. Father Ignatius had a broader vision than others: he wanted to form him and inform him precisely about the spirit and projects of the new order. In fact, when rumors began in 1551 that he might be made a cardinal, Borgia left Rome to seclude himself in the Basque mountains. There he made public that he was a professed member of the Society of Jesus, renounced everything in favor of his children, and named his son Carlos heir to his dukedom. He was ordained a priest and prepared himself to celebrate his first Mass.

Before fleeing Rome, he left alms to begin the college that would initially be known as "Borgia College" before being designated the Roman College, predecessor of the current Gregorian University. Nor did he forget to provide for the new church that Father Ignatius wanted—the future Church of the Gesù—which could only be built when Borgia himself was general of the Society, as second successor to Saint Ignatius.

His first Mass in Bergara was a major event, very well attended, with the possibility of participants gaining a plenary indulgence conceded by the pope for the occasion. From then on, in the style of the new order, he carried on his apostolic priorities by preaching in the area surrounding Oñate and proposing to Father Ignatius that the Hermitage of the Magdalene be converted into a retreat house from which to evangelize the region and in addition to gain new apostles and saints by means of the Spiritual Exercises.

Just to see him and to hear him preach with humility and the apostolic zeal of a saint was a profoundly moving experience, since everyone knew his background and what he had given up for the love of God. His mediation had an unparalleled moral authority with the courts of Spain and Portugal, with the nobility and authorities of Italy, and even with the pope himself. Within a few years, foundations multiplied in Spain and Portugal: colleges and even the occasional university. From 1554, he was commissioner of the Society for all the provinces of the Iberian Peninsula. It was then that he took a vow not to accept dignities unless commanded by the one who could oblige him under sin.

His incessant travels around the Iberian Peninsula took him from place to place where there were no houses of the Society. Nobles and ecclesiastical

Saint Francis Borgia adores the Eucharist and wears the symbols of his great mortification, the skull and the ducal crown that he renounced. On the banner, we can read: "Never again will I serve a lord who can die," words that he pronounced in front of the decomposed remains of Queen Isabella. Painting by Raúl Berzosa (2019).

authorities had confidence in the prestige, prudence, and virtue of this saintly commissioner. He gave spiritual assistance to Princess Juana and to the emperor himself, who wanted to have him as a confessor and executor in his retirement to the Monastery of Yuste. Saint Teresa of Jesus herself confided spiritual problems to him and remained satisfied with his responses as a person speaking from experience.

Both Ignatius and his successor as general superior, Diego Laínez, consistently put their total confidence in him. He, on the other hand, didn't see himself physically able to go to the Indies, nor as having the talents "to teach little children," but he was desirous "to die shedding his blood for the Catholic truth of the Roman Church." To free Borgia from the unjust problems created for him in Spain, Laínez intervened with Pius IV, so that he might be called to Rome for church affairs, and made him assistant for Spain in the Society's curia.

Becoming the Superior General

It did not take long for Borgia to be elected superior general at Laínez's death: at the Second General Congregation in 1565, he garnered thirty-one of the thirty-nine votes. His gesture at the close of the Congregation was impressive: he begged the assembled fathers that, since they had placed him in the highest office, they treat him like an "imbecile," and he humbly kissed their feet to demonstrate the love he bore them.

His seven years governing the Society coincided almost exactly with the pontificate of Saint Pius V (1566–72). He was the pope's right-hand man for many affairs of the universal Church, among others organizing two Congregations of Cardinals in the Roman curia: one dealing with separated Christians in northern Europe, the other dealing with the missions. In two instances of pestilence in Rome during his generalate, Pius V mandated him to direct and organize the care of the city's plague victims.

The moral authority that he had in the eyes of Philip II contributed to opening the doors of the missions in Latin America to Jesuits. In a few years, he sent various groups of missionaries. The first expedition, to Florida, was crowned with the martyrdom of Father Pedro Martinez (1566), after which the survivors had to flee to Cuba, and then to Mexico. The subsequent efforts, to Peru, Brazil, and Mexico, opened the way to a missionary venture that became typical of the Society: based in colleges and teaching doctrine, it would soon result in the Universities of Lima and Mexico, and blossom later into the reductions. He erected the Provinces of Peru and Mexico, and neither the martyrdom at the hands of Calvinists of Blessed Ignatius de Azevedo and his thirty-nine companions as they voyaged to Brazil, nor that of Father Juan Bautista Segura and his seven companions, once again in Florida (1571), stopped him. Rather, it succeeded in nourishing even more the missionary zeal of Jesuits

In the internal governance of the Society, following the mandate he had received from the general congregation that elected him, little by little and with prudence he extended the hour of prayer to the different provinces of the Society that fostered the interior life and the prayer proper to the *Exercises*, and had an impact on the apostolic life proper to the Society, of which he was himself a model, as can be seen in his spiritual diary. He was especially concerned that every province have its own novitiate, if possible in a location distinct from the colleges. He accepted Saint Stanislaus Kostka into the Society. He fostered the formation and the ministry of Saint Robert Bellarmine, the popular missions, and the Marian sodalities. At the same time, he moved ahead founding or inspiring colleges, particularly in France, the Low Countries, Germany, and Poland. He even thought he might realize the plans of Saint Ignatius to put foundations in Constantinople, Cyprus, and Jerusalem. He never forgot the recommendation of the general congregation to begin founding some professed houses, above all in the more developed provinces.

Last Mission

Finally, obedient to the pope, Borgia set out to accompany the papal legate Michele Bonelli in the mission he had received from Pius V to unite the Christian monarchs. With his prayer and good manners, he animated that mission spiritually and even managed to use the opportunity to resolve in passing some problems in the houses of the Society. That mission cost him his life: he contracted the grave pulmonary illness that led to his death two days after his return to Rome.

We can attest that Borgia was an example of universal and faithful collaboration in the affairs of governance of the Church with Pope Saint Pius V. This extended to his offering his life in fulfillment of the fourth vow of the professed of the Society of Jesus: an excellent message for Jesuits of all ages.

In general, he manifested in his life how humiliation and continuous prayer are not opposed to the apostolic vocation, but rather imbue it with its deepest energy and make it fruitful by means of the example of evangelical dynamism they imprint on apostolic action.

Manuel Ruiz Jurado, SJ[8]

Francis Borgia was declared blessed by Urban VIII in 1624 and a saint by Clement X on June 20, 1670.

The means which unite an instrument to God and render it ever ready to the touch of the divine hand are more efficacious than those which dispose it to be of service to man. These means are uprightness, generosity, and, particularly, charity and purity of intention in God's service. To these may be added a familiar intercourse with God in one's spiritual exercises and the purest zeal for the salvation of souls, which seeks nothing else than the glory of Him who created and redeemed them.

Saint Francis Borgia, quoting the Constitutions *in a letter to Jesuits*

---

8. Jesuits, *Yearbook of the Society of Jesus* (Rome, 2010), 46–48. Translation by John C. O'Callaghan, SJ.

Saint Stanislaus Kostka (1550–68)

PATRON OF THE NOVICES

Memorial on November 13

Stanislaus Kostka was not yet eighteen years old when, early one Sunday morning, August 10, 1567, he fled the city of Vienna to meet the Jesuit Provincial Peter Canisius in Augsburg. He had to walk some five hundred miles, which took him about fourteen days. He dressed as a beggar in order not to be recognized and also to be a bit like Jesus. That, in fact, had been the worst thing for his father in Poland, when he found out about it later. His son, his own flesh and blood, had disgraced the good name of the Kostka family by going along the roads of Europe begging.

What had gone before this? Three years earlier, in July 1564, Stanislaus had been sent from Poland to the Jesuit college in Vienna, which had just been founded by Canisius. He went there with his older brother Paul, their personal tutor, and some other wealthy boys, all accompanied by their servants. The young noblemen were to receive a thorough Catholic education, important at a time when Protestantism was gaining ground all over Europe.

Here, Life Was Full of Spirit

Initially, the young men lived in the college. Stanislaus was impressed by the way the Jesuits did things: the cordial and cheerful atmosphere among them; their panache and courteous elegance. It was all so different from home, where people tried to imitate the nobility of two hundred years ago with studied manners and much bowing, along with a surfeit of rules, customs, and etiquette. The Jesuit life, on the other hand, was full of spirit, not only in the way they prayed, but also in their mutual interaction, and in their treatment of the students and the subject matter in class. Stanislaus wanted to be like them, too.

Saint Stanislaus Kostka is welcomed by Saint Peter Canisius at the Jesuit college in Dillingen. Stained glass workshops of the Carmel of Le Mans Hucher & Fils (1878–80).

After six months, a section of the college buildings was requisitioned by the emperor. The students could no longer stay there. Paul found lodging for the entire Polish group, but they had to accept a Protestant as landlord. There, too, Stanislaus continued the way of life he had copied from the Jesuits. This brought him into repeated clashes with Paul and the other boys. Paul organized dancing lessons at the express wish of his father. Stanislaus participated with great reluctance, but otherwise tried to evade the student life of the group as much as possible. They began to mock him: "You little Jesuit!" Stanislaus replied by polishing Paul's boots, an exercise in humility that angered Paul even more: noblemen do not polish shoes; that is what servants are for.

Around Christmas 1566, Stanislaus fell seriously ill. The doctors thought he would die, but Paul, fearing the Protestant landlord, did not dare to call a priest for the last sacraments. Their tutor watched over him. Later he would tell that the ailing Stanislaus had cried out that he should kneel, for Saint Barbara was coming from heaven to bring him communion. He also saw the Blessed Virgin Mary with the Child Jesus, which she laid in his arms. That is how it feels to be close to Jesus. The next morning, Stanislaus was better, to the great surprise of the doctors. The whole episode strengthened Stanislaus's desire to become a Jesuit.

Only One Goal in Mind

Stanislaus spoke about his wish with the rector of the college. The latter replied saying he was welcome, but that he needed his father's permission first. Stanislaus knew his father would never give it. "But we don't want to make him our enemy. He might jeopardize the houses we just opened in Poland." In fact, it had been the rector himself who had founded those houses.

Then the empress's new confessor arrived at court, Cardinal Giovanni Francesco Commendone. Stanislaus knew him from his days in Poland, when the latter had sometimes visited their castle. The cardinal advised him to go to Father Canisius, the provincial superior of the German Jesuits. He would know what to do. Commendone gave him a letter of recommendation. Stanislaus had a tailor make him a beggar's dress, "for carnival," and no sooner had classes ended than he fled Vienna.

On the way to Augsburg, he noticed that in many places the churches lay in ruins as a result of the recent raids by Muslim Turks. Where they were still in use, they had often been taken over by Protestant ministers, usually former priests. And amid all this, he himself was on the run with only one goal in mind: to become a Jesuit.

When Paul realized that Stanislaus had disappeared, he ran to the father rector: "You have hidden him!" The rector firmly denied it: "He was asked to return to Father Canisius in Augsburg." The next day, early in the morning, Paul hired a four-horse carriage. In addition to the coachman, the tutor, and the landlord of their house accompanied him. Towards the end of the afternoon, they drove past Stanislaus at full speed, without recognizing him. He saw them and fled across the fields towards the woods. On the front seat of the carriage, the tutor said: "The beggar we just saw, was it not him? He is foolish enough to travel in disguise as a beggar." They turned back and saw that Stanislaus had almost reached the woods. The coachman spurred his horses to pursue him, but in vain. Despite the many lashes, the horses refused to move on. "This has never happened to me before!" Finally, Paul gave the order to stop the pursuit. Later he would say that he had the impression of opposing something sacred that frightened him. Back in Vienna, "the miracle of Stanislaus" was the subject of all conversations.

The Journey Ends in Rome

Father Provincial Canisius was not at home. He was in Dillingen, another thirty miles away. Canisius let Stanislaus stay with him for three weeks, enough to judge his character and vocation. He then sent him with two Jesuit students and a letter of recommendation to Father General Francis Borgia in Rome. Stanislaus had to walk another one thousand miles and more, but he came closer and closer to his ideal. On October 28, 1567, three days after his arrival in Rome, he was admitted to the Society of Jesus. Less than a year later, he died in the summer heat of Rome, on August 15, 1568, feast of the Assumption of the Blessed Virgin Mary.

Shortly thereafter, Paul Kostka arrived in Rome to take back his brother by force. But when the novice master told him that Stanislaus had died a saint, Paul's anger broke and he burst into tears. He went back to Poland full of remorse and instead of starting a family, he remained unmarried and passed his days in prayer and good works. He was present in 1605, when Pope Paul V permitted the local cult of Stanislaus, the first Jesuit thus honored. When

Paul was fifty-six, he asked to become a Jesuit, too. He was accepted, but died shortly before he could start the novitiate, on November 13, 1607. His death anniversary became the feast day of Stanislaus.

Dries van den Akker, SJ[9]

Stanislaus Kostka was beatified in 1605 and canonized by Pope Benedict XIII on December 31, 1726, together with Aloysius Gonzaga.

From a Letter of Saint Peter Canisius to the Superior General, Saint Francis Borgia

The young man who under Christ's leadership brings this letter is being sent to you from this province. He is a Polish noble and his name is Stanislaus. He is an excellent, intelligent young man whom our fathers at Vienna would not admit into the Society for fear of antagonizing his family. On his arrival here he was so eager to carry out his long-standing ambition—some years ago he committed himself unreservedly to the Society, though not yet admitted to it—that he was tested here for a time as a boarder in the college. He was faithful in the duties entrusted to him and showed himself persevering in his vocation. He was very eager to be sent to Rome to be as far away as possible from any harassment by his family, and also to advance as much as he could in the path of holiness. He never lived among our novices, though he serves them as a very good example of what a true probationer ought to be. We hope for great things from him.

Liturgy of the Hours, Second Reading for November 13

9. Translation by Marc Lindeijer, SJ.

Saint Aloysius Gonzaga (1568–91)

UNIVERSAL PATRON OF YOUTH

Memorial on June 21

To appreciate the richness and strength of the character of Aloysius Gonzaga, a number of myths must be disposed of. It is also essential to reconstruct the historical background of Aloysius's life to understand the magnificence and the misery of the famous House of Gonzaga and to interpret the source of our knowledge about the eldest son of the Marquis Ferrante. That is the only way to appreciate the evangelical challenge he offered to contemporary society.

Young Aloysius and His Destiny

Aloysius was born on March 9, 1568, at the Castle of Castiglione, near Mantua. He was a child with both a lively and open intelligence and the imperious character of the Gonzagas. From his earliest years, he lived among the aristocracy and was destined to become one of them under the title of the Imperial Marquis of Castiglione delle Stiviere. He was, therefore, subjected to the rules of etiquette of the courts of Castiglione, of Florence under the Medici (1575–78), of Mantua (1579–80), and finally the court of Philip II of Spain (1581–83).

It was in this frivolous world, where vanity and intrigue were the overriding standards of conduct, in this society addicted to pleasure and depravity, that Aloysius grew up; and it was against these that he deliberately rebelled. Under the care of his mother, whom he loved deeply but from whom, to his sorrow, he was often parted, he welcomed and responded to the voice of God speaking within him, the God who wanted him for himself. Aloysius, though still young, gave himself to God totally in the Church of the Annunciation in

Florence (1583). At the age of twelve, he met Saint Charles Borromeo, who prepared him for his first communion.

As time went by, that frivolous world became ever more unbearable, and Aloysius reacted against it. It was not simply that he did not conform. His was the rebellion of one whose ideal it was to follow Christ without any reserve, who wanted and chose the poverty of Christ rather than riches, insults with Christ rather than honor (cf. *Spir. Ex.*, 167).

His Answer to God's Calling

In 1583, when Aloysius was fifteen years old, he told his mother he had dedicated himself to God. He then had to face opposition from his father and his circle. At the risk of making a fool of himself, he defied and ridiculed the world that he rejected, riding, for instance, in a Milan pageant, not on a princely horse but on a donkey. The men and women of the court made a laughing-stock of him, but what he wanted was precisely to be with Christ who had once been treated as a madman, rather than to rank with the wise and prudent of the world (cf. *Spir. Ex.*, 167). In fact, the world in its heart of hearts admired his Christian courage, a courage it could not match, all of which makes it crystal clear that Aloysius was not a weakling nor a coward running away from life and from the world.

In his earliest years and in adolescence, Aloysius had given convincing proof of outstanding ability in learning languages and mathematics (later he also excelled in philosophy and theology), and in the subtleties of diplomacy. His father was immensely proud of him and for that reason was the more adamant in opposing his son's religious vocation, especially as he saw the youth as his own successor. Aloysius was well aware of his father's hopes, and he knew that his younger brother Rudolf's abilities did not measure up to his own.

The Difficult Decision

While on the one hand Aloysius felt the call of Christ to follow him in religious life, at the same time he could not escape the thought of the good he could do as marquis of Castiglione delle Stiviere among his own people and among the privileged classes on whom the people depended.

It was not an easy problem to solve. It called for exceptional intellectual and spiritual discernment, especially when men of rank in the world as well as the Church reasoned with him and tried to incline him toward the solution that, humanly speaking, seemed more prudent and beneficial to others. For Aloysius, however, the ultimate criterion was the will of God, and, once he was sure he knew what it was, nothing could turn him aside from it—neither his father's anger nor the thought of separation from his mother, still less honors and riches.

This was the reason why he chose the Society of Jesus and joined it in 1587. He had come to appreciate the love that made God become man to give life to men, and he had fallen in love with Christ crucified. So he longed to go out from himself, to give himself entirely to others in the life, apostolic and contemplative, of the Society of Jesus.

Complete Surrender: Service for Love

For that reason, his spirituality was permeated with the idea of loving service of the poor and suffering. But this service of God for the love of the neighbour was not to be identified with a purely external activity. He had understood that in the life of a religious and of a priest this service consists primarily of self-oblation, a transformation whereby, under grace, a person learns to make the standards of Christ one's own, to live by Jesus's life, and thus to become a true apostle.

In the years of his noviceship and at the Roman College, when Aloysius was preparing for his future priestly life under the guidance of Saint Robert Bellarmine, his love of Christ deepened and drove him on with growing insistence to abandon himself completely to the will of God, who continued to call him to himself. In this way, Aloysius grew quickly to Christian maturity and to the wisdom that knows that the grain of wheat, to bear fruit, must first die.

Under the impulse of this faith nourished by prayer and enlightened by mystical experience, with courage and unrestricted generosity, Aloysius volunteered to serve the sick when, in the spring of 1591, the plague broke out in Rome where he was studying theology.

Despite his labors for the plague-stricken poor, whom he visited and nursed in their homes, Aloysius did not catch the disease. All the same, he died on June 21, 1591 after a short period of rapidly increasing exhaustion. It was his

SAN LUIS
GONZAGA

Francisca Leighton Munizaga, Saint Aloysius Gonzaga carrying a plague victim to the hospital. Icon written after an eighteenth-century statue by Pierre Le Gros at the Santo Spirito in Sassia Hospital, Rome (between 2000 and 2015).

self-dedication that killed him, his love that drove him to respond to the cries of pain, that is, to the call of Christ who in his suffering brethren needs comfort and loving care: "What you did to one of the least of these my brethren, you did to me" (Mt. 25:40).

Paolo Molinari, SJ

Aloysius Gonzaga was beatified in 1605 and canonized by Pope Benedict XIII on December 31, 1726, with Stanislaus Kostka. In 1729, he was proclaimed Patron of Youth, especially of students. In Africa, the Jesuits who started the AJAN movement to serve people suffering from HIV/AIDS chose him as their patron.

From a Prayer of Pope John Paul II to Saint Aloysius Gonzaga

Saint Aloysius, poor in spirit,
we turn to you with confidence,
blessing our heavenly Father,
because in you he offered us
eloquent proof of his merciful love.
Humble and trusting worshipper
of the designs of the Divine Heart,
since you were a teenager you spoiled yourself
of all worldly honor and every earthly fortune.
You put on the sackcloth of perfect chastity,
you walked the road of obedience,
you made yourself poor to serve God,
offering everything to him out of love.

You, "pure of heart,"
set us free from all worldly slavery.
Do not let the young fall victim to hatred and violence;
do not permit that they give in to the temptation
of easy and illusory hedonistic fantasies.
Help them rid themselves of all sordid feelings,
defend them from the selfishness that blinds us,
save them from the power of the Evil One.
Make them witnesses of the purity of heart.

You, heroic apostle of charity,
obtain for us the gift of divine mercy,
which stirs hearts hardened by selfishness,
and keep alive in everyone the longing for holiness.
Let today's youth also have the courage to go against the grain,
when it comes to spending their life
to build up the Kingdom of Christ.
May they also share your passion for people,
and recognize in everyone, whoever they may be,
the divine presence of Christ.

Prayer pronounced on June 22, 1991, at the Sanctuary of Castiglione delle Stiviere

Saint John Berchmans

On the morning of August 13, 1621, in the sick ward of the Roman College, the Jesuit scholastic John Berchmans died, aged twenty-two. That same day, he was laid out in the Church of Saint Ignatius next to the college. Immediately, it was crowded by the faithful and by souvenir hunters. At the end of the memorial service, it appeared many had torn a piece from his clothes or from the cloth on the bier to keep as a relic. The corpse had to be dressed again. How was it possible that a young Flemish Jesuit, who had lived in Rome for his studies for less than three years, had become so famous and was posthumously venerated as a saint?

An Angel

More than a month before, on July 8, John had drawn attention to himself because, being the best student of the college, he was to participate in the public debate with which the academic year concluded. All clerical and other dignitaries of Rome were invited. John had to summarize from hearing the exposition of the opponents' questions, address their arguments one after another, and then show what was right in them or not. And all of that in Latin. Soft-spoken, he defended his case with amiability and firmness, with modesty and disarming humor. Someone in the audience whispered: "If I hadn't known better, I would have sworn an angel was standing there, rather than a young man."

A month later, on August 6, John had been allowed to represent the college in a similar debate at the Greek College. There, too, he had gained everybody's admiration through his charming performance. Immediately after that hard day in the heat of the Roman summer, however, he called on the nurse with a headache. In the following days, his health deteriorated quickly. He was completely exhausted. A week later, he died, with in his hands his crucifix, his rosary, and the Jesuit rulebook.

Catchily Cheerful

What was his secret? His Jesuit companions said that John was always kind and cheerful. They had nicknamed him "Frater Hilarius," the cheery brother. He was a diligent student. When unable to spend sufficient time on his studies because of his daily duties, one could see the light in his room burn until very late at night. He was courteous and did everything he was asked with a remarkable cheerfulness. One of his companions said: "I don't know how he does it, but whenever I am depressed, I seek his company and it's over in no time." John captivated people; nothing was too much for him. That, in the end, led to his death.

This became evident, too, when his rector, Virgilio Cepari, leafed through John's private notes. They showed how pious he had been, and how attached to his prayer life. How he tried to serve God in all things, especially in the ordinary things of everyday life. In the novitiate, he had learned that "the most important thing in life is not to do extraordinary things, but to do the ordinary things in an extraordinary way." Father Cepari discovered that John had suffered from headaches and chronic fatigue for months before his death. No one in the community had ever noticed, and John had consistently kept silent about it. His neighbors and his study were more important. And so he served God and offered up his pain to share in the sufferings of Jesus.

Youth Years

Father Cepari decided to write a book about John, as he had done thirty years earlier with Aloysius Gonzaga, who had also died at a young age. He sent two Flemish students back to their country to make inquiries about John's youth in Diest, where he had been born on March 13, 1599, and in Mechelen, where he had lodged as a student and completed his novitiate.

John's father was a master shoemaker and a member of the town council; his mother was the daughter of a mayor. John was the eldest of five siblings, all of whom had been born within a six-year period. When his mother fell ill,

IOANNES BERCMANS *Belga Diestemy natus in Societate* IESV *ita vixit, vt Angeli nomen mereretur. Deipara amore excellens ; propugnaturuseus; te immaculatam illius Conceptionem quantum per S. Ecclesiam liceret syngraphâ scriptâ firmavit. sub mortem , Crucifixum Rosarium et Regulas arctè complexus exclamavit , Hæc tria mihi carissima cum his libenter morior . Obijt Romæ anno* MDCXXI.

EXCELL. PRINCIPI PHILIPPO DEI GRATIA COMITI ARENBERGICO, DVCI ARSCHOTANO, BARONI ZEVENBERGÆ ET QVIEVRAINGY, EQVITI AVREI VELLERIS, CATHOLICÆ MAIESTATI À CVBICVLIS ET CONSILIO STATVS, PRÆFECTO TVRMÆ ÆQVITVM ORDINARIÆ. *B. et à Bolswert DD.*

Saint John Berchmans carries a crucifix, a rosary, and the book of the Rules of the Society of Jesus, of which he said: "All three are dear to me above all, I would die happy with them." Engraving by Boëtius Adamsz Bolswert (circa 1630).

he learned to lend a hand in the house, not to be too noisy, to do the odd chore, take the little ones out to play, and quietly withdraw in a corner when not needed. Already in those days he felt the growing desire to become a priest.

When he was ten years old, the children were placed into care. John was sent to a neighboring parish priest, who, given the boy's character and qualities, was pleased to take him in for a reasonable fee. Two years later, he moved to Mechelen, in order to attend school. There he lived with a canon and earned his living as a servant, taking care of two Dutch boys. Even though he was only thirteen, he did well; had he not been caring for children most of his life? When his duties took up too much time during the day, he would simply study at night.

Entrance in the Jesuit Order

When three years later a Jesuit college was founded in Mechelen, John wanted to go study there. Everyone around him was against it, but John went all the same. The same happened when he decided to enter the Jesuit order. This was preceded by a long period of reflection and prayer. He even spent the greater part of the money he had saved for books, on Masses to be said for obtaining the grace to make the right vocational choice.

What attracted him to the Jesuit order? We could think of the inspiring classes he got from the fathers at the college, bringing science and faith together. Those classes responded to his inquisitiveness and his desire for spiritual deepening; here, too, he was the best student of his year. Or we could think of the personal guidance the fathers provided in prayer and study. Or his membership of the college's Marian sodality, in which he could really bring into practice his great love for Our Lady. We could also think of the Jesuits' principled position toward the ever-spreading Reformation; they stood firm in the Catholic faith and insistingly opposed divergent doctrines. Later, when John told his parents that he wanted to enter the Society of Jesus, he called it "the hammer of all heresies."

But John himself would later say that he had not thought of entering until he read the biography of Aloysius Gonzaga. In it, John recognized how irresistibly God can captivate and attract a person, regardless of circumstances. He read how Aloysius, kindly and with pain in his heart, had resisted his father's anger. The latter had had very different ambitions for his eldest son than becoming a Jesuit. The same applied to John. After he decided to enter the Society, he wrote a letter to his parents. His father moved heaven and earth to dissuade him. But John, normally ever so compliant, was now adamant, without losing his kindness. After hardly a month in the novitiate, he received the message that his mother was dying: Would he not come home to say farewell? John did not go and wrote a pious letter instead. His parents were hurt by his refusal, yet a few months after his mother had died, John's father applied to the priesthood. One year later, he was ordained.

Saintly Gestures of Charity

What made John a saint? Was it his ability to subordinate his pain and physical discomfort to his daily duties and charitable services? As courageous as John's attitude in this matter may have been, and how much it may have been prompted by the enthusiasm of his youth, a critical note is appropriate here. Saint Ignatius always emphasized the importance of good health. According to the *Constitutions*, John should have been more open and transparent towards his superior on this matter. Also, the superior, as well as John's companions, should have been more attentive to his well-being.

Maybe we should seek his holiness more in his desire to turn even the most ordinary things into gestures of charity. In the spirit of Ignatius: to seek and find God in all things; to be a person of prayer. John's childhood years had been marked by his mother's illness. He had not known a home since he was ten. He had to obey, be helpful, be quiet, take care of little children, watch other people's needs, efface himself; he had to study at night when he was unable to do so during the day. God knows with how much pain he had acquired these virtues. And these were the very qualities with which John as a young Jesuit impressed other people. His life as a religious consisted in generously putting at God's service all he had learned as a child. To live for God—we might learn from John—does not mean doing things you are really unable to do. It means doing the things you can do in the service of the Gospel—doing ordinary things with love.

Dries van den Akker, SJ[10]

---

10. Translation by Marc Lindeijer, SJ.

John Berchmans was beatified by Pope Pius IX in 1865 and canonized by Pope Leo XIII on January 15, 1888.

Holy Mary, Virgin Mother of God, I choose you this day to be my queen, my patroness, and my advocate; and I firmly resolve never to leave you, and never say or do anything against you, nor ever permit others to do anything against your honor. Receive me, then, I beg of you, as your servant forever. Help me in my every action, and abandon me not at the hour of my death. Amen.

Saint John Berchmans

José de Anchieta (1534–97)

"APOSTLE OF BRAZIL AND MIRACLE WORKER OF THE NEW WORLD"

Memorial on June 9

José de Anchieta was born on March 19, 1534 in the city of San Cristóbal de la Laguna, on the island of Tenerife in the archipelago of the Canaries, part of Spain. His parents sent him to study at the University of Coimbra in Portugal. Anchieta developed his gifts as a student of rhetoric, poetry, Greek language and culture, dramaturgy, and other disciplines. These humanistic studies he later used effectively in his work in evangelization and catechesis.

He got to know the Jesuits in 1548, seven years before the Society assumed responsibility for the Faculty of Arts at Coimbra. His contact with the Jesuits quickly aroused interest on both sides. Anchieta entered the order three years later, when he was seventeen years old, and he excelled in the spiritual life. While still a novice, the contemplations of the month of Spiritual Exercises awoke in him a desire for the missionary life.

Missionary of the Missionaries

On May 8, 1553, Anchieta and six companions sailed for Brazil on the fleet that was under the direction of the second governor general, Duarte da Costa. After a journey of two months, they disembarked in Salvador, Bahia, and five months later he was sent to the southern region of São Vicente. On January 21, 1554, a group of Jesuits chosen by the provincial, Manuel da Nóbrega, undertook the major project of founding the College of São Paulo in Piratininga. José de Anchieta, who stood out because of his youth and great learning, was named teacher of Latin and humanities for the twelve Jesuits, including the superior. Thus, he began his apostolic activity not just as another missionary but as a missionary to missionaries: he was teaching men who were going to be priests without being a priest himself. He instructed them not only in the Latin needed for sacred orders but also in the indigenous language, which was the most important instrument for pastoral work in those times. He developed a grammar and other works in the Tupi language, and these opened the way toward new life for the Indians. Anchieta was a founder of the college and therefore also of the city of São Paulo, and for many years he was the soul of the college and the catechist of the region.

Anchieta the apostle was always actively seeking people's conversion, especially by means of his theater productions, in which he presented the Christian way of life in an entertaining and interesting way. He outlined major doctrinal points in detailed fashion in his *Catechism*, written in the native language, and in his *Dialogue of Faith*. His catechesis bore much fruit: "130 Indians of all ages and both sexes were admitted to the catechumenate, and thirty-six to baptism. They study Christian doctrine twice a day. On Sundays, they go to Mass, but the catechumens complain when they are dismissed after the offertory; as a result, they are often allowed to stay." Despite the excellent catechesis, the bad example of the Portuguese caused great difficulties. Moreover, the natives tended to be inconsistent. A culture of vengeance was deeply rooted in their mentality, and cannibalistic banquets were held simply to celebrate a victory over enemies.

A Peace Mission

The truce afforded by the Portuguese victories over the Indians in 1561 and 1562 was frequently disturbed by attacks from the Tupis and the Tamoios. After careful discernment, Nóbrega saw clearly that it was the will of God that he travel to the territory of the Tamoios in order to seek peace; he was ready to acknowledge the injustices committed by the colonizers. Since he had not mastered the native language, he asked Anchieta to accompany him. The two of them left São Vicente on the octave of Easter and traveled in canoe as far as Bertioga. There they stayed in the fort of São Tiago until setting off for Tamoio territory.

After six days, they left for Iperoig (the modern-day city of Ubatuba), where they arrived many days later. They did not leave their canoes but waited for the Indians to join them. Anchieta explained that they came on a mission of peace and that they would remain there as hostages while two Indians went to São Vicente. Nóbrega and Anchieta were received as guests in the lodge of Cunhambebe, an Indian chief who got along well with the missionaries and took good care of them. While living there in Iperoig, the missionaries lost no time; they gave catechesis to the children, some of which rubbed off on the adults who observed them from a distance.

During their two months of captivity, there were disputes and threats of death but also comforting moments such as the Masses and homilies for the Tamoio Indians. Finally, a peace agreement seemed to be reached. Conscious of the fragility of the accord, Nóbrega decided to leave on June 21 to talk directly with the interested parties in São Vicente. Anchieta insisted on remaining in Iperoig as a hostage of peace in order to provide security to the Indians.

The time in Iperoig was without a doubt his great moment of agony, struggle, anxiety, and option for God. All alone during those three months, without Mass or the sacraments, he fought against evil, and God remained by his side, giving him strength. During this time of testing, Anchieta had recourse to the Virgin Mary, asking her for special graces to overcome the countless trials. He promised her that he would compose a poem in recognition of the graces he received, and he set about doing so immediately, even before attaining the grace he asked for, so great was his faith that his request would be heard. This poem is still the longest one ever written to Mary; it contains six thousand verses and is filled with literal biblical citations, thus giving ample evidence of Anchieta's mastery of sacred scripture.

On September 14, 1563, Anchieta was finally freed, and he arrived in Bertioga on September 22. Father Luís da Grã presented the petition for his ordination, bearing witness to the worthiness of the candidate. In June 1566, he was ordained a priest of Christ by a former companion of Coimbra who was now the second bishop of Brazil, Don Pedro Leitão. He is famous for his saying: "The Society in Brazil is a golden ring, and Father José is its precious stone."

Pastoral Letters

In 1576, Superior General Everard Mercurian named Anchieta as provincial of Brazil, thus making him superior of the more than 140 Jesuits then living in the Americas. As provincial, Anchieta wrote and received countless letters. Some of his letters to Superior General Claudio Acquaviva tell of his relations

Saint José de Anchieta on the beach, perhaps that of Iperoig, where in 1563 he composed his famous poem to the Virgin Mary. Painting by Benedito Calixto de Jesus (1902).

with the black slaves and give evidence of his concern for their evangelization. He showed great interest in the spiritual lives of those who played a fundamental role in the construction of Brazil. His letters describe the harsh treatment of the slaves brought from Guinea, and he reports that in the year 1582 alone more than two thousand were brought to Salvador. He commented on their state of health and on the catechetical work being done with those who survived the crossing of the Atlantic, including the creation of the Guild of the Rosary. He also wrote about the pastoral work being done on the farms and in the towns.

Anchieta showed particular concern for the sick, as he did aboard the ship that brought him from Europe. He helped them get up and later put them to bed; he remained awake and attentive as long as the sick person needed him. Often he got up at night to prepare medicine or food for someone who was sick. And it was precisely the diligent care he was giving to a bedridden Jesuit that hastened Anchieta's death. He reached his final Passover on Sunday, June 9, 1597.

Cesar Augusto Dos Santos, SJ[11]

José de Anchieta was beatified by John Paul II in 1980 and canonized by Pope Francis on April 4, 2014. On July 10, 2010, the president of Brazil inscribed him in the Book of the National Heroes.

---

11. *Jesuits, Yearbook of the Society of Jesus* (Rome, 2015), 46–49. Translation by Joseph V. Owens, SJ.

From a Letter of Superior General Adolfo Nicolás

Of the forty-four years that José de Anchieta lived in Brazil, at least forty can be characterized by constant traveling, beginning in the region of São Vicente and Piratininga, between 1554 and 1564, when the founding and first years of the city of São Paolo took place. Named provincial in 1577, and later as superior, he visited houses and communities: father of the poor, healer of the sick and those who suffered, counselor for governors, but above all friend and defender of the Indians in their villages.

Certainly he was not moved to carry out this itinerant life by any spirit of adventure, but rather by a spirit of availability for the mission, of spiritual freedom, and of promptness to search and find in each moment the will of the Lord. A true apostolic fire accompanied him to the very end. "Since I do not deserve to be a martyr by any other way," he himself writes, "may death at least find me abandoned in one of these mountains and there to die for my brothers. My physical condition is weak, but the strength of grace is enough for me, which on God's part will never fail."

Should not itinerancy—with all that it implies of spiritual freedom, of availability, and of capacity to discern and make choices—be one of the indispensable characteristics of our apostolic body? The constant travels of Anchieta, almost a way of life, could in our day inspire and animate our search for apostolic mobility in order to respond to the challenges that new frontiers set before us.

Letter of April 3, 2014, to the whole Society, on the canonization of José de Anchieta

Saint Peter Canisius (1521–97)

DOCTOR OF THE CHURCH

Memorial on April 27

An Unstructured Jesuit Formation

Peter Canisius spent his life improvising. Because he joined the Society of Jesus in 1543, only three years after its founding, he had little choice: the structured stages of Jesuit formation did not exist during Canisius's formative years, and he was a founding member of every Jesuit institution in which he worked. When he took his first vows in the presence of Saint Peter Faber, scant days after making the *Spiritual Exercises*, the Society's *Constitutions* had not been written, nor was there a set vow formula for him to profess.

The Dutch-born Canisius was already a student of theology at the University of Cologne when he met Faber; he was ordained a priest three years later, in 1546, and invited as a theologian to the Council of Trent in 1547. After Trent, he made his way to Rome, where Ignatius of Loyola assigned him to make a reduced form of the *Exercises* in three weeks, to serve at menial tasks around the house, and to minister in local hospitals, which amounted to what would later be called Jesuit tertianship. Shortly thereafter, Canisius was one of the nine Jesuits who founded the first Jesuit college for lay students at Messina. But by 1549 he was back in Rome to make his solemn profession of four vows before being sent to the University of Ingolstadt to serve as a professor of theology.

This inaugurated his ministry among the German-speaking peoples of the Holy Roman Empire, whom he would serve for the rest of his life. He was dismayed by his first encounter in Ingolstadt with the wreckage left of the German Catholic faith in the aftermath of the Protestant Reformation. But he met this dismay with his confidence in the presence of God's Spirit at work in the Society of Jesus. Amid the frenetic, unstructured years of his unique formation, Canisius had made the Society's way of proceeding his own, and it became his way of serving the Church amid the tumultuous times in which he lived.

Moved by Love

Canisius felt the wounds of the Church deeply. The final chapter of the "Spiritual Testament" he composed in the last years of his life is a prayer "for the enemies of the Church." Canisius's harsh words regarding the "dark impiety of Satan" that blinds "infidels," and the seductions of the "plague" of heresy show him to be a man of thoroughly sixteenth-century religious sensibilities, unaware of the possibility of God's Spirit at work outside the Catholic Church. But if we look beyond this theology and his disconcerting rhetoric, his prayer reveals how moved he was by love for those whom he considered his enemies. He does not ask God to punish the Protestant Christians whom he names as "deserters and perturbators," but rather begs God to "have mercy on our false brothers, either knowingly or ignorantly sinning, that they may not be punished in this present or in the future age on account of their perfidy, but led back to true faith and charity, that they may be made sons of peace."[12] He desired not only peace and unity in the Church, but salvation for those who seemed to him farthest from it. For Canisius, this was no vain hope, but rather the driving inspiration behind much of his labor as a Jesuit.

And he was convinced that restoring unity to the Church demanded not endless argument, but deep spiritual renewal. Thus, although he participated in such events as the Colloquy of Worms in 1557 where he discussed the theological controversies of the day with the prominent Protestant reformer Philip Melanchthon, his heart lay not in debate, but in the spiritual formation of youth. Nearly as soon as he arrived in Ingolstadt in 1549, Canisius began to agitate both for the production of a Jesuit catechism that could be used in the instruction of youth and also for the foundation of Jesuit colleges among the German-speaking people. He published his first catechism, the *Summa doct-*

---

12. Julius Oswald and Rita Haub, eds., *Das Testament des Petrus Canisius. Vermächtnis und Auftrag* (Frankfurt am Main, 1997), 57. All translations are my own.

In 1546, Saint Peter Canisius pleaded before Emperor Charles V, the apostolic nuncio, and the clergy of Liège against the archbishop of Cologne, Hermann von Wied, who had broken with the Holy See. Soon after, von Wied was deposed and excommunicated. Stained glass workshops of the Carmel of Le Mans Hucher & Fils (1878–80).

rinae christianae, in 1555, and would go on to publish and endlessly revise catechisms for all levels of instruction throughout the rest of his life. By the time he died some forty years later, his various catechisms had gone through at least 347 editions and been translated into sixteen different languages. By any measure, they were phenomenally successful. At the same time, he involved himself in the foundation of well over a dozen different Jesuit colleges and worked hard for the financial support of the German College in Rome for the training of German diocesan clergy, as he also labored tirelessly as a preacher and teacher of catechism himself. He worked for many years as the official preacher at the cathedral in Augsburg, and this while also serving as the first provincial of the Superior German province, a post he held for fourteen years.

Another prayer Canisius composed gives particular insight into the thread that held these various labors together. It is his prayer for the Society of Jesus: "I commend to your Lord Jesus this body of our universal Society, that in its heads and in its members, in its healthy and its sick, in its progressing members and those who are falling away, in spiritual and temporal matters, it may be duly governed to the glory of your Name and the utility of the whole Church." The prayer testifies to Canisius's concern for every aspect of the life of the Society, as he beseeches God for an increase in Jesuit virtue, for a deepening of "the bonds of fraternal charity," as well as for the Society's benefactors and deceased members.[13]

Encounter with God

Canisius once described his experience of the *Spiritual Exercises* under the guidance of Faber as being like the call and conversion of Saint Matthew in the Gospel. On the surface, the comparison seems implausible: Canisius was committed to his faith from a young age, and certainly never engaged in the sort of public sin exemplified by Matthew the tax collector. But he understood the Exercises and his Jesuit vocation as that which had freed him from the "entanglements" of the world's confusion and temptations.[14] The Exercises allowed him the freedom to meet Christ and to know his will. He came to see

---

13. Otto Braunsberger, ed., *Beati Petri Canisii, Societatis Iesu, epistulae et acta* (Freiburg im Breisgau,1896–1923), 8:783.
14. *Das Testament des Petrus Canisius*, 37.

this Christian freedom, this encounter with the living God, as the great gift of the Society of Jesus to the Church. And so in his catechesis and his preaching, in the schools he founded and the books he wrote, Canisius strove to do much more than simply teach Catholic doctrine: he sought to form Catholics in faith so that they, too, could meet the Lord whom he had encountered in the *Spiritual Exercises*, and whose Spirit animated the Society to which he belonged.

This was why Canisius's catechism utilized a structure unlike any other catechism written before it. He organized his presentation of Christian teaching not merely according to the traditional topics he included—the Creed, the Our Father, the Ten Commandments, and the Sacraments—but as a protracted lesson in how to know God's wisdom and to pursue God's justice. Indeed, the two books of Canisius's *Summa* bore the names of "Wisdom" and "Justice." For Canisius did not see catechesis as primarily an exercise in memorization: it was an encounter with God that should lead people to a desire to live their lives in accord with God's goodness. Jesuit colleges, too, were meant not merely to inform students, but to form them in virtue.

This was the work of Canisius's life: not to assault Protestant theology, but to build up the body of the Catholic Church according to the spiritual methods he had learned in his Jesuit formation. There was no well-trodden path for him to follow in this work: he had to improvise at every turn. But the spiritual pattern of his life appeared as soon as he emerged from the Exercises and professed his vows before Peter Faber. From then on, he knew of no better way to serve the Church than as a Jesuit, and no surer place to encounter Christ than in laboring alongside him in his least Society.

Thomas Flowers, SJ

Peter Canisius was beatified by Pope Pius IX in 1864, and later canonized and proclaimed a doctor of the Church by Pius XI on May 21 of the Holy Year 1925.

From the Catechesis of Pope Benedict XVI on Saint Peter Canisius

This was a characteristic of Saint Peter Canisius: his ability to combine harmoniously fidelity to dogmatic principles with the respect that is due to every person. Saint Canisius distinguished between a conscious, blameworthy apostasy from faith and a blameless loss of faith through circumstances. Moreover, he declared to Rome that the majority of Germans who switched to Protestantism were blameless. In a historical period of strong confessional differences, Canisius avoided the harshness and rhetoric of anger and aimed only at presenting the spiritual roots and at reviving the faith in the Church. His vast and penetrating knowledge of sacred scripture and of the fathers of the Church served this cause: the same knowledge that supported his personal relationship with God and the austere spirituality that he derived from the Devotio Moderna and Rhenish mysticism.

Characteristic of Saint Canisius's spirituality was his profound personal friendship with Jesus. For example, on September 4, 1549 he wrote in his journal, speaking with the Lord: "In the end, as if you were opening to me the heart of the Most Sacred Body, which it seemed to me I saw before me, you commanded me to drink from that source, inviting me, as it were, to draw the waters of my salvation from your founts, O my Savior." Then he saw that the Saviour was giving him a garment with three pieces that were called peace, love, and perseverance. And with this garment, made up of peace, love, and perseverance, Canisius carried out his work of renewing Catholicism. His friendship with Jesus—which was the core of his personality—nourished by love of the Bible, by love of the Blessed Sacrament, and by love of the fathers, this friendship was clearly united with the awareness of being a perpetuator of the apostles' mission in the Church. And this reminds us that every genuine evangelizer is always an instrument united with Jesus and with his Church and is fruitful for this very reason.

The Christocentric spirituality of Saint Peter Canisius is rooted in a profound conviction: no soul anxious for perfection fails to practice prayer daily, mental prayer, an ordinary means that enables the disciple of Jesus to live in intimacy with the divine Teacher. For this reason, in his writings for the spiritual education of the people, our saint insists on the importance of the liturgy with his comments on the Gospels, on feasts, on the rite of Holy Mass, and on the sacraments; yet, at the same time, he is careful to show the faithful the need for and beauty of personal daily prayer, which should accompany and permeate participation in the public worship of the Church.

General audience of February 9, 2011

Saint Robert Bellarmine (1542–1621)

DOCTOR OF THE CHURCH

Memorial on September 17

The life of Robert Bellarmine played out in a century that was critical for Catholics. The Protestant Reformation provoked an explosion in the Western Church, and made clear the necessity of a profound renewal. This was the task of the Council of Trent, which was held between 1545 and 1563. But it took men like Bellarmine to bring the decisions of the council into reality so that the Church might emerge stronger through this challenge.

A Focused and Full Life

Born in Montepulciano, a small village in Tuscany, Italy, and educated in a school run by the Jesuits, Robert Bellarmine entered the Society of Jesus in 1560 and began his studies at the Roman College founded by Saint Ignatius.

Quite quickly, his brilliant mind, his prodigious knowledge, produced by endless studies, and the clarity and solidity of his thinking, led his superiors to commit him to the tasks of preaching and teaching. Even before his ordination to the priesthood in 1570, his superiors sent him to Louvain: the Catholics of this university city sought someone able to confront Protestant preachers who had become more and more influential in Flanders. Bellarmine spent seven years in Louvain at the heart of the great theological debates.

Having become quite famous, he was called back to Italy and took up increasingly important positions: professor, then rector of the Roman College, and finally provincial in Naples in 1594.

In 1599, Pope Clement VIII named Bellarmine a cardinal, an honor and burden he did all he could to evade. Once made a prince of the Church, however, he applied himself and became an active member of a number of congregations. Named archbishop of Capua, he spent three years there, which were rich in pastoral experiences. However, the pope preferred to have this great theologian near him. Bellarmine spent the rest of his life in Rome, where he gave a huge amount of energy at the service of successive popes, for whom he was the listened-to counsellor and spokesman, involved in all the debates of that time.

So, what are we to draw from this life so focused and full?

Great Theologian

First of all, Bellarmine was a great theologian during a time when the Catholic faith was rattled by Protestant attacks. At Louvain, and then at Rome, where he held the chair of controversial theology created to refute Protestant positions, he spent night and day studying the writings of the reformers to put in order responses to their arguments and stating clearly the positions of the Catholic Church as based upon scripture, the teaching of the church fathers, the councils, and the popes.

From 1586, his courses in controversial theology, which touched upon the burning topics of the time—grace, sacraments, the Church—were published and were met with immense success. By the appropriateness and depth of his thought, but also by the courteous and measured tone of the author, at a time when polemic had descended into an exchange of name-calling and slandering, his work had such persuasive power that it brought about numerous reconversions. The reformers, seeing the danger, multiplied their attacks.

Spiritual Master

Bellarmine was also a great spiritual master: as rector of the Roman College, as provincial, as spiritual director of many of his contemporaries, and as author of spiritual books. His teaching is fundamentally Ignatian: he insists without ever yielding on the necessity of exercising and mastering oneself. For him, continual prayer, renunciation, being prompt and careful in the service of God, kindness in word and act, and generous use of the world's goods, are basic necessities for anyone called by God to service in the Church.

And, what he taught, he lived. "Outside of his studies and letter writing, he spends all or most of his time in prayer," said his principal servant. A cardinal described in the following words what he admired most in Bellarmine: "A

ROBERTVS·BELLARMINVS·POLITIANVS·S·R·E·CARD·TIT·S·MARIAE·IN·VIA·ARCHIEPISCOPVS
CAPVANVS·ECCLESIAE·CATHOLICAE·ADVERSVS·HAERETICOS·PROPVGNATOR·ACERRIMVS
AETAT·SVAE·ANN·L·XII
Bellarminus hic est, geminas qui contudit hydras
Hinc laude ingenii, moribus inde piis.
Franciscus Villamena fe. Romæ Anno. 1604. Cum priuilegio Summi Pontificis et Superiorum authoritate.

Saint Robert Bellarmine is at his desk. In the background, we see the Church of the Gesù and a portrait of Saint Ignatius. Engraving by Francesco Villamena (1604).

great humility from which this vast knowledge, of which everyone is aware, allows nothing to be lost, an austerity in regard to himself which he never relaxes nor excuses himself. And yet he himself is of a friendly, peaceful, and joyful nature." At a time when the higher clergy were often corrupted by their appetite for power and riches, this prince of the Church gave an example of poverty, humility, and service. One might say that for the honor of the Church a cardinal should have an imposing sort of life, but Bellarmine never accepted that. He looked upon his servants as his children; his house was a refuge for all the poor devils of the streets. He treated all as one would a gentleman, which was seen as astonishing in Rome; he would give anyone anything, even his own mattress.

At Capua, like his contemporaries, Saints Charles Borromeo and Francis de Sales, Bellarmine was truly a pastor who tends his sheep, as the Council of Trent strongly reminded the Church after the abuse and decadence of earlier years: preaching everywhere, visiting remote villages to meet and instruct simple folk, reforming his clergy with gentle firmness, holding synods to organize the application of the council's decisions.

At the end of his life, in a little book titled *The Eternal Happiness of the Saints*, Bellarmine expressed a peaceful confidence in the wondrous destiny of the human race, created by God in his own image, beloved and saved by him, summoned to enter into joy: "We shall enter into an immense sea of eternal joy, which will fill us within and surround us on all sides."

And it was filled with this hope that on September 17, 1621, he "returned home," as he liked to say when he spoke of his death.

Colette Savart[15]

Robert Bellarmine was declared blessed by Pius XI in 1923 and a saint on June 19, 1930. This same pope declared him a doctor of the Church in 1931.

---

15. "Visages ignatiens," *Sources vives* 41 (1992): 46–49. Translation by Walter E. Boehme, SJ.

Charity is that with which no man is lost, and without which no man is saved.

Saint Robert Bellarmine

The Forty Martyrs of Brazil

BLESSED IGNATIUS DE AZEVEDO AND COMPANIONS

(†1570)

Optional Memorial on January 19

Ecclesial Apostolate and Ignatian Discernment

Ignatius de Azevedo was born around 1527 in Porto. His father, Manuel de Azevedo, was a nobleman, commander of São João d'Alpendurada. His younger brother, Jerónimo, would become viceroy of India. It was the golden age of Portuguese exploration. The campaign to spread the Gospel in the huge Brazilian continent was beginning to move from the coast to the interior. In a primitive society of poverty-stricken nomadic people who lived by scraping what they could from the land against a background of superstition, tribal war, and cannibalism, this apostolate was not limited to fervent, dedicated priests. It was shared by committed lay catechists, with family groups acting as the nuclei of social action and giving direction and unity to the enterprise. This was a new form of ecclesial apostolate, a prophetic preannouncement of modern missionary techniques.

Azevedo, with his upbringing at court and his education in the humanities, was of a haughty and independent temperament, and had to be won to the way of humility and gentleness for the Cross of Christ. Acting on the advice of a friend, Henrique Nunes de Gouveia, he went to hear the Jesuit Francisco Estrada preaching. He was struck by the transience of earthly ambitions in the light of eternal truth and decided to go to Coimbra to find out more about the Jesuits. He was twenty-two when he resolved to join the Society, but he wanted to base this resolution on clear, solid discernment and therefore made the

Spiritual Exercises for forty days. On November 28, 1548, he exchanged his life on his family estate at Barbosa for the modest lifestyle of the Jesuits. He continued his arts studies and went on to philosophy and theology. In February 1553, Azevedo was ordained a priest.

A Born Leader, Serving the Glory of God

The news of the Jesuit missions delighted him: first from Angola and Congo, then from India and Japan. However, he wanted obedience to have the last word. "I would not like to think," he wrote, "that any request or representation from me might be the reason for a decision by my superiors. The greater glory of God must be the supreme reason." He soon revealed unusual qualities of leadership, and these were given an outlet in the Colleges of Coimbra and Lisbon. Sent to Braga, he founded the schools there, which Archbishop Bartolomeu dos Mártires had asked the Society to open. He combined his administrative duties with pastoral activity, especially in the hospitals and prisons, and in the countryside. His great apostolic weapons were prayer, penance, and works of mercy.

His heart, however, was with the overseas missions. In Brazil, Father Manuel da Nóbrega was pressing for reinforcements and particularly needed a man capable of reorganizing the emerging Christian communities on a more solid basis. They thought of Ignatius: an active, enterprising, and energetic man. Sent to Rome as procurator for India and Brazil at the time of the Second General Congregation of 1565, he was appointed by the new superior general to be visitor of the Tierras de Santa Cruz (Brazil). The appointment called for dynamic and effective government in the south and in Bahia. The enterprise there had slowed down, and some restructuring was needed if progress was to be made. There was also a lack of personnel.

In 1568, Ignatius was again sent as procurator to Rome and this time also to Lisbon, and while in Portugal secured effective material aid. There was no greater prize than men, however, and in his travels round various houses and colleges Ignatius's powers of apostolic persuasion raised an enthusiastic response from the young. In Rome, he impressed Pius V and Francis Borgia. The pope gave him wide pastoral faculties, and the saintly superior general was struck so much by the urgent need to help Brazil that he wrote to the Spanish provinces encouraging them to be generous with missionaries and

V.V.P. Ignatius de Azevedo Lusit, et Soty 39. S.I. ad prædicandum Xti Evangelium in
Brasiliam misi pro Fide occiduntur ab Hæreticis, et in mare proijiuntur
18. July. 1570.

*Blessed Ignatius de Azevedo and his thirty-nine companions, on their way to Brazil to
preach the Gospel there, are attacked by Calvinist corsairs and thrown into the ocean
(seventeenth century).*

money to assist a region so lacking in resources. This recommendation was given added force by Azevedo's burning eloquence.

Gathering Apostles for Brazil

On his way back to Portugal, Ignatius was given, out of many volunteers, three men from Valencia, five from Madrid, and two from Medina del Campo. But the largest contingent came to him from the colleges and novitiates of Coimbra and Évora. In this way, he gathered an expedition of seventy-three priests and brothers, together with several lay workmen and servants; in all, about one hundred men. This heterogeneous mixture of people could only give positive results if inspired by deep apostolic unity.

As the plague spread in Lisbon, Azevedo concentrated his expedition, mainly composed of religious, at the farm of Vale de Rosal, a property of the College of Saint Anthony, south of the Tagus. In this healthy atmosphere of the countryside and the Atlantic beaches, he prepared his battalion of missionaries both physically and spiritually for the great evangelizing campaign in the Brazilian interior, which called for bodies of steel and hearts of gold.

Forging Missionary Souls

The months of waiting were passed in devotional practices, communal and individual, exercises in humility and penance, spiritual conferences, and hours of study or work, with intervals of music and song or walks in the open countryside or at the seaside, pilgrimages to the local sanctuaries and processions in the fields, according to the seasonal liturgy.

Azevedo was not merely the eloquent, inspiring voice of youthful enthusiasm. Following his unvarying method, he was the living example of all that he inculcated in asceticism and zeal. The hardest work, the humblest task, the service carried out with unchanging cheerfulness and generosity were all for him. The lives of the saints offer few more striking instances of such simple piety, jovial joy, and brotherly love, solidly founded on austerity of life.

On June 5, 1570, the peaceful army of seventy-four Jesuits sailed in three ships from the Tagus for the Island of Madeira. Life on board for laymen and religious was almost monastic; prayers and hymns were recited and sung in common at daybreak and nightfall, whenever the weather permitted.

A Heavenly "College" of Martyrs

On June 30, despite the reluctance of the governor of Brazil, Luís de Vasconcelos, but at the request of the traders of the ship *Santiago*, which was about to sail for the Canary Islands, Ignatius re-embarked with thirty-nine companions. With some forebodings of danger from pirates and of possible martyrdom, he called his group together before going on board. He wanted volunteers, not pressed men, to die for Christ. Some hesitated, but their places were immediately taken by candidates from the other ships.

After two weeks of travelling, while they were sailing from Tazacorte for Las Palmas, a fleet of Huguenot pirates came into view, commanded by Jacques de Sores (Sourie). As the defenders of the *Santiago* were few in number, the captain asked Azevedo for fighting men. His team, however, were priests and religious and as such could not fight. They could only help the wounded and encourage the defenders with prayer.

When the Huguenots took the ship and saw among the crew so many missionaries on their way to evangelize Brazil, they pressed home the attack. Azevedo met them, with an image of Our Lady in his hands, and declared he was a priest of Christ: "You are all witnesses that I am dying for the Catholic faith and for the Holy Roman Church." A soldier slashed at his head, leaving him covered in blood.

The other religious supported him with their prayers and also confessed their faith: their only sorrow was for the Brazilian missions, which would now be deprived of their help. Azevedo told them: "Do not weep, my sons: we shall not reach Brazil, but today we shall found a college in heaven." The enraged Huguenots slew Azevedo and Father Diogo de Andrade, the only other Jesuit priest on board, who was shielding him, and threw them into the sea. Afterwards, they slaughtered all the other Jesuits, except two: the novice brother Simão da Costa, who was held over till next day, and Brother João Sánchez, whom they made their cook. His place was taken by the captain's son, also named João, who wanted to enter the Society, and gave himself up as a Jesuit, so bringing the number of martyrs to forty. He was called, for this reason, *Adaucto* (added). All these martyrs died on July 15 and 16, 1570.

The death, at one blow, of such a large group of missionaries deeply impressed the whole of Christendom. Humanly speaking, it was a catastrophe for the evangelization of Brazil. But under divine Providence the martyrs were the forty living stones of a cathedral built as a splendid monument on the threshold of Christian Brazil, under the sign and promise of the Southern Cross.

Domingos Maurício, SJ

Pius IX confirmed the liturgical cult of Ignatius de Azevedo and his thirty-nine companions on May 11, 1854.

Saint Edmund Campion and His Two Companions

(✝1581)

On December 1, 1581 at Tyburn, London, a triple execution took place: that of the Jesuit Edmund Campion, his companion Alexander Briant, admitted to the Society in prison, and the diocesan priest Ralph Sherwin. The most famous of them was Campion: he had given up a promising career at Oxford and refused an invitation to enter Queen Elizabeth's service, in order to become a Catholic priest and minister to the abandoned English Catholics who greatly desired the sacraments.

To Live Openly as a Catholic

Campion was born in London in 1540, of Catholic parents who later became Protestant. He studied in Oxford, where he gained renown as a lecturer and a following of students who called themselves "Campionites." When he was twenty-six years old, he gave a speech of welcome to Queen Elizabeth in Latin on her visit to Oxford; he made such an impression on the queen that she and Lords Cecil and Leicester tried to recruit him for her service. He was ordained a deacon for the Established Church, yet the more he studied to be a priest, the more convinced he became that the Catholic Church had the true faith. He moved to Dublin in 1569, in an effort to find a place to live openly as a Catholic, but the Irish capital showed an anti-Catholic feeling that drove him back to London.

In June 1571, Edmund left England for Douai, in Northern France, where the recently founded English College trained seminarians for England. He finished his degree in 1573 and set out soon after for Rome with the intention of becoming a Jesuit. Within a month of his arrival in Rome, he was accepted into the Society. At that time, there was neither an English province nor an English mission, so he was assigned to the Austrian province and went to Prague and Brno to make his novitiate. He remained in Prague after he took vows and was ordained there, expecting to spend the rest of his life teaching in that city. He wrote and directed plays for his students and won renown as an orator.

His life changed course suddenly when the superior general in Rome decided to open a mission in England. Father Campion was one of the first to be assigned to it. He stopped in Rome on his way back to England and joined Father Robert Persons and Brother Ralph Emerson. They turned north and joined other recruits for the new mission at Saint-Omer in Flanders. English spies in Flanders learned of their impending departure and informed the English ports of entry, who awaited their arrival. Campion and Emerson left the continent on June 24. Campion disguised himself as a jewelry merchant. Port authorities were suspicious, but he answered their questions adequately, and they let the merchant enter.

It had been eight years since Campion had left England. He briefly remained in London, where he preached in a semi-clandestine manner and wrote a manifesto of the mission that has become known as "Campion's Brag" and was widely divulged in all the London prisons and in the countryside. Its influence in the English Church was inestimable. In it, the Catholics discovered a new type of priest: a man sent by the pope, equipped with all the sciences of the continent, armed against all weakness, loyal to his fatherland, as intelligent as he was saintly. A breath of hope calmed their restless hearts. But it was a challenge in the face of the political powers. From now on, the missionaries were condemned to the strictest underground existence.

Campion himself moved on to Berkshire, Oxfordshire, Lancashire, and Yorkshire. He would stay at a Catholic house for one or two nights or visit households where Catholics were employed. His pattern was to arrive during the day, preach and hear confessions during the evening, and then celebrate Mass in the morning before moving on to the next location. He continued to write and composed a book addressed to the academic world, entitled *Ten Reasons Proposed to His Adversaries for Disputation in the Name of the Faith and Presented to the Illustrious Members of Our Universities*. The book was printed by the end of June 1581. Many of the four hundred copies printed were left on the benches of Oxford's University Church of Saint Mary. Campion was still well-enough known that the book was eagerly read.

On one of his clandestine visits to a Catholic family, in July, a spy named George Eliot, who had posed as a Catholic, was present and left to denounce Campion. Some fifty soldiers surrounded the house and finally discovered the hole in which three priests had hidden themselves with some food. Through his sweetness and charm, Campion managed to win the friendship of his guards during his transferal to London; his traitor, on the other hand, was despised and rejected like a cursed man.

All Companions of Jesus in the End

The three were taken to the Tower of London on July 22, where Campion was put in a cell so small he could neither stand upright nor lie down. After three days there, he was brought to Leicester House, where he met Queen Elizabeth for a second time. She offered him the opportunity to renounce his Catholic faith and become a Protestant minister, with the offer of great advancement. He refused and was returned to his cell; five days later, he was tortured on the rack. He had four conferences with Anglican divines, something he himself had requested in the book *Ten Reasons,* but the disputations were inconclusive, partly because the first one was held shortly after he had been tortured. The government determined that he should be executed, but it needed a stronger charge than the fact that he was a Catholic priest.

On November 14, the priests were led to Westminster Hall, where charges were raised against them that they had formed a conspiracy against the life of the queen, had exhorted foreigners to invade the country, and had entered England with the intent of fomenting rebellion to support the invaders. Campion attempted to defend all the priests by pointing out their motives were religious, not political; but they were found guilty of high treason and condemned to be hanged, drawn, and quartered. The priests joined in singing the *Te Deum* when they heard the verdict. One of them was the Reverend Ralph Sherwin, born in 1550, who after his priestly ordination at Douai had spent three years at the English College in Rome, directed by the Jesuits. Back in England in August 1580, he had been arrested two months later and imprisoned in the Tower of London, where he was tortured on the rack and then laid out in the

Saint Edmund Campion was executed at Tyburn in 1581. The words on the banner are taken from his Challenge. Painting by Raúl Berzosa (2018).

snow. Later he was put into an isolation cell, without food. He is said to have been personally offered a bishopric by Queen Elizabeth if he converted, but he refused.

Campion and Sherwin remained in chains for another eleven days; then they were dragged through the muddy streets of London to Tyburn, together with Father Alexander Briant. The latter, born in 1556, had studied at Oxford, where one his teachers had been Father Robert Persons, Campion's companion. Briant had crossed the Channel in 1577 to attend the English College at Douai, where he was reconciled to the Catholic Church. Ordained a priest in 1578, he returned to his homeland in August 1579 and took up ministry in his native shire, Somerset, before being arrested by the priest-hunters on April 28, 1581. He was brought to the Tower and severely tortured, but did not talk. He wrote to the English Jesuits, saying that he kept his mind so firmly set on Christ's Passion that he felt no pain during the torture, only afterwards. He asked to be admitted to the Society and was accepted shortly before the opening of his trial. In his cell, Briant, who called himself "the soldier of the Cross," had carved a small wooden crucifix; he held it in his hand when he headed the procession of the accused priests—they were seven—to court. Like his fellow Jesuit Campion, Briant was accused of high treason and condemned to death.

At Tyburn, the three martyrs were hanged, then disemboweled and cut into pieces. The end of Father Briant was particularly cruel: he was still alive when he was disembowelled. As Campion forgave those who had condemned him, Father Sherwin on the scaffold again proclaimed his Catholic faith and prayed for the queen. His last words were, "Jesus, Jesus, Jesus, be to me Jesus (that is, Savior)!" He was the first member of the English College in Rome to be martyred.

Thomas Rochford, SJ[16]

Beatified by Leo XIII in 1886, Edmund Campion and Ralph Sherwin were canonized by Paul VI on October 25, 1970, together with thirty-eight other martyrs who had died for the faith in England and Wales. Among them also Alexander Briant, beatified in 1921 by Pius XI.

---

16. Revised by Marc Lindeijer, SJ.

From Campion's Brag, to the Members of the Privy Council of Queen Elizabeth I

Many innocent hands are lifted up to heaven for you daily by those English students, whose posterity shall never die, which beyond seas, gathering virtue and sufficient knowledge for the purpose, are determined never to give you over, but either to win you heaven, or to die upon your pikes. And touching our Society, be it known that we have made a league—all the Jesuits in the world, whose succession and multitude must overreach all the practices of England—cheerfully to carry the cross you shall lay upon us, and never to despair your recovery, while we have a man left to enjoy your Tyburn, or to be racked with your torments, or consumed with your prisons. The expense is reckoned, the enterprise is begun; it is of God, it cannot be withstood. So the faith was planted: so it must be restored.

If these my offers be refused, and my endeavors can take no place, and I, having run thousands of miles to do you good, shall be rewarded with rigor, I have no more to say but to recommend your case and mine to Almighty God, the Searcher of Hearts, who sends us his grace, and sets us at accord before the day of payment, to the end we may at last be friends in heaven, when all injuries shall be forgotten.

Liturgy of the Hours, Second Reading for December 1

The Martyrs of Aubenas, France

BLESSED JACQUES SALÈS
AND GUILLAUME SAULTEMOUCHE
(† 1593)

Optional Memorial on January 19

The religious ideas of Martin Luther and even more so of John Calvin had expanded in France and led a small group of Christians to separate from Rome. These newly created churches created some new tensions sustained by the upper classes and opposed groups: on one side were the Catholics, the so-called "Holy League"; on the other, the Huguenots. Assassinations and massacres followed with victims on both sides. It is in this context of mutual violence that the death of two French Jesuits from the Auvergne is situated, Father Jacques Salès and Bother Guillaume Saultemouche. The debate in which the theologian Salès got engaged with his Huguenot opponents, centered on the Eucharist.

Eucharistic Love

Jacques Salès was born in 1556, the year Saint Ignatius died, completed his studies in the Jesuit college at Billom and then at the Clermont Jesuit College in Paris. Even as a youth he had a very strong attraction to prayer. His Eucharistic devotion, already very remarkable, moved a priest to have him serve at his Mass every day.

Salès entered the novitiate at seventeen years of age. After his doctorate, his studies in the Society of Jesus allowed him to be a successful theology professor. But his health had always been weak: he suffered greatly from asthma and had to take food frequently to avoid fainting during the courses he was teaching. For this reason, his superiors sent him to the college at Tournon, located in a region with a better climate, in the south of France. There he was quickly relieved of teaching and spent his time editing doctrinal and apologetic treatises. Because of his special talent for explaining Catholic dogma and morals, he was also sent out to preach missions.

Being humble because of his social situation, Salès did this task despite his success as a professor. He was always available to anyone and to his superiors, who moved him around frequently and one day asked him to take on an unexpected task that delayed his ordination for three years.

As the years rolled on, his love for Jesus in the Blessed Sacrament grew, inspiring constantly his preaching and conversations with stunning results. The self-sacrifice that his life demanded was intimately connected to the sacrifice of the Mass, for him the center of everything. He spoke of this frequently and never let an hour pass without spending some moments kneeling before the Blessed Sacrament. As a professor of theology—and one who prayed his theology—he frequently and happily touched on the Eucharist according to Saint Thomas Aquinas and the recent Council of Trent. On this topic he drafted a paper in which he explained the Catholic position, so bitterly contested by the Protestants. It was this manuscript that he sent to the Protestant ministers in Aubenas who brought him to the day of his death, and it was this doctrinal point that was the explicit and indisputable motive for his martyrdom.

"Goodbye, for We Are on Our Way to Death"

The city of Aubenas had become Calvinistic in the middle of the sixteenth century. Most of its churches were destroyed, and priests were few in number. But towards the end of that century Catholics regained power. They asked the Jesuits to come and preach a long mission of four months, from Advent till Easter, not only to assure that the sacraments would be celebrated, but also to give the faithful the fundamentals of the Catholic faith.

Salès, well prepared for this difficult task, was missioned by his superiors. When he learned that he had been chosen for this task, it was the happiest news he could imagine, and he kissed the relic of the English Jesuit martyr, Edmund Campion, which he always carried on his breast, thanking him for having obtained this great favor. He also had a sense that this would bring him to a violent death. When leaving the college at Tournon, he said to one of his

Blessed Jacques Salès and Guillaume Saultemouche are about to be assassinated because of their profession of faith in the Blessed Sacrament. Mauméjean Frères workshop (circa 1934).

fellow Jesuits: "Goodbye, my brothers, pray God for us, for we are on our way to death," and, to one of his directees, "Goodbye, my son, for you will not see me anymore."

His companion on this mission was Brother Guillaume Saultemouche, also from the Auvergne, of the same age and a prayerful soul like Salès. One has to admire his great devotion to the Blessed Sacrament before which he frequently prayed. Guillaume was admitted to the Society of Jesus as a coadjutor brother at the age of sixteen. He was humble, silent, and worked as a porter, tactful and discreet, first at Pont-à-Mousson and later at Lyon. In this kind of work, he was both effective and mortified. He did this out of love for Christ crucified, and was prepared for his own supreme sacrifice. Sometimes you would hear some words from his mouth, which he would also murmur under the burden of blows from the citizens at Aubenas: "Hang in there, flesh, hang in!" He was on his way to the college at Tournon when he was chosen to accompany Salès on the mission to Aubenas.

Dying for the Truth

After arriving at Aubenas in December 1592, Father Salès, accompanied by Brother Saultemouche, gave themselves zealously to their task: to help the parish priest there to reestablish Catholic worship and the religious zeal of the parishioners, so broken down by years of random celebration of the sacraments, and to teach solid doctrine, thus putting an order into the life of the faithful, so that Protestants could be brought back to the faith.

Much fruitful success arose for several reasons. Father Salès joined great knowledge and spirited preaching with a sweetness and piety that was impressive even to the Huguenots. As for Brother Saultemouche, he impressed everybody through his exemplary humility and fervor. A number of Catholics, tepid and confused, returned to the Church and the practice of the sacraments. Some Protestants laid aside their church membership and asked to be readmitted into the Catholic communion. The Protestant pastors were infuriated by this success. Seeing that they were unable to match Salès in their discussions with him—he confounded their doctrine with arguments solidly based on the Scriptures and tradition—they resolved to silence this preacher in other ways.

On the night of February 6, 1593, a small group of about fifteen Protestant soldiers took control of the city without encountering any resistance. The two Jesuit companions started to pray. The next morning, Sunday, February 7, three soldiers forced their way into the Jesuit residence and found the two religious in prayer. They were brought to the Huguenot headquarters, where Salès was confronted by some Calvinist pastors who tried without success to get him to deny the Catholic faith. The pastor in charge of the interrogation decided that he was to be put to death. Some soldiers led Father Salès outside, where they met Brother Saltemouche, who insisted on accompanying his companion. When Salès suggested that he would best go on alone to his death, the latter refused, saying, "I will not leave you alone, dear Father, but I will die with you to witness the truth of the articles of faith you have defended."

At the main city square, Father Salès was asked once more to deny the real presence of Jesus Christ in the Blessed Sacrament. When he refused, a soldier shot him in the back and he fell to the ground. A soldier then stabbed him in the chest with his sword. Brother Guillaume took Salès into his arms and was then also stabbed to death.

The Calvinists then dragged the two bodies across the city. Six days later, the bodies were thrown into the ruins of an old church used as a rubbish dump. That same night, two Catholics came to recover the bodies and buried them in a nearby garden.

Jacques Fédry, SJ[17]

Jacques Salès and Guillaume Saultemouche were declared blessed by Pope Pius XI on June 6, 1926.

---

17. Translation by Walter E. Boehme, SJ.

Blessed Dominic Collins (1566–1602)

Captain

Dominic Collins was born around 1566 in Youghal, County Cork, an important English-speaking town on the south coast of Ireland. His father, John, and his brother were mayors of the town, so he came from a family of respected burghers. The family of his mother Felicity was Irish-speaking. Dominic grew up bilingually and picked up other languages very quickly. He had some contact with the Jesuits, because there was a small Jesuit school in Youghal for a short time during his childhood.

There were many political tensions in the region, and religious conflicts deepened in Ireland, when the government of Queen Elizabeth I extended its authority throughout the country and attempted to impose Protestantism. In 1560, the Irish Parliament had passed the Acts of Supremacy and Uniformity, making the queen head of the Church and declaring that the Book of Common Prayer was the only legal form of worship. There was widespread and successful resistance to this policy. Dominic could not envisage a career in his own country and went to Brittany at the age of twenty. He worked there for three years as a servant in two inns at Nantes, and saved the money needed to outfit himself as a soldier. He then joined the Catholic League's armies and served as an officer in the French wars of religion for nine years.

Realizing that the league did not have a future, Dominic left Brittany and retired to La Coruna, where there was a long-established Irish community. He received a good pension from the Spanish crown and lived very comfortably, with two servants.

Despite having retired in comfort, Dominic had no inner peace. He went to various friars for confession and mentioned his attraction to the religious life. All of them offered him a place in their novitiates and a path to priesthood. Meeting Father Thomas White, an Irish Jesuit, Dominic declared that he found consolation only with the thought of being a Jesuit brother. He had been impressed by the Jesuits he had met as military chaplains in Flanders, France, and Spain. He said that he had forgotten all his Latin and felt no call to the priesthood.

Novice

The Jesuit provincial of Castile was very impressed by the character of this solid Irishman, but he wanted him to be sure of his vocation to the Society. He asked Dominic to wait. After eight months, he was admitted to the novitiate at the Jesuit college of Santiago de Compostela, on December 8, 1598. He made a great impression during his first probation, with his handsome looks and his beautiful clothes. Soon, as a novice, he worked as a nurse, a cook, was in charge of the dispensary, and was the handyman of the community. When the house was hit by plague, all the healthy Jesuits fled, and Dominic remained for two months, nursing the seven Jesuits affected, one of whom died. Everyone was impressed by his courage as well as by his "obstinacy" (or determination), a trait noted by his superiors.

Martyr for the Faith

Dominic made his first vows on February 4, 1601. A few months later, to his surprise, he returned to Ireland, which he had left so many years earlier. Father James Archer, another Irish Jesuit, had requested him as his companion. Father Archer supported the cause of O'Neill and O'Donnell, two Irish chieftains in revolt against Elizabeth I: they had obtained the help of Philip II of Spain. Brother Collins sailed from Lisbon on September 3, 1601. He and Father Archer had never met; they travelled on two different ships, and Dominic's ship took much longer to reach Ireland.

The two Irish Jesuits met for the first time in January 1602 on the southern Irish coast, near Castlehaven. The Irish and Spanish forces had just been defeated by the English army at Kinsale, an important port town in County Cork. Father Archer and Brother Collins stayed to help O'Sullivan Beare, the local Irish chieftain, defend his castle at Dunboy. Archer left Dunboy Castle shortly before the English besieged it. Resistance was futile, so Dominic, who had not

Patrick Malone, Scenes from the Life of Blessed Dominic Collins: left, mercenary Collins before entering the Society of Jesus; center, Collins on the day of his execution; on the right, Collins caring for the plague-stricken during his novitiate in Santiago de Compostela (1992).

taken part in the fighting, surrendered on the evening of June 17, 1602. He was almost the only prisoner not immediately executed. He was taken to Cork, the regional capital, and tried by a court martial. Dominic was questioned at length, but even when threatened with torture, he refused to give any vital information.

Elizabeth I's officials in Ireland had used unlimited violence to control the south and west of the country. Surprisingly, Dominic was kept alive for four months. It was hoped that he would give some information, then enter the queen's service as an army officer and finally become a Protestant. His own family tried to persuade him to become a Protestant, while remaining Catholic in his heart. He refused. On October 31, 1602, Dominic was taken on the fifty-two-kilometer journey to his hometown of Youghal for execution, as part of the official policy of intimidation, because the townsfolk knew him and all his family. A poor fisherman was forced to carry out the sentence, while the soldiers contained the small crowd. None of the Collins family was present.

Dominic insisted on wearing his Jesuit cassock on the scaffold. He addressed the onlookers in Spanish, Irish, and English, saying that he had come to Ireland to preach the Catholic faith and that he would be very happy to die a thousand times for it. He then prayed in Latin. Dominic was hanged and his body was left in the gallows for three or four hours, until the rope broke; he then fell to the ground on his knees. His clothes were taken from him. The townsfolk did not want his naked body to be left there, so they took him away in the middle of the night and buried him in a secret place. Superior General Claudio Acquaviva, the Spanish and Irish Jesuits, those who had witnessed his execution, and many others immediately recognized him as a martyr for the faith.

Fergus O'Donoghue, SJ

Dominic Collins was beatified—along with sixteen other Irish martyrs—by Pope John Paul II on September 27, 1992.

From a Letter of Superior General Peter-Hans Kolvenbach

Dominic has left us no writings. Happily, however, his friends and even the enemies of the Catholic faith have given clear witness to a life that seems to have developed in accord with the spiritual rhythm noted by Ignatius in his contemplation on the Eternal King (*Spir. Ex.*, 91ff.)

In fact, from 1586 to 1598, Dominic lives in the ambience of the parable of "a human king, chosen by God our Lord himself" (id., 92). Forced to leave his native country, Dominic works for three years in various hostelries at Nantes, in France, so as to be able to enlist in the army of the Holy Catholic League fighting against the Calvinists. He put his whole believing heart into it. Having completed his service in France, Dominic, ever the "good subject" (id., 94), wants to answer the call of the most Catholic king Philip II, who wishes to "conquer" (id., 93) Ireland with his army and the Spanish fleet in order to defend the faith of the Catholic faithful.

It is at La Coruña, in Spain, that the call of the human king withers away in the face of the call of "Christ our Lord, the Eternal King" (id., 95). Just as Ignatius had noted in the parable, this call to make a more complete offering of his heart—"magis"—and "to distinguish himself in whatever concerns the service of the eternal King and universal Lord" (id., 97), evolved out of Dominic's capacity (proven in the service of the earthly king) to overcome "self": to reject the instinctive concern for self, preoccupied only with self-realization.

Shortly after pronouncing his first vows, this "offering of greater value and of more importance" (id., 97), Dominic is sent to Ireland as coadjutor brother to Father James Archer, chaplain of the Spanish expedition that is to aid the Irish Catholics. Brother Dominic finds himself again in the midst of soldiers, is present at the terrible battle of Kinsale, the cruel siege of Dunboy Castle, where he is taken prisoner. Brother Dominic is thus faced with the paradox of Christian life: he is in the army of a human king, though he is not part of it because he is at the service of the Eternal King; yet he finds himself in the thick of the battle for human liberation, so as to let the Eternal King carry out his work of liberation from eternal death and from the sin that leads to it.

Dominic bears all wrongs and all abuses for a greater service and praise of the Eternal Lord of all things (id., 98). May he obtain for us that grace never to be deaf to the call of Christ, but unreservedly and unambiguously "prompt and diligent" (id., 91) to profess and proclaim the faith, authentically and integrally.

Letter of June 21, 1992, to the whole Society, on the beatification of Dominic Collins

The Salcete Martyrs

BLESSED RUDOLPH ACQUAVIVA AND HIS FOUR COMPANIONS

(† 1583)

Optional Memorial on February 4

Martyrs, by the selfless sacrifice of their lives, bear witness to their spiritual heroism: their unconditional love of God, their uncompromising commitment to the faith, and their total allegiance to the Church. The five courageous Jesuit martyrs we commemorate here hailed from different parts of Europe: Rudolph Acquaviva from Italy, Alphonsus Pacheco from Spain, Peter Berno from Switzerland, Anthony Francisco and Francis Aranha from Portugal. They shed their blood on foreign soil, in the mission fields of India—"the Far East"—sanctified by Saint Francis Xavier. They were sent on mission to the church in Goa, India. They were appointed to the region of Salcete, which had twenty-five mission stations and fifteen Jesuits beside them posted there. All the five Jesuit martyrs were young, between the ages of thirty and thirty-five, when they generously surrendered their lives.

At the Emperor's Court

Acquaviva was born on October 25, 1550, in the family castle in Abruzzi, Italy. When he was seventeen, his father, the duke of Atri, took him to Rome, to visit his uncle Claudio Acquaviva, who had recently relinquished his position as papal chamberlain in order to join the Society of Jesus, in the hope of getting Rudolph the vacated position. While the duke went about his own business, Rudolph met his uncle at the Jesuit residence, expressed his desire to become a Jesuit, and asked Claudio to intercede for him. His father refused to grant him permission to join. It took Rudolph two months of consistent pleading, to

P. RVDOLPHVS AQVAVIVA *vande Societeyt* IESV *komt den eersten in t'Ryck Mogor om t'Gheloof te verkondighen, ende wort vanden Coninck wel onthaelt.*

"Father Rudolph Acquaviva of the Society of Jesus Arrives at the Mogul Court to Spread the Gospel and Is Well Received by the King" (1667).

convince his father that his decision was not an impulsive one, but had been made after serious reflection and prayer; the duke then gave his consent.

Acquaviva entered the novitiate of Sant'Andrea in Rome in 1568. In November 1577, his application for the Indian missions was accepted, and he left for Lisbon, where he was ordained a priest in 1578. He sailed for Goa on March 24 that year, arrived on September 13, and was assigned to teach philosophy to the seminarians at Saint Paul's College. In November 1579, he was specially chosen, with another Jesuit, to go to the court of Akbar in Fatehpur Sikri, in North India, at the request of the great Mughal emperor, Akbar, who had an unquenchable thirst for knowledge and truth. They arrived at the royal palace on February 28, 1580 and were welcomed warmly and provided comfortable lodgings. Acquaviva hoped that through his interactions with the emperor, he would influence him to convert to Christianity. After three years, he realized that this would never be possible. In early 1583, while remaining on friendly terms with Akbar, the Jesuits left Fatehpur Sikri for Goa, where they arrived in early May. He was appointed superior of the Jesuits in Salcete in early July.

Salcete had a predominately Hindu population that was hostile to the Christians, especially after punitive expeditions of the Portuguese colonists, which destroyed their shrines and temples. The Jesuits, however, in their zeal to establish the faith, decided to start a new campaign to promote conversions and to visit all of the peninsula's sixty-six villages. They planned to launch their venture in Cuncolim, a town in Salcete, under the leadership of Acquaviva. Accordingly, Acquaviva selected four Jesuits to team up with him for the task: Alphonsus Pacheco, Peter Berno, Anthony Francisco, and Francis Aranha.

Four Companions

Alphonsus Pacheco (1551–83) was a native of Minaya, Toledo, Spain. He entered the Society of Jesus at the age of sixteen, and volunteered for the Far East missions. He arrived in Goa in September 1574, where he was ordained a priest and appointed as assistant to the rector at St Paul's College. Three years later, he was made assistant to the provincial. He was highly gifted in human relationships. He was superior of the Salcete mission till 1583, when Acquaviva took over from him.

Anthony Francisco (1552–83) hailed from Coimbra, Portugal. In 1570, he was so deeply touched by the news of the brutal slaying of Father Ignatius de

Azevedo and his thirty-nine missionary companions that in 1571 he gave up his university studies and joined the Society of Jesus. He accompanied Pacheco, who had recruited him for the mission, to Goa in 1571, and was ordained a priest in 1583. After his ordination, at the consecration in all his Masses he always prayed for the grace to die as a martyr—a grace that he received sooner than expected.

Peter Berno (1552–1583) was from Ascona, Switzerland. His father, a fruit merchant, moved to Rome for better prospects. Peter, who had already begun his priestly studies, continued his training at the German College. On July 2, 1577, he entered the Jesuit novitiate of Sant'Andrea, and after four months, being assigned to the missions, he went to Lisbon, Portugal, to complete his novitiate. In April 1579, Berno left Lisbon and arrived in Goa in October, and continued his studies. He was ordained a priest in early 1580. He had a premonition that he himself would die for the faith.

Francisco Aranha (1551–1583), from Braga, Portugal, as a boy traveled to Goa where his uncle had been Goa's first archbishop. He was a carpenter by trade. Aranha entered the Society of Jesus as a brother on November 1, 1571. After two assignments at the colleges in Cochin and Goa, he was appointed to Salcete in 1577, to build or repair the chapels and residences as needed. He devoted himself with the greatest zeal and labored indefatigably at the work entrusted to him. He was called to build the church at Cuncolim.

Planting the Cross

Acquaviva and his team assembled at Orlim on July 15, 1583. They determined to make an apostolic excursion into Cuncolim, a neighbouring village that had revolted in 1581 and showed a great hatred toward Christianity. They planned to erect a huge mission cross on the summit of a hill as the site of a chapel to be built, and the people were invited to be present at the ceremony. The day chosen was July 25, the anniversary of the martyrdom of Azevedo and his companions.

On reaching the village, they found it deserted. Not disconcerted at such an inhospitable reception, they entered a deserted cabin to discuss their project and the site of the new church. After waiting some hours and hearing increasingly frightening shouts from the village, the Jesuits decided just to plant a cross on the site of a future chapel and to leave. Unfortunately, they chose a spot where a temple had stood until the previous year's punitive expedition had destroyed it. The people who had been secretly watching them summoned hundreds of angry villagers who surrounded the Jesuits and then brutally massacred them with swords, lances, and other weapons. The militants also killed fifteen of the faithful who had formed a shield around the missionaries. Acquaviva and three companions were killed praying for their murderers. One of them, Aranha, was found alive the next day. He was given a chance to venerate an idol and, on refusing, was tied to a tree and shot with arrows.

The bodies of the five Jesuit martyrs were thrown into a well, the water of which was afterward sought by people from all parts of Goa for its miraculous healing qualities. The bodies themselves, when found after two and a half days, showed no signs of decomposition. The martyrs were solemnly buried in the Church of Our Lady of the Snows at Rachol and remained there until 1597, when they were transferred to the Saint Paul's College in Goa, and in 1862 to the Cathedral of Old Goa. Some of these relics have been sent to Europe at various times.

Hedwig Lewis, SJ

The martyrs of Salcete were beatified on April 2, 1893, by Pope Leo XIII.

Saint Paul Miki and His Two Companions

PROTOMARTYRS OF JAPAN

(†1597)

Memorial on February 6

A Turning Point in Japan's History

Paul Miki and his fellow Japanese martyrs died at a time when the history of their country had reached a turning point. After the collapse of the central government of the Ashikaga shoguns, Japan was for a hundred years the scene of endless conflicts among the *daimyo* (as the feudal barons were called). In the second half of the sixteenth century, military leaders, especially Oda Nobunaga and Toyotomi Hideyoshi, little by little laid the foundations of national unity and peace, and the structures they worked for came into being under the rule of Shogun Tokugawa.

At that time, permanent insecurity and many dangers threatened the life of the individual and also any attempt to establish a social order. The decisive factor was military prowess and the code of chivalry (*bushido*). Powerful rulers struggled to gain control of the nation and to shape a new social order, and the fate of many people depended on their good will.

At the same time the national culture was developing, especially in building, painting and other arts, and in literature. The contact with the West, which had began in the middle of the sixteenth century by means of trade with the Portuguese, enriched the lives of many people in many ways. The search for inner composure and the cultivation of the self found its expression in the tea ceremony, which at that particular time was practised at various levels of society and found its greatest exponent in Sen no Rikyu (1522–91).

Development of the Church

The spread of the Christian religion, started by Francis Xavier in 1549, ran into many difficulties after initial success. Some local rulers considered that the importance of the Christian religion was too linked with the business interests of foreigners; moreover, the native forms of religion were closely connected with the history and culture of Japan and clashed with the alien Christian culture. Sudden and violent risings obliterated flourishing Christian communities, as, for example, in Yamaguchi.

Bit by bit, however, Christianity was able to establish a firmer footing, not only in the southern island of Kyushu, but even in central Japan. Influential personalities, such as Omura Sumitada, Otomo Sorin, Takayama Hida-no-Kami, and his son Takayama Ukon (beatified in 2017), became Christians and gave powerful support to the work of the mission. The Church now began to develop more quickly in various classes of society, and by the year 1582 there were already 150,000 baptized Christians.

The mission in Japan had been entrusted solely to the Society of Jesus for the past forty years, and hence the piety of the Japanese Christians was much influenced by Jesuit spirituality, above all by the *Spiritual Exercises* of Saint Ignatius. Father Alessandro Valignano, who came to Japan for the first time during the years 1579–82, as visitor in name of the superior general of the Society, was much impressed by the intense faith of the Japanese Christians and had the highest hopes for the future of the Church in Japan. He drew up extensive plans for the development of the mission work, for the "adaptation" of Christianity to the feelings and customs of the country, and for the training of Japanese workers in the mission field.

Storm

The military authorities who controlled events at the time at first seemed favorably disposed to Christianity, but in 1587 Toyotomi Hideyoshi suddenly changed his attitude, forbade the spread of the Christian religion, and ordered all the missionaries out of Japan. The reason for this measure may have been his anxiety that the growing influence of the Christian religion among the people could be a barrier to his claims to total authority, and he may have seen the missionaries as a means of infiltration by foreign powers. So the Church in Japan was deprived of its freedom and permanently exposed to threats of all kinds.

The Hideyoshi decree was probably put into effect with some leniency, and the work of the mission continued in some districts. Moreover, in 1593 a group of Franciscans arrived from the Philippines. They were allowed to remain in Japan and bear witness to the Gospel through their charitable work for the poor and the lepers, for whom they built a number of hospitals.

The position of the Church in Japan remained in danger, however, and an accident at sea and a war in Korea did nothing to help. A new crisis blew up in the autumn of 1596 when a Spanish vessel, the *San Felipe*, sailing from Manila to Mexico was wrecked on the Japanese coast. Its rich cargo was confiscated, and complaints were raised about hostile Spanish intentions against Japan—thanks to some unhappy remarks by the ship's pilot. Hideyoshi made the most of it and condemned six Franciscans (three of whom were priests) and fifteen of their Japanese lay helpers to be crucified. Paul Miki, who was a Jesuit scholastic, and two lay helpers of the Society, John Soan (from Goto) and Diego (James) Kisai, all three of whom were at that time in the Jesuit residence in Osaka, were added to the list of the condemned. In addition, two other Japanese Christians, who on the journey to the place of execution at Nagasaki offered their assistance to the condemned men, were also condemned to death. The result was that on February 5, 1597 a total of twenty-six Christians died as martyrs.

Imitation of Christ

The first martyrs of the Society of Jesus in Japan were intimately involved in the changing destinies of the Japanese church in that era.

Paul Miki was born in 1564, thirteen years after Xavier's death. His parents, both from the Japanese nobility, had become Christians when Paul was five years old, and they had been baptized along with their child. A few years later, they sent him to the Jesuits for his education. In 1586, when Paul was twenty-two, he entered the Jesuit novitiate at Arie (Nagasaki Prefecture), where in 1588 he took his first vows.

During his studies, Paul showed himself a good catechist and preacher, and was outstandingly effective in dialogue with the adherents of non-Christian religions. He began his apostolate in the southern islands, then went up

Pedro Garcia Ferrer, Martyrdom of Saints Paul Miki, John Soan, and Diego (James) Kisai, (around 1627, probably for the beatification of the martyrs).

to the capital Miyako (now Kyoto). He traversed several provinces preaching, catechizing, and preparing for baptism. He had great concern for the salvation of souls, and one day did not hesitate to climb into the cart of a condemned man, whom he converted and baptized on the way to his painful death. Many people embraced the faith by listening to it. According to a contemporary, Manuel Ribadeneyra, "the common voice attributed to the young missionary the greatest number of conversions made at that time."

During the new wave of persecutions of 1596, Miki was arrested in Osaka and transferred to Miyako, then led for a month to the other end of Japan, to the extreme west, to Nagasaki. His way of life was characterized by a continuous growth in the imitation of Christ and the service of the Gospel, as appears from his letters from prison and his final profession of faith in Christ, on the cross, before he died.

Miki's companions, John Soan and Diego Kisai, differed in age and the fortunes of life, but they had one thing in common: their loyalty to Christ and their desire for martyrdom.

John Soan was nineteen years old and the son of Christian parents, a pupil of the Jesuits and their collaborator in mission. He took his Jesuit vows shortly before his death. His parents watched closely at his torture and begged him to hold on.

After a varied life, Diego Kisai departed to Osaka to put himself at the service of the Jesuits as porter and servant. He became catechist, then brother in 1596. On December 9, at the age of sixty-four, he was arrested with Miki. He had given himself to Christ and loved to meditate on the Sorrowful Mysteries of Our Lord.

In this way, the first martyrs of Japan took to heart the call of Christ to take up his cross and follow him (cf. Mt. 16:24–25): their death was truly that "offering of greater importance" that is at the heart of the Jesuit vocation.

Paul Pfister, SJ[8]

18. Revised by Jacques Fédry, SJ.

The twenty-six protomartyrs of Japan were beatified as early as 1627, by Urban VIII, at a time when Japanese Christians were still being hunted and executed. Their canonization by Pius IX took place on June 8, 1862.

From an Account of the Martyrdom of Saint Paul Miki and His Companions

The crosses were set in place. Father Pasio and Father Rodriguez took turns encouraging the victims. Our brother, Paul Miki, saw himself standing now in the noblest pulpit he had ever filled. To his "congregation" he began by proclaiming himself a Japanese and a Jesuit. He was dying for the Gospel he preached. He gave thanks to God for this wonderful blessing, and he ended his "sermon" with these words: "As I come to this supreme moment of my life, I am sure none of you would suppose I want to deceive you. And so I tell you plainly: there is no way to be saved except the Christian way. My religion teaches me to pardon my enemies and all who have offended me. I do gladly pardon the emperor and all who have sought my death. I beg them to seek baptism and be Christians themselves." Then he looked at his comrades and began to encourage them in their final struggle.

Others kept repeating "Jesus, Mary!" Their faces were serene. Some of them even took to urging the people standing by to live worthy Christian lives. In these and other ways, they showed their readiness to die. Then, according to Japanese custom, the four executioners began to unsheathe their spears. At this dreadful sight, all the Christians cried out, "Jesus, Mary!" And the storm of anguished weeping then rose to batter the very skies. The executioners killed them one by one. One thrust of the spear, then a second blow. It was over in a very short time.

Liturgy of the Hours, Second Reading for February 6

Saint Bernardine Realino (1530–1616)

Optional Memorial on July 2

Bernardine Realino belonged to the second generation of Jesuits, those men who joined the Society in the years immediately following the death of Saint Ignatius and whose religious life was molded by men who had known him intimately and instilled the Ignatian spirit into their lives. This second generation included in its numbers men of outstanding ability who fitted harmoniously into the new institute during a period of rapid expansion while rules were still being formulated and the atmosphere was that of the "primitive Apostolic Church," to use Bernardine's own phrase. In Italy, men like Robert Bellarmine, Antonio Possevino, Claudio Acquaviva, and Matteo Ricci had a real influence on the tone of religious life in the new order.

"Men with Experience of the World"

Bernardine was born in Carpi, near Modena, in 1530. He studied at the Academy of Modena, then in Bologna. After graduating in law in 1556, he became mayor of Felizzano at the age of twenty-six, thanks to family connections. This position allowed him to carry out his profession as a judge. At the end of his term of office, the inhabitants asked him to continue in this position, because they found in him a perfect and upright judge, but also a committed Christian. He was then appointed tax collector in Alexandria and became mayor of Cassine. Upon his return to Milan in 1562, his reputation as a competent magistrate preceded him, so much so that the marquis of Pescara took him to his service by appointing him mayor of Castelleone. Realino was certainly one of those men whom the then general superior of the Jesuits, Diego Laínez, considered most suited for the progress of the Society. "Give me men with experience of the world," he used to say, "for they are the men we need."

For the naturally optimistic nature of Bernardine Realino, it was easy to respond to the ideals of the Italian Renaissance, then at its most mature. These ideals were embodied in the fundamental concept of the "dignity of man," a synthesis of human virtues with a Christian core, essentially optimistic, seeking to get the best out of every dimension of human nature by sublimating it: goodness was of more account than good fortune; nobility was the fruit of effort; knowledge was the handmaid of action; the place of human labour was high; glory was the reward of right conduct; love consisted of the gift of oneself.

These were the characteristics of the humanism of the fifteenth and sixteenth centuries. We can discover them in Bernardine's writings; we find them more particularly in his choice of a career in the service of his fellow men; in the defense and promotion of the common good through his judicial and administrative work. In the course of his career, the realities of life, professional disappointments, and private sorrows like the loss of his much loved wife, brought spiritual maturity and an ever more conscious effort to act on Christian principles. So when, providentially, he met in Naples, in the person of Alphonsus Salmerón, the new order founded twenty years before by Ignatius of Loyola, Realino immediately recognized in it the perfect embodiment of the ideals he had developed for himself.

Despite the lucrative posts he occupied, Realino wrote to his brother: "I have no desire for the honors of this world, but only for the glory of God and the salvation of my soul." As a good Christian, he considered himself an instrument of divine Providence, and he distributed his wages to the poor. Because of his honesty and fame, the marquis of Pescara appointed him in 1564 superintendent of his properties in the Kingdom of Naples. He arrived in the city of Naples in July of the same year. But not for long.

In the Footsteps of His Lord and Captain

A month later, as Bernardine was passing through the city, he came across two Jesuit novices whose conversation and behavior caught his attention. He inquired about the order to which they belonged: the Society of Jesus, newly arrived in Naples. Then one Sunday he went to a Jesuit church, where he was struck by the preaching of the priest. Three days later, he returned to the preacher for a general confession. The preacher suggested that he follow an eight-day Ignatian retreat, during which Bernardine experienced intense spiritual consolation. Afterward he received a vision of Our Lady, who asked him to

The magistrates of Lecce beg Saint Bernardine Realino, on his deathbed, to become the patron of the city when he arrives in heaven. Lithograph after the painting by Giovanni Gagliardi produced for the beatification of Realino in 1895 (1947).

join the Jesuits. The brilliant jurist did not delay: unhesitatingly, he abandoned his profession and his humanistic studies (retaining, however, their highest ideals) and chose for himself "the knowledge of Christ and him crucified." By denying himself, renouncing his own will, and taking up his cross, he would run his course in the footsteps of his Lord and Captain, Jesus Christ. In order to give himself without reserve to God, he chose life in the Society. This he described to his father as "a good life grounded on sound doctrine, with few of this world's possessions but spiritual wealth in plenty, together with zealous love for God and man."

Bernardine entered the novitiate on October 13, 1564. His humility and readiness to serve led him to believe he was only capable of carrying out subordinate tasks. He then asked to become a brother, but his superiors refused to allow him to do so. The noble and discreet service, in the Society of Jesus, of the Triune God, with Christ, in the Church, in the ministry of souls redeemed by his blood, presented itself to him as a personal Christian vocation ever more certain, urgent, positive, and supernaturally obvious.

In October 1566, Bernardine was asked to prepare for priestly ordination on May 24, 1567. Shortly after his ordination, Superior General Francis Borgia appointed him master of novices, while he was still studying theology. But his prudence and good judgement made up for his lack of formal ecclesiastical formation. At the same time, he began the work that would occupy him for the rest of his life. He preached and catechized, visited slaves on the galleys of the port of Naples, and spent long hours in the confessional. In the company of Jesuits, he would find his "paradise on earth" and live with "great joy of spirit," glad to be able to reverence and "serve his neighbor for the honor and glory of God." Contentment and consolation deriving from the action of the Spirit were the themes recurring constantly in his letters and in the memories of those who lived with him.

Patron of the City

Realino was sent to Lecce in Apulia in 1574, with a view to the possible establishment of a Jesuit house and college. The inhabitants were so pleased with the Jesuits' arrival that they offered them a residence and then began to build a church in which Father Realino would exercise a pastoral apostolate for forty-two years. There as in Naples, he was spiritual advisor to a great number of people; like many Jesuits in the first fifty years of the Society, he counseled them in personal interviews, by letter, in the confessional, and through the Spiritual Exercises. With minimal organization, he was able to maintain a great many personal contacts, and it was through these contacts that his own virtues of faith, hope, and charity shone out and enlightened those who sought his advice.

Long bouts of sickness and periods of petty misunderstandings on the part of some of his own brethren, especially during the first years at Lecce, purified and refined this apostle of spiritual consolation right up to the end of a long life when, according to his last superior, "because of extreme old age, he could no longer exercise the ordinary ministries of the Society, yet still continued to help many people by his prayers and by his advice and shining example." It was a mortification to him not to be able to do any more work, and this led him to sign his name "useless old Bernardine Realino." But in the eyes of God and in those of his fellow men, he had faithfully completed his mission as the "servant" of those he called the "servants, or rather the sons, of God."

In June 1616 he contracted the disease that would carry him to his grave. The town magistrates twice visited him to ask him to become their heavenly patron. He was too weak to answer, but a sign he made was interpreted as a consent to continue taking care of the people of Lecce.

Mario Gioia, SJ[19]

Bernardine Realino was beatified by Pope Leo XIII in 1896 and canonized by Pope Pius XII on June 22, 1947.

---

19. Revised by Jacques Fédry, SJ.

Saint John Francis Regis (1597–1640)

"APOSTLE OF THE VELAY AND OF THE VIVARAIS"

Optional Memorial on July 2

The Call of a Wholly Consecrated Life

One year before the Edict of Nantes put an end to the wars of religion, a child of blessing was born, John Francis Regis, in Fontcouverte, halfway between the cities of Narbonne and Carcassonne, on January 31, 1597. He was the second of four boys and grew up in a deeply Christian family.

At the age of fourteen or fifteen, John Francis went to the Jesuit college in Béziers, where he showed himself to be both studious and pious, as well as a cheerful companion. When the boy heard God speaking to his heart, calling him to a life wholly consecrated to God's love and to the service of mankind, he responded with great generosity. After completing his studies, he asked and obtained admission to the Society of Jesus. He was nearly twenty years old when he entered the novitiate in Toulouse. It was December 8, 1616, the feast of the Immaculate Conception.

For twelve years, John Francis let himself be shaped by the religious formation that the Society of Jesus demands from its sons. On the outside, nothing distinguished him from his brothers in religion, except a greater regularity, a profound spirit of penance and humility, and above all a marked taste for teaching catechism and practicing ascetical and spiritual exercises. Interiorly, Regis renounced himself day after day and grew in love for Jesus, a love that would be the guiding principle of his life.

First Missions

His superiors noticed his fiery word and intrepid zeal, along with his unfaltering virtue—a combination that promised him to become a perfect missionary one day. John Francis was physically a man of very tall stature and uncommon vigor. Lively, cheerful, simple, and attractive, he carried within him all the riches of the southern temperament.

At the beginning of the summer of 1632, Regis was assigned as a missionary to the college of Montpellier. Although he stayed there only two years, his devotion to the poor and sinners was highly praised. There was also much talk of his marvelous mission in Sommières and the surrounding area, in particular his fearlessness when one day he had stood in front of a church door all alone halting a band of looters.

In the spring of 1634, he and another Jesuit were assigned to the bishop of Viviers to assist him in the visitation of the southern part of his diocese. A more difficult mission was reserved for him in 1635–36: the mission of Boutières. Here, the wars of religion had caused great material and moral damage. Blood had been spilled everywhere and misery reigned. Attached to the college of Aubenas, Regis and his companion Father Broquin evangelized Privas and Le Cheylard. On top of that, he traversed the region all by himself, village by village. Once, it is said, he was blocked in the mountains by a snowstorm. Only God knows what he had eaten and how he had slept. In fact, usually he lived on milk and black bread, and slept on the ground.

He preached and confessed everywhere, in barns, stables, even on the roads. People always found him welcoming. One day, he was leaving the church, tired after the mission's morning exercises. A group of people arrived from a place far away to profit from his instructions. "Come, my children," he said without hesitation, "come, I carry you all in my heart." In a few months, the country had changed beyond recognition. Even the Calvinists, won over by his kindness, sought his guidance, almost as much as the Catholics.

In Le-Puy-en-Velay

In 1636, Regis was attached to the college of Le Puy. From then on his time was divided between the city and the countryside. In Le Puy, his activity was focused particularly on three areas: teaching catechism, aiding the poor, and converting sinners.

His way of teaching catechism has remained famous. In the church of Saint -Pierre-du-Monastier, four to five thousand people would be present, not only

Michel-Ange Houasse, *Saint John Francis Regis, newly ordained priest, distributes communion to plague victims in Toulouse in 1631 (before 1722).*

poor people, who were always his favorites, but people of standing, priests, and religious. They all enjoyed the simplicity of his words—a rare quality in those days of baroque preaching—words that were warm, colorful, lively, stirring the depths of the soul: in short, words of a saint.

The wars and famines, so frequent at that time, caused many poor people to seek a better life in Le Puy. Regis's heart was moved by them. He brought together pious ladies whom he charged to seek out the needy in each neighborhood and come to their aid. He himself went from door to door, begging, collecting money, gifts in kind, or simply work for his poor. In the college, he had a room that he called his "treasure trove." There, he collected clothes, tools, furniture, objects of all kinds, which he then distributed.

Even more than the poor, the sinners touched the heart of John Francis. His kindness was well-known. In the college church, his confessional was besieged. He was strict only with the hardened and the corrupt. Impurity in particular plagued the city. Regis, strengthened by his trust in God, attacked this evil with heroic zeal. He founded a home for "lost girls" whom he rescued from vice. The passions he tried to eradicate were unleashed against him: he was mocked, insulted, slandered, whistled at, beaten up, even threatened with death. But he carried on, unfaltering, with a smile, attentive only to his divine Master and the salvation of souls.

In the Missions

Le Puy did not take up all of Regis's activity. In the periods that he did not have to teach catechism, he went on mission to the people of the countryside, especially in winter, when they had more time to spare. From 1636 to 1640, he evangelized the regions to the east and northeast of the diocese of Le Puy. In these mountainous regions, winter is harsh. Nothing, however, ever stopped the Jesuit. Sometimes he arrived exhausted and with his clothes covered with snow. But, without any concern for himself, he went up to the pulpit or into the confessional.

He prayed to God continuously and with all his heart. Often he appeared radiant, as if rapt in ecstasy. The tabernacle attracted him irresistibly. Sometimes he was found standing in front of the closed door of a church, seemingly unaware of the snow and the freezing wind.

Such love of God made his apostolic zeal inexhaustible. So much so, that in April, 1640, he wrote to the superior general in Rome: "Please allow me to travel the countryside with one of our brothers and devote, in these missions, what remains of my life to the salvation of the peasants ... Allow this to me, I beg you in the name of God, every year, for at least five or six months." "One cannot explain the fruits brought about by this kind of mission," he wrote. This time, the superiors approved, and Regis, full of hope, saw before him new harvests. But then God, in his mysterious ways, suddenly stopped him.

Death

In September 1640, Regis left for four months of missions. The last ones were those of Montregard, Montfaucon, and Raucoules. Before leaving Raucoules, he had announced that he would be at La Louvesc for Christmas. However, on December 17, he took the road to Le Puy. He arrived there unexpectedly the following day and told a confidant: "I have interrupted my missions to pre-pare myself to die well. I have reserved three days for myself. I want to make a confession of my whole life, as detailed as possible, because I am sure that it will be the last one. Be good enough to help me in this important matter ..." When three days later he made his general confession, his feelings "clearly indicated that he was no longer of the earth and that he was approaching heaven."

John Francis left Le Puy on December 23. The journey through snow and ice was very difficult. The next day, upon his arrival at La Louvesc, he went to the little church and without further delay started the mission. For three days, he worked as never before. He preached seven times and confessed almost without pause. On December 26, after the two o'clock Mass, he was unable to return to his confessional, so compact was the crowd and so weakened was he. So he sat down near the altar and began to confess again, bareheaded, under a poorly closed window. In the evening, Regis suddenly collapsed. He was taken to the parish house. There, near the fire, he still found the strength to hear about twenty confessions. Finally, unable to take it anymore, he went to bed. He still had five days to go in this life.

On the last day of the year, shortly before midnight, John Francis told his companion Brother Bideau that he "felt worse." And immediately afterwards: "Ah, dear brother, I see Our Lord and Our Lady opening the gates of paradise to me." Then he began to repeat the words of Christ on the cross: "Father, into your hands I commend my spirit." With these last words, he also finished his life. He was forty-three years and eleven months old.

The Shrine of Lalouvesc[20]

John Francis Regis was beatified by Pope Clement XI in 1716 and canonized by Clement XII on April 5, 1737.

20. Cf. the biography on www.saintregislalouvesc.org (abridged). Translation by Marc Lindeijer, SJ.

From a Letter of Superior General Peter-Hans Kolvenbach

When he died at the age of forty-three, John Francis Regis had brought the Good News of Christ again in the villages of the Vivarais—doubtlessly one of the most battered regions in France at the time—through an exceptional ministry that had lasted less than ten years. In these villages, constantly subject to the ravages of the plague, as well as to injustice, and material and moral misery, Father Regis tackled as a matter of course the concrete problems of the villagers, in the name of the One who had sent him to evangelize the poor.

It was not part of Regis's charism to set up or organize groups. He did not have the time for it. Yet his presence, brief as it may have been, abounded in such activity and in such charity that it inspired the creation of charitable and social initiatives. The leaders of Le Puy recognized this fact in a lapidary statement: "He taught us to love our neighbor."

In Saint John Francis Regis, defender of the poor and apostle to the mountain villages, it is not difficult to recognize the One who sent him, and to understand that the goal of his mission was to proclaim the Good News in that region, where Jesus Christ was little or no longer known. Making the best use of the time he had at his disposal, he spoke about Christ, the Living One, with a passion as intense as the altruism with which he had risked everything, had left everything to make him known through his catecheses, which deepened the sacramental life once lost and now found back again. Because he lived his mission humbly and generously to the point of total self-giving, Regis could meet concrete social needs without encroaching on his pastoral duties, and live out his intimacy with the One who sent him without sacrificing any of the human traits of his southern temperament.

We, too, are servants of Christ's Mission, laboring with him and sharing his preferential love for the poor. Regis sets us an example, which each should follow in his own way. Regis leads the way in the evangelizing mission of the Church, in which the Good News is announced in many gestures of love for all and every person, made tangible in the various spheres of human existence.

Letter of January 9, 1997, to the whole Society, on the four hundredth anniversary of the birth of Saint John Francis Regis

New Martyrs as a Result of Divisions Among Christians

Saint Nicholas Owen and His Two Blessed Companions
(†1606)

Memorial on December 1

Well-Hidden Jesuits

Nicholas Owen, son of a carpenter and brother of two priests, was a Jesuit brother whose talents as a mason and carpenter provided priests with concealed hiding places—known as priest holes—in the homes of Catholics. These enabled priests to avoid capture despite the most thorough of searches. He served as servant to Edmund Campion, who was arrested and executed in 1581, and was briefly arrested himself the following year when he spoke out on behalf of Campion's innocence. Then he came to work with Father Henry Garnet, the mission superior, in London.

Owen employed great ingenuity in devising the priest-holes and even hid his activities by working openly during the day as a regular carpenter and working on the hiding places only at night. Even the house servants would be ignorant of his real activity. Only he and the owner of the home would know where he had created a hiding place by chipping through stone walls or burrowing into the earth. Some of the places were big enough to accommodate six to ten people; others were concealed inside another hidden room to throw the priest-hunters off the scent. It was hard work to do by oneself, and he suffered injuries in the process.

In 1588, Father Superior Garnet wrote a letter expressing the hope that his carpenter might someday enter the Society. No names were used, so it is not certain that he was writing about Owen, who never did make a formal novitiate; the exact date he became a Jesuit remains unknown. Owen was briefly detained in 1594, when he was caught with the Jesuit priest John Gerard, but the police did not realize they had in custody the mastermind behind the hiding places. They released him, and he immediately returned to his work.

Catholics looked forward to the end of persecution when Queen Elizabeth died and James I became king in 1603. He had promised that he would be more tolerant, but in fact, the persecution increased. Some angry Catholic laymen, among them Guy Fawkes, plotted to blow up the Houses of Parliament during the king's visit there on November 5, 1605. Discovery of the "Gunpowder Plot" intensified hatred of Catholics. The government was determined to implicate Jesuits in the plot, despite the fact that the men behind it had already been captured. In December, Father Garnet decided to leave London and, together with Brother Owen, seek shelter at Hindlip Hall, a manor near Worcester. There they joined two other Jesuits, Father Edward Oldcorne and Brother Ralph Ashley; the two priests went into one hiding hole, the two brothers in another.

The Mission Station at Hindlip Hall

Ashley's place and date of birth are unknown. He was a cook at the English College at Reims, which he left in April 1590 to take up the same job at the English College in Valladolid, Spain. There he entered the Society of Jesus as a brother and spent his first years of religious formation. In 1597, he was urged to return to his homeland to recover his good health. Once in England, in March 1598, Brother Ashley accompanied and assisted for some time the mission superior, Henry Garnet, before being sent to Hindlip Hall, not too far from Worcester, to help Father Edward Oldcorne, whom he would assist for eight years.

As for Oldcorne, son of a non-Catholic father and a Catholic mother, he was born in York in 1561. Impressed by the courage of his mother when she was imprisoned for her faith, Edward dropped his medical studies to travel to Reims, France, in August 1581 in order to study for the priesthood. In 1583, he moved on to Rome, where he finished his studies and was ordained a priest. Soon afterward he became a Jesuit and after a shortened novitiate returned to England in November 1588. He was welcomed by Father Superior Garnet and

Blessed Nicholas Owen holds a model of Hindlip Hall, where he made eleven "priest holes" before being arrested there in 1606. Icon by Francisca Leighton Munizaga, (between 2000 and 2015).

after a few months assigned to Hindlip Hall, where he would enjoy one of the longest periods of any Jesuit ministering in England.

The master of Hindlip Hall was an ardent Catholic, who was in prison and had left the property in the care of his sister Dorothy, a Protestant who had been at Queen Elizabeth's court and merely tolerated the presence of the priest guests in her brother's residence. Several priests had tried unsuccessfully to convert her back to her family's Catholicism, but she resisted all efforts. Finally Oldcorne began fasting for her conversion; when she learned of his fast, she yielded to God's grace and became an encouragement for many others in the shire to return to the Catholic religion. Hindlip Hall became Father Oldcorne's base of operations, where many people came to seek the sacraments and hear his preaching. With more hiding places than any other mansion in England thanks to the work of Brother Owen, the hall seemed to be the safest haven for Owen and for Father Garnet, fleeing from London and seeking to hide himself in December, 1605.

Dead for Their Religion

On January 20, 1606, the sheriff of Worcestershire raided Hindlip Hall with over one hundred men; they spent several days fruitlessly searching for the priests. A man arrested for being involved in the Gunpowder Plot tried to curry favour by telling authorities he could lead them to Father Oldcorne. Finally, on the fourth day, hunger forced Brother Ashley and his companion, Brother Owen, to leave their hiding place. They tried to pretend to be the priests, but could not fool the searchers, who uncovered a dozen hiding places before finally apprehending the two priests. All four Jesuits were imprisoned in the Tower of London.

When efforts to spy on the conversation between the prisoners failed to yield any damning evidence, Oldcorne was tortured on the rack five hours a day for five consecutive days. He refused to say anything. When Oldcorne and Brother Ashley were put on trial, the Jesuit priest denied the charge of being involved in the Gunpowder Plot so well that the charge against him was changed to simply being a Jesuit priest. He was found guilty of high treason and ordered to be executed.

Owen, too, was tortured. The king's men realized they had the only person who knew the location of the hiding places and residences of priests all over the kingdom. They were eager to force him to uncover the Catholic underground, but he was even more firm that he would not betray those whom he had spent so much time protecting. He was tortured on the rack for hours a day, several days in succession, but maintained his silence. In frustration, the torturers kept adding weight to his feet, but went beyond all limits: on March 1, his abdomen burst open and his intestines spilled out. Owen lingered on for one painful day before dying in the early hours of March 2. The rack-master tried to cover his behavior, excessive even under the harsh standards of the day, by saying that the Jesuit had committed suicide. Clever and hard-working in his life, Owen remained courageous and faithful in his death.

Oldcorne and Ashley were hanged, drawn, and quartered on April 6 at Red Hill, Worcester. Just before Oldcorne was hanged, the man who had betrayed the priest asked for pardon, which the latter readily granted. The Jesuit also prayed for the king and royal family, for his accusers, the judge, and the jury who had condemned him. He was pushed from the ladder but was cut down before he was dead; he was then beheaded and quartered. As Oldcorne waited on the ladder to die, Brother Ashley kissed his feet and said, "What a happy man am I to follow the steps of my Father unto death." When Ashley followed him on the scaffold, he also prayed and asked for forgiveness, and made it known that he was dying for his religion and not for being a traitor.

Thomas M. Rochford, SJ[21]

Edward Oldcorne and Ralph Ashley were beatified by Pius XI on December 15, 1929, as was Nicholas Owen. The latter was canonized by Paul VI on October 25, 1970, in the group of forty martyrs of England and Wales.

---

21. Revised by Marc Lindeijer, SJ.

From a Homily of Pope Paul VI

In its long and glorious history, Great Britain, an island of saints, has given the world many men and women who have loved God with this sincere and loyal love: this is why we are pleased to have counted forty other sons of this noble land today among those whom the Church publicly recognizes as saints, proposing them with this to the veneration of his faithful, and because these portray a vivid example from their lives.

Like many of their fellow countrymen who died in similar circumstances, these forty men and women of England and Wales wanted to be, and were, loyal to their homeland that they loved with all their heart. But this was precisely the high tragedy in the lives of these martyrs, namely that their honest and sincere loyalty to the civil authority came into conflict with their fidelity to God and with what, according to the dictates of their conscience illuminated by the Catholic faith, they knew to involve the revealed truths, especially on the Holy Eucharist and on the inalienable prerogatives of the successor of Peter, who, at the behest of God, is the universal pastor of the Church of Christ.

Faced with the choice of remaining steadfast in their faith and therefore dying for it, or of saving their life by denying that faith, without a moment's hesitation and with a truly supernatural strength they sided with God and joyfully confronted martyrdom. But such was the greatness of their spirit, so noble were their feelings, so Christian was the inspiration of their existence, that many of them died with prayers on their lips for their beloved homeland, for the king or queen, and even for those directly responsible for their capture, their sufferings, the ignominious circumstances of their cruel deaths.

The Church and the world today have the greatest need of such men and women, of every state of life: priests, religious, and laity, because only people of such stature and holiness will be able to change our tormented world and to give that spiritual and truly Christian orientation to which every man intimately yearns—even sometimes without being aware of it—and of which we all so much need.

May God, in his love, grant that today, too, centers of study, formation, and prayer flourish and develop, able to prepare holy priests and missionaries, as did in those days the Venerable Colleges of Rome and Valladolid, and the glorious Seminaries of Saint-Omer and Douai, from which ranks came forth many of the forty martyrs. For as one of them, a great personality, Saint Edmund Campion, said: "This Church will never falter as long as there are priests and pastors to tend their flock."

Homily of October 25, 1970 at the canonization of the forty martyrs of England and Wales

Saint Robert Southwell (1561–95)

Memorial on December 1

Robert Southwell, one of England's many poets but one of its most illustrious martyrs, was killed during the reign of Queen Elizabeth I.

Every Time Too Young

Robert was born at the end of the year 1561 at Horsham Saint Faith (Norfolk) to a well-to-do family of aristocratic stock but had to move to the continent to study in a Catholic school. In May 1576, he enrolled in the English College at Douai, Flanders; he later studied in Paris, where he met the English Jesuit Thomas Darbyshire, who became his spiritual guide. Southwell asked to join the Jesuits, but was turned down at first because he was too young and the novitiate itself was closed due to fighting in nearby areas. With great determination, the young Englishman walked to Rome, where he was accepted into the novitiate at Sant'Andrea al Quirinale on October 17, 1578.

After finishing his novitiate, Robert studied philosophy and theology at the Roman College. At the same time, he was tutor at the English College in Rome, which the Society had just started in 1579. When Father Robert Persons, short of men for the English mission, asked that Southwell be sent to him, the superior general refused; again he was judged too young. Southwell was ordained a priest in 1584 and served for another two years as prefect of studies at the English College, also in Rome, preparing men to be priests for England. Finally, at his insistent demand, he was assigned to the mission in his homeland and left Rome on May 8, 1586, along with Father Henry Garnet.

A Living Legend

The two Jesuits landed on a secluded coast to avoid capture in the ports of entry. Southwell was assigned to minister in and about London, living at first with the Vaux family and then in the household of Lady Anne Howard, whose husband Sir Philip, twentieth count of Arundel, was imprisoned in the Tower for maintaining his allegiance as a Catholic. Southwell's ministry included visiting the dozen or so prisons in the city, sending seminarians to the continent, and helping young priests who had just entered the country. When Father Garnet, his traveling companion, also came to London, Southwell started visiting Catholics in the outlying counties. He also helped direct the printing of Catholic catechisms and devotional books published by a secret press that Garnet had established; it was the sole source of religious literature for English Catholics. Southwell put together several letters he had written to Sir Philip to encourage him in prison; these letters were revised and published in 1587 as *An Epistle of Comfort*. He had a good pen: his writings and poems, often copied, were spread anonymously in the clandestine Catholic world and were of great comfort to many people. But his great popularity also made him one of the priests most searched for by the government agents, who wanted to arrest him at any price.

For six years, Southwell escaped from the priest-hunters and exercised a fruitful ministry, becoming a living legend, until he was betrayed by a Catholic woman, Anne Bellamy, who had been imprisoned after she refused to attend Protestant services. She had been made pregnant by Richard Topcliffe, a priest-hunter noted for torturing his prisoners. Topcliffe promised to marry her and win pardon for her family if she would persuade Southwell to go to a designated spot where the trap would be set. When she was released from prison in June, 1592, she wrote the Jesuit asking him to meet her at her parents' home. Southwell went there, thinking she wanted to receive the sacraments. Instead, Topcliffe and his men were waiting. Southwell managed to slip into a concealed room before they could catch him, but he eventually gave himself up rather than betray the family.

Dead without Applause

Topcliffe was overjoyed to have captured Southwell, whom he regarded as the biggest catch of his career. Bound in chains, the Jesuit was led to Topcliffe's residence next to Gatehouse Prison and put in the private torture chamber that Topcliffe had there. Several excruciating days of torture failed to force

Saint Robert Southwell, together with the English martyrs Saint Anne Line and Blessed John Robinson, diocesan priest, was locked up in the Tower of London (in the background) and hanged at Tyburn (also depicted). Line was similarly hanged at Tyburn six years later, while Robinson was executed at Ipswich in 1588. Stained glass window by Margaret Edith Aldrich Rope (1945).

Southwell to reveal the name of any Catholics or priests. He remained steadfast despite being tortured thirteen different times; finally his captors threw him among the paupers to face cold, hunger, and thirst. Southwell's father managed to visit him in the paupers' prison and was horrified at his son's condition. He petitioned the queen to treat him like the gentleman he was, either releasing him or condemning him to death. The queen allowed him to be moved to the Tower, where he was better cared for but still could not receive visitors. He did continue, however, to write the poems that expressed his deepest feelings and were later collected and published as *St. Peter's Complaint*.

For two and a half years, Southwell endured the solitude of his imprisonment, and then finally petitioned the queen's chief advisor William Cecil, First Lord Burghley, to be released, be allowed visitors, or be brought to trial. The latter was granted, and he was tried on February 20, 1595, at Westminster Hall. The Jesuit readily admitted being a Catholic priest but denied he had "entertained any designs or plots against the queen or kingdom, let alone to participate in them." If he had come back to his country, he said, it was only "to administer the sacraments of the Catholic Church to those who desire them." He was found guilty of high treason and executed the very next day.

For the three-hour journey to Tyburn, Father Southwell was tied to a hurdle and dragged through the streets to the gallows, where he made the sign of the cross. Allowed to address the crowd, he admitted he was a Jesuit priest and prayed for the salvation of queen and country. As the cart was drawn away from under his feet, he commended his soul to God with the words of the psalm, "In your hands, Lord, I commend my spirit ..." But the noose being improperly placed on his neck, Southwell did not die immediately. The hangman took mercy and hung on his feet to end the agony; then he was beheaded and quartered. As his head was displayed to the crowd, no one shouted the traditional "Traitor!"

Once, Robert Southwell had been considered too young to join the Society of Jesus; then he was deemed too young to be sent to the dangerous English mission. Now, at the mere age of thirty-four, he had matured into a martyr.

Thomas Rochford, SJ[22]

---

22. Revised by Marc Lindeijer, SJ.

Robert Southwell was declared blessed by Pius XI in 1929 and canonized by Paul VI on October 25, 1970, as part of the forty martyrs of England and Wales.

We therefore are under an obligation to be the light of the world by the modesty of our behavior, the fervor of our charity, the innocence of our lives, and the example of our virtues. Thus shall we be able to raise the lowered prestige of the Catholic Church, and to build up again the ruins that others by their vices have caused. Others by their wickedness have branded the Catholic faith with a mark of shame, we must strive with all our strength to cleanse it from its ignominy and to restore it to its pristine glory. Amen.

Saint Robert Southwell

Saint John Ogilvie (1579–1615)

MARTYR IN SCOTLAND

Optional Memorial on January 19

John Ogilvie was born in 1749 at Drum-na-Keith in Banffshire, Scotland, the first son of Walter Ogilvie, a noble and well-to-do Calvinist gentleman. Little is known of the saint's early years, but it has been established that when he was twelve or thirteen years old he was sent by his parents to the continent to complete his education. In 1592, we find him in Germany, entering the University of Helmstedt, newly founded and already earning its reputation as a stronghold of Protestantism.

Four years later, in 1596, Ogilvie was admitted to the Scots' College of Louvain, Belgium. It must have been around this time that his conversion to Catholicism took place, mainly under the guidance of Father Cornelius van den Steen (1567–1637), who later won fame for his volumes on scriptural exegesis under the name of Cornelius à Lapide.

In 1598, the young convert left Louvain to reside first in Regensburg, then in Olomouc, Moravia. Here he asked to be admitted into the Society of Jesus in 1599. On November 5 of that year, he was received in the novitiate of the Austrian province at Brno, where another famous Jesuit martyr, Edmund Campion, had been a novice too. He pronounced his first vows on December 26, 1601, at Graz, and continued his academic formation first in this city and then in Olomouc. According to the custom of the Society, his studies were interrupted for a period of practice teaching, and he was assigned to teach grammar in the Jesuit college in Vienna. Renowned for his genuine and manly piety, he was sought after for his extraordinary gifts of counseling and inspiring young people, especially those in the Marian sodality, fostering in them an ardent love of commitment to God and neighbor.

Missionary Work Day and Night

Ogilvie had always hoped he could return someday to his homeland to give heart to his fellow Catholics there, so ruthlessly persecuted on account of their faith. Accordingly, after his ordination to the priesthood in Paris in 1610, the young apostle repeatedly and earnestly begged to be missioned to Scotland. However, in obedience to his superiors' wishes, he spent the first three years of his priestly life in pastoral ministry in the city and diocese of Rouen.

It was not until the year 1613, that Superior General Claudio Acquaviva granted him the mission yearned for and enjoined him to sail secretly for Scotland to comfort his countrymen in their trials, to confirm them in their faith, and to reconcile those who had faltered. Posing as an army officer returned from the wars in Europe and now wanting to settle down as a horse merchant, Ogilvie landed in Scotland and set out for the Highlands. Shortly after, he took a brief and rather mysterious trip back to France to consult with his superior, and, upon his return to Scotland, he threw himself wholeheartedly into his missionary work, mostly around Edinburgh, Glasgow, and Renfrewshire. He labored day and night in a whirlwind of missionary activity, never sparing himself, never inhibited by the threat of death that hung over him wherever he went. It was not surprising that eventually someone betrayed him to the Protestant authorities. He was arrested in Glasgow on October 14, 1614, and imprisoned in the castle of the reformist archbishop John Spottiswoode.

The following day, he was brought before his judges and was confronted with the main "crime" for which he would eventually be sentenced to the scaffold. "Having been asked," we read in the martyr's own signed confession, "whether the pope's jurisdiction in spiritual matters extended to the king's dominions, he steadily maintained that it did, and declared he was ready to lay down his life for his conviction."

In the long, exhausting grilling that followed, Ogilvy defended his faith valiantly and with exceptional skill in the art of debate. He nursed no illusions of eluding the hangman's noose, yet he never lost his calm serenity and that keen sense of humor common among Scots. His accusers' blandishments to induce him to apostatize were of no avail, nor was he swayed by fiendish tortures, among others that of being kept awake for eight days and nine nights. Nothing could break his heroic spirit.

In 1615, Saint John Ogilvie endured nine consecutive nights of "guardianship," that is, the torture of sleep deprivation by stings with sharp needles and knives (1933).

Ogilvie was condemned to death on March 10, 1615, and at four o'clock in the afternoon on the same day, he was hanged. Shortly before his death, the martyr publicly professed his loyalty to the king in all matters pertaining to his legitimate jurisdiction, but he left no doubt that he was going to his death because of his religious convictions. He faced his ultimate trial with courage and serenity, forgiving his persecutors and praying to the last.

His remains were cast into the common grave for criminals outside the city.

For Freedom of Conscience

John Ogilvie is the first Scot canonized since 1250, and even though he lived four centuries ago, his life and martyrdom have an important pastoral significance today.

If his generous and clear-minded loyalty to the faith is an example for all of those who, despite rampant religious indifferentism, take their faith seriously and are willing to make the greatest sacrifices for it; if the heroic conduct of this martyr is a clear proof of the power of the Holy Spirit that Our Lord promised would never fail those who sincerely seek his will in all of life's travails, then the example of John Ogilvie is particularly inspiring to our generation, because it shows how Christians should stand up to the totalitarian and absolutist claims of any political power exerting pressure directly or indirectly on religious conscience.

Ogilvie repeatedly, even to his death. proclaimed his loyalty and obedience to his king and to the state in all that pertains to their legitimate authority, but he could not, nor would he, concede that they had any authority in spiritual matters. And he was put to death because he defended to the last his right to freedom of conscience.

At this time, Ogilvie's canonization has a particular ecumenical relevance. Today, all Christian denominations are as one in refusing to identify political with spiritual power and are now arranged together battling for the right of each person to follow one's own conscience and to live one's own faith.

Obviously this canonization must not become an occasion for outdated vindications; that would be pointless and divisive. Actually, there seems to be no such danger, since we all know that Catholics were not the only Christians that suffered in the persecutions that made John Ogilvie a martyr.

Apostolic Sanctity

If the above considerations demonstrate why Ogilvie's example transcends his time and offers a pastoral message of particular significance in our times for all people of goodwill, it is no less evident that his canonization is all the more relevant for those who live the same Ignatian charism that inspired this saint to dedicate himself unconditionally to the service of our Lord and his Church.

Deeply imbued with the spirit of the *Spiritual Exercises*, this saint lived intensely the ideals proposed by Ignatius in the Meditation of the Kingdom: the invitation to follow Christ, sharing his labor and sufferings, making one's own the attitude of Christ's heart to the point of professing "to be considered foolish and of no account for Christ, who himself first chose to be so considered, rather than wise and prudent in this world" (*Sp. Ex.*, 167). A man of action by temperament, he became through the *Exercises* a man of prayer, a true "contemplative in action."

Spirited and critical by nature, Ogilvie gave heroic example of humility and obedience, distinguishing himself as a true son of Ignatius, above all by his sincere and loyal attachment to the Chair of Peter, and to the teaching authority of the supreme pastor, for whose spiritual supremacy he laid down his life.

Finally, it is significant that Superior General Pedro Arrupe, announcing Ogilvie's canonization to the whole Society of Jesus, concluded his letter with the following words: "May our martyr, who soon will join the ranks of the saints, help us by his intercession so that our Society, true to the charism of Ignatius, might be a genuine source of apostolic sanctity in the church today, serving the Lord and the Church, his Spouse, under the Roman pontiff, the vicar of Christ on earth."

Paolo Molinari, SJ[23]

John Ogilvie was beatified in 1929 by Pius XI and canonized on October 17, 1976 by Paul VI.

---

23. Jesuits. *Yearbook of the Society of Jesus*, 1976-1977, p. 85-88.

The Martyrs of Košice

STEPHEN PONGRÁCZ, MELCHIOR GRODZIECKI, AND CANON MARK KRIŽEVČANIN
(†1619)

Optional Memorial on January 19

The early seventeenth century had an unpromising start for the Kingdom of Hungary and for Catholicism in that country. Hungary was divided into three parts: the Ottoman Empire occupied one-third of it; Transylvania had become an autonomous principality; and the kingdom itself consisted of the western strip of the earlier Hungarian country and what is now Slovakia. The Protestants, in the majority at the turn of the century, were hostile to the resurgence of the Catholic Church and used every available means to stop it. Gábor Bethlen, a Protestant Transylvanian prince, took advantage of the difficulties created by the Thirty Years' War and in 1619 conquered a large part of the territory belonging to the kingdom. It was during this campaign that three Catholic priests were martyred in the town of Košice (currently in Slovakia).

None of these three priests has left any well-authenticated writings. The established facts that offer an insight into their spirituality are that they belonged to the sodality of Our Lady from their early youth, that they spent four or five years in the priestly ministry, and that they underwent a cruel death for the Catholic faith. Pope Pius X, in the decree of their beatification, sums up their spirituality in a passage from Saint Paul: "The grace that has been granted you is that of suffering for Christ's sake, not merely believing in him" (Phil. 1:29).

"Ready to Die at Once"

The youngest of the three, Mark Stephen Križevčanin, aged thirty or thirty-one, was born in the diocese of Zagreb. He had been a pupil of the Jesuits in Vienna and Rome, and was a close friend of his future fellow-martyrs. After he became priest in 1615, he returned to the diocese of Zagreb. He was then called to lead the seminary of Trnava and was appointed canon of Esztergom Cathedral. At the beginning of 1619, he was called to manage the former Abbey of Széplak, near Košice.

Father Melchior Grodziecki, born in Silesia of a family of Polish origin, had reached the age of thirty-five or thirty-six when he was martyred. Like the future canon, he was a pupil of the Jesuit college in Vienna. There he became a member of the sodality of Our Lady, an experience that caused him, so he said, a "great joy." He entered the Society of Jesus on May 22, 1603, and did his novitiate in Brno (in Moravia), where he befriended the man who would become his companion in misfortune, Stephen Pongrácz. After studying for the priesthood in Prague, he was ordained a priest in 1614 and remained in the same town for the first years of his ministry, He preferred controversy and casuistry to speculative theology, and he had a liking for music. His ministry consisted of educating poor boys and preaching. He was prevented by the circumstances of the time from completing his tertianship: after the thirty-day retreat, in December 1618, when the Jesuits were expelled from Bohemia and Moravia, he was sent to the college of Humenné in Slovakia. He pronounced his final vows there on June 26, 1619. Shortly afterwards, Grodziecki was appointed chaplain to the Bohemian and German Catholics at Košice.

Father Stephen Pongrácz was a year older than Grodziecki. He came from a noble Hungarian family, and was born and studied in the Principality of Transylvania. The Jesuit college at Cluj, in modern Romania, was going through difficult but apostolically effective years. On leaving school, Stephen went to the Jesuit novitiate. He spent the early years of his religious formation in Bohemia and then went to Austria for his priestly studies, in which he showed great brilliance. After his priestly ordination in 1615, he returned to Hungary as prefect of studies at the college of Humenné. He was also a very able preacher. At the request of the governor of Košice, he also served as pastor for the small Catholic community of this largely Calvinist city, which was located

The blessed martyrs of Košice, led by Canon Mark Križevčanin, receive the palm of their victory from an angel. In 1904, the Church of the Sacred Heart received a relic of Blessed Melchior Grodziecki, who was born there in 1584. Anonymous painting (around 1905, probably for the beatification of the martyrs).

in an unstable region of the eastern part of the Austro-Hungarian Empire, the scene of violent inter-ethnic and religious conflicts. The Hungarian Calvinist pastor at Košice, himself a distinguished preacher, complained of Stephen: "As long as this Jesuit is alive, the Reformed Church cannot hope for any peace." In July 1619, Pongrácz did the Ignatian Spiritual Exercises with Križevčanin, his fellow-martyr. When the army of Prince Bethlen was approaching Košice, Pongrácz left the countryside for the town to join the other two priests in giving encouragement to the Catholic inhabitants

The commander, George Rákóczi, reached Košice with his troops on September 3, 1619. Once in the town, they put the three priests under arrest in the king's palace where they had their residence, and for three days gave them nothing to eat or drink; they were only offered, on purpose, a piece of meat on Friday, which they refused. The commander tried, unsuccessfully, to persuade the canon to become a Calvinist by offering him a benefice.

On the evening of September 6, the soldiers demanded a ransom from the three, but they were unable to pay it. "Get ready to die, then," they were told. "But why must we die?" "Because you are papists." "For that sacred cause, we are ready to die at once." But the soldiers had not yet received authorization to carry out the execution. The three priests made their confession to each other and prayed out loud.

Martyrs for the Unity of the Church

On the following day, September 7, a captain appeared again with some soldiers shortly after midnight: they were accompanied by the Calvinist pastor Peter Alvinczi. Pongrácz, who opened the door, was struck to the ground and tied up. The two Jesuits were ordered to adopt Calvinism. Pongrácz was hung up by the hands to the joists of the building and castrated; a rope was pulled tightly round his head; he was burned with torches until his internal organs began to appear. Grodziecki was pierced through the body several times. Canon Križevčanin was invited to join those who professed the "Hungarian religion" and opposed the "foreign tyranny" (of the Habsburgs). "God preserve me," he replied, "from being the enemy of those who work for the good of the country." Hearing this apparent surrender, Pongrácz took fright, but the Calvinists must have realized at once that the canon had not been "converted," for they flew into a rage, burned him too, and cut off his head. Grodziecki likewise finished up by being beheaded. Their heads were thrown into a cesspool. Pongrácz was violently beaten on the head twice and then reunited with his companions.

Apparently, the sacristan could observe the whole scene from his hiding place. When the soldiers left, he came closer and heard some groaning: Father Pongrácz had regained consciousness and was asking for help. The distraught sacristan did not dare to intervene, and the poor Jesuit lay dying there for another twenty hours, praying Jesus and Mary. He expired on the morning of September 8.

Even the Protestants of the town admitted with some dismay that the three priests, with all their zeal and their gentleness, had not deserved this barbaric treatment. News of the martyrdom spread rapidly and shocked the whole country. But Prince Bethlen chose to ignore the requests made by many Catholics to give the martyrs a decent burial. He persisted in his refusal for six months until, at a dinner he gave in honor of the palatine of the kingdom, in the very palace where the martyrs had died, the palatine's wife, Countess Katalina Pálffy, when she was asked by the prince to dance with him, agreed only on condition that she was allowed to give the three martyrs a proper funeral. The Jesuit cardinal Peter Pázmány, who a few years earlier had appointed the young Križevčanin a canon of Esztergom, carried out the canonical investigation and, on behalf of the local hierarchy, asked Pope Urban VIII in 1628 to authorize public veneration of the three martyrs.

In an age very different from our own, and in a manner appropriate to that age, the martyrs of Košice were champions of what is today known as ecumenism. They labored and sacrificed themselves to bring about peace between rival Christian denominations and the peoples of the Danube Basin.

Ferenc Nagy, SJ[24]

Stephen Pongrácz, Melchior Grodziecki, and Mark Križevčanin were beatified in 1904 by Pius X. They were canonized on July 2, 1995, during the visit of Pope Saint John Paul II at Košice.

---

24. Revised by Marc Lindeijer, SJ

From a Letter of Superior General Peter-Hans Kolvenbach

Melchior, István, and Marko were called to a rather exceptional form of martyrdom, but the tortures they endured came only after the kind of martyrdom to which each of us is called: the testing of our faith that consists in a permanent conversion of our hearts of flesh toward the attitudes of the Heart of Jesus; both we ourselves and those whom the Lord has entrusted to our care, have to turn away from the idols of all times. In this way, dialogue and compassion, respect and solidarity, the search for unity and reconciliation, efforts that are peaceful and patient —all achievements of the undeniable pluralism of our times and highly recommended by General Congregation 34—will nonetheless not bring to a halt the great conflict between truth and falsehood, love and hatred, life and death, that the martyrs of Košice went through. As "servants of Christ's mission," to use the expression introduced by General Congregation 34, they loved to the very end the men and women who are in the world, knowing full well that their passion for the true life of the world involved a struggle with that same world, so filled with violence, inhumanity, and bound to the earth even today. Far from being militant and aggressive fanatics with a fundamentalist approach, István, Marko, and Melchior were passionate men; they did not seek division or heroic deaths, but neither were they willing to treat like common merchandise the only treasure they had—the Lord. When, in the light of Christ, the moment came to manifest their disagreement and thus suffer tribulation and even death, they did not turn back; without reservation or ambiguity, they gave witness to the very end to the name of the One who alone justified their "yes" and their "no": Jesus.

Letter of May 16, 1995, to the whole Society, on the canonization of the martyrs of Košice

Blessed Charles Spinola, Sebastian Kimura, and Their Seven Companions

(†1622)

Optional Memorial on February 6

From time immemorial, the Japanese mission has been regarded by the Society of Jesus as a mission field dear to its heart. One reason naturally is that this mission was established by Saint Francis Xavier himself. But a second reason is the numerous martyrs of the order who have offered up their lives and their blood in the service of Christ in times of persecution.

One of the typical figures of that period is Blessed Charles Spinola. It is true that there were martyrs in the Japanese mission who endured greater torments, but there were certainly few who from their very youth had such a heartfelt longing for martyrdom.

The Calling

Born in Genoa in January 1564, eight years after Ignatius died, Charles spent the greater part of his childhood in Spain. After his return to his native Italy, his education was entrusted to his uncle, Cardinal Philip Spinola, bishop of Nola, who sent him to the Jesuit college there.

Hearing of the martyrdom of Blessed Rudolph Acquaviva in 1583, Charles made up his mind that he too wanted to go to the Indies (the name given in those days to the whole of the Far East) to do God's work there and to die a martyr's death. Even if this desire was then only a youthful romantic aspiration, it never deserted him. Again and again, this longing shows itself in all his prayers and activities, and under every trial.

When his family heard of his intention to enter the Society of Jesus, a storm of protest arose. But he stood fast and turned to his uncle, the cardinal, for help: "If Your Eminence is of the opinion that I should wait until my father gives his consent, I should only like to say that I do not think that his permission is necessary. He will never sway my decision, whether he gives his consent or not. And if I have asked Your Eminence about this matter, it has not been because I thought it necessary to have your permission, but only because I thought I should do it out of respect for you ... I hope that a cardinal of our Holy Mother the Church will not use the influence of his high office to deprive his nephew of such great happiness. And what right would there be for Your Eminence to refuse help for me in my vocation, when you have supplied help and support to many others in their vocation?"

Finally, his father gave permission to enter the novitiate when Charles was twenty. It was at that time, in 1584, that he wrote his famous "Dedication," in which, toward the end, the desire for martyrdom becomes apparent again: "Fill my heart with spiritual comfort that I may always find you, in all things, at all times, in every place, and that finally I may be united to you by the martyr's death."

The Missionary

In 1594, Spinola was ordained, and one year later he was selected for the Japanese mission. Once more, his family used every means to prevent his departure for the missions, and when the ship ran onto a rock and returned to Genoa, this was a providential sign for his relatives that he ought to remain in Italy. But Charles passed the time composing a litany of the Jesuit martyrs. He wrote on December 6 to a Jesuit in Milan: "I used these days to put together a sort of litany of all those members of the Society of Jesus who have given their lives for Christ. In the life of Francis Borgia, I found the names of the forty martyrs who were thrown by the heretics into the sea. In addition, I discovered the names of nine others who received the palm of martyrdom in Florida. I send you a copy of this litany so that you may beg these holy martyrs to procure for me the grace to imitate their virtues ... My dear Father, when will the time come when the same destiny will be assigned to me!"

The journey took no less than six years, eight ships, and much patience: shipwrecks, pirate attacks with a forced stay in England ... He finally arrived in 1600 in Malacca, Malaysia, and in 1602 in Japan, the land of his desires.

Prisoner for Christ

After learning the language, he was appointed minister at the Jesuit college and professor of mathematics. Seven years later, he was summoned to Nagasaki and appointed procurator of the province, in charge of material matters.

The growing number of Christians—two million—was perceived as a threat by the country's leaders, and in 1614 a general persecution was unleashed. About a hundred Jesuits left the country, but a few remained, including Spinola, who managed to escape the priest hunters for four years. During the night of September 14, 1618, he was arrested with his companion, Brother Ambrose Fernández. The latter was born in 1551 in Portugal and entered the novitiate at Nagasaki in 1579. He then remained in that city to perform various administrative duties and to serve as an interpreter for his brothers. Ambrose was the first of them to die, on January 7, 1620, after thirteen months of captivity.

As for Father Spinola, after a first interrogation in Nagasaki he was conducted along with two Dominicans and three Japanese Christians to the prison at Suzuta near Omura. He felt that the long cherished desire for martyrdom was soon to be fulfilled. He wrote on February 20, 1619: "At last I was arrested and dragged through the streets like a criminal, while all the people came flocking round. Now I am living here in joy and contentment and full of thanks to the Lord who has granted me such a great grace." The happiness and pride to resemble the suffering Savior fills the many letters that he wrote from prison and that were always signed: "Charles imprisoned" or "Charles captive for Christ."

But he still had a long time to wait for the crown of martyrdom. He and his companions had to endure four long years of privation in captivity, which, from the evidence of Father Porro, were like a living martyrdom but were regarded by Father Spinola himself as a preparation for the final consummation. "What I have suffered is not very much. I long for even greater afflictions. The first year of my novitiate is coming to an end; but since I hope that I shall achieve my profession in heaven I am ready to endure many other different trials." In fact, in the course of time several of his fellow captives who were Japanese, mostly former students of the seminary and catechists, asked to be received into the Society of Jesus, and with the permission of the

Stained glass workshops of the Carmel of Le Mans Hucher & Fils, Blessed Charles Spinola at the stake in Nagasaki in 1622 (1878–80).

provincial, seven of them, after the completion of their "novitiate" in prison, were allowed to take their vows.

In the narrow cell, described by Spinola as a "birdcage," seventeen prisoners were packed together, then twenty-four, and finally thirty-three. In the end, there was so little space left that it was impossible for anyone to lie down at night or to make the slightest movement by day. Since they had no sanitation there and for the whole time could neither wash themselves nor change their clothing, and despite the gaps between the timbers, the air was permanently foul. "Every sense has here its own particular torment," Spinola wrote to the provincial. Despite the strict surveillance, the Christians succeeded in smuggling into prison all the necessary equipment for Mass, so that every day one of the priests was able to celebrate. At Father Spinola's suggestion, the rest of the day was divided up into a regular routine—meditation, the recitation of the Little Hours, the rosary, and spiritual reading. After the prisoners' miserable meals, there was a "recreation," sung vespers, and examination of conscience. In this way, they were not only able to counteract the torture of doing nothing but used the time in a positive way, deepening their spiritual sense and making interior progress.

The Holocaust

On August 28, 1622, Father Spinola wrote a farewell letter to the provincial: "Yesterday, quite unexpectedly, the prison officers burst into our cell with great violence. Because of rumors which had reached us, we thought that they intended to kill us straightaway. But their purpose was to count the prisoners and make a list of their names ..." The signature of this letter is as follows: "Charles, condemned to death for the sake of Jesus's Name."

On September 9, the twenty-five prisoners were conducted to Nagasaki. They arrived there on the following day and were taken to the "Holy Mount," the place where in 1597 the twenty-six holy protomartyrs had died. It is called Nishizaka, the site of the present Jesuit residence. Another group of thirty Christians from Nagasaki arrived an hour later, so that the total number of martyrs rose to fifty-five. Thirty of them were beheaded, twenty-five were burnt to death. Father Spinola was the first to be given to the flames and ended his life as a holocaust for Christ, in the fullest sense of the word.

The last to die was Father Sebastian Kimura. He was one of the two Japanese Jesuits who in 1601 had been ordained as the first native priests by Bishop Luís Cerqueira. He came from Hirado, where his grandfather had been baptized in 1550 by Francis Xavier.

The other Jesuits who died in the great martyrdom were those Japanese who had been received into the Society of Jesus by Father Spinola while they were in prison. Their names are John Chugoku, Peter Sampo, Michel Shumpo, Gonsalves Fusai, Louis Kawara, Thomas Akahoshi, and Anthony Kyuni.

Hubert Cieslik, SJ[25]

Charles Spinola, Sebastian Kimura, and their seven companions were beatified with Ambrose Fernandes and 194 other Japanese martyrs by Pope Pius IX on July 7, 1867.

---

25. Revised by Jacques Fédry, SJ.

Blessed Francis Pacheco and
His Seventeen Companions
(†1626)

Four years after the martyrdom of Charles Spinola and twenty-nine years after Paul Miki's, Francis Pacheco died for Christ at the very same place: the "Holy Mountain" of Nagasaki. There, the persecution against Christians was displayed for more than forty years from 1597.

Missionary Charism

Francis Pacheco was born in Ponte de Lima, in the archdiocese of Braga (Portugal), about 1566. While still a young child, he heard of the martyrs of the early Church, and in his innocence vowed to be one himself. The solemn ceremonies carried out at Lisbon every year when missionaries embarked for the missions of the East or of Brazil added to his determination. Another stimulus to the call of grace was the example of his maternal uncle, a heroic missionary in Japan. To imitate him, Francis joined the Society of Jesus in Coimbra on December 30, 1585. He studied philosophy there and was appointed to the mission of India in 1592.

The Dream of Japan

Francis went through his theological course in Goa and was ordained a priest. At that time, the Japanese missions were the most promising, though not the easiest, in the East. Pacheco begged to be allowed to share in the work of evangelizing those regions. Posted to Macao, he taught theological subjects there for some years, and made his final vows in 1603. The following year, he saw his hopes crowned: he settled down to a thorough study of the Japanese language and for four years worked in Osaka and Miyako (now Kyoto), which was previously Japan's capital. But he had to return to Macao in 1608 to be rector of the college.

In 1612, he returned to Japan, where the bishop, Luís de Cerqueira, recognizing his wisdom and amiability in dealing with all sorts of people, made him his vicar-general. When the prelate died in 1614, a fierce persecution broke out and the missionaries were expelled. Father Pacheco had become apostolic administrator of the diocese, but since he was too well-known to be able to carry on running the diocese, he had to withdraw to Macao; however, in June of the following year, 1615, he returned to Japan dressed as a merchant, with other Jesuits disguised as sailors. He resided first in Takaku, then on the islands of Amakusa, and finally moved to Kani, in 1619.

In 1621, Pacheco was appointed provincial superior. He moved to the port of Kuchinotsu in Arima to make the visit of his companions easier. Francis lost none of his zeal for preaching the Gospel, though by now he was worn out and his eyesight was failing. A missionary of the Church of Silence and of the pastorate of the catacombs, he lived in continuous isolation in his last years, preaching and administering the sacraments at night in the worst weather and always in danger of betrayal.

Meanwhile, as provincial superior and apostolic administrator, he gained universal esteem and admiration because of the selflessness with which he cared not only for his own subjects but for all the missionaries of the various religious institutes, and gave them all possible help in such difficult circumstances. His aim was to achieve in everything and among them all something greater than personal or even group motivation, namely the union of charity. His affability and patience overcame all the obstacles, and he achieved and maintained a remarkable degree of harmony in the missionary community.

Danger grew upon the Jesuits in 1625, when more and more spies were sent by Shogun Iemitsu. However, it was no spy that denounced Father Pacheco but rather an old friend, a Christian apostate. He revealed the priest's residence to the district governor, who sent two hundred soldiers on December 18, 1625 to surround the house. With Pacheco, they found two catechists, Paul Shinzuke and Peter Rinscei. The soldiers arrested the three of them, along with the occupants of the neighboring house: Brother Caspar Sadamatsu and

SB Franciscus Pacecc Balthasar Torres. Io Baptista Zeli
Carerichus, Petrus Rinxet, Vincentius Caun Ioannes
Chincoco Paulus Semeuche Michael Toro Sebal
Gaspar Sandamatzu Coai Denn. S I Mancius
Matuaz Petrus Susanna Ioannes Catharina Ioannes
Mbarca. Aloisius puer bospites et bambares MM

Odoardo Persichini, Blessed Francis Pacheco is tied to the stake, with seventeen Jesuit and lay companions, in 1626. Engraving after a drawing by Tertulliano Giangiacomo (circa 1870).

another catechist, John Kisaku, as well as the father and the families who gave them shelter. They were taken to Shimabara and placed in a cold, wet dungeon where Father John Baptist Zola, a native of Brescia (Italy) was also imprisoned.

The Eve of Martyrdom: Prayer and Penance

Forbidden to celebrate the Eucharist or recite the Canonical Hours, the prisoners passed the time in prayer and penance, catechizing even the warders themselves, who were filled with admiration at their captives' patience and happiness. "For the martyrs," as one of them said in a letter written with orange juice, "prison was a paradise." At rest in the arms of Jesus Christ and the Father of Mercies, who consoles in tribulation, they felt themselves awaiting the blessed hope and the coming of martyrdom. During those months of imprisonment, the provincial, Father Pacheco, received into the Society Peter Rinscei, with three other catechists: Vincent Kaun (from Korea), Paul Shinzuke, and John Kisaku.

Finally, on June 17, 1626, the governor returned from a visit to the *shogun* with the order to put them to death. In Nagasaki, the sixteen prisoners of Shimabara met two others who had been based in Omura: Father Balthasar de Torres (born 1563 in Granada), as well as his catechist Michael Tozo, captured on March 20, 1626, in a small village near Nagasaki; in the prison, Father Torres had received Michael in the Society. At the entrance of the city, the Christians came out to greet the confessors of the faith and recommend themselves to their prayer. They replied that they wished them perseverance to the end.

On the Steps of the Altar of Sacrifice

Reaching the place of execution, Pacheco and his eight Jesuit companions knelt down to venerate the altar of their sacrifice and to give thanks to God for the grace that they were allowed to give witness to Christ with their lives. The wood caught fire, and the victims, invoking the names of Jesus and Mary, achieved the martyrdom they had desired. Their ashes were collected and scattered at sea. It was June 20, 1626. Pacheco's childhood vow had been fulfilled. The missionary charism had borne fruit for him and his comrades in all its fullness.

The governor forced the laypeople to watch the death of the martyrs as a terrifying lesson. But they did not change their mind and were sent back to prison, until on July 12 they, too, were martyred. These were Mancius Araki, his brother Mathias, and seven other Christians: Peter Araki Chobyoe, John Nagai Naizen, and John Tanaka, who died on a slow fire; their wives Susan, Catherine, and Monica, beheaded along with the child Luis, the son of Monica and John Nagai. With true Christian hospitality, they had taken the preachers of the Gospel into their homes. Martyrs of faith, they were also martyrs of charity.

Domingos Maurício, SJ[26]

Francis Pacheco and his companions were jointly beatified by Pius IX on May 7, 1867 to show that anyone, can bear witness to Christ in the furthering of his Kingdom.

---

26. Revised by Jacques Fédry, SJ.

Blessed Julian Nakaura (1568–1633)

An Epochal Journey

Julian Nakaura was born around 1568 in the village of Nakaura, today part of the municipality of Saikai, in the prefecture of Nagasaki. His father Kosasa Jingorō, lord of Nakaura Castle, died in 1568, shortly after Julian's birth. At the age of twelve, the boy entered in the minor seminary of Arima, which the Jesuits had opened for training Catholic *samurai* youth to become future teachers, catechists, and priests. This initiative had come from Father Alessandro Valignano, visitor to Japan. Two years later, in 1582, Valignano put forward the idea of sending some fine young samurai from the student body to Rome as showpieces of the Japanese Church.

Julian and three other young noblemen were chosen to be part of the embassy, which was sponsored by Omura Sumitada, the first Japanese *daimyo* (local feudal lord) who had converted to Catholicism; two other *daimyo* joined in—Arima Harunobu and Otomo Sorin. After a long and dangerous journey, they disembarked in Lisbon in August 1584 and traveled to Madrid, where they were received with full honors by King Philip II. They finally arrived in Rome on March 22, 1585. Pope Gregory XIII, who anticipated the Japanese delegation with great joy, sent the Jesuit superior general Claudio Acquaviva ahead to the Flaminian Gate to welcome them. Julian had been struck by malaria on the way but wanted nothing more than to assist at the papal audience: on the long journey, he had even had a dream of seeing the pope. In his faulty Latin, he assured the medical doctors: "If they lead me in front of him, I am sure I will recover." At last, a private meeting was organized before the public audience. The aged pontiff recognized in the young Julian, burning with fever and enthusiasm, the fruit of his efforts to open colleges and seminaries in different parts of the world and embraced him with great emotion. Julian, too, responded with tears. A short while later, Pope Gregory fell gravely ill, but even on the day of his death (April 10, 1585) he asked to pray for the health of the "little Japanese boy" that he had received like a son.

During his stay in Rome, Julian and his companions visited the Jesuit novitiate at Sant'Andrea, where they prayed in front of the tomb of the saintly novice Stanislaus Kostka, who had died there in 1568. His life moved them so much that on the same evening they asked to see the superior general to tell him that they wanted to remain in Rome to enter the Society of Jesus. Prudently, Father Acquaviva suggested that they first conclude the diplomatic mission and then consult their guide and advisor Father Valignano. The boys accepted the answer, but Julian had already made up his mind and would maintain his decision in the face of a thousand difficulties.

In early June, the new pope, Sixtus V, offered the young ambassadors a boat trip to the seaside at Ostia. They were to embark at the port of Ripa Grande, in which vicinity stood the Church of Santa Maria dell'Orto. When told that it housed a much venerated image of Our Lady, they entered the church for a short prayer, after which the party sailed along the river to Ostia. For their return to Rome, the pope sent some small, festively decorated boats with musicians and singers to accompany them, but when they wanted to strike up the music, a heavy storm rose, which threatened to shipwreck them all. Remembering the Madonna dell'Orto, the young samurai invoked her help with great fervor. They did not have to wait for the miracle to happen: instantly the wind stopped, the sea became calm like a lake, and they were all safe. Comforted in body and spirit, the delegation sailed back to Rome, singing the *Te Deum* in thanksgiving. In the Church of Santa Maria dell'Orto, the memory of this miracle is still kept alive.

"The One Who Was in Rome"

When the four ambassadors disembarked again at Nagasaki in 1590, Japan had become a very different country. Formerly a conglomerate of largely independent feudal states, with some of their lords ardent Catholics, Japan was now ruled by one man, the warlord Toyotomi Hideyoshi, who in 1587 had banned the Christian religion. Arima Harunobu, one of the embassy's sponsors, had bravely invited the Jesuits of Nagasaki to his castle-town of Arima,

Dry ionghe Iaponoische Princen, ghesanten van dry Christene Iaponoische Coningë, nemen
afscheyt van hunne moeders, ende vertrecken naer Roomen, om den Paus te herkennen

Blessed Julian Nakaura and two other "Japanese princes, ambassadors of three Christian
Japanese kings, bid farewell to their mothers and embark for Rome, to recognize the pope
there as the Vicar of God on earth." Engraving by Jacobus Bruyneel, after a drawing by
Abraham van Diepenbeeck (1667).

but this, too, was becoming an ever more risky place. In light of this, the Jesuits moved the minor seminary and novitiate first to another town in his domain and then to Kawachinoura, in the Amakusa Isles. There, on July 25, 1591, Julian and the other three young samurai entered the Society of Jesus.

When Julian had finished the first part of his studies, he was sent to Yatsushiro. There, between 1598 and 1600, he took part in an evangelization campaign, which abruptly ended with the defeat of the *daimyo* of Yatsushiro, Augustin Konishi Yukinaga, at Sekigahara. Julian then went to Macao, the Portuguese colony in south east India, to complete his theological studies. In 1608, he returned to Japan, where he was ordained a priest. In 1614, when the Tokugawa *shogun* Hidetada ordered all missionaries to leave Japan and more than half the clergy left the country, Julian was asked by his superiors to remain hidden in Japan.

From 1614 until 1626, he was based in the Arima domain, first at Kuchinotsu, in a house near the port, and then at Kazusa, in the residence of a local leading citizen, in which he even had a clandestine chapel. From here, he served a wide "parish" territory; once a year, he made a pastoral visitation of the various places for which he was responsible. As the years passed by, his health declined, making it difficult, if not impossible for him to walk, so his parish helpers carried him in a bamboo basket like the ones used by peasants to transport farm products.

Up till 1621, the clandestine Japanese missionaries in the Arima territory could work in relative quiet, but then a period of troubles set in. That same year, Julian made his final vows and wrote at the bottom of the sheet: "February 21, 1621, during the Japanese persecution," a clear sign that he was determined to live out his vocation to the bitter end. The next year, he reported: "Still the persecution continues unabated; because of it we cannot take a minute's rest ... The feudal lord hopes to uproot the teaching of the Gospel from this domain and see to it that not even one person remains who maintains the faith and thus violates the command of the Tenka—the ruler of all Japan." Twenty-one Christians in Kuchinotsu had already been killed, but Julian adds, "Thanks to the grace of God, I still have sufficient health and strength of spirit to shepherd the Christian charges of the Society of Jesus."

Finally, in 1627, Julian moved to Kokura, only to be captured five years later and sent to the Cruz-machi Prison at Nagasaki. There, Julian met several acquaintances, to whom many others would be joined. And while they, one after the other, met a martyr's death, Julian was kept in custody for more than ten months: since he was well-known, it was only logical that the persecutors tried with all their means to induce him to apostasy. On October 18, 1633, however, for him, too, the prison doors opened to martyrdom.

He would not die alone, but with seven other Jesuits and Dominican missionaries. They were herded up Nishizaka Hill, Julian with his hands tied behind his back and his legs atrophied because of infirmity. Yet while his body was weakened, his spirit remained strong, so much so that he could bear his illnesses and be filled with great courage. Led to the place of execution, in the face of the two governors of Nagasaki who wanted to enjoy the show, he proudly presented himself with words that would become famous: "I am Father Julian Nakaura, the one who was in Rome."

The martyrdom that Julian underwent was terrible. For him and his companions, a new, extremely sadistic way of execution was devised: coiled tightly in rope from the feet up to the chest, they were hanged upside-down from a gallows into a hole filled with filth; to increase their agony, their executioners cut them at the ears, so that they would slowly bleed to death. One of Julian's companions, the Jesuit provincial, broke down after five or six hours. The executioners came and told Julian: If his superior had apostatized, why not also give in? But Julian persevered for three days, until October 21. A witness heard his last words, saying that he withstood his sufferings for the love of God. Like so many other martyrs, his body was cremated and his ashes thrown into Nagasaki Bay.

Julian Nakaura, priest and martyr, is a powerful symbolic figure, an emblem of the cultural exchange between East and West; an emblem of the strong ties that bind the Japanese Church to the Holy See; a symbol of the highest and most noble ideals for young people, and of fidelity to God's calling to the religious life and to the priesthood.

Domenico Rotella[27]

Julian Nakaura was beatified at Nagasaki on November 24, 2008, together with 187 other Japanese martyrs, among whom three Jesuits. It was the first ever beatification ceremony in Japan.

---

27. Cf. the biography on www.santamariadellorto.it. Adapted and translated by Marc Lindeijer, SJ.

The Martyrs of the Reductions

SAINTS ROQUE GONZÁLEZ, ALONSO RODRIGUEZ,
AND JUAN DE CASTILLO

(†1628)

Memorial on November 16

In Service of Faith

Roque González de Santa Cruz was born in the year 1576 in Asunción, which was then the capital of the vast administrative area of Río de la Plata, today's Paraguay, and was ordained at the age of twenty-two. Some ten years later, he entered the Society of Jesus, and from that moment spent his life "in seeking out Indians, converting them, teaching them doctrine, and settling them in townships. His labours were great, and he often went naked and hungry, and lacking even the necessities of life," as Brother Luis de Bolaños, a Franciscan missionary in Paraguay, attested after his martyrdom.

It was really Father Roque who organized and built San Ignacio, a village that had been started some years before. This is his account of what he did there: "We had to build this village from its very foundations. To remove what is normally an occasion of sin, I decided to build it along the lines of Spanish villages, so that each man had his own house with its own definite boundaries. A house and a church were built for our own use. Getting all this organized meant a great deal of work; but we labored with far greater enthusiasm and far more diligently to build temples for God Our Lord that were not made of bricks and mortar. I mean the spiritual temples that were the souls of these Indians. We put all our energy into this task. On Sundays and feast days, a sermon was preached during Mass, and before Mass the catechism was explained."

In Service of Justice

Father Roque baptized the natives and built them a village, preached to them, and gave a structure to their townships. His constant struggle was to free men from sin in all its forms, and he had to offer robust opposition to two types of oppressors who attempted to enslave the Indian: the witchdoctors and the *encomenderos*, Spanish colonists who "protected" their Indian vassals.

These colonists had on several occasions tried to get the Jesuits expelled, even in the very earliest days of the Indian mission. Roque wrote in a letter that was to become famous: "These *encomenderos* and soldiers have long held it against the Jesuits that we defended the Indians and their right to remain free: their complaints are nothing new." And further on: "The day is not far off when injustice will be punished, especially offenses against the poor. On that day Your Honour will see that the *encomenderos* (doubtless deceived by their greed) have hardly given you the full story when they say that the Indians have nothing with which to pay the many years' tribute they owe them. This I find astonishing, since I know that, even if the *encomenderos* were to beggar themselves, they could not repair the enormous debt they owe to the Indians. And this immense blindness is the reason why people who know them are reluctant to hear their confessions; and for myself I will not give any of them absolution, since they have done evil and have no desire to recognize it, still less to make amends and restitution for it. They will realize this on the Day of Judgment, if they do not change their ways and make it up to the Indians, when they stand before him who cannot be deceived, for he knows everything."

In Service of Villages

From San Ignacio, Father Roque moved up toward the Paraná, and for ten years did extraordinary work as an explorer, founding many villages between 1615 and 1619 in what is now Argentina: Santa Ana del Iberá (now Itati), Itapuña (origin of Posadas and Encarnación), and Concepción (north east of Corrientes).

Epidemics, assisted by famine, periodically devastated the area; on occasions, the attentions of Spanish soldiers on forays against the Indians had equally devastating effects. We can guess at the anxiety this caused Roque González from this letter to his provincial: "I have no thought or desire other than to do Your Reverence's will, for in doing that I do the will of God. My existence here is a living death ... but I order mind and heart to God's greater glory."

The effects of this heroic self-giving were astonishing. Large numbers of Indians came to be baptized and began leading a more civilized life. The governor of Buenos Aires received Father Roque with an artillery salute when he sent for him in order to entrust him with the task of civilizing the Indians of the province of Uruguay. Later on, in 1627, González and his provincial founded Yapeyú to serve as a bridge between the missions and Buenos Aires.

Roque taught the Indians to sing and dance and paint, and gave them their first lessons in agriculture, industry, and commerce.

In Service of Truth

In the last years of his life, Roque had the assistance of two young men, Alonso Rodriguez, born in Zamora in 1598, and Juan del Castillo, born in 1596 in Belmonte, near Cuenca. The first entered the Society at a very young age, the other during his law studies at the University of Alcalá, but both immediately offered themselves for the missions. Coming from Spain via Buenos Aires, they had reached Córdoba in 1616. They were students in what was soon to become the foremost university in the Argentine and had degrees in philosophy and theology; they had said their first Masses in Córdoba. Juan del Castillo went to Concepción, in Chile, to teach literature for two years.

Then came the year 1628. With the two young men, Roque González carried the light of the Gospel more toward the southeast, founding two new villages. An Indian witch doctor called Nezú lived near one of these villages, and it was he who hatched the plot that led to the death of the three missionaries.

In Service of Love

On November 16, Father Roque, having just said Mass, came out to put a new bell on a log that Alonso and a large number of Indians had dragged down from the mountains. He stooped to attach the bell's clapper, and while he was in that position, one of the conspirators struck him with a stone axe. Such was the force of the blow that the victim was killed outright.

Father Alonso was preparing to say Mass when they threw him to the ground, trampled him, and shattered his skull. The two bodies were mutilat-

"We work for justice," proclaims the banner above Saint Roque González. He was killed by a tomahawk while supervising the installation of a new bell for the mission of All Saints Church in Caaró. His murderers then defaced all the pious images in the chapel, in particular the painting of the Virgin known as La Conquistadora, which the saint took with him into non-Christian territory. Painting by Raúl Berzosa (2019).

ed and burned. The assailants then caught Father Juan del Castillo, who was nearby, and killed him with appalling tortures on November 17.

These three martyrs offer an abiding example of priests at the service of humanity. Their profound understanding and preaching of the Gospel meant for the Indians a new social organization and liberation from all kinds of oppression.

Alberto Ibáñez Padilla, SJ[28]

The three missionaries were beatified by Pius XI in 1934 and canonized by John Paul II on May 16, 1988 in Asunción, Paraguay.

---

28. Revised by Jacques Fédry, SJ.

From a Letter of Saint Roque González

I soon returned there and found somewhere to stay in a small hut near the river; soon afterward, they offered me a slightly larger hut made of straw; but two months later the rector sent me to Father Diego de Boroa. He arrived on Whit Monday, and we were both very consoled as we thought of the way the love of God had brought us together in such a remote and out of the way place. We then divided our tiny house in two by means of a wall of reeds, and added a chapel a little broader than the altar where Mass was to be celebrated. It was because of the power of this supreme, divine Sacrifice, in which Christ offered himself to the Father on the Cross, and even now is among us in glory, that the demons who used to appear to the inhabitants of this place have no more dared to display themselves. We have this on the authority of some of the natives.

Still we decided to remain in our hut, despite our lack of all necessaries. The cold there was so severe that we could hardly sleep. Food was utterly primitive: we ate wheat or a meal made out of something they call *mandioque*, which they live on. Because we go out looking for the herbs the parrots eat, the natives call us "parrots" by way of a joke.

While things were going on in this way, the demons were afraid that the entrance of the Society in these regions would mean the loss of their own long-held power; so they tried to spread a rumor throughout the whole Paraná region that we were spies and magicians, and that we brought death with us in our books and statues. So strong was this view that, when Father Boroa was trying to explain the mysteries of the faith to the pagans, some of them were afraid to stand near our holy statues in case somehow death passed from the images to themselves. Bit by bit, they are learning the faith, especially as they can see with their own eyes that we are true fathers to them, willingly letting them have anything we may have at home and helping them day and night in their labors and sicknesses, spending ourselves for the healing of their bodies, and—what is more important—their souls.

The love the Indians have for us has now been established, and we have decided to build a church, small and very low, and thatched with straw, yet as far as these poor men are concerned a royal palace. They are amazed when they look up at the roof. As they did not know how to make bricks for the church, we had to dirty our own hands and show them how to do it. So the church was finished for the feast of Saint Ignatius last year, 1615. On that day, we celebrated the first Mass in the church and renewed our vows, adding other festive rites that the poverty of the place allowed. We even tried to train the young men to dance, but they are so primitive that they could learn nothing. Then we erected a little wooden tower and hung a small bell up high, which amazed the people, who had never seen or heard anything like it before. The cause of the greatest devotion was the cross that the natives themselves had set up in front of the church; for when we had explained to them why we Christians adore the cross, they all genuflected with us before it. My hope in the Lord is that this cross, which has arrived so recently on these shores, may lead to the erection of many others.

Liturgy of the Hours, Second Reading for November 14

Saint Alphonsus Rodríguez (1533–1617)

PATRON OF JESUIT BROTHERS

Memorial on October 31

Two Stages of a Life

Alphonsus Rodríguez, the second child in a family of seven sons and four daughters, was born in the Spanish city of Segovia in July 1533, while Ignatius of Loyola was studying in the University of Paris and arousing the interest of some of his companions with his apostolic ideas.

It was not until he was thirty-eight that Alphonsus became a Jesuit. His *Memorial* explains what turned him to God: "When he was immersed in worldly concerns, God inflicted a series of disasters on him which aroused in him a deep sense of his own evil life and a contempt for the world ... and with this self-knowledge the knowledge of God came too."[29] A succession of domestic calamities—the death of his wife and of two of his three sons, and heavy financial losses—prepared the way for God's grace.

His first request for admission to the Society of Jesus in 1568 was refused: he was too old, in poor health, and had not completed the studies required for priestly ordination. Two years later, he applied again for admission. If he could not be a priest, he would gladly be accepted as a brother coadjutor. Despite the negative advice of his consultors, the provincial accepted him with the words: "Let him enter, we will admit him as a saint!"

In January 1571, at the age of thirty-eight, he started his novitiate. While still a novice brother, he was sent in August of that year to the College of Our

---

29. Alonso Rodríguez, *Autobiografía o sea memoria o cuentas de la conciencia escritas per el mismo santo por mandato de sus superiores*, ed. V. Segarra (Barcelona, 1956), 15.

Francisco de Zurbarán, Saint Alphonsus Rodríguez, supported by his guardian angel, re-ceives from heaven the outpouring of love from the hearts of Jesus and Mary (1630).

Lady of Monti-sión, in Palma de Majorca, where he would spend the remaining years of his life until God called him to himself on October 31, 1617. The image of Alphonsus performing the duties of a doorman and other humble services over many years is very familiar.

Outwardly, Alphonsus's life seems to reflect the unruffled calm of the beautiful island where he lived, without any major preoccupations, given the few responsibilities he had, in a framework of monotonous routine, and with few opportunities to practice the heroism that usually makes the saints. Apparently, he was just a good brother among the other brothers. A very different Alphonsus is revealed in his writings, however, and especially in his *Memorial or Accounts of Conscience*, which is, in effect, his autobiography.

Self-knowledge and Knowledge of God

The way to holiness is through knowledge of self and knowledge of God, and Alphonsus never stopped growing in this way in the course of his life in the Society. In his writings, he continually repeats the phrase of Saint Augustine: "Lord, let me know Thee, let me know myself."[30] Self-knowledge had a constantly purifying effect on his soul and confirmed him in his very profound humility. It was an active humility, however, that led him to live in union with God and to strive to be content in everything with God, a humility that Alphonsus calls "humility of heart" as distinct from "humility of the understanding."[31] His faults, his human limitations, his physical infirmities, and the tests his soul went through, all helped him to build on self-knowledge and led him to strive to overcome and mortify whatever in him could be an obstacle to a perfect encounter with God.

Since by the favor of heaven Alphonsus was able to understand, at least imperfectly, "who God is," he wanted nothing more than that his entire life should belong to God. As he wrote, "Looking at himself and at the great majesty of his God, to whom he has been disloyal, bad, and traitorous, he abhors the state in which he sees himself; and this comes from the great love that he has for God and from the remorse he senses for having offended him; for

---

30. Ibid., 23.
31. Alonso Rodríguez, *Cartas espirituales y plàticas*, ed. I. Quiles (Buenos Aires, 1944), 68.

love awakens the soul, that it may perceive what evil it has done in offending against God who is so good."[32]

Drawing Nearer to the Lord

"Through clarity, humility, and love of God comes the surrender of the whole soul to God. This alone is sure, and he holds everything else in suspicion and fears it, such as visions, revelations, interior and exterior voices, and spiritual gifts."[33] The continual favors in prayer and contemplation that God now grant-ed him marked new stages in Alphonsus's spiritual ascent, without altering the clarity of his ascetic vision or falling short of Ignatius's criterion "that love ought to show itself in deeds rather than words" (*Spir. Ex.*, n. 230).

Praying continuously, Alphonsus made sure to do God's will as perfectly as possible, with the help of his grace. His entire daily activity, so repetitious and monotonous over so many years, was for him an opportunity for an ever greater fidelity to God. This explains the pure love of obedience that makes his spirituality so distinctive. Obedience, understood as he wanted to understand it and as he described it in his writings, is faithful and complete performance of the superior's suggestions or commands, for the love of God, whom he always saw present in the person giving the order.

Alphonsus tells us that some people took him to task over his exaggerated and literal obedience: "Because he obeyed exactly and promptly, he had many long arguments with those in the house who were of a different opinion; but he broke off the arguments for the sake of obedience."[34] He was never able to compromise on this point: "This obedience that our Blessed Father [Ignatius] asks of us is such a lofty thing that few can penetrate it and know its greatness, and still fewer have it implanted in their hearts like our Blessed Father."[35]

A Heart the Size of the World

This concrete love that Alphonsus sought to give to God, led him to desire and ask also that not just he but all mankind and the whole of creation should love

---

32. *Autobiografia*, 129–30.
33. Ibid., 130.
34. Ibid., 154.
35. Ibid., 63.

God and not fall away from his service. "So this person, moved with a desire for the salvation of the whole world, with great emotion used to make this offering of himself to God, that he would write to everyone in the world to help them to greater service of God."[36]

With a heart the size of the world, in 1608 Alphonsus recapitulated the desires of his soul thirsting for love: "This person's prayer is a petition to God and to the Blessed Virgin for four loves, which are, first, the love of God; second, the love of Jesus Christ Our Lord; third, the love of the Blessed Virgin, Our Lady; fourth, the love of one another, until the end of the world. And however many people there are or will be in the world until it ends, I beg you to grant us these four loves without limit, so that we may serve you with them."[37]

Mary was always very much a part of Alphonsus's intimate relationship with God. She invariably comes to his aid, telling him: "Where I am, there is nothing to be afraid of," reassuring him as a mother reassures her son. At the age of seventy-five, Alphonsus writes: "As time went on and with the passing of the years, his love and devotion to the Virgin Our Lady grew so much that when he was talking to her on various occasions, he would ask her to ask her Blessed Son to make him very devoted to them both and to make him imitate them. This person's love of Our Lady eventually grew so great that one day he said these words to her: 'He loves her more than she loves him,' and Our Lady replied, 'No, I love you even more.'"[38]

A Contemplative in Action

Alphonsus's two aspirations were to live for God and to bring the whole world to him. In his fidelity to his actual mission at the college of Montesión, as he tried to fulfill it with increasing perfection, his life became simply the working out of his deep love of God, and took on an unbounded apostolic meaning and scope.

Seeing him so united with the Lord, so full of God, many people went to him for advice and spiritual enlightenment. He encouraged many to be gener-

---

36. Ibid., 175–177.
37. Ibid., 116.
38. Ibid., 112.

ous toward God and maintained with some a faithful correspondence, full of common sense and the desire to communicate what he had come to know of God and to do what was right for everyone.

His best known spiritual son was Peter Claver. Under Alphonsus's influence, Claver developed his ambition to become an apostle to the slaves in South America; when he decided to follow this road, he was doing what Alphonsus himself longed to do. Claver's heroism, his utter selflessness, and his compassion for the abandoned and afflicted slaves, are a reflection of the greatness of Alphonsus's soul.

All Jesuits, especially the brothers of the Society and those of other religious orders, have been stimulated and encouraged by Alphonsus in their vocation as contemplatives in action; he has taught them his own cheerful readiness to obey every manifestation of the will of God. While he was porter at Montesión, he tells us: "When people knocked at the door, he would make acts of joy on the way, as though he were going to open the door to his God, and as though it was he who had rung the bell, and on the way he would say: 'I'm coming, Lord.'"[39]

Cándido Gaviña, SJ

Beatified by Pope Leo XII in 1825, Alphonsus Rodríguez was canonized by Pope Leo XIII on January 15, 1888, with Peter Claver and John Berchmans.

---

39. Ibid., 155.

Jesus, love of my soul, center of my heart! Why am I not more eager to endure pains and tribulations for love of you, when you, my God, have suffered so many for me? Come, then, every sort of trouble in the world, for this is my delight, to suffer for Jesus. This is my joy, to follow my Savior, and to find my consolation with my consoler on the cross. This is my happiness, this is my pleasure: to live with Jesus, to walk with Jesus, to converse with Jesus, to suffer with and for him. This is my treasure.

Saint Alphonsus Rodríguez

From a Letter of Superior General Arturo Sosa

Jesuit brothers offer a prophetic witness within religious communities, in the Church, and in the diversity of social situations in which the apostolic work of the Society of Jesus is realized. Following Christ in the evangelical radicality of religious life, they give clear witness to the free gift of the whole person to the service of other human beings. Brothers in the Society today engage fully in a wide variety of ministries and hold positions of leadership in them. They remind us, not so much of functions, but of the depth of consecration, the loving, joyful dedication of one's whole self to the Lord in the vows of poverty, chastity, and obedience. It is as consecrated persons who are not clerics that brothers become a prophetic sign to both ordained members of the Society and lay partners in mission. It is no surprise that, in his final speech before his resignation, Father Pedro Arrupe said: "I want to remind the whole Society of the importance of the brothers; they help us to center our vocation on God." This is the wisdom that one discerns in Saint Alphonsus Rodríguez. It is that "element of wisdom" that comes with being a brother in the Society, as pointed out by Pope Francis in the dialogue he had with the members of the General Congregation 36 on October 24, 2016, and that he earnestly asked us to preserve in the apostolic body.

Letter of October 31, 2017, to the whole Society, on the four hundredth anniversary of the death of Saint Alphonsus Rodríguez

Saint Peter Claver (1580–1654)

"SLAVE OF SLAVES"

Memorial on September 9

On April 15, 1610, the Spanish galleon *San Pedro* set sail from Seville for Cartagena de Indias, now a city of Colombia. On board, together with some other missionaries, was a Catalonian Jesuit scholastic, born on June 26, 1580, at Verdú in northeastern Spain.

A Saint on His Way

The Jesuit was not yet a priest. He was thirty years old, and his name was Peter Claver. His missionary vocation to the New World had been prompted by a saint, Alphonsus Rodríguez, porter at the Jesuit college of Montesión in Palma Majorca.

One day, Brother Alphonsus had told him: "Your mission is in the Indies. It is a great thing ... Ah! dear Peter, why don't you go too, to work there for Our Lord?" And Claver went to the New World. He had inherited the Spaniard's soberness, austerity, and realism, and God gave him the gift of contemplation in action. His spirituality became centered on the apostolate of the slaves. He took his lead from his master Alphonsus, whose teachings he had collected in an exercise book that Claver took with him everywhere and clutched to his heart as he died.

Claver's missionary charism was marked by the profoundly Christocentric spirituality of Saint Alphonsus Rodríguez. His apostolic strategy was much influenced by the work of another Jesuit whom he met in Cartagena, Father Alonso de Sandoval, whose book *On the Salvation of the Blacks* became Peter's catechetical manual and the basis of his pastoral ministry.

Claver was ordained a priest in Cartagena in 1616 and worked in its slave markets until his death in 1654—thirty-eight years dedicated to the black slaves, who were the most downtrodden sector of contemporary society. He baptized and instructed more than three hundred thousand of them, using methods far in advance of the time: working through native interpreters, their tribal structures, and with visual aids.

Slave of Slaves

On the day of his final vows, April 3, 1622, he wrote in his own blood the words that would become the hallmark of his life: "Peter Claver, slave of the black slaves for all time." And he fulfilled those words to the fullest in a difficult and paradoxical age.

Three Key Questions

Claver was a man of few words. When travelers arrived from overseas, he would ask them, "Is there peace in Europe? What news of the pope? How goes the work of the Society of Jesus?" Peace, the papacy, and the Society: these three sum up his own deepest concerns and reflect the age in which he lived, an age to which he owed a good deal.

He was born in 1580, in the last years of the brilliant sixteenth century, the golden age of his native Spain, when art and literature flourished and great spirits were abroad. He died in 1654, halfway hrough the seventeenth century, with its marked decadence of all religious orders and its contrasting morals— rigid Jansenism versus ostentatious hedonism. The century of Claver's active life was marred by a certain loss of faith, a thirst for gold, the slave trade, and great national rivalries. New worlds were being opened up, full of adventure and easy opportunities for enrichment.

"Is there peace?" There was the Thirty Years' War, a war in Peter's own little Catalonia, and struggles for power among the leaders of Christendom.

"What news of the pope?" After the Renaissance and the Council of Trent, the papacy was being renewed. In France, there were great men like Vincent de Paul, John Eudes, John Francis Regis, and also the austerities of Jansenism. Their contemporaries were two quite different representatives of renewal, Saint Charles Borromeo, the saint of the reform of the Church, and Saint Peter Canisius, the apostle of Northern Europe. The pontificate of Gregory XV

Giuseppe Vitta, *Saint Peter Claver baptizes one of the black slaves, of whom he is aptly called "the apostle." Intaglio engraving after a painting by Pietro Gagliardi (1888, for the canonization).*

(1621–23) witnessed the creation of the Congregation for the Propagation of the Faith and flourishing missionary work in Asia and America. Saint Teresa of Ávila and others like her had disappeared, but what they had started had retained its vigor. Saints like John of God and Camillus de Lellis were pursuing their apostolate of charity. Gregory XV, Urban VIII, and Innocent X left a profound impression.

"How is the Society of Jesus?" Ignatius and Francis Xavier had been canonized in 1622; Saint Robert Bellarmine was dead, like two others who had influenced Claver, the theologian Francisco Suárez and the catechist Juan Martínez de Ripalda. He himself was the contemporary of great missionaries like the Jesuits of the reductions in Paraguay, Roberto de Nobili in India, John Francis Regis in Europe—the Ignatian second generation.

The spirit of Ignatius was alive and flourishing in the missionary villages. The letters of Jesuits to their brethren made the story known throughout the world. Claver was one of the great American missionaries, "the greatest of the seventeenth century," according to one author. He was not an important figure in political history; his apostolate was no more than a spiritual footnote in its pages, but he made a deep impact on the social level.

A Dynamic Mystic

The essence of Claver's spiritual impact was his unconditional gift of himself to others, and his preference for the wretched, though he did not work exclusively for them. He also lived an intense spiritual life. "He was a dynamic mystic."

Some of his sayings are preserved: "Speak little with men and a great deal with God." "See God in all men and serve them as his image and likeness." "Let us seek God in all things and we shall find him by our side."

His mysticism was thoroughly realistic and was marked also by a great freedom of spirit. On his couch were Father Bartolomeo Ricci's *Considerations on the Whole Life of Our Lord Jesus Christ* (1625), Father Louis de La Puente's newly published book *Meditations on the Mysteries of Our Holy Faith*, and the works of Saint Teresa.

He was a man of prayer: "Great prayer is a precious gift; blessed is he who has it," he used to say.

He was often misunderstood, even by his companions. He had his share of deep despair. He also had difficult superiors. Here is a report sent to Rome not long before his death, from the Annual Letters of 1651: "Peter Claver. A good disposition, poor judgment, lacking in prudence. Little experience of life or affairs. Some progress. Melancholic temperament. Remarkable work with the Ethiopians (blacks). Great advance in the spiritual life." What a contradictory and paradoxical assessment!

"Any time left over from hearing confessions, and from catechizing and instructing the blacks, he gave to prayer; he spent much of the night in prayer." One of his fellow workers noted that they heard him saying over and over again: "Lord, I love Thee very much ... very much."

His Great Charisma: A Total Gift to Others

His love was not just a matter of talk. The austerity of his life is quite remarkable; the "folly of the cross" is another distinctive mark of his holiness. It took on all kinds of forms in his life, from the cross-shaped end of his staff and the cross around his neck, "made of rosewood, called the cross of miracles," to the cross as sacrifice and the gift of self, sharing in the sorrow of the poor.

He was obsessed with the tragedy of the slaves. "He saw and wept bitterly over the great tragedy of the slaves packed into their huts, looking out sadly, like animals without hope." He saw himself as the liberator of an oppressed race. "He would go to the sick," his companion tells us, "and saw how they had no wish to eat but desired only to die. Then he went to them and cared for them." This great love of his is the chief mark of his apostolate. "His heart went out to the suffering," of whom there were many: captives, heretics, slaves, lepers—those were the people he felt most at home with.

He was by nature melancholic, but he had only kindliness for the poor, especially his catechists. "No mother was ever as watchful for her children as Peter Claver was for his catechists." He described them as "my right arm"; they were "his friends."

"He had immense compassion for these black slave-women who had nobody of their own. They always came first with him, and he used to make great ladies wait long hours among the rows of slave-women who came to confess to him."

He had a clear sense of racial and human integration based on love and self-sacrifice. This was the great charism that made him a hero and a saint for today. The best epitaph for him is the cry of the slaves when they heard of his death, which occurred on September 8, 1654: "Our best friend is dead."

Angel Valtierra, SJ[40]

Peter Claver was beatified by Pope Pius IX in 1850 and canonized by Pope Leo XIII on January 15, 1888, with his master, the brother porter Alphonsus Rodríguez. In 1896, Claver was proclaimed universal patron of the mission to the blacks by Leo XIII, who once said: "No life, after the life of Christ, has moved me as deeply as that of that great apostle, Saint Peter Claver."

To do the will of God man must despise his own: the more he dies to himself, the more he will live to God.

Saint Peter Claver

---

40. Revised by Marc Lindeijer, SJ.

From the Allocution of Pope Francis at Cartagena de Indias

In this Church of Saint Peter Claver, we will pray to Mary, who referred to herself as "the handmaid of the Lord," and to Saint Peter Claver, the "slave of the blacks forever," as he wanted others to know him from the day of his solemn profession. He waited for the ships from Africa to arrive at the New World's main center of commerce in slavery. Given the impossibility of verbal communication due to the language difference, he often ministered to these slaves simply through evangelizing gestures. For a caress surpasses all languages. He knew that the language of charity and mercy was understood by all. Indeed, charity helps us to know the truth and truth calls for acts of love. These two go together, they cannot be separated. Whenever he felt revulsion toward the slaves —they came in a repulsive state—Peter Claver kissed the wounds.

He was austere and charitable to the point of heroism. After consoling hundreds of thousands of people in their loneliness, he died without honors and was not remembered, having spent the last four years of his life in sickness and confined to his cell, which was in a terrible state of neglect. This is how the world paid him, yet God paid him in another way.

Saint Peter Claver witnessed in a formidable way to the responsibility and care that we should have for one another. Furthermore, this saint was unjustly accused of being indiscreet in his zealousness, and he faced strong criticism and persistent opposition from those who feared that his ministry would undermine the lucrative slave trade.

Here in Colombia and in the world millions of people are still being sold as slaves; they either beg for some expressions of humanity, moments of tenderness, or they flee by sea or land because they have lost everything, primarily their dignity and their rights.

Our Lady of Chiquinquirá and Peter Claver invite us to work to promote the dignity of all our brothers and sisters, particularly the poor and the excluded of society, those who are abandoned, immigrants, and those who suffer violence and human trafficking. They all have human dignity because they are living images of God. We all are created in the image and likeness of God, and the Blessed Virgin holds each one of us in her arms as her beloved children.

Allocution preceding the recitation of the Angelus of September 10, 2017

Part 3

THE CONTROVERSIAL SOCIETY (1640–1773)

"Paraguay, Where the R.R.P.P. of the Society of Jesus spread Their Missions. By the S.r. d'Anville, Geographer Ord.re du Roi, October 1733."

Jean-Baptiste Bourguignon d'Anville (1697–1782)

Reassured by the celebrations of their first century, the Jesuits moved with confidence into their second. Although the Japanese mission, of which they were particularly proud, ended in tragedy, that failure was an exception. In virtually every other place where they had established themselves, they seemed to move ever more deeply into the religious and cultural fabric and further develop enterprises earlier undertaken. Vocations to the Society continued to grow, even when those to other orders began to decline. The Austrian province, for example, expanded to include some 1,800 members.

In parts of northern Europe, the religious controversies continued as bitterly as ever, and martyrs such as Andrew Bobola in Poland and Thomas Whitehead and his companions in England still paid with their lives for the Catholic cause. As the period progressed, however, such overt viciousness diminished.

In both Europe and Latin America, the schools flourished, as did the important publications on sacred and secular subjects that flowed from them. Large congregations filled the Jesuit churches. The missions to hamlets and villages in Europe flourished and became ever more elaborate and popular. Itinerant Jesuits such as Julian Maunoir, Francis Jerome, and Anthony Baldinucci became as renowned for their dedication to this ministry as for the holiness of their lives.

The mission of the French Jesuits to North America proved particularly difficult. It exposed the Jesuits to uncommon hardships and dangers, as the extremely cruel martyrdoms of Isaac Jogues, John de Brébeuf, and others makes unmistakably clear. Nonetheless, the Jesuits persevered and, along with missionaries from other orders, finally established the Church in present-day Canada.

The reductions in Spanish America won praise even from quarters unfriendly to Catholicism. The accommodation experiment in Beijing succeeded in winning almost unwavering imperial favor. The experiment in India undertaken by John de Britto, however, ended in the tragedy of his martyrdom.

In Southeast Asia, Jesuits and other Catholic missionaries had their most lasting success in the Philippines. In 1688, the Jesuits there even began their own mission in the Marianas. The Spanish Jesuit Diego de San Vitores and his valiant catechist Pedro Calungsod set out to evangelize the territory of Guam, where they met strong resistance and became its first martyrs.

Successes and failures thus marked the period. The balance, however, swung strongly in favor of success. Yet, as the period advanced, it gradually soured. The Jesuits' very successes generated envy, suspicion, and resentment in certain quarters of the Church.

Catholic culture itself began to undergo significant shifts. The Peace of Westphalia, 1648, ending the Thirty Years' War, initiated one such shift. It marked the end of the religious militancy of the Reformation and Counter Reformation. Catholic rulers and many churchmen wanted to put dogmatism and religious wars behind them. They were ready to pay attention to innovative thinkers such as Descartes and even to Protestants such as John Locke and Isaac Newton. They set the stage for the Enlightenment.

No cultural phenomenon was more characteristic of the period than the Enlightenment. Multiform though it was, basic to it was confidence in the power of human reason. For some Enlightenment thinkers, this premise did not exclude the possibility of the transcendent, but for others it certainly did.

By the middle of the eighteenth century, the latter undertook a veritable crusade against the Church. Catholics, including the Jesuits, had at first accepted many of the Enlightenment's proposals, but acceptance became increasingly difficult as time wore on. The anti-Catholic thinkers of the Enlightenment hated the Jesuits because they saw them as the most qualified of their adversaries to challenge them.

Meanwhile, Gallicanism, another movement that became inimical to the Society, took formal shape in 1682 with the publication by the Assembly of the French Clergy of the *Four Gallican Articles*. Although essentially a reaffirmation of the ancient tradition of episcopal collegiality, Gallicanism began to stand for limitations of papal authority and the right of secular authorities to regulate religious affairs. Those two aspects of the movement became especially prominent in the third quarter of the eighteenth century, and neither of them boded well for the Jesuits, who were traditional defenders of papal authority.

Jansenism explicitly and intentionally took aim at the Society of Jesus. Its point of origin was Louvain, where in 1640, the Jesuits' jubilee year, Cornelius Jansen's treatise *Augustinus* was posthumously published. Jansen hoped to save Catholicism from the worldliness and loose morality promoted by the Jesuits and make it a model of probity, similar to that of the Puritans.

According to Jansen and his later followers, the Jesuits by their emphasis on free will denied the efficacy of grace in the mystery of salvation and sanctification. By teaching that in moral matters Catholics might, under certain conditions, follow less probable (and less strict) opinions, they made sin easy. By promoting theater and dance in their schools and by the exuberant baroque of their churches, the Jesuits fostered worldliness. By accommodating Christianity to Chinese culture and rituals, the Jesuits betrayed the Gospel.

The battle lines between the two sides were drawn. In the very first instance, the Jesuits appealed to the Holy See for condemnation of the *Augustinus,* and with success. The movement nonetheless took off. Its center moved to Paris, and it soon became a pan-European phenomenon. Although the number of its adherents remained relatively small, it proved particularly appealing in higher circles of Church and society.

The papacy continued to issue condemnations of the movement, and the Jansenists continued to find ways to evade them. They held the Jesuits responsible for such actions by the Holy See, which increased their bitterness and animosity. The religious scene grew ugly as Catholics turned against themselves.

In the midst of this rancor, however, a series of events in a Visitation Convent at Paray-le-Monial in France eventually became interpreted as a Catholic antidote to the coldness of Jansenist piety. In the 1670s, Sister Margaret Mary Alacoque received a number of visions in which Christ pointed to his heart as a symbol of his love for humanity and asked to be venerated for it.

The Jesuit Claude La Colombière counseled Sister Margaret Mary and became convinced of the authenticity of her visions. Other Jesuits became similarly convinced and began to preach and teach about the Sacred Heart. In a relatively short time, "Devotion to the Sacred Heart" became an identity mark for Jesuit spirituality, to the horror of the Jansenists.

A few decades before Margaret Mary's visions, the Beijing mission found itself in serious difficulty. Reports reached the Holy See that the Jesuits allowed Chinese converts to continue their pagan religious practices. When in 1645 the Holy See condemned the "Rites," as the controversy is known, the Jesuits appealed. They argued that the rites in question were civil, not religious, and therefore licit. They won the case, and the matter seemed settled.

Twenty years later, however, the issue rose again and ignited decades of arguments and counter-arguments. Finally, in 1704, Pope Clement XI condemned the Rites; all efforts by the Jesuits to change the decision availed nothing. The decision enraged Emperor Kangxi and spelled the end of Christian missions to China until the next century. The Jansenists' glee at the condemnation was unbounded, and they took it as vindication of their accusation that the Jesuits were destroying the Church.

In Spanish America, the reductions continued their peaceful and productive existence until 1750, when a treaty between Spain and Portugal redistributed parts of the territories there. Seven of the reductions suffered the consequence by being required to pull up stakes and move to other locations. The native inhabitants, who had long had royal permission to carry firearms in defense against the slave traders, refused to move, and war broke out between them and the government forces. After a valiant effort, the natives lost the "War of the Seven Reductions," and the reductions were destroyed.

In Europe around the same fateful year of 1750, a new generation of royal ministers came into power in Portugal, Spain, France, and satellite countries. They were intent on exalting the power of the crown and of crushing real or imagined challenges to it by any foreign authority. They set their eyes on the Jesuits. Whereas the local superiors of other religious orders were elected locally, the superior general of the Jesuits, a foreign authority, appointed those of the Society. Beyond the Jesuits lay the papacy with its traditional international claims, intrusions into the sovereign rights of the nation.

Among this new breed of royal ministers was the Marquis de Pombal in Portugal. He seized upon the War of the Seven Reductions as proof positive of Jesuit perfidy and danger to the state. By a series of deft moves, he brought about in 1759 the unthinkable, the suppression of the Jesuits in Portugal and its dominions. He thus showed, to his great satisfaction, the impotence of the papacy to save this large and highly respected religious order.

The enemies of the Jesuits—Jansenists, Gallicans, and the anti-Christians of the Enlightenment—smelled blood. Prelates, many of whom were creatures of the crown, fixed their eyes on Jesuit properties and were therefore loath to raise a voice in protest.

Pombal had shown that the unthinkable could be done. France followed his lead. In 1764, a reluctant Louis XV took the final step by suppressing the Jesuits in France. The momentum was building. Spain, the Kingdom of the Two Sicilies, and others fell into line.

A worldwide suppression of the Jesuits by the papacy itself still eluded their enemies. Their opportunity came in 1769 when Pope Clement XIII died. The anti-Jesuit forces were determined that a pope pliant to their objective be elected, which meant that the fate of the Jesuits dominated the conclave. Finally, after 185 ballots, the cardinals chose Cardinal Giovanni Ganganelli, who took the name Clement XIV.

The new pope had his own reservations about the Jesuits, and before his election he somehow let it be known that he considered their suppression a possibility. Nonetheless, once elected, he shrank from the deed. The ambassadors especially of Spain and France, however, applied unremitting pressure to him and hinted at the possibility of schism if he failed them.

After three years of agonizing hesitation, Clement XIV, on August 15, 1773, issued the brief of suppression, *Dominus ac Redemptor*. The secular powers had humiliated the papacy by forcing it to do their will. They had at the same time got rid of the Jesuit pests. The Society of Jesus was no more. When the news of the brief reached the Spanish court, the ministers ordered the singing of a solemn *Te Deum* in jubilation.

John W. O'Malley, SJ

Servant of God Vincenzo Carafa (1585–1649)

GENERAL OF THE CONTROVERSIAL SOCIETY

Deceased on June 8th

Erudite and Devout

Born in 1585 as second son of the duke and duchess of Andria (Bari), Vincenzo Carafa was destined for a splendid clerical career. Instead, when studying at the Jesuit college in Naples, he chose the religious life. The dramatic loss of his father, murdered when caught in adultery with the wife of the prince of Venosa, may have guided young Vincenzo's decision to leave the world. Initially, he was drawn to the Capuchins because of their penitential spirituality, but when he was praying Our Lady in a period of desolation, he perceived a call to become a Jesuit. He entered the Society in 1604 and was soon noted for his great piety; people who had known Aloysius Gonzaga, deceased in 1591, were struck by the similarities between the two young noblemen.

After his priestly ordination in 1613, Father Carafa taught philosophy at the college in Naples, until his superiors discovered his talents for governance. He was first appointed rector and novice master in Naples (1620–25), then provincial (1627–30), twice superior of the professed house (1630–33, 1637–40), and in between once again rector of the college. He would have been made provincial of Sicily and rector of the Roman College had a lobby of local nobles not forced the hand of the superior general to keep him at Naples. In 1641, Carafa had become the beloved director of their Marian sodality, introducing them to the new cult of the Five Wounds and to the Good Death Confraternity; he also wrote pious booklets for their use under the pseudonym of Aloysius Sidereus. His major work, though, dated from 1634: the *Camino del cielo* (Way to heaven), a manual of the spiritual life, was the fruit of his conferences for the novices and for the Jesuits of the professed house. Erudite, devout, and evidently written from experience, Father Carafa's books were read in Italy and abroad until the nineteenth century. Only his praise of Our Lady was deemed somewhat excessive; the second volume of his *Camino* was posthumously put on the Index of Forbidden Books until its orthodoxy had been proven.

A Short but Intense Generalate

Carafa participated in the general congregation of 1645, which had to elect a new general. It started badly with a letter of Pope Innocent X, demanding that they first consider a list of eighteen grave problems. Had the order not become too large and too widespread to be properly governed by one man? Had it not lost much of its original vigour and discipline? The fathers took several weeks to study the matter and at the end managed to persuade the pope that there was no need for structural changes: the Constitutions, Rules, and traditions of the Society met most of his worries. The general did not have to go and visit the provinces, for example, for the best guarantee of the order's unity was the nearness of the general to the pope as vicar of Christ. On January 7, 1646, Vincenzo Carafa was elected as seventh superior general of the Society of Jesus, with over sixty percent of the votes in the first round.

His generalate, which lasted only three and a half years, was intense; its challenges would dominate the life of the Society until its suppression in 1773. In the early 1640s, the Jansenist controversy had begun, as well as the troubles over ecclesiastical jurisdiction and political power with the bishops Juan de Palafox in Mexico and Bernardino de Cárdenas in Paraguay. In the latter case, Carafa witnessed the expulsion of the Jesuits from their reductions in March 1649. Even though they made their comeback six months later, it was a sign that the Society's fortunes were on the decline at the court of Madrid, after the order had supported the independence of Portugal from Spain. The reputation of the Jesuits in Spain was not much aided either by the great scandal that occurred because of unsuccessful business speculations by a brother coadjutor. In France, a Jesuit priest openly apostatized to Calvinism. To refute the growing accusations against the order, which were often inexact or unfounded, Superior General Carafa asked the noted Jesuit historian Sforza Pallavicino to write his *Vindications of the Society of Jesus*, which would appear in 1649, shortly after the general's death. He also insisted that Jesuits be as prudent as possible in venting their opinions on secular rulers, even in private correspondence, which could so easily fall into wrong hands.

Not unsurprisingly, the first and only letter that Carafa wrote to the whole Society, in 1646, was a fervent call to return to "the original state, spirit, and vigor," reminding its members that they were "without any doubt called to a state of life of the greatest perfection." He demanded that the provincials be more severe with Jesuits who did not observe the rules. As a provincial, Carafa had sent a Jesuit scholar caught with profane books back to the novitiate for some time, with the happy effect that the chastened father became an excellent missionary among the heathens. In the same manner, Superior General Carafa pointed his men towards the ministry of the popular missions as "most proper" to the Society, decreeing that in each province a mission prefect should be appointed, who at least once a month had to report to the general and collect edifying news for the annual letters. In his instruction on tertianship, Carafa recommended the itinerant ministry as a preferential option for the newly professed. He also promoted the Good Death Confraternity, as he had done in Naples, thus making it one of the order's characteristic devotions, together with the Marian sodality.

The Good Death

Carafa's own death was worthy of his life. When in 1649, Rome was visited by famine and accompanying disease, the general procured generous help for them. From April 1, a daily distribution of food was organized in Via degli Astalli, at the back of the Gesù—the same place where the Jesuit Refugee Service is nowadays aiding the poor, offering them a meal and shelter. Despite his age, his frail health, and his many occupations, Father Carafa himself lent a hand, too, just as he took it upon himself to organize the relief for the needy men and women housed by Pope Innocent X in both the Lateran Palace and in Saint Peter's Square. A mere five weeks later, on June 6, Vincenzo Carafa died from exhaustion.

His charity had impressed many, who promptly sought his intercession in their needs now that he had gone to his eternal reward. The fame of miracles he acquired was sufficient for the order to commission Jesuit historian Daniele Bartoli to write an edifying biography in 1651, and to start a canonization cause. The process was suspended in 1693, though, when the saintly general's

CARAFA NEAPOLITANVS PRÆPOSITVS GENERALIS VII. SOCIETATIS IESV · R P VINCENTIVS

Electus in Congreg:
die Septima
Obyt. 8 · Iuny 1649

Generali octaua
Ianuary An: 1646·
ętatis Suę 65·

Arnold van Westerhout (1651–1725), Vincenzo Carafa. Engraving belonging to the series of portraits of Jesuit superiors general published in Rome in 1748.

memory had fallen into oblivion with the passing of the generation that had known him. Then again, for Carafa, fully aware of being but a pilgrim on earth, a good death had always been more important than posthumous glory. In his book on the dignity and duties of the priest, Saint Alphonsus de' Liguori, also from Naples, tells the story of Father Carafa visiting a sick friend who had just been appointed to a high position full of moral risks. Asked to pray for the restoration of his health, Carafa answered the man: "No, my friend. God forbid that I should violate the love that I bear you: your sickness is a grace from the Lord, who wishes to save you by sending death, now that your soul is in a good state. Perhaps you might not be in such a state hereafter, should you enter on the office that has been given you." The friend died, so the story ends, and died full of consolation.

Marc Lindeijer, SJ

Saint Andrew Bobola (1591–1657)

Optional Memorial on May 16

It is ironic that a missionary who lived an outstanding saintly life, who served humanity with unswerving selflessness, upheld his faith with heroism in the brunt of persecution, surrendered his body to abominable tortures to bear witness to his undying commitment to his Lord and Master Christ, would lie buried—literally—out of sight and mind for almost half a century. Such was the case of Andrew Bobola. Adverse political forces blotted out his existence, but Providence brought it back to life and crowned Bobola with the halo he so truly had merited.

"All Things to All Men"

There are sparse records of Bobola's early upbringing. He was born on November 30, 1591, in Strachocina, southern Poland. From the age of fifteen, he attended the Jesuit schools at Braniewo and Vilnius, capital of Lithuania. He entered the novitiate of the Society of Jesus at Vilnius on July 31, 1611. After the novitiate, he was sent to the famous Vilnius Academy for courses in philosophy and theology. He was ordained a priest on March 12, 1622, the day Ignatius of Loyola and Francis Xavier were canonized, and was appointed assistant pastor at the Jesuit church in Nesvizh. In 1624, he was transferred to the Church of Saint Casimir, Vilnius. He proved himself as an outstanding preacher and devoted himself entirely to his pastoral duties. He encouraged lay-collaboration. As director of several Marian sodalities, he recruited sodalists to help out in catechism classes for children and in visiting the poor and the prisons.

His sterling qualities as a caring and compassionate pastor shone forth during the devastating plague of 1624, when he reached out to the victims with boundless devotion. There were no doctors, nurses, or hospitals, and the ailing were often abandoned by their own family, who sought safety in flight. Bobola

Stained glass workshops of the Carmel of Le Mans Hucher & Fils, Saint Andrew Bobola in the hands of the Cossacks (1878–80).

did not fear contagion; he went from village to village comforting the sick; he was priest, doctor, and nurse, all in one. When a second plague ravaged the city in 1629, he was up to the task once more. "He became all things to all men. With unfailing cheerfulness, he made light of the danger of contracting the plague and dedicated himself to nursing the sick and above all to their spiritual welfare," said Pope Pius XI in his homily at Bobola's canonization Mass.

In 1630, Bobola was transferred to Bobruisk, in Eastern Poland, near the border of the Polish–Lithuanian Commonwealth and the Russian Empire. Most of the Catholics in the region, having been left without priests or churches, had converted to Orthodoxy. It was tough going for him at the beginning. He had to face opposition from the majority non-Catholic populace. Elders would encourage children to heckle the priest in the streets, calling him names such as "Robber of Souls"; and they would try to shout him down as he preached. Bobola showed no signs of annoyance or impatience. Strong-willed and spiritually grounded as he was, he intensified his resolve to win them over with loving kindness. And he succeeded in doing so. Soon enough, he managed to construct a much-needed church, which provided space for Catholics to gather for worship. It eventually became the hub for all wayward Catholics. Two entire villages returned to the Catholic faith through his preaching.

Pope Pius XI summed up Bobola's exemplary pastoral approach: "He worked to strengthen everyone in Christian virtue. He strove to bring light and consolation to minds that were in the grip of perplexity or superstition. He taught Christian doctrine unsparingly in both town and country. By frequent visits to the squalid hovels that served as houses to the poor, he endeavored to win over the hearts of the people, so that they would allow him to speak to them as friends about the teachings of the Church. He did not overlook convicts and the sick." Bobola drew his strength from the long hours he spent in the chapel, before the tabernacle of the Lord's Presence, whenever possible.

Never Miss an Opportunity to Save a Soul

In 1643, Bobola was sent to Pinsk, in Belarus, a little city in which there were barely forty Catholics out of a population of thirteen thousand. Prince Radziwill had built a college, and Bobola was appointed its rector and prefect. Bobola's influence transformed Pinsk. The families entrusted the education of their children to him, and the anti-Catholic prejudices began to vanish.

In the political and religious struggle between Poland and Russia, the Jesuits became marked men. Eventually, the Polish Jesuits were driven from their churches and colleges and had to take refuge in the forests and wetlands. The Cossacks invaded and pillaged Pinsk, destroying five thousand houses and killing four thousand inhabitants. They razed the college to the ground and reduced the church furniture and roof to ashes. In the aftermath of the turmoil, Bobola was asked to return there in 1652 to restore the faith. He accepted the invitation, although he knew that Pinsk was an even more perilous location.

One of Bobola's biographers noted: "Never did Andrew Bobola miss an opportunity to save a soul. He would overtake travellers on the road and walk along with them, in the hope of converting them or strengthening them in their faith. He would seek out the sick to console them, and the dying to give them the last sacraments. Everywhere he would spread especial devotion to Our Lady and the Holy Eucharist ..."

Bobola accounted for conversions to the faith by the tens of thousands. At times, he won over whole dioceses with their bishops, which had broken away. Pope Pius XI turned the opprobrious phrase, hurled at Bobola by his enemies, into a glorious tribute and called him "the Huntsman of Souls."

Imitation of Christ

Bobola's success in converting schismatics drew upon him the rage of those in high authority, and the adherents of Orthodoxy decided to centralize their forces in Polesia, the region between Belarus and Ukraine. On May 16, 1657, the Cossack cavalry attacked Janów and massacred Catholics and Jews. Bobola was away in Peredil, but an informer helped the Cossacks find him. They apprehended Bobola, and tried to pressurize him into embracing the Orthodox religion. When he remained undeterred, the fanatics resorted to physical torture. The stripped him, tied him to a hedge, and began to whip him until the blood flowed from his body. Then, mocking his faith, they placed a crown of twigs on his head, bound him by a rope to the pommels of their horses, and made him stumble back to Janów behind them.

Once in the town, they took him to a butcher's shop, stretched him on the butcher's table, and because he still refused to abjure Catholicism, the angry Cossacks made him undergo excruciating torture for two full hours. They tore his skin from his hands and head, and in imitation of the chasuble that the priest wears at Mass, they scorched and tore the skin from his chest and back. The prayers he uttered to Jesus and Mary further infuriated his executioners. In imitation of Christ's crucifixion, they cut holes in the palms of his hands. They jabbed a butcher's awl into his chest near the heart. They strung him up by his feet and killed him with a saber blow. They cast his mutilated body on a manure pile. Shortly after, a band of Poles arrived at Janów in a vain attempt to rescue him. They took his lifeless body back to Pinsk where they placed it in the crypt beneath the Jesuit church—into obscurity.

In 1702, Bobola appeared in a vision to the rector of the Jesuit college in Pinsk, who ordered that the body should be found. After two days of search, it was discovered, buried in one of the damp crypts of the church. The coffin and garments were decayed, but the body was unharmed. It was totally incorrupt, and with a "fine fragrance," even though it had never been embalmed for forty-five years. The wounds and mutilations were still clearly visible on the supple flesh. The martyr was made presentable with new attire, placed into an elegant casket, and interred with fitting honor.

Hedwig Lewis, SJ

Andrew Bobola was beatified in 1853 by Pope Pius IX and canonized on April 17, 1938 by Pope Pius XI.

Blessed Thomas Whitbread and
His Six Companions

(†1679)

Six Jesuits, including Thomas Whitbread, the provincial superior, and a lay collaborator were falsely accused of plotting to assassinate King Charles II and overthrow the government. They were themselves the victims of a plot hatched by the infamous Titus Oates, a man whom the provincial had refused to accept into the Society. No plot against the king was ever planned, but the plot against the Jesuits was all too successful.

The Titus Oates Plot

Whitbread was born in Essex in 1618, but attended the Jesuit college at Saint-Omer in Flanders. He entered the Society of Jesus in 1635 and was ordained a priest in 1645. Two years later, he returned to England and enjoyed a fruitful apostolate of more than thirty years. In 1678, during the first year of his term as provincial superior of the Jesuits in England, Father Whitbread visited the communities on the continent that trained Catholics from England. At Saint-Omer, he encountered Titus Oates, a student at that school who asked the provincial to be admitted into the Society of Jesus. Oates had been an Anglican minister but had been dismissed because of poor behavior. Then he converted to Catholicism and studied at the English College in Valladolid, Spain, but was thrown out of that school. Whitbread did not trust Titus's character or motivation, declined to accept such a candidate, and ordered him to be expelled from Saint-Omer because of unsatisfactory behavior there.

Oates returned to London, where he joined forces with another Protestant minister, Israel Tonge, who harbored suspicions of the Jesuits' plotting against the king. Tonge and Oates invented the story of a plot by the Jesuits to assassinate the king, overthrow the government and the established religion, and reinstate Catholicism. They were able to present this accusation to the king in mid-August, 1678, but he did not find it credible. So Oates fabricated more details and presented the revised accusation to the king's Privy Council on September 27, setting into motion a deadly chain of events.

The Two Martyrs of January 24, 1679

The first step was the arrest on September 28, 1678 of two Jesuits, John Fenwick (1628–79) and William Ireland (1636–79), and of their lay collaborator John Grove. Titus Oates himself came in the middle of the night with an armed force of parliamentary soldiers. Fenwick had lived in London since 1674, Ireland since 1677, and the two occupied themselves with the mission finances. Mr. Grove was the proprietor of the house where they found refuge and took care of their practical need. Then, Oates and his men wanted to arrested Whitbread and his socius Edward Mico, but these two Jesuits had contracted the plague on their recent trip to Antwerp and were too ill to move; they were also under the protection of the Spanish ambassador in whose residence they lived. By December, Whitbread's health had improved enough for him to be moved to Newgate Prison, where Fenwick and Ireland were; as for Father Mico, he had already died of maltreatment on December 3.

Meanwhile, the wild accusations Oates made fanned a flame of fear that made people hysterical with tales of Irish and French Catholic conspirators crouching in cellars, ready to jump out and slit the throats of good Protestant subjects of the king. The general outcry was enormous; before it ran its course, some thirty-five innocent people had been executed; hundreds more perished in prison, some of them victims of the plague.

The three Jesuits were brought to trial on December 17, 1678 at the Old Bailey. Oates testified that he had seen the three priests at a tavern planning to kill the king, overthrow the government, and re-establish the Catholic religion. The three men had indeed met from 24 to 26 April, at St. James's Palace, where the Jesuit Claude La Colombière was chaplain to the duchess of York. Their topic was picking a Jesuit to travel to Rome and present the regular triennial report on the province to the superior general.

Oates had probably heard of the meeting when he was at Saint-Omer, but he was certainly not present at St. James's Palace. When the only other witness failed to corroborate completely Oates's testimony, there was insufficient evidence to find the Jesuits guilty. The court then took the extraordinary step of suspending their trial to a later date, despite the fact that all the witnesses had already been heard. The Jesuits went back to prison, except for Father Ireland and John Grove. Even though Charles II never believed that they were involved in a plot against him, he allowed the executions to take place out of fear of popular anger. Ireland and Grove were taken to Tyburn on January 24, 1679 as the populace pelted them with stones and insults. They were hanged until dead; then, their bodies were drawn and quartered.

The Five Martyrs of June 20, 1679

In 1679, three more Jesuits were arrested on the basis of more false evidence provided by Stephen Dugdale, a convicted embezzler. In January, Father John Gavan (1640–79) was caught in London, most of whose apostolic work had centered on Staffordshire, where he enjoyed great success in bringing people to conversion, as well as Father Anthony Turner (1628–79), who had served Catholics for eighteen years in the Worcestershire area. The latter had journeyed to London hoping to find a companion who would give him the money to get out of the country. His search was unsuccessful, so he gave the last of his coins away to a beggar and then turned himself in as a priest and Jesuit. The third was Father William Harcourt (1610–79), treasurer of the English province from 1671 till 1677 and superior of the London Jesuits since 1678. He had urged other Jesuits to leave the country and seek safety abroad, but felt himself responsible to remain in London and attempt to care for his brothers in prison. A woman servant at one of the houses where he took refuge betrayed him to the police, who arrested him on May 7, 1679.

At the second process, held on June 13, 1679, Harcourt, Gavan, and Turner were included in the original charge of plotting against the king. Oates again claimed that he had witnessed the meeting at the White Horse Tavern. Father Gavan served as the spokesman for the Jesuits, and answered the deceitful claims of the prosecution. The defense produced sixteen witnesses from Saint-Omer testifying that Oates had been at the college on that day and not in England. Despite the clear weight of the evidence on the side of the defense,

Jan Luyken, "In London the Jesuit William Ireland Is Hanged and John Grove Cut to Pieces for Plotting against the King" (1698).

the court instructed the jury to believe the prosecution witnesses rather than those of the defense. The jury returned a verdict of guilty, condemning the five Jesuits to die for treason.

The execution took place on Friday, June 20 at Tyburn. Father Whitbread affirmed their innocence and forgave the men whose false testimony led them to their deaths. He was followed by the other Jesuits, Fenwick, Harcourt, Gavan, and Turner, who made their final statements. Then they all stood quietly in prayer on the gallows, nooses around their necks, waiting for the cart to pull away from them. Suddenly a rider burst onto the scene crying, "A pardon! A pardon!" He gave the sheriff a document announcing the king would pardon them provided they admit their guilt and tell all they knew about the plot. The martyrs thanked the king for his merciful intentions but firmly noted that they could not acknowledge any guilt for a plot that never existed. They would not accept pardon if it meant they had to lie. They paused for private prayer again, and then the cart pulled away. The bodies were pulled down and quartered, but friends were able to claim them and give them burial in the churchyard of St. Giles-in-the-Fields.

Thomas Rochford, SJ[41]

The six Jesuits and their lay collaborator were beatified by Pope Pius XI on December 15, 1929.

---

41. Revised by Marc Lindeijer, SJ.

The North American Martyrs

SAINTS JOHN DE BRÉBEUF, ISAAC JOGUES, AND COMPANIONS

(† 1642–49)

Memorial on October 19

The eight martyrs of North America had devoted themselves, at the cost of hard work, to the missionary apostolate to the Hurons. Five of them, all priests, courageously endured a horrible martyrdom in what is now Canada: John de Brébeuf (died March 16, 1649), Antoine Daniel (died July 4, 1648), Gabriel Lallemant (died March 17, 1649), Charles Garnier (died December 7, 1649), and Noël Chabanel (died December 8, 1649); three others, a priest, Isaac Jogues (died October 18, 1646), and two laypeople "given" to the Society, René Goupil (died September 29, 1642) and Jean de La Lande (died October 19, 1646) gave their lives with heroic courage in a place that today is on the territory of the United States.

Conditions of Evangelization

The Huron mission, where Brébeuf, Jogues, and their companions chiefly exercised their apostolate, was one of the most demanding in missionary history. These men encountered the worst conditions of climate, hunger, and exposure. In the vast territories of North America, they covered distances of hundreds of miles in fragile canoes made of skin, which had to be carried overland from one river to another. There were treks through forests, the scourge of mosquitoes, the difficulty of replenishing their stores, the Indians' ignorance of hygiene. In winter, after long walks with snow-shoes on their feet, they found as their only lodging either windswept, pinewood huts or miserable cabins without windows where men and animals huddled together, the air heavy with the smell of fish, the smoke attacking the throat, nose, and eyes.

Then for years there was the hard apprenticeship of a new language, without any link with European tongues, so that they had to compose, with endless effort, their own dictionary and grammar to help them stammer in Huron the rudiments of the Christian religion. Added to these trials was the even more formidable specter of opposition to any progress they might make. After quite an encouraging start, the missionaries met among those they had come to convert a growing and obstinate resistance. Brébeuf attributed this to three factors: the Hurons' immorality, their attachment to their customs, and the successive epidemics that the missionaries were blamed for and that, in a few years, reduced to twelve thousand a population of twelve thousand souls.

From 1636 to 1641, the mission lived in a constant climate of threats, persecution, and attempted murder. The rate of conversions was desperately slow. It was only in 1637, after six years of backbreaking work, that Brébeuf could baptize one healthy adult. In 1641, the mission still only counted sixty Christians. At the beginning of 1642, a network of Iroquois invasions enveloped the land of the Hurons. Then began the great disasters which came to succeed each other up to 1649—attacks on convoys, seizure of correspondence, Hurons and Frenchmen captured, tortured, and massacred, villages pillaged and burned. The climax was the tragic defeat of the Hurons and the martyrdom of those who had given their lives to preach the Gospel.

Spiritual Sources

In such a context, there was no room for mediocrity. The missionary could only opt for heroism or leave the mission. In fact, the missionaries had all been men of outstanding religious observance. Many of those who did not receive the grace of martyrdom were worthy of it; and those who were martyred were saints before they died. All these men had been formed by the *Spiritual Exercises* of Saint Ignatius, which remained for them the formative influence of their lives. Some of them (like Brébeuf, Jogues, and Garnier) had not made their tertianship, but all of them lived the spirit of the *Exercises*. What they had derived from this source was above all else an ardent and invincible love of Christ, who for them was a living presence: their companion on the journey, in solitude, in the work of the apostolate, in suffering, in martyrdom. Every line of their writings speaks of the presence of Christ. Like Saint Paul, they were "seized" by Christ and lived only for him. Their love went out especially to Christ crucified. Several of them had asked for the Canadian mission because they could suffer for Christ more generously there. Men like Brébeuf and Jogues had a true vocation to the cross.

Among the numerous influences in the spiritual life of the martyrs was that of Father Louis Lallemant, whose strong personality dominated a whole generation of Jesuits. Directly or indirectly, his work had affected most of the Jesuits in the Huron mission: notably Jogues and Daniel, his novices, and Brébeuf, whose spiritual director he was. Lallemant's impact spread by a kind of osmosis through conversation, spiritual exhortations, and retreats. In fact, the spiritual principles of Father Lallemant appear distinctly in the martyrs' writings: purity and custody of the heart, continual recollection, union with God, love of Christ, docility to the Spirit.

Dominant Figures: Brébeuf and Jogues

The two dominant figures of the group were Brébeuf and Jogues. Three major texts scan the spiritual development of the former: in 1631, a promise to serve Christ to the point of martyrdom; between 1631 and 1639, the vow never to refuse the grace of martyrdom; in 1645, the vow to do the most perfect thing. So the life of John de Brébeuf seems to have been impregnated with the sign of the cross, spanned from end to end by the grace of martyrdom that arose in the first days of his religious life and burst into the flame that consumed him. "Jesus Christ is our true greatness," he wrote in 1635, "it is him alone and his cross that one should seek among these peoples." During a period of persecution, when he had been insulted, jeered at, beaten, and attacked by diabolical power, the Lord confirmed him in his vocation to the cross: "Turn to Christ Jesus crucified, and may he be from henceforth the principle and foundation of your contemplations" (Retreat of 1640). He lived from that time on as a victim consecrated to death. "I see nothing more frequent in his memoirs," says his companion, Paul Ragueneau, "than the sense that he has to die for the glory of Jesus Christ ..., a desire he goes on repeating eight out of ten days on end." Martyrdom, at the end of such a life, is only a recapitulation and final offering. In Brébeuf, two extremes meet and are reconciled: on the one hand, the man who is a realist, lover of tradition, the minister of a college, the

Joseph Chiwatenhwa is one of the first believers of the indigenous people of Canada, baptized by Saint John de Brébeuf in 1637. He too was martyred in 1640. Saint Gabriel Lalemant considers him a great catechist within his people, "their apostle." Artistic Glass Workshop (2002).

mission organizer, the humble religious; and, on the other hand, the apostle dedicated to the folly of the cross.

The personality of Isaac Jogues offers a contrast. He was not a founder or superior of a mission. He was always the lieutenant. Had he not been captured, his whole apostolate would have passed into obscurity. His was a delicate soul, of an exquisite sensitiveness, easily moved; the soul of a humanist, anxious to express himself well; a man distrustful of himself and his own judgment, of his own initiatives. Yet grace has made a saint out of him. Conscious of his own weaknesses, he admired his companions and was generous to them. His obedience fired him with a silent courage. His sensitiveness inspired his tenderness towards the wild men who put him to death. Born for great friendship and compassion, he developed a passionate love of Christ, above all the suffering Christ. Like Brébeuf, he had received a special call to the cross and was granted mystical experiences characterized by the expectation of martyrdom.

"The Blood of Martyrs, the Seed of Christians"

The Huron mission died with the martyrdom of its founders. In 1650, only a few hundred Hurons survived. Their dispersal had the effect of spreading the faith throughout the basin of the Great Lakes of Canada and among the peoples living on the banks of the Hudson. These converts formed the nucleus of the Christian communities later founded by the Jesuits among the Iroquois and the inhabitants of the West. By a mysterious act of providence, the salvation brought to the Hurons by the blood of the martyrs took root and spread through North America, and light shone in the darkness.

In each era, the Church rediscovers Christ, and this rediscovery is marked by a new missionary zeal. The seventeenth-century French Jesuit missionaries, formed by the Ignatian *Exercises*, had rediscovered Christ under the sign of his supreme appeal to charity: the cross. Only a passionate love of Christ, sacrificed for men under this sign of the greatest love, can explain the presence in North America of this group of young missionaries and their burning enthusiasm.

René Latourelle, SJ

John de Brébeuf, Isaac Jogues, and their six companions were beatified in 1925 by Pius XI and canonized by the same pope on June 29, 1930.

From the *Spiritual Diaries* of Saint John de Brébeuf

For two days now, I have experienced a great desire to be a martyr and to endure all the torments the martyrs suffered.

Jesus, my Lord and Savior, "what can I give you in return for all the favors you have first conferred on me? I will take from your hand the cup of your sufferings and call on your name." I vow before your eternal Father and the Holy Spirit, before your most holy Mother and her most chaste spouse, before the angels, apostles and martyrs, before my blessed fathers Saint Ignatius and Saint Francis Xavier—in truth, I vow to you, Jesus my Savior, that as far as I have the strength I will never fail to accept the grace of martyrdom, if some day you in your infinite mercy would offer it to me, your most unworthy servant.

I bind myself in this way so that for the rest of my life I will have neither permission nor freedom to refuse opportunities of dying and shedding my blood for you, unless at a particular juncture I should consider it more suitable for your glory to act otherwise at that time. Further, I bind myself to this so that, on receiving the blow of death, I shall accept it from your hands with the fullest delight and joy of spirit. For this reason, my beloved Jesus, and because of the surging joy that moves me, here and now I offer my blood and body and life. May I die only for you, if you will grant me this grace, since you willingly died for me. Let me so live that you may grant me the gift of such a happy death. In this way, my God and Savior, "I will take from your hand the cup of your sufferings and call on your name": Jesus, Jesus, Jesus!

My God, it grieves me greatly that you are not known, that in this savage wilderness all have not been converted to you, that sin has not been driven from it. My God, even if all the brutal tortures that prisoners in this region must endure should fall on me, I offer myself most willingly to them and I alone shall suffer them all.

Liturgy of the Hours, Second Reading for October 19

Blessed Diego Luis de San Vitores
and Saint Pedro Calungsod

(†1672)

PROTOMARTYRS OF THE MARIANAS

Optional Memorial on October 6

In the latter part of the seventeenth century, as the fervor of the Spanish Empire's expansionism to gain global and economic power and Christian conversion spread, Diego Luis de San Vitores sailed to Guam and established the first Catholic Church in the Marianas. In the span of merely four years, through his heroic commitment and Christ-like compassion, he altered the social, cultural, and religious landscape of the fifteen-island archipelago—at the cost of his life.

"Be a Good Jesuit, or Else ..."

Vitores was born in 1627 at Burgos, Spain, of noble parentage. When he was eleven, he was sent for studies to the Jesuit Imperial College in Madrid. He developed a great desire to join the Jesuits, but his father, who wanted him to follow a military career, strongly opposed his vocation. The determined lad sought the intercession of the Blessed Virgin Mary through incessant prayer, and succeeded in breaking the stalemate. Interestingly, his father gave his approval with a proviso: "Be a good Jesuit and grow in holiness, or else you will no longer call yourself my son." The boy never forgot this admonishment.

Diego entered the novitiate of Villarejo de Fuentes, near Madrid, in 1640, when he was about thirteen years of age. He did his studies with distinction and was ordained a priest in 1651. He was assigned to teach theology in Madrid for the next five years, but made time for preaching retreats and missions. His experiences in the latter ministries, made him volunteer for the foreign missions: "From my earliest childhood, I recall that I always had a desire for the conversion of souls and for martyrdom. That early desire grew within me steadily and I could never put it out of my mind. ... I declare that I am ready to give up not only my life but also any kind of honorable death if by so doing I may win even one soul for Christ." His request was granted, and he was assigned to the Philippines missions in 1659.

Vitores embarked at Cádiz, Spain, on May 15, 1660 and arrived at Veracruz, Mexico, two months later. He had to wait eighteen months for a ship bound for the Philippines, during which time he was immersed in preaching and giving retreats. In April 1662, Vitores, with thirteen other Jesuits, set sail from Acapulco for Manila. As the vessel entered the waters off the island of Guam, it briefly halted at the "Thieves' Islands," as the Marianas were known at the time. Vitores sighted the indigenous Chamorro people and felt an immediate desire to "bring the light of Christianity" to what he regarded to be godless islanders.

On arrival in the Philippines, Vitores began learning Tagalog and was then assigned to the Jesuit college of Manila to teach theology. During the five years he spent there, he was made master of novices and dean at the university in Manila, yet all the while his heart was set on the Marianas. He used his father's influence to get the support of Mariana of Austria, queen of Spain. Finally, her husband King Philip IV issued a decree on June 24, 1664 ordering the missions to begin in the "Thieves' Islands" archipelago. Vitores was appointed its pioneer and first superior, and he prepared himself for the mission by learning Chamorro, the local language.

Led Along by a Rope

On June 16, 1668, Vitores and five other Jesuits arrived off the shores of Guam's primary village, Hagatna, with about thirty lay helpers and three Spanish soldiers. In appreciation for her support, he renamed the archipelago the Mariana Islands, in honor of Queen Mariana. He subsequently renamed the other islands in honor of saints.

The lay helpers included boys trained and employed by the Jesuits in the Philippines as catechists and assistants for the Marianas mission. Pedro Calungsod, a thirteen-year-old, was one of them. He must have received his elementary education at a Jesuit boarding school. For the mission, he would

Saint Pedro Calungsod carries the Catechism and the palm of martyrdom. In the background, we see him teaching his young compatriots.

have had to master the catechism and learn to communicate in Spanish and Chamorro. He would have been trained in the skills of drawing, painting, singing, acting, and carpentry, all necessary in missionary work. He would also have been an altar server. Calungsod became Vitores's close assistant.

On landing at Guam, the local chief, Kepuha, offered food and shelter to the Jesuits and their helpers, and told them that they were free to go about preaching their religion. The Jesuits planted a cross in the ground as a sign of their consecration of the island. Vitores, who had learned their language and had even written a simple catechism in Chamorro, established the mission headquarters at Agana, with small wooden huts to serve as residence and church. Eventually, the Jesuits went out to the islands, adopting the simple life of the natives.

Vitores wore a conical palm-leaf hat on his head, hung a large rosary around his neck, and carried a long wooden pole with a crucifix attached to the top. Though very near-sighted, he refused to wear his glasses, considering it a luxury; instead, he had to be led along by a rope tied to his waist. He carried only a small satchel containing his breviary, a Bible, the holy oils, and sugar lumps and biscuits that he would give out to children who could recite their prayers and catechism lessons without a mistake.

Calungsod, his faithful assistant, used to hold the rope around Vitores to guide him and prevent him from stumbling. This, of course, indicated the deep trust the priest had in him. "Pedro saw in Father Diego, not just an authority to obey, but someone who was his father, his partner in mission, his friend in the Lord, to use the words of Saint Ignatius."[42]

Life in the Marianas was tough because the jungles were too thick to cross; the cliffs were very steep to climb, and the islands were frequently visited by devastating typhoons. Despite the hardships, the missionaries persevered, and religious work with the Chamorro people was enthusiastic and reassuring. The mission was blessed with many conversions. After six months, the Jesuits counted thirteen thousand people who had been baptized. Vitores wrote: "All 180 villages of these islands have been visited, one by one, two or three times."

---

42. Adolfo Nicolás, SJ, homily given on October 19, 2012.

Their Final Song

After Chief Kepuha's death in 1669, relations between Spain and the Chamorro leaders deteriorated. The local leaders, priests, priestesses, and medicine-men felt threatened, with their status being side-lined. There was resentment over their culture and language being drained. Christian values conflicted with their own. In 1672, Chamorro resistance increased. Rumors were rife that the water used for baptism was poisonous and caused illnesses.

On April 2, 1672, Vitores left for Agana along with Calungsod. On the way, they stopped at Tumon, where he met Matapang, a Chamorro noble and old friend whose life he had once saved and whom he had converted. Though Matapang had abandoned the faith, Vitores offered to baptize his newborn daughter. The man refused, saying he did not wish her to die, and then stalked off. While he was gone, Vitores entered the house and baptized the sick child. He knew his former friend would be furious at him for this, but felt that the salvation of the child outweighed the threat upon his own life. To give Matapang some time to cool down, Vitores and Calungsod gathered the children and some adults of the village at the nearby shore and started chanting with them the truths of the Catholic faith. They invited Matapang to join them, when he returned with a friend, both of them armed.

Calungsod, a valiant youth, could have warded off the assailants if he had a weapon, but the missionary never permitted him to carry arms. He could have made good his escape, but he chose to stand beside his father. Without warning, Matapang threw a spear into the boys's chest. Vitores, realizing his own end was imminent, too, grabbed his crucifix, fell to his knees, and uttered a prayer of forgiveness for his assailants. He had barely enough time to kiss his crucifix before the two men were on him; one of them split the priest's skull with a stroke of the cutlass, while the other buried a spear in his heart. Matapang then stripped him of crucifix and cassock, tied stones to the naked body, and took it far out in the bay where he cast it into the sea.

Hedwig Lewis, SJ

Diego Luis de San Vitores was beatified by John Paul II on October 6, 1985. It was also John Paul II who beatified Pedro Calungsod, on March 5, 2000. Benedict XVI canonized the catechist martyr on October 21, 2012.

From a Homily of Pope John Paul II

"If anyone declares himself for me in the presence of men, I will declare myself for him in the presence of my Father in heaven" (Matthew 10:32). From his childhood, Pedro Calungsod declared himself unwaveringly for Christ and responded generously to his call. Young people today can draw encouragement and strength from the example of Pedro, whose love of Jesus inspired him to devote his teenage years to teaching the faith as a lay catechist. Leaving family and friends behind, Pedro willingly accepted the challenge put to him by Father Diego de San Vitores to join him on the mission to the Chamorros. In a spirit of faith, marked by strong Eucharistic and Marian devotion, Pedro undertook the demanding work asked of him and bravely faced the many obstacles and difficulties he met. In the face of imminent danger, Pedro would not forsake Father Diego, but as a "good soldier of Christ" preferred to die at the missionary's side. Today Blessed Pedro Calungsod intercedes for the young, in particular those of his native Philippines, and he challenges them. Young friends, do not hesitate to follow the example of Pedro, who "pleased God and was loved by him" (Wisdom 4:10) and who, having come to perfection in so short a time, lived a full life (cf. Wisdom 4:13).

Homily of March 5, 2000, at the beatification of Pedro Calungsod

The Martyrs of Zenta

BLESSED JUAN ANTONIO SOLINAS
AND PEDRO ORTIZ DE ZÁRATE

(†1683)

Optional Memorial, November 16

Father Juan Antonio Solinas was born on February 15, 1643 in the village of
Oliena, on the island of Sardinia, now part of Italy. On June 12, 1663, he entered the Society of Jesus in Cagliari. Having completed his theological studies, and after his ordination in Seville in 1673, the following year, together
with three other Sardinian Jesuits, he was sent to the old province of Paraguay (which then corresponded to what is now Paraguay, southeastern Bolivia,
northern Argentina, southern Brazil, and Uruguay). After his tertianship in
Santa Fe, he was first sent to the Guaraní reduction of Santa Ana and then to
Itapúa. An elderly missionary, who was often his preaching companion, wrote
about him in 1679: "Father Solinas has worked and is working wonderfully,
both in the confessional and from the pulpit. Many days, he gives sermons
and teaches catechism to children and all categories of the population. God
gave him health and strength, and with these he works day and night for the
good of souls, without any distraction in other things." In 1682, Juan Antonio
made his final vows.

Father Pedro Ortiz de Zárate was born in San Salvador de Jujuy (northwest
Argentina) on June 29, 1626. He married and had two children. In 1654, after
the sudden death of his wife, he took the road to the priesthood in the diocese
of Tucumán. He studied at the Jesuit college in Córdoba (Argentina) and was
ordained in 1657. In his duties as a priest, he dedicated himself to a consistent
apostolate, tending to the ill and administering the sacraments to all. After

several postings, he was appointed parish priest of Jujuy in 1659. His sole desire, however, was to spread the Gospel among the Chaco people. He often spoke about it with his bishop, Nicolás de Ulloa of Tucumán, and even wrote about it to the king of Spain, Charles II. Eventually, he would obtain authorization to start this mission, together with the Jesuits who had a similar idea in mind. In a letter addressed to the king of Spain in 1682, referring to him, Bishop Nicolás reported that in Jujuy he had found "a venerable and elderly priest, a great priest, very zealous for the honor of God, a great lover of the Indians and their benefactor."

Blessed the Peacemakers, Blessed the Persecuted

Moved by their desire to evangelize, the Jesuits had set out to find a way to link the villages of Chiquitania (in Bolivia) to their other missions, extending as far as the borders of Patagonia. But the Chaco region, known as the "green desert," which stretches from southern Bolivia to northwestern Argentina, became a greater apostolic challenge. A group of native peoples populated that region where Solinas preached and confessed in Guaraní, evangelizing Indians and Spanish settlers in several provinces of northern Argentina. The Chaco Gualamba, south of the Pilcomayo River, was also a place of injustice and ambition, fierce indigenous resistance, and armed repression. In the same area, in 1639, the Jesuit fathers Gaspar Osorio Valderrábano and Antonio Ripari had been murdered; and a few years earlier, in 1628, a little farther away, in what is now Brazilian territory, the saints of the Guaraní reductions, Roque González de Santa Cruz, Alfonso Rodríguez Olmedo, and Juan del Castillo, had been martyred. By 1763, more than twenty Jesuits would lose their lives violently in those missions.

After a failed military campaign to conquer the territory, Father Pedro Ortiz de Zárate, concerned for the Chaco people and worried about the atrocities the military could commit, pleaded instead for a spiritual campaign to help convert the local indigenous population. When in April 1682 approval came for the mission, the bishop of Tucumán suggested allocating the Jesuits to it, due to their missionary experience. In May 1683, Juan A. Solinas was assigned to the expedition, organized by Ortiz de Zárate and consisting of over seventy people. Solinas had stated that he was willing to evangelize these groups and stay with them, not abandoning them, giving them "the necessary food and all other possible assistance." Indeed, according to the testimony of a contemporary, Solinas, who was self-effacing, accustomed to suffering, docile and gentle in character, and much loved by his companions, "was a help to the poor, to whom he provided sustenance and clothing; a doctor for the sick, whom he cured with great gentleness; and a universal remedy for all the ills of the body. For this reason, the Indians venerated him with the affection of sons." The Sardinian Jesuit ended his letter: "May God take care of us."

The missionary expedition tried to establish peace with the indigenous groups that had ravaged the borders of Jujuy and to bring about reconciliation between the Creoles and the native peoples. Three Jesuits were part of the expedition that crossed the Zenta Valley (present-day Orán), east of Jujuy: Fathers Juan Antonio Solinas and Diego Ruiz, and Brother Pedro de Aguilar. In October, Fathers Ortiz de Zárate and Solinas pitched their tents near the chapel of Our Lady of Jujuy, about five leagues from Fort San Rafael. With them, in a group of two Spaniards and sixteen natives, were a mulatto, a black man, an indigenous woman, and two girls.

While they were celebrating the peace, some five hundred Toba, Mocoví, and Mataguayo Indians appeared, along with several *caciques* (native chiefs). For several days, they surrounded and threatened them. On the morning of October 27, 1683, the priests prayed and celebrated the Eucharist. Afterward, they spoke of God with their besiegers in a friendly tone. In the afternoon, apparently spurred on by sorcerers from their clans, the attackers charged with arrows, spears, clubs, and sticks against the missionaries and all their companions, cruelly murdering them. They were posthumously stripped naked and had their heads cut off, with arrows thrust into their bodies. As an aboriginal from the mission who was able to escape on horseback tells us, when Spanish troops arrived from Salta ready to carry out justice, Father Diego Ruiz prevented them from doing so: "We have come to convert infidels, not to kill them."

A Joint Mission

With the death of these martyrs, we are celebrating a mission in which members of the diocesan clergy worked closely together with the Society of Jesus in a joint and ambitious ecclesial project, which unfortunately unraveled. There was so much to do that Ortiz de Zárate and Solinas had asked the provincial for one more Jesuit, with the following profile: "First, he must be totally detached from the world and resolved to face dangers and difficulties; second, his charity must be supreme, not at all fearful, with a cheerful face, a big heart …" The missionaries were well aware of the difficulties, but, at the same time, they lived their vocation with enthusiasm, devoted to the natives, as is shown by the fact that a good number of these—whose names are unknown—were killed at the same time. We can see, then, how the faith transmitted by the missionaries had permeated the lives of these eighteen laypeople: men, women, and children, Indians and Spaniards.

Solinas's European origins remind us of how the Society has always favored the most urgent missions at any given time, putting at its service the varied origins of the Jesuits who were sent, regardless of the great distance—physical and in terms of customs and habits—that separated them from their destination. Their detachment from habits acquired in their homeland and their inculturation, whether here or there, allowed for a communication of the Gospel that responded to the needs and circumstances of those who received it. This required of the missionary—as we have seen with this Zenta mission—attributes and virtues that characterized, among others, Juan Antonio Solinas—particular qualities that can in no way be improvised, but are generated and cultivated in the daily concern for the love of God and one's neighbor, right from the childhood and formation of the Jesuit.

The faithfulness of these martyrs in persevering in their commitment to reconciliation between different groups in the area, going so far as to be willing to give their lives for this and to forgive their assailants, allows us to see their hierarchy of Christian values. On the other hand, the attention given to the person on the part of Solinas and his companions—as doctors of body and soul—makes it clear how spreading the Gospel, directed by the grace of God, aims to respond to the yearnings of every human being, communicating to them the complete life offered by Jesus Christ.

Arturo Sosa, SJ
Superior General of the Society of Jesus

Juan Antonio Solinas and Pedro Ortiz de Zárate were proclaimed blessed by Pope Francis on July 2, 2022.

Saint John de Brito (1647–93)

Optional Memorial on February 4

Two words polarize and sum up the life of João (John) Heitor de Brito: missionary and martyr, a twin destiny put before him from early childhood.

Page at the Court of Kings and Martyr of Christ

The Brito family was highly placed in seventeenth-century Portuguese society, and at nine years of age John went to the court of King John IV of Portugal as page to the prince who was later to be King Peter II. Among his fellow pupils at the College of Saint Anthony in Lisbon, John stood out because of his seriousness, moral refinement, and conscientiousness. He put up with the insolence of some of the rougher characters with a degree of patience that earned for him the nickname, in the royal household, of "the martyr," a forecast of what he was later to achieve in India.

When John fell gravely ill, his mother prayed to Saint Francis Xavier. If her son were cured, she said, he would wear the Jesuit cassock for a year as a mark of gratitude. He recovered, and the new clothing he wore among the court pages earned him another name, this time *apostolinho*, the little apostle, the popular name for the Portuguese Jesuits of the time.

At sixteen years of age, on December 17, 1662, he accepted God's call and entered the novitiate. On Christmas Day, he placed at the feet of the Child Jesus an ingenuous letter asking the new-born Savior to be sent on the mission to Japan. The call to the missions was now growing strong in John's soul.

After taking first vows, he was sent to the University of Évora to study philosophy. The climate did not suit him, and he had to transfer to Coimbra, where he recovered his health and made excellent progress with his studies. In 1668, he begged to be sent to the Indian missions. The reply from Superior

Stained glass workshops of the Carmel of Le Mans Hucher & Fils, The beheading of Saint John de Brito in Oriyur, India (1878–80).

General Oliva was long in coming. John de Brito was appointed to teach in the College of Saint Anthony, where he had studied humanities. He was told to preach the panegyric on Saint Francis Xavier, and did so with a fervor that deeply impressed his audience. Father Balthasar da Costa had just come from Madurai to Portugal, emphasizing the needs of the mission and exhorting the young to undertake the arduous labour entailed. John was greatly affected by the missionary's example.

In the Footsteps of Xavier

His theology course began, and he was ordained a priest in 1673. Shortly after this, John was finally posted to the Indian missions. Overcoming great opposition from his family, he embarked for Goa, where he finished his theological studies. Following Xavier's example, he preached so boldly against immorality that he was attacked and seriously injured by some of the local boys.

It was put to him that he could teach theology courses, for which he was well qualified. He refused: he had gone to India to be a missionary, not a professor, and he made a vow to devote himself to the missions of Madurai, the most difficult missionary area in the East.

To solve the caste problem and preach the Gospel to all, he followed the principle of "adaptation," through which his friend and predecessor, Father Balthasar da Costa, had achieved the most spectacular results. He became a *pandara swami*, that is, an ascetic and penitent, and in this way he enjoyed the privilege of dealing with all ranks of society, even of living with the pariahs.

The Secret of Missionary Adaptation

Although caught up in a net of local conventions, with nothing beyond the barest necessities of food and clothing, he spent a year in pastoral preparation for missionary life in Ambalacata and fixed his base in Colei, near Gingee. He wore an ample cloak dyed red ochre, with a kind of scarlet turban on his head and wooden sandals on his feet, and he carried a long seven-jointed bamboo stick for his journeys. He slept on a simple cloth or tiger skin stretched out on the floor, and for meals would eat a handful of rice cooked in water and spiced with pepper, bitter herbs, some vegetables, a little milk and butter. His life was wholly devoted to prayer, spiritual reading, and catechesis. Living like an anchorite, he would write to his brother Fernando, on September 22, 1692: "I live very happily in this exile, with little homesickness for my native land, though I do feel some homesickness for heaven."

His apostolate was favored by his condition as a *pandara swami*, and he quickly won a high reputation with a prodigious increase in the number of catechumens he instructed. In 1676, the Colei base had to be divided up. Brito extended his energy and wisdom not only to large numbers of pariahs, for whom he built a church, but to the rulers, immersed in political troubles and inter-state wars. Conversions ran into hundreds, confessions and communions into thousands. Persecution obliged the missionaries to leave the region of Maravar.

In 1686, named superior of the mission, Brito decided to go beyond the frontiers of the country, again shielded only by the arms of the spirit. In less than three weeks, he baptized more than three thousand people. They called him from the north to administer baptism to numerous catechumens. In Mangalam, however, he was imprisoned with his catechists. Bound to tree trunks, they were subjected to cruel torture. They later received the same treatment in Manarcoil and Pagani. Finally they were condemned to death, but this sentence was not carried out, as the sovereign called the would-be executioners to court. An eloquent defense of the faith by John de Brito gained him freedom to preach the Gospel to the Christians, and to teach it openly. The missionary martyr was left with deep scars from the tortures he had undergone.

Madurai Bush or Portuguese Palace?

Returning to the mission, he was called to the Fishery Coast and ordered to return to Europe, to report on the state of Christianity in the East and on its most pressing needs. In 1687, in the company of the viceroy of India and count of Alvor, Francisco de Távora, he embarked for Europe, making a stopover in Brazil. In Portugal, the court venerated him as a martyr for Christ. Still dressed as a *pandara swami*, he expounded with great simplicity the most urgent problems of Madurai, Maravar, and the Fishery Coast in Lisbon, Évora, Coimbra, and Porto. With fiery eloquence, he appealed to young men to respond to the call of the Lord and the hunger for souls, and at the same time gave a living illustration of the new methods of missionary adaptation.

Difficulties arose to prevent him from going to Rome. He was thinking of returning to the East, when the king and queen chose him as tutor for the princes. When he learned of this plan, the missionary reacted strongly. "I love heaven more than earth, and the bush country of Madurai more than the palaces of Portugal," he was to write in April 1691. A diocese was suggested, but his refusal was equally swift. He could not abandon his catechists and neophytes.

On November 3, 1690, he reached Goa. On June 20 of the following year, he wrote from Vadugapatti: "I have been here for a fortnight and I have already heard nearly a thousand confessions and baptized four hundred people." The apostolic miracle was happening again. What was the missionary's secret as the instrument of divine grace? The austerity of his life, limitless dedication, and a remarkable simplicity in catechizing: "The truths of the faith preached in their purity bear more fruit than subtle concepts or polished words," he wrote in 1692 to his friend Father Luis Pereira.

He was appointed visitor to the mission and traveled all round it. The last fifteen months of his life were to be proportionately the most fertile. He evangelized the Colers and in conditions of fear and privation founded the mission station of Muni, baptizing more than eight thousand people. "It is often horribly frightening," he said, "and I travel through the bush without house or hut to reach the Christians."

Final Immolation

He was threatened with martyrdom, to which he replied with a smile: "We will go to heaven more quickly." The conversion of Tariadevem and the fidelity of the prince to the laws of Christian marriage gave rise to renewed persecution. While John was in the forest of Muni, surrounded by catechumens, he was seized by police spies from Rauganadevem on January 8, 1693, and led to the court, suffering the greatest ill-treatment on the way. Condemned to death and sent back to Oriyur, he stayed there to await execution. At this time, he made these notes for his provincial, with striking simplicity: "I was put on trial. I confessed faith in God at a lengthy hearing process. They put me in prison again, where I am now awaiting the good day." It dawned the following morning, February 4, 1693, when he was beheaded, mutilated, and had his hands and feet cut off. The missionary vocation of John de Brito was consummated with his martyrdom.

Domingos Maurício, SJ

Beatified by Pius IX on August 21, 1853, John de Brito was solemnly canonized by Pius XII on June 22, 1947.

Saint Claude La Colombière (1641–82)

Memorial on February 15

There is no doubt that placid Claude La Colombière enjoys a fine reputation and great popularity in the Society of Jesus. That will not surprise one who remembers that the task of spreading devotion to the Sacred Heart was entrusted to the Society. The man who was called "the faithful servant and perfect friend" of the Heart of Jesus could not help but be special. But is that the only basis for his popularity? Is there not some other consideration as well? The life and personality of Saint Claude, the role he played in Christian spirituality, the message he spread—they are obviously of immense influence.

A Calling against His Will

Claude La Colombière, third child of the notary Bertrand La Colombière and Margaret Coindat, was born on February 2, 1641, at Saint-Symphorien d'Ozon in the Dauphine, in southeastern France. After the family moved to Vienne, Claude began his early education there. He competed his studies in rhetoric and philosophy at the Jesuit college in Lyon.

During this time, he sensed his vocation to the religious life in the Society of Jesus, but nothing is known about the motives that led to this decision. In one of his early notes, he writes: "I had a terrible aversion to the life I embraced." This affirmation is consistent with Claude's closeness to his family and friends, and with his inclination to the arts and literature, and to an active social life. But Claude was not a person to be led by his sentiments alone.

When he was seventeen years old, Claude entered the Jesuit novitiate at Avignon. In 1660, he moved to the college in Avignon, where he pronounced his first vows and completed his studies in philosophy. He remained at the college for another five years, serving as professor of grammar and literature.

In 1666, Claude went to the College of Clermont in Paris for his studies in theology. Already noted for his tact, poise, and dedication to the humanities, he was assigned by his superiors to the additional but important responsibility of tutoring the children of Jean-Baptiste Colbert, minister of finance under Louis XIV.

After his ordination to the priesthood and the completion of his theological studies, Claude returned to Lyon. For a time, he taught in the college there, then he became full-time preacher and the moderator of several Marian sodalities.

Claude was known for his solid and serious sermons: instead of losing himself in abstract ideas, he addressed himself concretely to his listeners. Faithful to their Gospel inspiration, his sermons communicated serenity and confidence in God. In print, too, they produced significant spiritual fruits in the soul of his readers, then and now. In fact, given the context in which they were delivered and the brevity of his ministry, they seem surprisingly fresh in comparison with those of better known contemporary preachers.

"Faithful Servant and Perfect Friend"

The year 1674 was a decisive one for Claude. He did his tertianship at Maison Saint-Joseph in Lyon, and during the customary month given to the Spiritual Exercises, the Lord prepared him for the mission for which he had been chosen. Claude's spiritual notes during this period allow one to follow step by step the battles and triumphs of his spirit, which was so extraordinarily attracted to everything human and yet so generous with God.

At the end of this retreat, Claude made a vow to observe the Constitutions and Rules of the Society of Jesus to the letter. The intent of this vow was not so much to bind him to a series of minute observances as to reproduce the clear ideal of the apostolic person so richly described by Saint Ignatius. So magnificent did this ideal seem to Claude that he adopted it as his program of sanctity. That this vow was indeed an invitation from Christ himself was evident from Claude's subsequent experiences of interior liberation and broadened apostolic horizons, to which he witnesses in his spiritual diary.

On February 2, 1675, Claude made his solemn profession and was named director of the College of Paray-le-Monial. People wondered at the assignment of this talented young Jesuit to such an out-of-the-way place. But his superiors knew that in Paray lived a humble religious of the Monastery of the Visitation,

Saint Claude La Colombière, imprisoned in King's Bench in London, finds consolation in the contemplation of the crucified Christ and sinks into the love of the Sacred Heart. Maumé-jean Frères workshop (circa 1934).

Margaret Mary Alacoque (1647–90), to whom the Lord was revealing the treasures of his Heart. Overcome by anguish and uncertainty, she was waiting for the Lord to fulfill his promise to send her his "faithful servant and perfect friend," to help her realize the mission for which God had destined her: that of making known to the world the unfathomable riches of this love.

After her first conversations with Father Colombière, Margaret Mary opened her soul to him and told him of the many communications she believed she had received from the Lord. The Jesuit assured her that he accepted their authenticity, and he urged her to put in writing everything about them. Claude did all that he could to support her in fulfilling her mission. When, after prayer and discernment, Claude became convinced that Christ wanted devotion to his Heart to be spread, he pledged himself without reserve to this cause. From his spiritual notes, it is clear that even before he became confessor to Margaret Mary, Claude's fidelity to the directives of Saint Ignatius in the *Exercises* had brought him to the contemplation of the Heart of Christ as a symbol of his love.

A Very Delicate Assignment

In 1676, after a year and a half in Paray, Father Colombière was sent to London. He had been appointed preacher to Mary of Modena, duchess of York and future queen of England. It was a very difficult and delicate assignment, because of the conditions prevailing in England at that time.

Before the end of October, Claude already occupied the apartment reserved for him in Saint James's Palace. In addition to the sermons he preached in the chapel, he spent much time in giving spiritual direction, both in person and in writing. He also dedicated much of his time to giving thorough instruction to the many people who sought reconciliation with the Church they had abandoned. Despite the dangers he faced, he had the consolation of seeing many people returned to the Roman Church, so much so that after a year he commented: "I could write a book about the mercy of God that I have seen him exercise since I arrived here."

The intense pace of his work and the damp northern climate combined to undermine Claude's health; symptoms of serious pulmonary disease began to appear. Claude, however, made no changes in his work or lifestyle.

In November 1678, Claude was unexpectedly and calumniously accused of conspiracy in the aftermath of the Titus Oates "Popish Plot" and was arrested. Two days later, he was put in the sinister King's Bench Prison, where he would remain for three weeks in extremely severe conditions, until he was expelled from England by royal decree, in January, 1679. Such suffering further weakened Claude's health, which deteriorated rapidly after his return to France.

During the summer of 1681, Claude, already gravely ill, returned to Paray. Here, in the evening of February 15, 1682, the first Sunday of Lent, Claude suffered the severe hemorrhage that ended his life.

Messenger of the Sacred Heart

The Ignatian expression *aficionarse* (to acquire a liking for) found authentic realization in the life of Saint Claude who, from his youngest days, concentrated his attention on Jesus Christ. And according to the spirit of the *Spiritual Exercises*, sought to obtain an interior knowledge of Our Lord who for the love of us became man, in order to be able to love him better and follow him more closely (cf. *Sp. Ex.*, 104). The natural result of this personal and affective bond with Christ was to open La Colombière to the disposition of heart that was characteristic of the Incarnate Word: serene interior joy at partaking of the insults, opprobrium, and suffering of our Lord (cf. *Sp. Ex.*, 167).

It is this that explains the freedom and delicacy of spirit that characterized him and that are at the root of his singular capacity for discernment. As is well known, that capacity made him a spiritual guide of very special quality, not because he was surrounded by a cloud of admirers, but because he was the right person to guide in the divine life one who had an important role to play for the good of humanity.

Paolo Molinari, SJ[43]

Pope Pius XI beatified Claude La Colombière in 1929. John Paul II canonized him on May 31, 1992.

43. Jesuits, *Yearbook of the Society of Jesus* (Rome, 1993), 38–39 (abridged).).

My God, I am so convinced that you keep watch over those who hope in you, and that we can want for nothing when we look for all in you, that I am resolved in the future to live free from every care, and to turn all my anxieties over to you.

Saint Claude La Colombière

Blessed Bernardo de Hoyos (1711–35)

A Dark Night of the Spirit

Bernardo de Hoyos, the first apostle of the Sacred Heart of Jesus, was born at Torrelobatón (Valladolid) on August 21, 1711. He did his early studies in the Jesuit high schools at Medina del Campo and Villagarcía de Campos. It was in the latter place that he entered the Society of Jesus in 1726. Because he was so young, he had first of all, and after some resistance, to get permission from his family and to convince the Jesuit provincial. He was barely fifteen years old and of a very young appearance.

While in the novitiate (1726–28), Aloysius Gonzaga and Stanislaus Kostka were canonized and proposed as models for the young Jesuits. But it was above all the figure of John Berchmans, who was in the process of being canonized, that most influenced Bernardo. For him, the novitiate was an introduction to the mystical life, and, during his three years of philosophy at Medina del Campo (1728–31), he experienced purification via a "dark night of the spirit."

The devil tempted this young scholastic violently: "You will see, you pious hypocrite, what it costs to mock God; you will fall into his hands and you will see." His mind was filled with images of a God who angrily judged him. He became discouraged. His taking communion and all his penances, instead of comforting him, left him even unhappier. His earlier gifts and graces came to appear to him as ridiculous. Even being at recreation with his novitiate companions was torture. He felt himself pushed violently to blaspheme God, the Blessed Virgin, his favorite saints. He was filled with obscene imaginations and more and more convinced that all his previous graces were nothing but illusion.

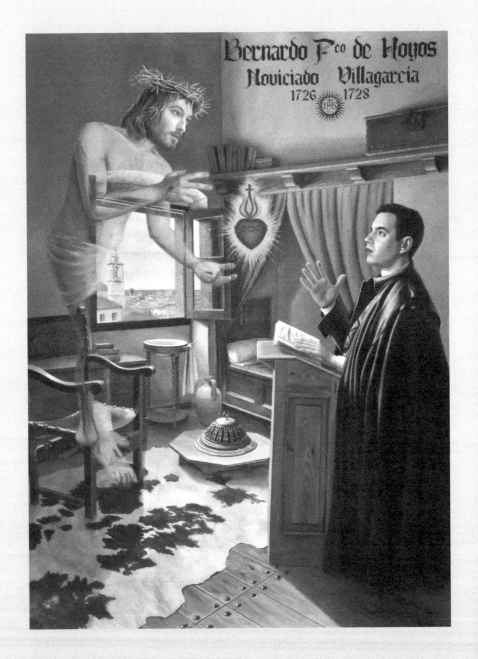

Blessed Bernardo de Hoyos had his first mystical experience when he was a novice in Villagarcía: Jesus appeared to him and offered him his Heart. Painting by Miguel Galván (2013).

But, the Lord was watching over him and did not allow him to say or do anything that would have shocked his companions.

Consecration to the Sacred Heart

Very much an exception, Bernardo immediately began his four years of theology (1731–35) at Saint Ambrose in Valladolid after three years of philosophy. It was here that he quickly grew spiritually and moved into a life of true mysticism. In a letter written to his spiritual director, Father Juan de Loyola, he wrote: "I see that my soul is drawn toward God as steel toward a magnet. It loves God, seeks God, aspires only to God." Given the clarity with which he perceived and described his spiritual movements, his director affirmed, "This young man is far beyond any knowledge that books could have given him." In addition, his companions were astounded by his strength of character, his cordiality, and his ability to form deep relationships. He also had great ability in preaching.

On May 3, 1733, when he was twenty-two, the Lord gave him a task that would become the major objective of his life: to propagate the cult of his Sacred Heart as a path to personal holiness and apostolic effectiveness. A friend of his, Father Agustín de Cardaveraz, who had been asked to preach on the feast of Corpus Christi at Bilbao, asked him to send some information from a book titled, *The Excellence of Devotion to the Adorable Heart of Jesus Christ*, by a French Jesuit, Joseph Gallifet. This book could be found in the community library. "I had never heard of anything like this and began to read this history of the origins of the cult of the Heart of our beloved Jesus. I sensed in my being an extraordinary movement, strong but sweet, nothing violent or impetuous. I at once ran to the Lord present in the Blessed Sacrament, offering myself to work with all my strength, even if only through prayer, to the spreading of this devotion."

Personal Devotion and Work with a Team

The first thing Bernardo did was to consecrate himself to the Heart of Jesus on June 12, 1733, using a formula written by Saint Claude La Colombière. Two weeks later, in prayer, on the feast of Saints Peter and Paul, he met with the two of them about the matter of the Sacred Heart and declared that he would not be satisfied with their answers until he received from

Saint Peter the assurance "that one of his successors would establish for the whole Church a feast of the Heart of Jesus." Saint Ignatius, on his feast day, July 31, told him that, as Bernardo later related, "Divine Providence wanted that the members of the Society would receive in part the honor of promoting and propagating the cult of the Sacred Heart of Jesus: and that they would obtain from the Church the establishment of this desired feast." He added that, "Our Lord had already chosen me as an intermediary in promoting this cult."

Aware of the magnitude of the task and of his main duty to pursue seriously his theology studies, he decided to set up a work group with some of his companions. He begged Father Juan de Loyola to lead the team. "I refused," his spiritual director would later record, "because of my incapacities and because I had too much work. But the young man overcame all these difficulties. His fervent prayers to the Sacred Heart of Jesus contributed more than anything, to my mind, to prepare me for this work. Why I do not know," he said, "but I decided to write a small book. I sensed some things in me that were not of me. Despite my work and the demands of my students, a few weeks later I sent Bernardo the little book he so desired." The outline and soul of this book was certainly Bernardo's. He corrected, lengthened, and embellished it. After some difficulties, the book finally appeared October 21, 1734 under the title *Hidden Treasure*.

Next, Bernardo's method consisted in spreading around texts and images just about everywhere, founding confraternities and associations in honor of the Sacred Heart, seeking conversation and preaching on this topic, and asking bishops and even King Philip V, that they support the request to the Holy See that a new and special liturgical feast be declared. Philip renewed his request of 1727 and received an encouraging response that gave hope of gaining a feast of the Sacred Heart for the kingdoms of Spain.

A Special Gift of Prayer

In the autumn of 1734, Bernardo began his fourth year of theology at Valladolid. This was for him a time of preparation for ordination that was blessed by revelations and divine communication that repeated and confirmed the message at Paray-le-Monial on reparation. "Every Friday I feel the highest degree of bitterness and sadness," he wrote. "This gift not only brought to my soul the grace and fruit of suffering itself, but it brought other benefits: compassion at seeing the suffering of the Heart of Jesus, the desire to avoid even the smallest of faults—the cause of such great suffering—but also an ardent desire to see the whole world come to know the Sacred Heart and press itself to repair all the evil done to him, and, especially, a firm resolution to spare no pain in the service of souls in this priestly life to which he has called me."

On January 2, 1735, Bernardo de Hoyos was ordained a priest at Valladolid at the youngest permissible age of twenty-four years; he celebrated his first Mass on January 6 in the church at Saint Ignatius College. A few months later, he began his tertianship, but he was not able to finish, dying of typhus on November 29, 1735, at twenty-four years of age. He was asked by a Jesuit companion on several occasions if he wished to die. To this, Bernado invariably responded, "When the Sacred Heart wants." His superior, Manuel de Prado, who had been his master of novices, was watching over him and heard him say several times, "How good it is to live in the Heart of Jesus."

In a letter on December 7, Father Prado communicated the news of his death to the communities of the province. He reported that, "his level of perfection was more than just ordinary, with a very special gift of prayer through which God opened up to him the most hidden mysteries of the Trinity, and, during his final years, a most special and tender devotion to the Sacred Heart of Jesus."

Bernardo's reputation for sanctity expanded after his death. But the difficult situation in which the Society of Jesus began to find itself because of the strong opposition of the Jansenists and the political powers of Europe made it impossible to begin a cause of beatification. The suppression of the order in 1773 caused the loss of any memory of him. It was not until the nineteenth century when the success of the devotion to the Sacred Heart brought about the rediscovery of this young Spanish apostle.

Jacques Fédry, SJ[44]

---

44. Translation by Walter E. Boehme, SJ.

Bernardo de Hoyos was beatified by Pope Benedict XVI; the ceremony took place in Valladolid on April 18, 2010.

From a Letter of Superior General Adolfo Nicolás

Bernardo de Hoyos's passion for the Heart of Jesus faithfully corresponds to the devotion that Saint Ignatius felt for Jesus poor and humble, before whom he asks that our affections be moved in order to accompany him in each step of his life: "As companions with him on mission, his way is our way" (GC 35, d. 2, 14), so that "in what we do in the world there must always be a transparency to God, (ibid., 10).

On the occasion of this beatification, I invite the whole Society, together with our collaborators, to renew our personal love of Jesus Christ and to open ourselves to the grace of identifying ourselves with him, so that in Nadal's words, "we might understand with his understanding; will with his will; remember with his memory; and that our entire being, living and doing be not centered in us, but in Christ" (cf. GC 35, d. 2, 14), as the cornerstone of the particular vocation to which each of us has been called.

Bernardo de Hoyos was a man of God, an apostle with ideas and strategies for planning. He was enthusiastic about "companionship with others" (GC 34, d. 26), a faithful son of the Church to which he tried to transmit the fire of his ardent fervor. Dead at the age of twenty-four, along with the other young Jesuit saints, he shows us that from early on in life and from our first years in the Society, we can and should allow Christ to dwell in our hearts, take root in us, and build us up in his love.

Letter of April 12, 2010, to the whole Society of Jesus, on the beatification of Bernardo de Hoyos

Blessed Julian Maunoir (1606–83)

Optional Memorial on July 2

Julian Maunoir was born in 1606 in Saint-Georges-de-Reintembault, in the far eastern part of Brittany. Sent to the Jesuit college in Rennes at the age of fifteen, he joined the novitiate in Paris at the age of nineteen. Ordained a priest in Bourges, he returned to Brittany, to Quimper, in 1640. As a friend and disciple of the diocesan priest Michel Le Nobletz, he decided to follow in his footsteps and evangelize Lower Brittany. Maunoir carried out his first mission in Douarnenez in 1641. He continued without interruption for forty-two years, during which time he travelled through the whole of Brittany, carrying out 438 missions. He died in 1683 in the presbytery of Plévin. His tomb soon became a place of pilgrimage where the faithful crowded.

A Sign from Heaven

Julian Maunoir walked the roads of Brittany for more than forty years, preaching missions from parish to parish, with intense times of prayer and conversion using songs and painted images that could draw crowds of several thousand people. He had dreamed of setting off for Canada, like his fellow scholastic Isaac Jogues. But as it happened, his native region was to be his field of action—especially where the Breton language was spoken.

While teaching as a scholastic in the college in Quimper, Julian had learned Breton so as to give catechism lessons to the local peasant children; he took to it with an ease that even to him seemed miraculous. Had he not asked the Blessed Virgin for this grace in the chapel of "Ti Mamm Doue" (the house of the Mother of God)? And the following week, he gave catechism in Breton. Was it not perhaps a sign from heaven? Le Nobletz, the itinerant priest who refused all benefices and evangelized the poor, recognized in Maunoir a successor sent by Providence. Yet Julian hesitated for a long time, until he was struck by an illness from which he could not hope to recover, and promised God he would dedicate himself to the Breton missions. He recovered and kept his promise.

Widespread Misery

There were many obstacles: opposition from the bishop of Quimper, suspicion among the diocesan clergy, skepticism on the part of Julian's Jesuit companions, the complete lack of financial means. But he was certain of the will of God, and with only Father Pierre Bernard as a companion (twenty years older than he was and unable to speak Breton), he threw himself into the venture. Immediately crowds responded to his appeal. They flocked in the tens of thousands to hear him and receive the sacraments.

Most of them were peasants and fishermen. Poor and hard-working, they were not the savages described by some historians who fail to distinguish the ordinary local people from the gangs of ruffians who pillaged the region. The once wealthy province had emerged ruined from the civil war; destitution was widespread. The population remained Christian, though its faith was dormant as religious instruction had been neglected. There were many more priests than were needed to serve the parishes. They were not all able to live from stipends or endowments: they worked with their hands and the priest-craftsman, gardener, weaver, or basket-maker was a common sight in a Breton village. They had not been to the seminary, and, with rare exceptions, their theological equipment was slender.

The special work of Blessed Julian was to adapt to this situation the ideas he had received from Le Nobletz. An essential element in the work of the mission was catechetical instruction, without which the Christian life can have no sound foundation. This gradually became an occasion of priestly formation as well, for it was up to the priests to carry on the work begun in the parishes by the missionaries.

A Mission Day

Father Maunoir called together those who had agreed to help him; they came in twenties and thirties, sometimes even more. For a month, they shared his life: rising at 4 o'clock, reciting the Little Hours together, meditating. Then they would all proceed to the church, where the crowd had already gathered, to

Workshop of Prosper Florence, "The Venerable Michel Le Nobletz Institutes Blessed Julian Maunoir as His Successor in the Breton Mission" (1900).

celebrate the Eucharist and hear confessions. Maunoir or one of his companions would strike up a dialogue with the congregation—asking and answering questions. In that way, he could be sure of catching his listeners' attention and not speaking over their heads. This would be followed by a singing practice in a private room or outside: they learned hymns composed by Julian himself; these were in fact the catechism lessons, put into verse and sung to familiar tunes. Everyone would come back to the church for a second instruction. After lunch, there would be a conference for priests. Julian liked to entrust this to fellow Jesuits like Fathers Jean Rigoleuc or Vincent Huby, while he returned to the faithful for catechism class. He considered this one of the most important exercises of the mission. In those classes, he made use of the famous symbolic pictures left to him by Le Nobletz. The remainder of the afternoon would be given over to confessions and prayer in common: the rosary, hymns, interspersed with instruction. A final sermon was followed by Benediction. Then the missionaries recited Matins and Lauds in common and after supper attended another conference. The mission was closed with a costume procession, meant to show the stages of human salvation. There, too, Maunoir's aim was to instruct rather than impress.

Such was the life of the man who, throughout his long apostolic career, was the principal architect of religious renewal in Brittany. He left behind him parishioners strengthened in their faith and pastors equipped to carry on his work. Crowds came to him, drawn no doubt by the many wonders he worked, but especially because of his ability to communicate to the simplest people the truths for which he lived. They held on to the striking charity of this man who made himself one of them and showed them the way to God. For the Breton people, Julian Maunoir was and remains the "Tad Mad," the good Father.

Henri Marsille, SJ[45]

Julian Maunoir was beatified by Pope Pius XII on May 20, 1951.

---

45. Revised by Jacques Fédry, SJ.

Almighty and all-good God, who has so much love for us and who so ardently desires that we love you, we most humbly beg you, by the love you bear for the angels and saints, and by the love they bear for you, and by the prayers they make to you on our behalf, that you would be pleased to give us all your holy love: pure love, strong love, perfect love, constant love, so that having loved you in this world, as you command us, and as we desire with all our heart, with all our soul, with all our strength and with all our mind, we may go after death to love you forever in heaven with all the blessed. We pray this through Jesus Christ our Lord, who, being God, lives and reigns with you in the unity of the Holy Spirit, for ever and ever.

Blessed Julian Maunoir

Blessed Philipp Jeningen (1642–1704)

Johann Philipp Jeningen was baptized in the Eichstätt cathedral parish (Germany) on January 5, 1642. His exact date of birth is not known, but it is likely to be within a short time of his date of baptism. Philipp grew up as the fourth child of eleven children of the goldsmith and mayor Nikolaus Jeningen and his wife Anna Maria in simple circumstances in the town of Eichstätt, which was almost completely destroyed by the Thirty Years' War.

Companion of Jesus

From 1651 to 1659, Philipp attended the Jesuit grammar school there. In 1654, he was accepted into the Marian Congregation. At the age of fourteen, Philipp already harbored the desire to become a Jesuit. After graduating from the grammar school, he earned a master's degree in philosophy in a two-year course of study (1659–61) at the University of Ingolstadt. On January 19, 1663, at the age of twenty-one, Philipp entered the Landsberg novitiate of the Society of Jesus. The focus of his formation was the initiation in the practice of religious life, especially through the Spiritual Exercises of Saint Ignatius.

Jeningen studied theology in Ingolstadt from 1668 to 1672. In Saint Francis Xavier, he saw his great missionary model. During a serious illness, he had a vision of the saint, who seemed to invite him to follow in his footsteps. Several letters to his superiors from this time, but also from later years, attest to Philipp's ardent wish to be sent as a missionary to other continents. However, this heartfelt concern was later to be fulfilled in a different way: Germany would be "his India."

In 1672, Jeningen was ordained a priest in Eichstätt Cathedral. After his tertianship in Altötting, he worked in the colleges of Mindelheim and Dillingen for the next seven years (1673–80), teaching Greek, Latin, and religion.

In 1677, he made his final vows and was fully incorporated into the Society of Jesus.

God, Jesus, and the Blessed Mother

In 1680, Jeningen was missioned to Ellwangen. There he was initially responsible for hearing confessions in the Marian shrine on the Schönenberg, a second "Loretto" created by the Jesuits in 1638, and in the collegiate church, today's Basilica of Saint Vitus. In a letter, he describes his main concern in serving his fellow human beings as "to impress God, Jesus, and the Blessed Mother on the heart of his neighbors," to lead them out of indifference and superficiality and help them develop a heartfelt relationship with God, Jesus Christ, and the Blessed Mother. It was precisely the relationship with Our Lady, her closeness, which he experienced especially in adoration, that shaped his spirituality. Gifted with visions of her, but also of Jesus, Joseph, and other saints, from whom he received many messages, he nevertheless was most cautious not to act upon them, unless he was convinced of their veracity. In the central experiences, however, which determined his life, he knew no doubt.

In order to cope with the influx of pilgrims going on pilgrimage to the Schönenberg, Father Philipp suggested replacing the chapel there with a larger shrine. When on September 14, 1681 lightning struck a town house during a thunderstorm and threatened the entire city, the prince-provost, Johann Christoph Adelmann von Adelmannsfelden, promised his friend Father Jeningen to build a new church if the city was spared through the intercession of Our Lady. Between 1682 and 1685, a baroque pilgrimage church was built on the Schönenberg, for which Philipp himself begged the necessary money.

His epitaph in the cloister of the basilica describes Father Philipp as "an untiring missionary in the Ellwangen district and far in the whole surrounding area in four dioceses." In fact, his activity as a missionary constitutes his real work: from Ellwangen, he conducted about fifty missions each year in what was then the border area between the dioceses of Augsburg, Würzburg, Constance, and Eichstätt. The Catholics living in the Protestant areas had no pastors of their own, and the Catholic places were also in need of support. The pastoral focal points of his missionary work were caring for the sick, administering the sacraments, confession, and catechesis. Living entirely from the spirituality of the *Spiritual Exercises*, he helped many people to renew their

Father Philipp Jeningen. 2003 oil painting by Gerhard Stock.

lives. Over the years, he would visit about a thousand places in the area.

Philipp Jeningen was not nor did he want to be a great speaker after the fashion of the Baroque orators. He once wrote: "There are preachers who believe they are on stage, like actors. They talk, make great gestures, and put themselves on display. Afterwards, they find nothing in themselves." It was rather the combination of simple sermons, a convincing lifestyle, and human kindness that touched the hearts of his audience. People felt that he believed what he said and—even more impotantly—that he did not demand anything of them that he did not do himself, and do in excess. Towards the end of his life, he himself said: "There is nothing more I can do than lay down my life for my beloved Ellwangers."

In His Footsteps

His ascetic lifestyle, which included strict fasting and physical penance exercises, increasingly weakened his already fragile health. A few days before his death on February 8, 1704, he began his last *Spiritual Exercises*. They accompanied him throughout his entire religious life. He lived and worked in their spirit and he also died in their spirit.

Father Philipp Jeningen's work left a lasting impression on the people of Ellwangen and the surrounding area. Despite his outward successes, he remained the simple, modest priest he had always been. He helped the people wherever he could, visited the sick, and accompanied those sentenced to death on their way to the place of execution. His relationship with God and with people was always characterized by a lively and heartfelt devotion. The people loved the "good Father Philipp" and called him "the saint" even during his lifetime.

Soon after his death, his veneration began, which also survived the suppression of the Society of Jesus in Ellwangen in 1773. Today, every summer, mainly young people make a five-day pilgrimage from Eichstätt to Ellwangen under the name "Action Spurensuche", to walk in the footsteps of Philipp Jeningen.

Toni Witwer, SJ

On June, 19, 2021, Pope Francis recognized the miracle attributed to the intercession of Philipp Jeningen, necessary for his beatification.

Saint Francis Jerome (1642–1716)

Optional Memorial on July 2

In founding the Society of Jesus, Ignatius and his first companions set themselves to outline the chief characteristics of their way of life in the Church for the service of God and man. This was to be a spiritual service through the ministries proper to the priesthood, that is, an apostolic ministry according to the Gospel of Christ and entrusted to the Society by his vicar on earth; a service of prayer and of the word explained and enriched by the Formula of the Institute.

Saint Francis Jerome's life, in the letter and in the spirit, was the exact model of the life of Ignatius and his companions that they proposed to use as a way leading to God. Jerome lived in a period when the Society had already grown to maturity, and toward the end of his life certain trends were already at work, inside and outside the Society, that half a century later were to lead to its suppression (1773).

"Foreign Mission"

Eldest son of eleven children, Francis was born on December 17, 1642, into a middle-class family of Grottaglie, in the far south of Italy. While still very young, he felt a vocation to the priesthood and his acceptance of that call led him, first as a boy and then as a youth, to study in Taranto and Naples, when the latter was the capital of the Spanish-ruled Neapolitan kingdom. He met a number of Jesuits in both places, and, after ordination in 1666 and further studies in theology and canon law, he asked for admission to the Society.

He entered the novitiate in 1670 and in the following year was sent to take part in a country mission in the "Heel of Italy," the type of mission frequently given by Jesuits in those parts. This proved to be a difficult but useful start for what was to be his life's work: giving missions and bringing the Gospel to the people of Naples. Recalled to the capital in 1674 to finish his studies, he was to remain there on what he called his "home Indies" until his death in 1716.

Scene of Contrasts

The social conditions in the largest city in southern Italy in the second half of the seventeenth century were appalling. Some two hundred thousand persons were squeezed into the restricted city center with its ten boroughs, or squatted as best they could in miserable settlements round the bay. Like all contemporary European capitals, Naples was the scene of glaring social contrasts. On the one hand, there were the magnificent medieval, Renaissance, and baroque mansions and churches of the main streets and squares, and on the other the unsanitary squalor of the neighboring side-streets, alleyways, and passages with their dreadful common lodging-houses and dark slums, where the greater part of the population lived in shocking promiscuity. As with the buildings, so with the people who lived in them; on the one hand, the luxurious life of the idle, quarrelsome rich, and on the other the privations and drudgery of the masses, the artisans, traders, and fisherfolk who formed the productive class. To these must be added those who were drawn for one reason or another as though by a magnet to the large city: the homeless and unemployed trying their luck; the quacks hawking their nostrums; poor peasants from the surrounding country hoping to make money; the idle and feckless; mercenary soldiers and galley-birds who haunted the port area; thieves and assassins. This fluctuating mass was engaged in an unceasing struggle for survival in which all human, let alone Christian, dignity was destroyed.

The apostolic preferences of Francis Jerome brought him precisely to these slum-dwellers, who had in common a certain childlike sincerity, a cheerful indolence, and an irresistible will to live. This would be the scene of his priestly ministry for forty years. He loved the Neapolitans with a truly Christ-like love and wanted to share their life: hence, the street became the common scene of his apostolic work.

Meeting God

Apart from the few hours a day that Francis gave to prayer and sleep, he spent all his time with the "marginalized" in the most insanitary and disreputable streets and squares of the city. His was an unending city mission. But through the ministry of the Word, of the sacraments of Penance and the Eucharist, he brought about a real moral reformation that lasted long after his death.

The great successes of his ministry in the 1680s also aroused mistrust and jealousy. Some felt that a priest who preached in the streets and frequented sinners was not suitable for giving retreats to priests and nuns who sought perfection. The archbishop forbade him to preach in the streets, until he discovered that the complaints against the Jesuit came from jealousy. He apologized and renewed the pastoral authorizations granted to Francis.

Then the Jesuit superiors tried to limit his activities, because they encroached too much on the time he spent in community. He lived these years of humiliation as a "period of spiritual growth." In the end, however, the provincial superior gave in and gave the green light to Father Jerome for his apostolate among the Neapolitans, which he exercised from 1694 to 1702. Then he devoted half of his time to missions outside Naples.

For his work, Jerome had the valuable help of some two hundred laypeople drawn from the ranks of the small artisans and traders and from his own "converts." With them he worked, like Our Lord in the Gospel, among sinners and prostitutes. They were his favorites, and he brought many of them to the feet of the crucified Savior where they made their peace with God. He was the means for them to hear the voice of God "today" and to listen to that voice, the voice of mercy, the refuge of the poor, of the sick, of prisoners, and of slaves.

Francis Jerome was buried in the Church of the Gesù in Naples. On the Sunday following his death, which occurred on May 11, 1716, more than forty-two thousand were at Mass and communion in that church—the sacrament that had been the main-spring of all his work for Christ, work that did not cease with his death.

Mario Gioia, SJ[46]

Francis Jerome was beatified by Pius VII in 1806 and canonized by Gregory XVI on May 26, 1839.

---

46. Revised by Jacques Fédry, SJ.

When Mount Vesuvius erupted on August 2, 1707, the people of Naples carried the reliquary bust of the patron saint of the city, Saint January, out of the cathedral. The torrent of lava and ash stopped after Saint Francis Jerome blessed the inhabitants with the Most Blessed Sacrament. Icon of Francisca Leighton Munizaga (between 2000 and 2015).

Blessed Anthony Baldinucci (1665–1717)

Anthony Baldinucci lived during a period of cultural and political decadence in Italy. He was born in Florence on June 19, 1665, of a noble Florentine family that had lost its wealth and whose lifestyle contrasted sharply with the luxury of the grand-ducal court, still one of the richest in Europe.

Florence still preserved the magnificence of its golden age. The reigning grand duke was Cosimo III de' Medici (1642–1723). During his reign, more than half-a-century long, conditions in the city, whether moral or material, did not improve; on the contrary, the excessive luxury of the court and the self-seeking of a few noble families led to a sense of growing discontent among the humbler folk who lived in miserable conditions and formed the majority of the population.

The Jesuits were a major presence in town, corresponding to the apostolic choices made by Ignatius and Diego Laínez in the early days of the Society. The College of San Giovannino was established there, for the education of the youth, and two retreat houses, one called Holy Savior House, which also housed the tertianship, and the other located near the ancient Basilica of San Miniato.

Baldinucci, of delicate health, was only thirteen years old when the idea of dedicating himself to God first occurred to him. This was when his eldest brother, Gian Filippo, who was very close to Anthony, became a Dominican. Anthony wanted to follow his brother into the Order of Saint Dominic, but for some reason his father strongly objected. It was this objection, and a retreat based on the Ignatian *Spiritual Exercises*, that made him realize that regardless of the external circumstances he was really called to the Society of Jesus. He thus entered the novitiate at Sant'Andrea in Rome on April 21, 1681; he was not yet quite sixteen.

Preacher Because of Poor Health

Still in formation, Anthony dreamed of following in the footsteps of the great Jesuit missionary Saint Francis Xavier and repeatedly asked to be sent to India, China, or Japan, but to no avail. A limiting factor was his uncertain health, which also kept him away from that other important work of the Society, the colleges. What remained was the apostolate of the pulpit, preaching Advent and Lent in the churches of Italy, as did the great orators of his day. He abhorred the theatrical and bombastic eloquence of the baroque, however, and even more heartfelt was his dislike of the fulsome attentions paid to well-known preachers.

Little by little, however, and especially during his fourth year of theology, he began to reflect on the people he had met in the countryside on the numerous occasions of necessary repose that had interrupted his studies so often. There were shepherds and small farmers, all the villagers of the Roman countryside and of Upper Lazio, in fact, who lacked everything, often—he well knew—because nobody had thought of bringing them the word of God. Why not make this his field of action and his mission?

Serving the Poorest in the Countryside

The popular missions had been a typical ministry of the Society of Jesus right from the time of Saint Ignatius, who had mentioned in his Formula of the Institute as its purpose "to strive especially for the progress of souls in Christian life and doctrine and for the propagation of the faith by the ministry of the word, by spiritual exercises and works of charity, and specifically by the education of children and unlettered persons in Christianity." Men like Silvestro Landini (1503—54) and Saint John Francis Regis, who had died in 1640, had dedicated their lives to this ministry, which was considered "proper to the Society." In 1599, following the Fifth General Congregation, Superior General Claudio Acquaviva had issued precise instructions on this point: all priests, especially the professed, should annually give missions to the people, and in every house at least two Jesuits should be set aside for this work alone. Mission houses should be set up on a temporary basis as centers for such work, which from time to time had to be moved to other places, to avoid their activity being limited to a few towns or regions.

P. ANTONIVS BALDINVCCI Soc. Iesu Missionarius vitæ
austeritate pietate morum, animarum zelo cultuq. erga Dei p.
Virginem insignis: natus Florentiæ 10. Iunij 1665. Societ. ingres-
sus Romæ 21. Aprilis 1601. obijt Pophis die 7. Nov. 1717.
Iav. Guttierez del. et sculp Sup. permis.

"Father Anthony Baldinucci, Missionary of the Society of Jesus, Eminent in Austere Life,
in Pious Morals, in Zeal to Save Souls and Devotion to the Virgin Mother of God. Born in
Florence on June 19, 1665, He Entered the Society in Rome on April 21, 1681 and Died in
Pofi on November 7, 1717." Engraving by Giovanni Guttierez (1720).

The golden age of popular missions in Italy was the half-century from 1681 to 1730. It was to this kind of ministry that his superiors appointed Baldinucci, ordained a priest on October 28, 1695. He was first sent for a short time to Viterbo, in 1697, and the next year transferred to Frascati, where he remained until his death on November 7, 1717, during a mission in Pofi near Frosinone. In those twenty years, Baldinucci visited thirty dioceses and carried out an average of twenty-two popular missions a year. He lived the Gospel in his own person, taking the word of God to the smallest hamlet, devoting himself to the poor and the dying, bringing peace to disturbed consciences, reconciling enemies, putting himself entirely at the disposal of those who needed his help. He was not alone: during his travels, he always carried with him an image of Our Lady "Refuge of Sinners," said to be miraculous, and he worked hard to promote devotion to the Blessed Virgin.

Baldinucci gave himself completely to this exhausting work, fully dedicated as he was to the Kingdom of God. He thus showed how much he had "put off his own will and inclination in order to put on Christ" and had joined the ranks of the men Ignatius wanted, men who "in labors, in wakes, in privations, in chastity and in knowledge, in patience and in gentleness, in the Holy Spirit, in charity unfeigned ... through honor and dishonor, through ill repute and good, and in brief through good times and bad, they themselves march with great strides toward their heavenly country, and, using all the means at their disposal, carry others along with them, their sole aim being the greater glory of God."

Armando Ceccarelli, SJ[47]

Anthony Baldinucci was beatified by Pope Leo XIII on April 23, 1893.

---

47. Revised by Marc Lindeijer, SJ.

Part 4

THE SUPPRESSED SOCIETY (1773–1814)

Jan Marcin Bansemer, map of Poland after the first partition of the country in 1772 (1837). In the small green-colored region to the east, which had been annexed by Russia, the Society of Jesus was able to survive its suppression.

The suppression of the Society of Jesus was a tragedy for the Jesuits but also a tragedy for the Church at large, as it lost the single greatest intellectual asset it possessed. The Jesuits were as a body the most broadly learned clergy in the Church. Their often-magnificent libraries were dispersed or pillaged, their artworks confiscated, and their more than seven hundred schools either closed or passed to other hands.

In Spain and especially in Portugal, the suppression was particularly brutal. The Portuguese herded the Jesuits into ships that carried some one thousand of them to Italy, where, uninvited, they were left to fend for themselves. Another 180 were not so lucky. Transported to Portugal from the missions, they were stuffed into underground dungeons, where they were left to rot away.

In other places, the governments treated them better, but the former Jesuits suffered a deep sense of loss and dislocation. Some joined the diocesan priesthood and continued to function as ministers of the Gospel. They prayed for the miracle that the Society someday might be restored. The Spanish Jesuit Joseph Pignatelli worked so consistently and resourcefully for that seemingly impossible eventuality that he is sometimes considered a second founder of the Society.

The papal brief required promulgation by the bishops of localities in which a Jesuit community existed and then implementation by the government. In places like Britain and its American colonies, there were no bishops and, more important, the British government had no interest in implementing a papal brief. In those parts, therefore, the Jesuits in dutiful obedience to the pope's express wishes suppressed themselves. Their lives changed little, and they retained their properties. They could not, however, accept novices, which meant that their days were numbered.

An altogether different situation prevailed in Prussia and Russia, where Frederick the Great and Catherine the Great refused outright to obey the brief. The Society thus continued to exist in Prussia until the government changed hands and suppressed it. The Prussian interlude had, therefore, no long-range consequences, which was altogether different from what happened in Russia. Catherine's actions were the means by which the Society not only survived but in time achieved full restoration.

As a result of the First Partition of Poland in 1772, Catherine had come into possession of territory in what is today Belarus and with it into possession of four colleges and two residences staffed by two hundred Jesuits. Like Frederick, she appreciated the contribution the Jesuits made to cultural life and, imperious person that she was, she saw no reason to implement in her empire a decree from a foreign government.

Catherine's refusal to carry out the papal brief threw the Jesuits into a moral dilemma. Were they not obliged to suppress themselves? Catherine would not hear of it. In desperation, the superior, Stanislaus Czerniewicz, appealed in 1776 to the new pope, Pius VI, for guidance.

Fearful of the reaction of the powerful monarchies that had demanded the suppression, Pius VI delayed responding until he finally hit on an enigmatic reply: "May the result of your prayers, as I foresee and you desire, be a happy one." Czerniewicz correctly interpreted the reply as allowing the Jesuits to continue as they were and conform to the empress's wishes. He informed her, however, that the Jesuits could not continue unless they could accept novices.

Catherine acquiesced in the founding of a novitiate, a decision that threw the Jesuits' enemies in Portugal, France, and especially Spain into a rage. They protested vigorously to the empress, who refused to back down. With that, the future of the Society seemed assured in that part of the world.

Shortly thereafter, the French Revolution broke out. Especially after the execution of King Louis XVI and Queen Marie Antoinette, the Jesuits' enemies had more serious things to worry them than Catherine's obstinacy. The revolution thus benefited the Jesuits in Belarus.

Many Catholic clergy had shared the ideals upon which the revolution based itself, but they soon turned against the revolution as the revolution turned against them. Liberty, equality, and fraternity turned out to be, in their eyes, a recipe for carnage and chaos.

The number of priests and nuns executed during this period is so great that it defies counting. Former Jesuits did not escape the scourge. Especially notable are those massacred with 191 other priests in the Carmelite monastery in Paris in September 1792, and those among the 542 who between 1794 and 1795 died in prison boats at Rochefort because of harsh treatment and malnutrition.

At the same time, the French government was bent on conquest. In 1792, French troops under the command of Napoleon invaded Italy and forced Pius VI into a humiliating and costly defeat. Some years later, the French took Pius prisoner and exiled him to Valence in France, where he died in 1799. The cardinals, themselves in exile from Rome, elected a new pope in Venice, who took the name Pius VII.

Once Napoleon gained dictatorial power, he saw that peace with the Church was to his political advantage. This situation allowed Pius on March 17, 1801, to issue the brief *Catholicae fidei* confirming the legitimacy of the Society of Jesus in Belarus. Former Jesuits and younger men with no previous association with the Society now had an institution with which they could affiliate. Thus did the order become restored in England in 1803, in the Kingdom of the Two Sicilies in 1804, and in the young United States in 1805.

Relations between Pius VII and Napoleon eventually soured: in 1809, French troops seized the pope and carried him into exile in France, where he was held until Napoleon's defeat in 1814. With that defeat, Europe entered an entirely new era. In it, the tide began to turn in the Jesuits' favor even among some of their former enemies.

Once Pius returned to Rome, he set about reversing *Dominus ac Redemptor*. On August 7, 1814, the pope, after celebrating Mass at the altar of Saint Ignatius in the Church of the Gesù, decreed through the bull *Sollicitudo omnium ecclesiarum* the restoration of the Society of Jesus worldwide. He thus, with the stroke of a pen, ended the Jesuits' long nightmare.

John W. O'Malley, SJ

Blessed James Bonnaud and
His Twenty-Two Companions
(†1792)

Optional Memorial on September 2

"Enemies of the People"

In 1789, the National Constituent Assembly in France decided to seize the properties and land held by the Catholic Church, and the following year it abolished religious vows and prohibited religious orders from accepting new members. Then the assembly passed the Civil Constitution of the Clergy, requiring priests to take an oath of fidelity to the Constitution, which created a national Church independent of the pope. If they refused to take the oath, they were prosecuted as "enemies of the people."

When in July 1792 Prussia and Austria invaded France, the assembly decided to deport the refractory priests (i.e., those who refused to take the oath) to South America. Jacques Bonnaud (1740–92), appointed vicar general of the diocese of Lyon in 1788 but back in Paris in 1791, was one of fourteen former Jesuits imprisoned at the Carmelite Monastery because of his public defense of the rights of the Church. There he was martyred on September 2, 1792, with ninety-four other priests. They were led outside two by two and invited to sign the Civil Constitution of the Clergy; those who refused were thrown down the stairs of the chapel and handed over to a crowd waiting for them, which attacked them with swords, bayonets, clubs, and rifles.

The next day, the Parisian crowd attacked the makeshift prison set up in the Saint Firmin Seminary buildings, where ninety priests were incarcerated. Among the eight former Jesuits present there was Alexandre Lanfant (1726–92), formerly preacher at the court of Empress Maria Theresa and then, from

1789 to 1791, preacher at the court of Louis XVI and confessor to the king. When the prisoners were taken out into the street, he was recognzed by the crowd, which rushed upon him and massacred him. The others were taken back to the seminary, where each priest appeared before a court. In one hour, seventy-two priests were massacred for refusing to take the oath of fidelity to the Civil Constitution.

The following day, the crowd went to La Force, a prison for unwanted politicians and aristocrats, where some priests were incarcerated. Among them was François Le Livec de Trésurin (1726–92), former treasurer of the Jesuit college in Brest. First a hospital chaplain in Tours, then a chaplain of the Daughters of Calvary in Paris, he was arrested in August 1792, and imprisoned at La Force. On September 4, Father Le Livec, the last of the twenty-three martyred companions, was beheaded there, along with two diocesan priests.

Martyrs on the Cheap?

In the glorious series of Jesuit martyrs, these men might, we must admit, look rather like "poor relations." They were massacred without glory by their fellow countrymen; their death, the inevitable outcome of events stirred up by angry passions, might seem to have been the result of a natural hazard and to leave them apparently trailing behind so many of their brethren who died in their epic missionary ventures in faraway Canada, India, or Japan. Most of them were men of no great standing either; even their number compels us to limit ourselves to the essential facts and precludes any attempt at depicting individual characteristics. The ultimate disgrace is that the papal suppression of the Society of Jesus twenty years before their death questions their right to be called Jesuits.

Authentic Jesuits

Let it be clear from the outset that, although some have called them "ex-Jesuits," a description taken up again in the decree of beatification, they were still members of the Society at the time of their death. There was, it is true, a decree passed by the Parlement of Paris in 1762 and subsequently adopted by most of the provincial parlements, which was the result of a powerful and protracted wave of anti-religious feeling, that compelled Bonnaud and his companion martyrs (including twelve scholastics) to leave their residences. They were reduced to destitution in this way, because of their refusal to take an oath renouncing their past commitment, and of their consequent disqualification from holding any office or benefice. But neither this decree, nor even Clement XIV's brief suppressing the Society eleven years later, could release them from their original obligations. For the brief of suppression to be valid, it had to be promulgated in the houses of the Society, and, even if the bishops had been willing to do this, the houses in question had long ceased to exist.

So Bonnaud and the rest were still members of the order and remained faithful to their religious obligations as far as circumstances permitted. However, they were known and recognized by most people as former Jesuits: by the authorities, since "ex-Jesuit" was their title to the modest pensions that had finally been allotted to them and that they regularly came to collect; by the enemies of the faith, who found formidable adversaries among them because of their preaching and writing; by the religious communities, the sick, and the prisoners whom they visited; by the ordinary faithful, finally, who flocked to their pulpits and confessionals.

It was still the love of Christ and the spirit of Saint Ignatius, drawn from the Exercises over a long period, that continued to inspire their apostolate and to sustain the fidelity of the scattered members of a great religious body. This humble fidelity was to prove itself quite naturally, with serenity and even eagerness, when the moment of their supreme sacrifice came, their martyrdom being no more than the crown of their lives as confessors. Such was the vitality of their spirit that, although the Society had been officially dead in France for thirty years, it could count among its orphaned sons incomparably more martyrs than any other religious family of men.

Authentic Martyrs

Furthermore, they were authentic martyrs, like their other companions. The primary reason for their arrest and death was their refusal to subscribe to the Civil Constitution of the Clergy. The original intention of legitimate social reform had soon been replaced by an explicit plan to create a national Church entirely withdrawn from the authority of the pope; this was only a first step, as later events were to show, towards the complete suppression of Catholicism and indeed all religion. It was out of loyalty to the pope and out of love of the

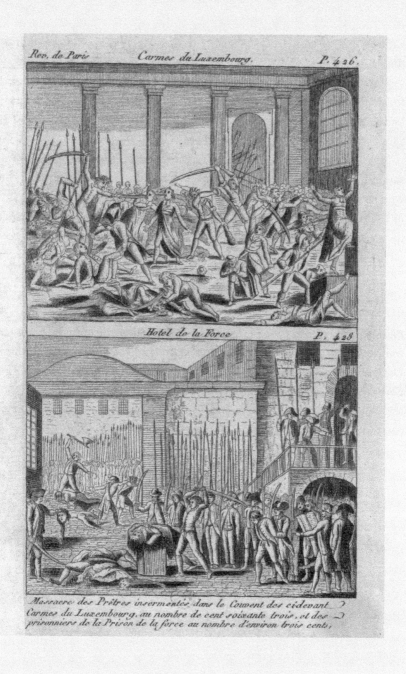

Massacre of refractory priests in the Carmel of Luxembourg and at the Hôtel de la Force in Paris on September 2 and 3, 1792. Engraving from a contemporary magazine.

Church that these men went readily to their death. The class prejudices of their executioners and the slanderous charges of treason and plotting with foreign enemies must not be allowed to obscure this basic fact: the Jesuits died for their faith; the blasphemies of those who killed them and the repressive anti-religious enactments of those in authority in the latter part of August, 1792, bear ample witness to this.

Their martyrdom was without glory; they were humble martyrs, one might say, but they are the perfect model for the countless martyrs of modern times who have been accused of disloyalty to their country and branded as enemies of the people. They were martyrs in the traditional sense, too, following in the wake of the early Christians, those "enemies of the Empire," and a host of others throughout the ages.

Rémy de Ravinel, SJ[48]

Killed for their fidelity to the Church and to the supreme pontiff, the twenty-three companions of Jesus were recognized as martyrs by the Church and beatified on October 17, 1926, by Pope Pius XI, along with many other priests, Capuchins, and Carmelites, victims of the excesses of the French Revolution.

---

48. Revised by Jacques Fédry, SJ.

The Martyrs of the Rochefort Prison-Ships

BLESSED JEAN-NICOLAS CORDIER AND JOSEPH IMBERT
(†1794)

Optional Memorial on September 2

Numerous Jesuits died during the French Revolution. In fact, twenty-three Jesuits were massacred during the atrocities of the Terror. Jean-Nicolas Cordier and Joseph Imbert had survived the initial furor, but they both fell victim to the violence of the deportation that later followed.

The Life and Calling of Jean-Nicolas Cordier

Jean-Nicolas Cordier was born on December 3, 1710 near Souilly in the Meuse. At the age of eighteen, on September 28, 1728, he entered the Jesuit novitiate at Nancy. After teaching as a regent in the college at Nancy from 1730 till 1733, he studied philosophy for two years at the University of Pont-à-Mousson. Finally, he became a full professor in the Jesuit colleges at Dijon (1735–37), Auxerre (1737–38), and Autun (1738–39). Returning for further education at Pont-à-Mousson, from 1739 until 1743, he became a doctor of theology.

While professor of philosophy at the College of Laon (1743–46), Cordier made his final religious profession on February 2, 1746. Next he was a professor of philosophy at Strasbourg (1746–48) and also a confessor in that same city. At Pont-à-Mousson, he worked as professor of Scholastic theology (1749–50), prefect of the boarding students (1750–57), and finally as prefect of studies (1757–61). Subsequently he was superior of the Saint-Mihiel residence in the Meuse until the suppression of the Society in Lorraine in 1768.

Facing Martyrdom

After the suppression of the Society, Cordier remained at Saint-Mihiel and

Refractory priests are crammed into one of three floating prisons off Rochefort, waiting to be deported to prison in French Guiana. In 1995, Pope John Paul II beatified sixty-four of them. Watercolor by Camille Mériot (1913).

became chaplain for the Annunciation sisters. He fulfilled this task for twenty years until the suppression of all religious orders in France in 1790. His vigorous opposition to the Civil Constitution of the Clergy of 1790 gave witness of his unshakeable faith. Next he went to live with a canon at Verdun.

On October 28, 1793, despite his advanced age of eighty-three and infirmities, he was arrested and put in prison. Less than a month later, seals were put on his house doors, and he remained imprisoned at Bar for nearly six months.

On April 15, 1794, at the age of eighty-four, he was deported on the fourth convoy of priests from the Meuse. At Rochefort, Cordier was put on the *Washington*, an old slave ship, to be deported with other priests to Africa.

Poorly treated, deprived of his breviary, he still gathered courage. He underwent, along with other deportees, horrible sufferings in the filthy and crowded holds of the ship. During the day, they were allowed to come up to the bridge of the ship, but the space there was so crowded that all they could do was to stand up one against the other. One meal of rotten food was given them each day. Every night, several of the priests died; epidemics raged.

Given these conditions and his advanced age, Jean-Nicolas Cordier quickly fell ill and died on September 30, 1794, in one of the hospital tents set up on the notorious Île Madame on the Atlantic coast of France.

The Life and Calling of Joseph Imbert

Joseph Imbert was born on September 5, 1719, in Marseille. He entered the Society of Jesus at the novitiate at Avignon in 1748 and was ordained to the priesthood in 1754. Successively, he taught at several colleges in Chalon-sur-Saône, Besançon, and Grenoble until the suppression of the Society in 1762. After that, as a diocesan priest, he was attached to one of the city churches in Moulins in central France. In 1791, he asked the director of the Allier department to obtain the remuneration due him as a former Jesuit.

Facing Martyrdom

Joseph Imbert entered the diocese of Moulins but was forced to leave his parish because he refused to sign the Civil Constitution of the Clergy. Since all the legitimate bishops had been expelled from France, the pope named Imbert as apostolic vicar of Moulins. In that office, he became more and more attached to the faithful, and, as a consequence, he became more and more exposed to persecution by the revolution.

It did not take long before he was arrested and imprisoned along with other priests, in 1793. Arriving at Limoges, he was subjected to a mocking and anti-religious masquerade and the execution of a priest. Sent to Rochefort, he endured long months in prison at Saintes. Known as a humorous person, they say it was there that he composed the words of the "Marseillaise of Priests." "During his detention at Saintes with his confreres of Allier, and before they embarked, he wanted to expiate in some way one of the errors of the seductive art of music by adapting the melody and words of the 'Marseillaise,' words that are so full of poetry and enthusiasm, with different words filled with an energy and enthusiasm of an entirely different kind: that of religion and apostolic zeal. We sang them whenever we could in the early days of our time on the ship, so that we would be ready and eager to plant the faith among the infidels that lived on the coasts of Africa."

Having embarked at Rochefort on April 13, 1794, on an old slave ship hired to take priests to Africa, Imbert succeeded despite the situation to absolve a priest they were about to shoot. Just as with Father Cordier, his age combined with the horrible and filthy conditions on board got the best of him. Joseph Imbert caught typhus and died in early 1794.

Beside the tragic circumstances of their deaths, these two martyrs had in common an unshakeable faith and undeniable courage. In fact, neither ever took an oath demanded by the revolutionaries to save their own lives and never ran away, but rather continued as long as they could exercise their priesthood with zeal. And further, neither advanced age, nor imprisonment, deportation, or persecution could prevent them from carrying on. They remained faithful and worthy until their deaths.

Barbara Baudry[49]

Joseph Imbert and Jean-Nicolas Cordier were beatified by Pope Jean Paul II on October 1, 1995.

---

49. Translation by Walter E. Boehme, SJ.

From Resolutions Drawn Up by the Priest Prisoners on Board the *Deux Associés*

They will never give themselves up to useless worries about being set free. Instead they will make every effort to profit from the time of their detention by meditating on their past years, by making holy resolutions for the future so that they can find, in the captivity of their bodies, freedom for their souls. ...

If God permits them to recover totally or in part this liberty that nature longs for, they will avoid giving themselves up to an immoderate joy when they receive the news. By keeping their souls tranquil, they will show they support without murmur the cross placed on them, and that they are disposed to bear it even longer with courage and as true Christians who never let themselves be beaten by adversity.

If there is question of receiving back their personal effects, they will show no eagerness in asking for them; rather, they will make the declaration that may be required of them with modesty and strict truth. They will receive without lament what is given to them, accustoming themselves, as is their duty, to despise the things of the earth and to be content with little after the example of the apostles.

They are not to satisfy curious people they might come across; they will not reply to superficial questions about what happened to them; they will let people glimpse that they have patiently supported their sufferings, without descending into detail, and without showing any resentment against those who have authored and been instrumental in their suffering. ...

They will sentence themselves to the severest and most absolute silence about the faults of their brothers and the weaknesses into which they happened to fall due to their unfortunate situation, their bad health, and the length of their punishment. They will preserve the same charity toward those whose religious opinion is different from their own. They will avoid all bitter feeling or animosity, being content to feel sorry for them interiorly and making the effort to stay on the way of truth by their gentleness and moderation.

They will not show grief over the loss of their goods, no haste to recover them, no resentment against those who possess them. ...

From now on, they will form but one heart and one soul, without showing distinction of persons, and without leaving any of their brothers out, under any pretext. They will never get mixed up in the new politics, being content to pray for the welfare of their country and prepare themselves for a new life, if God permits them to return to their homes. There they will become subjects of edification and models of virtue for the people by their detachment from the world, their assiduousness in prayer, and their love for recollection and piety.

Liturgy of the Hours (France), Second Reading on September 2[50]

---

50. Translation: www.thesixbells.blogspot.com, August 18, 2004.

Saint Joseph Pignatelli (1737–1811)

THE "GOLDEN LINK" BETWEEN THE OLD AND NEW SOCIETY

Memorial on November 14

An Encounter in Rome

The month of May is normally a beautiful month in Rome, but it wasn't so in the year 1769, at least not for the Jesuits. Between 1762 and 1768, they were banished from Portugal, Spain, Parma, and Malta, and suppressed as a religious order in France, Naples, and Sicily, all territories ruled by various branches of the royal House of Bourbon. In May 1769, a conclave was about to elect a new pope, successor to Clement XIII, who had protected the Jesuits through thick and thin.

The head of the order since 1758 was Father Lorenzo Ricci, a man of wide academic background but little experience in governance. It was with great pleasure that he received in that same month of May a slender Spaniard of princely Italian stock, thirty-five years old, Father Joseph Pignatelli. He had entered the order at the age of fifteen, had been ordained in 1762, and then worked as a teacher in the Society's college in Zaragoza and as a chaplain to the local prisoners. His gentle ministry to condemned convicts had earned this grandee of Spain the singular title of "padre of the gallows." It all ended in April 1767, when King Charles III expelled the Jesuits from his kingdom.

First the rector of the college and then the provincial delegated their authority to Father Pignatelli, thus making him, who had not even pronounced his final vows, responsible for some six hundred Jesuits. He certainly lived up to their confidence, providing for his exiled brothers on sea and on land, until at the end of 1768 they had reached Ferrara in the Papal States.

On May 18, 1769, the new pope was elected, Clement XIV. For nearly four years, he was able to withstand pressure from the ambassadors of Spain, Portugal, and France, but they did not let up. Every concession inevitably brought nearer the fulfillment of their one desire, the complete suppression of the Society, effected on July 21, 1773 when Clement XIV under considerable duress signed the brief *Dominus ac Redemptor*. The only real motive given was the preservation of Christian peace, and it was precisely that which the pope did not obtain.

"The Time Will Come ..."

Joseph Pignatelli, who had pronounced his final vows in February 1771, binding himself forever to a body whose mere existence was threatened, would comment on the suppression only once, on the day the brief was read to the Spanish Jesuits in Ferrara. "Why," he asked his stricken brothers, "why should ours be the hearts to bleed in this affliction? Why should ours be the eyes to weep in sorrow? We know that we have committed no fault in all this unhappy business. Those who have caused our suppression or contributed to it, it is they who have reason to be downcast, not we." And recalling the sacrifices of so many Jesuits, especially in the colleges, he concluded: "The time will come, when they will cry out for these fathers to return to them, but their cry will be in vain; they shall not find them."

The suppression of the Society of Jesus did not bring peace upon the Church. "We have killed the son," declared one of the Spanish agents in Rome, "now nothing remains for us to do except to carry out like action against the mother, our Holy Roman Church." Pius VI was unable to stand firm against military power and revolutionary ideas. He lacked support from the old enemies of the Jesuits within the Church, who favored a moralist, enlightened religion in a national Church.

In February 1798, the French army occupied the Eternal City and proclaimed the Roman Republic. The pope refused to renounce his temporal power, was taken prisoner and escorted from the Vatican to Siena, and thence to a monastery near Florence. When the news reached Pignatelli, he was deeply saddened. From 1773 till 1797, he had lived in Bologna, comforted by the signs of approval that Pope Pius VI had given regarding attempts to continue or restore the Society of Jesus, the latest being the return of the order in the

Saint Joseph Pignatelli bears the Formula of the Institute of the Society of Jesus. We see through the window the Church of the Gesù in Rome, in front of the saint, a statue of Our Lady of the Pillar from his native city of Zaragoza and on the desk, a statuette of Saint Ignatius. Icon of Francisca Leighton Munizaga (between 2000 and 2015).

Duchy of Parma in 1794. Pignatelli had gone to Parma, and there he had renewed his vows on July 6, 1797 to fight under the standard of the cross, to be sent at will by Christ's vicar.

Now the newly professed, a beggar himself, hurried to Florence with all the money he possessed and offered it to the chained pontiff. It might have been on this occasion that the pope gave permission to Father Pignatelli to open a novitiate at Colorno, Italy, the only Jesuit novitiate in Western Europe at that time. The first six novices arrived in November 1799. In the meantime, Pius VI had died in a French prison, the cardinals were dispersed, the enemies of the Church boasting that they had buried the last of the popes.

That Most Charitable Beggar

As novice master, Pignatelli stressed above all the necessity of the spiritual life in union with Christ, without forgetting the practice of solid virtues and mortification. It sufficed to look at his example: he swept the corridors of the house, replaced anyone when necessary, including the cook; he went forth into the streets, begging alms from the passers by; he visited the hospitals and prisons. The only pleadings he did not listen to were those of his brothers asking him to restrain his zeal.

His greatest shock, on the other hand, was his appointment as provincial of Italy in 1803. In that capacity, it befell to him to discuss with King Ferdinand, son of Charles VII, the re-establishment of the Society of Jesus in Naples. This time the pope, Pius VII (elected in 1800), gave his approval in writing, on July 30, 1804, confirming the concessions made in favor of the Jesuits in White Russia and extending them to the Kingdom of the Two Sicilies.

God's blessing on Pignatelli's work was demonstrated not only by the spiritual fervor of the Jesuits but also by the divine providence whereby his faithful servant was able to spend enormous sums in charity. But the cross was not far away either: in February 1806, Napoleon's army entered Naples, and despite Pignatelli's diplomatic maneuvers, he and his men had to leave the kingdom. They made their way to Rome, where Joseph immediately obtained an audience with Pope Pius VII. The latter directed that the exiled Jesuits should take up quarters in Rome, in the Gesù and in the Roman College.

In the Shadows of the Coliseum

The presence of so many Jesuits in Rome was likely to prove a constant source of irritation to the enemies of the Society. Hence Pignatelli sought and found other apostolates for them outside the Papal States, staffing several diocesan seminaries, and he moved his own quarters to the Hospital of Saint Pantaleon, in the shadows of the Coliseum, close to the Church of Our Lady of Good Counsel. Here, the seventy-year-old Jesuit lived a hidden life of intense mortification and assiduous prayer, assisting high dignitaries of Church and state with advice, and many poor with alms that never seemed to outrun his resources.

In June 1809, Pignatelli was given another opportunity to demonstrate his unshakeable loyalty to the pope. The French army had again occupied Rome, to overcome the sovereign pontiff's resistance to Napoleon's policy of Church domination. Pius VII retired to the Quirinal palace, a voluntary prisoner, and refused to negotiate with the emperor, who in revenge seized all the pope's possessions. When Pignatelli heard about the pope's dire condition, he immediately put together a huge sum of money that he sent to the Quirinal. When Pius heard that it came from the provincial, in name of the Society of Jesus, with a tactful gesture he refused to take more than half of it. Shortly thereafter, the pope was abducted from Rome and held a prisoner at Savona for three years.

Pignatelli would not see the pontiff again, nor would he see the day, in 1814, when Pius VII fully restored the Society of Jesus. Pignatelli died at Saint Pantaleon's on November 15, 1811, worn-out in the service of the Church and the Society of Jesus, with a preferential option for the poor, the prisoners, and the exiled. His last words were a plea to be left alone, to spend what remained of his life with God.

Marc Lindeijer, SJ[51]

Pope Pius XI beatified Joseph Pignatelli in 1933, remembering his acts of mercy toward his predecessors. Pius XII canonized him on June 12, 1954.

---

51. Jesuits, *Yearbook of the Society of Jesus* (Rome, 2012), 12–15 (abridged).

My God, I do not know what must come to me today. But I am certain that nothing can happen to me that you have not foreseen, decreed, and ordained from all eternity; that is sufficient to me. I adore your impenetrable and eternal designs to which I submit with all my heart. I desire, I accept them all, and I unite my sacrifice to that of Jesus Christ, my divine Savior. I ask through his name and through his infinite merits, patience in my trials, and perfect and entire submission to all that comes to me by your good pleasure. Amen.

Prayer attributed to Saint Joseph Pignatelli
(actually by Jean Pierre de Caussade, but recited daily by Pignatelli)

From a Letter of Superior General Adolfo Nicolás

Joseph Pignatelli preserved unbroken his love for the Society and for the Church. He never gave in to family pressures to abandon his vocation, because of the difficulties he suffered, or because of the greater evil that was first foreshadowed and then realized when the Society was suppressed on July 31, 1773.

Trusting in God's providence, Joseph undertook the mission of keeping the dispersed Society united. When changing political and ecclesial circumstances permitted, he dedicated himself to bringing his brothers together in common life and to undertaking apostolic work enjoined by obedience, thus putting an end to the individualism that many had adopted after a prolonged period of acting in isolation.

When some urged a revival of a glorious Society of Jesus, his attitude was firm and clear: to continue to keep "the least Society" tightly bound to the Holy Father, as Saint Ignatius had intended. Indeed, he intuitively understood the frequent temptation to power and success that we have suffered in our history. It is likewise a challenge for us today to rediscover what Saint Ignatius meant by "the least Society."

In the midst of many activities and numerous relationships with people of social and economic power, he never neglected those in need. Joseph Pignatelli searched out the poor and helped them with generous alms. He also visited those in prisons and hospitals to the point of becoming known as the "father of the poor."

Without doubt, the life of Joseph Pignatelli was an example of love received and of love given. He wore himself out in his devotion to the Church and to a Society whose restoration he envisioned in the near future, but which he never saw.

Letter of November 15, 2011, to the whole Society, on the bicentenary of the death of Saint Joseph Pignatelli

Part 5

THE NEW SOCIETY (1814–PRESENT)

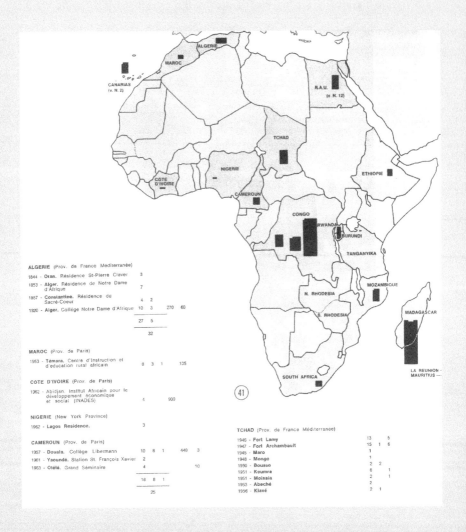

Jesuit Africa in 1964, Annuarium Societatis Iesu 1964–65 (Rome, 1964).
The bars in the diagram represent the number of priests, brothers, and scholastics working in the different countries: 435 people in the province of Central Africa (Congo, Rwanda, Burundi) and 337 in the vice-province of Madagascar.

Restored, the Jesuits now had to rebuild their order. They had few resources to help them do so. The documentation telling them what it meant to be a member of the Society was, in comparison with today, sparse. It consisted essentially in the *Exercises*, the *Constitutions*, the *Common Rules*, a few letters of Ignatius, especially the famous letter on obedience, and a handful of other documents. Although these provided the fundamental guidelines the Jesuits needed, they were bare bones, without the living tradition that could help them fully understand and interpret them. The members of the Society who had survived the long years of the suppression and rejoined the order were of only minimal help in that regard. They were old, often frail, and few in numbers.

Nonetheless, the Jesuits resolutely set about the task of trying to be as true to the original inspiration of the Society as they could. In this task, they were aided by able superiors general, among whom John Philip Roothaan was particularly important. Two things seemed clear to them: Jesuits ran schools, and Jesuits were missionaries.

The history of the Society in this era is largely the story of how they pursued these two ideals and how they in so doing came to a more copious understanding of their vocation. It is, once again, largely a story of success, but also a story of frustrations, missteps, and failures, a story of persecutions and martyrdoms.

The world into which the Society had now been reborn was a world altogether different from the world before the suppression. The French Revolution had brought with it the new, and hotly contested, ideal of liberty, equality, and fraternity. The ideal meant the end of monarchy and hierarchy. It looked to the future and wanted to cast off the shackles of the past. Progress became its watchword.

Leaders espousing these ideals were known as liberals. Even in traditionally Catholic countries, the liberals were often bitterly hostile to the Church and within the Church especially hostile to the Jesuits. Conservatives responded to the liberals with equally bitter hostility.

The history of Europe and Latin America during the nineteenth century seesaws, therefore, back and forth between liberal and conservative regimes. In this turbulent situation, the Jesuits suffered uprooting and, again, suppressions. They found themselves expelled from their native lands, only to be invited back when the political temper changed. They with great difficulty founded schools, had to abandon them, and a few years later had to found them anew. In a few countries of Spanish America, such as Ecuador and Mexico, liberal regimes did more than expel Jesuits. They saw to their execution.

Even in this situation, Jesuits in large numbers labored quietly and effectively in the schools. They were for the most part unsung heroes, their humdrum labors not worthy of notice, exemplified by the Spanish brother Francis Gárate, whose devotion to students was legendary, and the Irish Father John Sullivan, who ministered to the sick and the poor in the vicinity of the Jesuit school.

No matter which ideology dominated in the European governments of the nineteenth century, virtually every country wanted to establish overseas colonies, thus initiating another wave of globalization. In this wave, Africa proved especially tempting to them. Native populations there and elsewhere resented and resisted such efforts as best they could, which often resulted in violent and bloody confrontations.

Jesuits and other European missionaries on one level benefited from this hunger for colonies, because even governments hostile to them saw them as indirectly helping them reach their objective. The missionaries, now identified by the native peoples as foreign agents, got embroiled in ugly situations that sometimes led to their death.

One of the earliest and strangest such incidents was the killing of missionaries in China during the Boxer Rebellion, a war resulting from the actions of Great Britain, a country without any relationship to Catholic missionaries. The incident thus shows how complex and unpredictable martyrdoms in the new colonies often were.

If the occasionally benign attitude of European governments towards missionaries seemed to help the Jesuits' commitment to missions, their hostile attitude towards Jesuits in Europe helped the missions in another way. Jesuits expelled from their own countries found themselves free to pursue a missionary vocation they had perhaps nourished for a long time. Jesuit refugees thus constituted an important element in the multiple and geographically wide-ranging missionary ventures of the Society of Jesus in the nineteenth century.

In that regard, Africa deserves special mention. Jesuit ventures there before the order's suppression were few and ill-fated, but starting in Madagascar in 1832 they have become one of the most successful. Today, in both Anglophone and Francophone sub-Saharan Africa, the Jesuits serve a well-established Church.

In Europe by the middle of the century, a new fissure in the fabric of society had occurred. The Industrial Revolution was in full swing, dividing society not so much between political liberals and conservatives but between rich capitalists and a downtrodden, ruthlessly exploited urban proletariat. Seven-day workweeks, ten to twelve hour work days in factories and mines, women and children toiling alongside men, barely subsistent wages—such had become the life of countless thousands.

The break came in 1848 when Marx and Engels published their *Communist Manifesto* with the cry: "Workers of the world unite! You have nothing to lose but your chains." It was a cry that rang true to many ears. The program that lay under the cry was based, however, on a materialist philosophy. It promoted class conflict and a militant atheism.

The Church could not act as if the "social problem" did not exist. In 1891, Pope Leo XIII not only took notice but also actively engaged in the debate with his landmark encyclical *Rerum novarum*. In it, he asserted the right to private property but at the same time made clear the responsibility of property holders to act justly and compassionately toward those they employed. He asserted the right of labor to a just wage and humane working conditions. He also asserted labor's right to organize in order to secure those goods.

Some Catholics strenuously and vociferously criticized the encyclical. They argued that the social problem was none of the Church's business and especially that the Church should not promote such potentially disruptive institutions as labor unions and the like. Nonetheless, the encyclical survived the criticism and laid out the fundamentals of Catholic social teaching that subsequent popes enlarged and developed. It inspired Jesuits and others to devote their lives to the "social apostolate."

Jesuits' traditional devotion to the "works of mercy" never flagged during this period, as Jan Beyzym's heroic devotion to the lepers in Madagascar makes clear. When much later, in 1980, the Servant of God, Superior General Pedro Arrupe, founded the Jesuit Refugee Service, he powerfully reasserted the Society's tradition in that regard. Nonetheless, the teaching of the popes on social problems transformed the "works of mercy" into a new mode, appropriate to an increasingly industrialized and capitalistic society.

Within a short time after Pope Leo's encyclical, the Society began to mobilize in support of it. Then in 1931 came Pope Pius XI's follow-up encyclical, *Quadragesimo anno*. Seven years later, Jesuit General Congregation 28 (1938) published a long document on "the social apostolate." Jesuits around the world went to work making the Church's social teaching known and effectual in their locality. Saint Alberto Hurtado in Chile stands for the hundreds of Jesuits who followed a similar path, a few of whom were also of recognized sanctity.

Communism did not go away. As a virulently anti-Christian force, it took on new vitality with its success in the Russian Revolution of 1917. Now with a firm territorial base, it was able, especially after World War II, to expand into Eastern Europe. At the same time, the Communists won control of China and pursued the same expansionist and anti-Church policy in Asia.

The number of Christians who suffered beatings, long imprisonments under unspeakable conditions, and even death in the struggle against Communism is beyond counting. The phenomenon was not confined to China and Eastern Europe, but produced martyrs in the Spanish Civil War just before World War II. Jesuits opposing the Nazi regime in Germany, which was ideologically the polar opposite of Communism but in brutality its twin, suffered in the same way. Rupert Mayer barely survived the regime and died in 1945 while preaching on the Beatitudes.

Meanwhile, especially in parts of Spanish America, oppression of the poor by the rich became ever more evident and ever more vicious. The situation was particularly grave in El Salvador. For the Society, the matter came to a head in General Congregation 32 (1974–75). After long debate and discernment, the congregation published its famous Decree 4, "On the Service of Faith and the Promotion of Justice."

The principal proponents of the decree were Jesuits working in El Salvador. Both they and Superior General Arrupe realized that for Jesuits to pursue this course would cost the Society dearly in certain areas of the world. Jesuits were now not only practicing the works of mercy but acting as agents to oppose institutions that exploited the powerless.

In El Salvador, the regime quickly reacted. In 1977, just two years after the congregation concluded, the government in El Salvador organized the assassination of Father Rutilio Grande. Other brutal assassinations followed shortly thereafter.

Controversy and confrontation, therefore, marked this long period of Jesuit history, but a remarkable vitality and achievement also marked it. No matter what the situation, saints played a leading role. Meanwhile, Jesuits had continued to work for a more capacious understanding of their charism. They knew that to achieve that goal they had to recover fuller documentation from the Society's earliest years than they had at their disposal in 1814.

In the late nineteenth century, a team of Jesuit historians in Spain led the way in this quest by publishing in their series, the Monumenta Historica Societatis Iesu, critically edited texts of all the extant documents from the foundational period. By 1930, the team had published most of the primary documents—such as twelve volumes of Ignatius's correspondence, the surviving portion of his spiritual diary, and his so-called autobiography, a text removed from circulation by Father General Francis Borgia. It also published two volumes of Xavier's correspondence, a collection of Nadal's letters and his exhortations to Jesuit communities, and a host of other important texts.

Beginning around 1930, Jesuit scholars especially in France and Spain went to work studying and analyzing these texts, eliciting from them a deeper understanding of the charism and spirituality of the Society. They called their finds "Ignatian spirituality," a new term then that is now in common use. When in 1970 Father Arrupe founded the Center for Ignatian Spirituality in the Jesuit curia in Rome, a landmark in our understanding of Jesuit sanctity had been reached.

John W. O'Malley, SJ

Servant of God John Philip Roothaan (1785–1853)

GENERAL OF THE RESTORED SOCIETY

Deceased on May 8

Destined to Be the Society's Second Founder

John Philip Roothaan, twenty-first superior general of the Society of Jesus, was born in Amsterdam on November 23, 1785, third son of Matthias Egbert Roothaan and Mary Angel ter Horst. Since an early age, John with his mother began to attend the church of Krijtberg, which was served by a small group of priests from the suppressed Society of Jesus. Father Adam Beckers, who was superior of the mission restored in Holland in 1805, in addition to being spiritual director of the young Roothaan, taught him Latin. Finishing his studies with awards in the secondary school, John entered the famous Athenaeum of Amsterdam, where he had as a teacher and professor the well-known Latinist David Jacob van Lennep. Greek language and literature were his favorites in this period of study and with them he helped many students.

Roothaan entered the Society of Jesus on June 30, 1804. Since the order had been approved in White Russia by Pope Pius VII, this action made it possible for a group of sixty novices to begin their training as Jesuits. They all came from different countries such as Poland, Russia, Lithuania, Belgium, Italy, and Holland. During his novitiate, he made use of his talents to learn new languages such as Polish. According to one of his co-novices, "Roothaan was an excellent young man in every aspect of life, which hinted that one day he would become general of the Society of Jesus and its second founder, since following the Constitutions and driven by Ignatian spirituality, he would give a spiritual and apostolic impulse to the restored order."

Roothaan was ordained on January 25, 1812 and sent by his superiors first to the college of Pusza and then to that of Orsa, where he combined his classes of rhetoric with pastoral work. In 1820, the Jesuits were expelled from White Russia. It was thus that Roothaan together with others was sent to a small town in southern Switzerland, called Brig. There he worked as a teacher of Greek and rhetoric to the juniors as well as in a pastoral ministry. In 1823, he was sent to Turin as superior and rector of the new college, which gave him the opportunity to adapt to the new situation in Italy, as he had done in the other places where he had worked. Father Roothaan and his fellow Jesuits had to face the burdens of the anti-Jesuit propaganda that was spreading throughout Europe. Nevertheless, despite such slander, his students went from thirty in the first year to two hundred in theology and philosophy in a few years. From Turin, he went on to become vice-provincial of Italy.

After the order was restored by Pope Pius VII in 1814, one of the most dynamic and important superior generals was Roothaan, whom some of his contemporaries and historians have called the second founder of the order. General Congregation 21 elected him general superior on August 17, 1829. From that moment, Roothaan recommended in a special way the study and observance of the Constitutions to maintain the unity and *esprit de corps* of the order.

Roothaan gave new life to the apostolic spirit of the order by translating from the original Spanish into Latin the *Spiritual Exercises* of Saint Ignatius with an introduction and explanatory notes. In 1832, he published a new edition of the *Ratio studiorum* through which he emphasized the benefits of Jesuit education. Finally he promoted the missionary spirit of the order. In 1833, he wrote a document *De missionum exterarum desiderio* in which he invited his brethren to become involved in foreign missions. This invitation was widely received, since by the end of his generalate Jesuits were working in the Americas, Asia, and Africa. These three proposals were made by the congregation that elected him as superior general. From the outset, he invited all Jesuits to live fully their vocation in the service of the Eternal King and to hold on to it strongly despite all the problems and persecutions unleashed in Europe again the Catholic Church and the newly restored order.

Suffer with Christ Crucified

Roothaan was witness to many expulsions of the Jesuits from different European countries and in South America; in 1848, he himself had to flee from
Rome owing to the revolutionary uprising of the unification of Italy. This
allowed him to visit the pastoral and intellectual ministries of his Jesuit brothers in other countries such as France, Belgium, the Low Countries, England,
and Ireland.

Since the restoration of 1814, the Jesuits had suffered persecution in various
countries. This was due in great part to the spread of anti-Jesuit propaganda
throughout the whole of Europe. The list of expulsions began in Russia, where
the Society had survived during the years of its suppression: in 1815, the Jesuits were forbidden and in 1820 expelled. In the Austrian Empire and the territories of Venice and Lombardy, the doors were closed to them. They were not
allowed in the Low Countries and Belgium, and the novitiate that had been
opened in Belgium was closed in 1816. Its colleges and popular missions were
forbidden by the governments, and the Jesuits were finally expelled violently
in 1818.

In Spain, the Jesuits were restored in 1815 but, because of political instability, suppressed again in two periods, in 1820 and 1835. In France, the existing
colleges were closed in 1828, owing to a debate on the freedom of teaching
in secondary schools. During the French Revolution of 1830, the Jesuits were
victims of governmental excesses, in the context of the persecution of the
Church. As superior general, Roothaan was a direct witness of the persecution
that erupted in Italy against the Papal States and against the Society, which led
to the closure of many colleges.

In Portugal, the Jesuits were welcomed in 1829 and set themselves up in
the old College of Coimbra amid great signs of joy from the people, but later
on they were declared enemies of the Portuguese Constitution and in 1834
were prohibited. When Spain and Portugal closed their doors to the Jesuits,
they were invited by the governments of Argentina in 1836 and Colombia in
1842 to open colleges and restart the prosperous missions they had before
their expulsion by King Charles III in 1767. But they were expelled from both
these countries and moved to Ecuador between 1850 and 1852, when they
were expelled again. Faced with these adversities, they moved to Guatemala
from 1850 to 1871, when that government decided to expel them.

Brother Frans Quartier, SJ, John Philip Roothaan, twenty-first superior general of the Society of Jesus. Painting made during his visit to the novitiate of Tronchiennes, Belgium (1849).

In the midst of the problems the Society was experiencing, Superior General Roothaan encouraged his brethren to experience the Passion of Jesus Christ, as Saint Ignatius recommends in the third week of the Spiritual Exercises, and to work tirelessly for the greater glory of God in the colleges and pastoral missions.

Yet despite these problems, during his generalate the number of Jesuits grew considerably from 2,137 to 5,209 (from 727 priests to 2,429; from 777 men in formation to 1,365; from 633 brother coadjutors to 1,415). Jesuit colleges increased from fifty to one hundred between 1844 and 1854. The Society of Jesus expanded geographically in North and South America, Asia, Africa, and Australia. The number of Jesuits overseas increased significantly from 119 in 1829 to 1,014 in 1853.

"I Thank You for All the Benefits"

Without doubt, in the work of Superior General Roothaan the Society experienced a new birth in the midst of the problems of the nineteenth century. This was possible because of his leadership and his call to live fully the spirit of the Constitutions and the Spiritual Exercises. The exhortations of John Roothaan were directed towards an evangelization for the greater glory of God. With him, the Society rediscovered the spirit that had characterized it in the time of Saint Ignatius.

Throughout his life, Roothaan gave witness to the love of God, and for his contemporaries he died with a reputation of sanctity. His spiritual diary gives witness to the spiritual depth that guided all his actions, his intentions, and his achievements.

"God, my most loving Lord and Father: In union with the most pure affection of the most holy Hearts of your beloved Son Jesus and of his most holy Mother Mary, and one with the hymns of praise that are always intoned and will be intoned to your divine Majesty by all your saints and chosen ones, although most unworthy of your divine presence, I thank you for all the benefits you have given me truly infinite in number and greatness; above all for that special and most sweet Providence by which you have called and guided me, through wonderful ways, to that most holy religion and for the singular benefits that the religious state has brought me ..."

Jorge Enrique Salcedo Martínez, SJ[52]

---

52. Jesuits, *Yearbook of the Society of Jesus* (Rome, 2014), 73–75 (abridged). Translation by Michael Campbell-Johnston, SJ.

Saint Jacques Berthieu (1838–96)

PROTOMARTYR OF MADAGASCAR

Memorial on June 8

Did he die for the faith of the Catholic Church or because of the political stance of a colonial power? In our day, with a more acute sensitivity for the cultural, economic, and political factors of the history of salvation, this will be one of the first questions asked when the subject arises of the violent death of French Jesuit Jacques Berthieu in Madagascar of 1896. It is true that his missionary life was dominated by the politics of his mother country, and it is a fact that his death occurred in the midst of the second war waged by the people of Madagascar against France, which had broken out just two years previously. But it is no less true that Father Berthieu sought only the Kingdom of Heaven. In 1873, he wrote, "I don't want to possess any land but a little heart to love people in the divine heart of Jesus." And that's what happened. In that very year, Berthieu entered the Society of Jesus. Born in Montlogis (Auvergne) in 1838, he was ordained to the priesthood in 1864 and worked as a modest and contented associate pastor for a good nine years before joining the Society with the request to be sent to the missions. Two years later, he told one of his fellow scholastics, "I am destined to become a future apostle of the Malagasy people." He certainly did not think that he would also become their proto-martyr.

From One Station to Another

Naturally, the beginnings of his missionary life were not easy for this thirty-seven-year-old Jesuit. Climate, language, culture were all totally new things that made him exclaim, "My uselessness and my spiritual misery serve to humiliate me, but not discourage me. I await the hour when I can do something, with the grace of God." On the Île Sainte-Marie his first work-assignment,

Father Berthieu gave himself totally to teaching catechism, visiting the poor and the lepers, baptisms, preparation for First Holy Communions, and regularizing marriages. At the same time, he helped the native people cultivate their fields in an effective way—from which he was able to draw the means to sustain his school for children.

In 1881, a decree from the French government expelling religious forced him to leave his mission. "My poor little people," he wrote in his diary, "May the good Lord watch over you in his mercy and soon give you other shepherds to save your souls." That sentiment, full of love for his Malagasy people and with no lamenting his own situation, could serve as the refrain of the following years in which he would be chased from one mission to another. Berthieu went first to Tamatave and then to Tananarive (Antananarivo), until his superiors sent him to the far-off mission of Ambohimandroso, near Betsileo.

But the outbreak of the first French–Hova war in 1883 forced him to depart. After a stay in Ambositra of five years, he went to Andrainarivo in 1891. This post was northeast of the capital Tananarive and had eighteen mission stations to look after, situated in the most remote and inaccessible places. Here, as elsewhere, he tried to make himself "everything for everyone." He wrote, "Evenings and mornings I teach catechism; the rest of the time I dedicate to receiving people, or visiting everyone in the vicariate, friends and enemies, to gain them all to our Lord." The faithful flocked to him, just to have contact with a truly religious man. They said of him: "He was a father who never abandoned his children." To Christians, he was fond of repeating, "Do not fear those who kill the body, but those who can kill the soul." Or, "Even if you were to be devoured by a crocodile, you would rise again."

In 1894, the second war against France broke out, and once again Berthieu had to leave his dear Malagasy people, returning only after a year, but in time to be able to share their worry because of the news of the violence of the rebels directed not only against the French authorities but also against missionaries. The latter, because they bore Christ, could deprive idols and amulets of their power! So the rebels planned to eliminate once and for all the bearers of Christian religion.

Saint Jacques Berthieu offers his life for his people. In the background, we see the Mananara River, in which his murderers threw his corpse, food for the crocodiles. Painting by Eric Armusik for the canonization in 2012.

Ready to Die

In March 1896, the village where Father Berthieu lived was evacuated by the French army as indefensible. The Jesuit, then almost sixty years old, remained in the midst of his "good Christians," who were, he wrote, "happy for my presence ... and ready to die with me, if necessary, in order not to be untrue to their conscience." Tired and sick, he reached Tananarive at Easter time and recovered his strength there, passing long hours on his knees before the Blessed Sacrament. But he could not stay far from his flock and returned to them on May 21. On his return to the residence, he confided to a sister, "I don't know what awaits me, but whatever happens I am ready. I made my retreat as if it were to be my last."

Two weeks later, the missionary again received notice of the need to evacuate the place. The refugees now numbered some two thousand. Preceded by French soldiers, they began the trip to Ambohimila. As the march went on, little by little the file was strung out: the soldiers had the lead, but the sick, old and children fell always farther behind their protectors. One of the mission's employees, no longer able to walk, cried for help; profoundly moved, Father Berthieu gave him his horse and continued the march on foot. Going forward that way, he completely lost sight of the soldiers. When some groups of the rebels rushed them, Berthieu fled with some Christians to the nearby village of Ambohibemasoandro. He spent the night there and celebrated Mass the next morning, June 8. It would be his last Mass. Some hours later, the rebels invaded the village and captured the compassionate and courageous missionary.

Father Berthieu was struck by axes on his shoulders and chest and fell onto his knees. But then he rose and wiped off the blood with his handkerchief, saying: "Don't kill me, my children, I have good things to say to you." Some wanted to kill him right away, but the majority preferred to take him to their camp some fifteen kilometers distant to present him to their leader. Outside their village they stripped the Jesuit of his cassock, and seeing the crucifix he wore around his neck, one of the officers yanked it off him, crying, "Here is your amulet! It's this that serves you to hoodwink our people!" Then they asked him, "Will you continue to pray and make the people pray, yes or no?" Father Berthieu replied, "I will certainly continue to pray, right up to my death."

As if the violence and the sacrilegious words of the rebels weren't enough, the missionary who had dedicated himself for a good twenty years to his Malagasy flock was abandoned by all of them. When the troops arrived at Ambositra, a village that Father Berthieu had converted, it was raining. "My children," he begged, "would you give me a blanket to cover myself? I'm cold!" But the villagers didn't dare to help him. Passing in front of the church where he had administered the sacraments countless times, he asked to be allowed to enter, but he was refused. So he knelt down at the door and said the *Our Father* and the *Hail Mary*, holding a rosary in his hand and kissing its cross. The march was taken up again, with insults and curses.

Evening was upon them, and some of the group wanted to go home. The easiest solution was to kill the prisoner. Father Berthieu asked to be able to pray for his killers. "Renounce your evil religion," was the response, "Don't hoodwink the people any more and we will take you with us and make you our chief and our counselor, and we will not kill you." He replied: "I absolutely cannot agree to that, my son; I prefer to die." A first and second shot, each fired by two men, missed; even a fifth shooter did not succeed in killing him. Then the captain went up to him and fired a shot into his neck. It was the *coup de grâce*. For fear of the French soldiers, the murderers threw Berthieu's body into the nearby River Mananara, infested with crocodiles. It vanished forever. In that way, the words so often repeated by Jacques Berthieu in his catechesis of his dear Malagasy people came true: "Even if you were to be devoured by a crocodile, you would arise."

Marc Lindeijer, SJ[53]

Jacques Berthieu was declared a blessed martyr for the faith and for chastity by Paul VI in 1965, during the Second Vatican Council. He was canonized by Benedict XVI on October 21, 2012 on the occasion of World Mission Sunday.

---

53. Jesuits, *Yearbook of the Society of Jesus* (Rome, 2013), 30–32 (abridged). Translation by John J. O'Callaghan, SJ.

The Martyrs of the Boxer Rebellion

LEO IGNATIUS MANGIN, MARY ZHU-WU,

AND THEIR FIFTY-FIVE COMPANIONS

(†1900)

Memorial on July 9

Three Persons

Zhujiahe is a small village situated in the vast plain at the border of the northern Chinese Provinces Zhili and of Shandong. Its name translates to the "River of the Zhu Family." Several members of that family had converted to Catholicism during the eighteenth century, when the Jesuits from Beijing progressed deeper into Zhili province. In the early tenth century, the Zhu family had settled near the river and given it its name. In 1900, the village had some three hundred inhabitants living in low cottages built of clay, nestled among sprawling sorghum fields and was dominated by a simple church with a flat roof and high façade; its cross towered over the countryside.

The French Jesuit Leo Ignatius Mangin, forty-two years old and a missionary in China since 1882, was the pastor of the Catholic community of Zhujiahe. He was helped by a middle-aged village elder, Zhu Dianxuan, an able administrator who also happened to be skilled in the art of warfare. His fifty-year-old wife, Mary Zhu-Wu, was much esteemed by the villagers: a gentle woman of great faith, she gave priority to helping the poor in her service of God. Never looking for notoriety or glory, these three people would become the center of the most violent massacre of Christians during the Boxer Rebellion.

The Fortified Village

The history of the uprising itself, the political machinations and warfare that ignited it, need not be explained here. They mattered little to the people of Zhujiahe, when in the summer of 1900 they took in thousands of Catholic refugees from the neighboring villages. This increased the population to three thousand, ten times its usual size, when on July 17 they were attacked by 4,500 heavily armed men, the combined forces of the Boxers and the imperial army.

A few days earlier, the villagers, protected behind the ramparts that Zhu Dianxuan had constructed, had still been able to ward off the attacks and even seized a cannon from the enemy. Father Mangin and his fellow-Jesuit, Paul Denn, who had also fled to Zhujiahe, had offered Mass each morning and heard confessions throughout the day; during the evenings, they relieved the night watchmen on the ramparts.

The next day, Zhu Dianxuan, the only experienced leader among the one thousand-odd men who were able to defend the village, climbed the ramparts to train the cannon on the enemy forces. But that same evening, when already more than half of his men had died in battle, the cannon backfired onto Zhu Dianxuan's chest. Mangin, who was standing nearby, ran toward the dying man and gave him Extreme Unction. By the third day, as the situation seemed hopeless, those who could escape did so, leaving behind those who were too weak to flee, especially women and children.

Massacre in the Church

When on the early morning of July 20 the soldiers took the village, the first people they killed were a group of parish virgins and women catechists. Eighty-five other women and children fled in panic to the orphanage and jumped into its well, where they drowned or suffocated. Their cries and screams for help continued for two days.

Most of the villagers, around one thousand of them, had taken refuge in the church, spiritually assisted by the two Jesuit priests. Too pressed to offer a final Mass, Mangin and Denn sat on the steps before the altar and heard confessions, while most of the people knelt in prayer or simply waited. Mary Zhu-Wu, presumably grieving for her husband, nevertheless remained calm, exhorting everyone to trust God and to pray to our Heavenly Mother.

Fathers Leo Ignatius Mangin (on the left) and Paul Denn are in the burning church. In front of Mangin, Mary Zhu-Wu protects him with her body. Drawing by Pierre-Dié Mallet (1934).

Around nine o'clock in the morning, the attackers broke through the door and began firing at random into the church, until it was filled with smoke. Panic ensued, while people were being killed, but the priests managed to unite them in prayer, reciting together the *Confiteor* and the *Act of Contrition*, and then gave them general absolution as the guns continued to fire on the people.

Here, Mary Zhu-Wu rose to singular greatness: she stood up and positioned herself with outstretched arms in front of Father Mangin to shield him with her body. Not long afterwards, a bullet struck her and she fell at the altar railing. Mangin, praying the rosary with one hand and grasping a crucifix in the other, soon fell victim to the gunmen, too. Then the Boxers barricaded the church and set it on fire. Most of the refugees inside died from smoke inhalation, the last ones—with Mangin and Denn—burning to death as the church roof finally collapsed.

A mere five hundred Catholics managed to survive the massacre by fleeing or apostatizing; a few others, women especially, were sold as slaves or led away as captives to Beijing, where they may have ended up in a brothel. But Mary Zhu-Wu continues to live on at Zhujiahe, the "River of the Zhu family", now turned into a river of blood. While her husband defended the village against the external enemy, she strengthened the interior faith and courage of the people, even giving up her life to save their pastor.

Marc Lindeijer, SJ[54]

In 1955, Pius XII declared Mary Zhu-Wu blessed, together with the two Jesuits and fifty-three other martyrs. They were all canonized by John Paul II on October 1, 2000.

---

54. *L'Osservatore Romano*, September 1, 2015.

From the Last Letter of Saint Leo Ignatius Mangin to His Family

The events that are taking place here are certainly of a nature to alarm you, too; I will not try to hide them from you.

The telegraph must have brought you the news of the massacre of two of our fathers at Ou-I, at a six-hour distance from here. The whole northern part of the mission is put to fire and sword; every day unfortunate fugitives are coming here, whose houses have been burned down; the dead are numerous, and how many are missing!

If we lack human help, we still have God and our trust in him. We have come here for his cause: our settlements, all our works exist only to make him known and to serve this people. Will he allow the loss of so many men and works? If so, we will nonetheless bless him. And those of us who will escape from ruin, or those who will come to replace us, will start again with the same courage and the same trust in God.

In this village, in addition to the five hundred Christians who live there, we have at least three hundred refugees. We make a rampart; we buy the necessary food, gunpowder, ammunition for an attack that, humanly speaking, cannot fail to occur. God's will be done! I make the sacrifice of my life for the salvation of souls and the good of my whole family. If you hear of my death, pray for me and thank God that he has deigned to select our family to ask for this sacrifice.

My beloved brothers and sisters, I thank you for the affection you have always shown to me.

I apologize for any grief I may have caused you. Whatever happens to you, remain good and faithful Christians, worthy of our beloved parents.

I bid you farewell, embracing you all with all my heart and blessing you all in the name of the Father, the Son, and the Holy Spirit.

Fiat! All yours in Our Lord.

Liturgy of the Hours (France), Second Reading on July 9

Blessed Francis Gárate (1857–1929)

Optional Memorial on September 10

Domestic, Infirmarian, Porter

Gárate, the second of seven brothers, was born in a modest family of country people on February 3, 1857 in a farmhouse near Azpeitia, not far from the castle of Loyola. When he was fourteen, he went to Orduña (Vizcaya) to work as a houseboy in the College of Nuestra Señora de la Antigua, which was under the direction of the Society of Jesus.

In 1874, he entered the novitiate, which the Jesuits at that time, exiled from Spain, had established at Poyanne in southern France. On February 2, 1876, he pronounced his first vows in religion, and the next year he was appointed infirmarian at the College of Santiago Apostolo at La Guardia (Pontevedra). He remained in this post for ten years, looking after the health of the boys and taking care of the sacristy. His personal interest and his loving solicitude for the sick soon won him the admiration of all.

After pronouncing his final vows on August 15, 1887, Brother Gárate was assigned to Deusto (Bilbao) in 1888, to be doorkeeper of the College of Higher Studies—the university. He filled this post uninterruptedly until his death, on September 9, 1929. How did Francis bear the burden of his day? With equal thoughtfulness and the same smile he received both the needy poor and the rich; he treated everybody with the same cordial warmth; with unfailing and uncomplaining dedication, he went up and down the stairs of the huge building that housed the university, carrying messages for the fathers and the professors or looking for students.

General Włodzimierz Ledóchowski, describing the characteristic qualities of this brother, highlighted what struck everybody who had anything to do with him: "Admirable discretion exercised in the testing conditions of more than forty-one years' service in a busy doorkeeper's lodge where he had to deal with people of every age and social standing; humility adorned with a natural charm; and charity which by a kind of spiritual instinct perceived and anticipated the service that was needed ..."

The Most Outstanding Figure of the University

One of those who remembered him from his own student days was Father Pedro Arrupe. On the occasion of the fiftieth anniversary of the death of Francis Gárate, in 1979, Arrupe related how he saw, esteemed, and loved him. Father General first of all noted a striking thing: in the close to one hundred years of the university's existence, its most outstanding figure, the most universally known and admired, is not an eminent writer or professor, nor is it one of the prominent graduates like a judge or a politician. It is this humble brother who spent forty-one years attending to the many simple things that keep the porter busy.

Three special traits are indicated by Father Arrupe to give some idea of what Brother Gárate was really like. These are characteristics noted by various kinds of people who knew him, like students, professors, the families of students, friends, beggars, and so many others.

First of all, Brother Gárate was a man of God. This shone through when he was cheerfully busy at his work. And what an endless round of work! Cardinal Pietro Boetto, SJ said that the porter's office where Brother Gárate worked was more like a busy seaport than the entrance to an academic institution. All sorts of people were coming and going with all kinds of requests, and the telephone never seemed to stop ringing. And in the midst of this sea of activity, Brother Gárate remained a man of God—ever present, ever calm, ever ready to help. This was not because of any external acts of piety, but rather because throughout his whole life, his actions radiated a deep-seated faith. And this was visible to all—students, professors, visitors. It was this witness of his daily life that impressed people the most.

The second characteristic was neatly described by a graduate who called Gárate "the saint of the ordinary." His place of work was very simple, and he met all with his friendly smile while trying to answer the same banal questions, fulfill the same repeated requests. His world was that of the "daily grind," the endless round of doing the same jobs, the same monotonous duties. Those

Blessed Francis Gárate at the University of Deusto in Bilbao (Spain). Detail from a Spanish painting (circa 1930).

who knew him say that he worked every day at the same ordinary things, not as one simply fulfilling his duty but rather with a youthful idealism, and happily and steadily. When Cardinal Boetto asked him how he managed to stay so calm and serene in the midst of all the activity, he replied: "I do very willingly what I can; the rest the Lord does, who can do all." Undoubtedly he had assimilated well the words of Father Balthasar Alvarez: "Holiness does not consist in searching for new things, but in following the old roads unerringly."

There was a popular nickname for him, and this is the third note that in the eyes of Father Arrupe really caught the personality of Brother Gárate. He was known as *Hermano Finuras*, which could be translated as "Brother Thoughtful." This name pointed to his spirit of attentiveness, of exquisite and effective charity, his smile and gesture of welcome, the kind word he had for all, poor or rich, young or old. And yet, there was nothing artificial, nothing of the "plaster saint" about him. As those who knew him insist, "He was a real live human being."

Father Arrupe's final point is that his recollections of Brother Gárate are still vibrant and strong, even though they date back to the years when he was studying at Deusto and visiting his spiritual director. But the important point is that the holy life led by Brother Gárate is as relevant now as it was in the 1920s. It comes down to living one's deepest religious convictions, to bringing them to bear on the sanctification of one's daily life, to succeed in determining one's relations and contacts with others by the great commandment of love. That is the lesson taught by Brother Gárate during his forty-one years as doorkeeper. Is there anything more evangelical? Is there anything more needed today?

Jesuits[55]

Brother Francis Gárate was beatified by Pope John Paul II on October 6, 1985.

---

55. Jesuits, *Yearbook of the Society of Jesus* (Rome 1983), 109–10; (Rome, 1986), 89–90. Adapted by Marc Lindeijer, SJ.

From a Homily of Pope John Paul II

The message of holiness that Brother Francisco Gárate Aranguren has left us is simple and clear, just as his sacrificial life as a religious in the porter's lodge of a university center at Deusto was simple. From his youth, Francis opened his heart wide to Christ who was knocking at his door, inviting him to be his faithful follower, his friend. Like the Virgin Mary, whom he loved tenderly as a mother, he responded with generosity and boundless trust to the call of grace.

Brother Gárate lived his religious consecration as a radical openness to God, to whose service and glory he gave himself (cf. *Lumen gentium*, 44), and from whom he received inspiration and strength to show a great goodness toward all. This was confirmed by so many persons who passed by the porter's lodge of "Brother Delicacy," as he was affectionately called at Deusto University: students, teachers, employees, parents of the young residents, and people from all walks of life, who saw in Brother Gárate the welcoming and smiling attitude of someone whose heart is anchored in God.

He gives us a concrete and contemporary witness to the value of the interior life as the soul of every apostolate and also of religious consecration. In fact, when one is dedicated to God and one's life is centered on him, the apostolic fruits are not long in coming. From the porter's lodge of a house of studies, this Jesuit brother coadjutor made God's goodness present through the evangelizing power of his quiet and humble service.

Homily of October 6, 1985 at the beatification of Francis Gárate

Blessed John Sullivan (1861–1933)

Optional Memorial on May 8

John Sullivan was born in Dublin on May 8, 1861. His father, the future Lord Chancellor of Ireland, Sir Edward Sullivan, was of the Church of Ireland tradition, his mother, Bessie Josephine, was Roman Catholic. John and his three brothers were raised in the Protestant tradition of their father and, his only sister in the Catholic tradition of their mother.

A Distinguished Gentleman

In 1873, John was sent to Portora Royal School, Enniskillen, following in the footsteps of his older brothers. His years in Portora were happy. In later years, he admitted that he went to Portora for the first time "bathed in tears" but when the time came to leave he wept "more plentiful tears!" Contemporaries of the young John Sullivan recall him as a popular boy who was always gentle and kind to the boys who found their new life in a boarding school to be difficult.

After Portora, John went to Trinity College, Dublin. He does not seem to have been an active member of the many societies that flourished in Trinity at the time, but he did distinguish himself in his studies; in 1883, he was awarded the Gold Medal in Classics. After achieving a Senior Moderatorship in Classics, John started to study law. It was at this time that his father died suddenly, in April 1885. The shock had a devastating impact on John. The promising young scholar left Trinity and continued his studies at Lincoln's Inn, London, where he was called to the Bar in 1888.

At this time, due to his inheritance, he was very comfortable in financial terms, noted for his fashionable dress and handsome good looks. He travelled a great deal and was a keen cycling enthusiast.

We are now at a period where very little is known of his inner feelings. Like many young adults, he probably set out on the marvelous adventure of life not very sure of where it would lead him. There must have been some times of uncertainty, but he continued to search. This is the time when he went on continental trips across Europe and on walking trips in Greece and Asia Minor. In 1895, John was appointed to a Royal Commission that was set up to investigate a massacre that took place in Adana in Asia Minor. It was while he was in Greece that he visited a Greek Orthodox monastery at Mount Athos. He spent three months there and considered joining the monastery as a monk. This gives one of the very rare insights into his spiritual thinking at this time.

Great Surprises

In December 1896, at the age of thirty-five, he made a momentous decision: he decided to become a Catholic. He was received into the Roman Catholic Church in the Jesuit church, Farm Street, London. The family was "shell-shocked" when the news reached Dublin. Not that they were in any way hostile to John's decision; after all, his mother, whom they all loved, was a devout Catholic. It was simply that John had never expressed any great interest in theological matters and seemed to be a "typical Protestant" of the best possible kind!

On his return to Dublin, John's life took on a dramatic change. From the young man known as "the best-dressed man" in Dublin, his new style was of the simplest. He stripped his room of all comforts, of anything that reflected luxury or ostentation. Drawn toward the poor and the needy, John visited the schools and the night refuges of the homeless. He was always a welcome visitor to Our Lady's Hospice for the Dying. His good works brought him into contact with some of the convents and religious houses in Dublin, where he made some lasting friendships.

Then, in 1900, the family got another profound surprise. John decided to become a priest and to enter the Society of Jesus. His training as a Jesuit followed the usual pattern. It began with two years novitiate at Tullabeg, County Offaly. This was followed by studies in philosophy at Stonyhurst (Lancashire) and then theology in Milltown Park, Dublin. From the beginning, it was remarked that he was different. John gave himself completely to his new way of

John Sullivan's image is placed above the high altar of Saint Francis Xavier Jesuit Church in Dublin, Ireland, for the beatification celebration on May 13, 2017. Photo by Paula T. Nolan (2017).

life. All who lived with him could not fail to notice his holiness and devotion to deep prayer. Throughout the years of formation, he never paraded his superior intellectual gifts, and he was always available to help, especially in the most menial of tasks.

John Sullivan was ordained priest at Milltown Park on July 28, 1907 and then sent to join the community at Clongowes Wood College, County Kildare, to begin a life of priestly, pastoral service. Apart from the period 1919–24, when he was rector of Rathfarnham Castle, the rest of his Jesuit life was spent in Clongowes. In the solitude and the beautiful surroundings of Clongowes, John must have remembered the Portora of his youth.

Many of the boys who were in his care remembered him as someone "different" and "special." He was a good counsellor, but not a good teacher. The boys often considered that they passed their exams more through the power of his prayers than through the quality of his teaching, despite his brilliant mind and intellectual achievement. The brilliant scholar is not always the best teacher, but a holy man is always a holy man. For many of his former pupils, it was only in later years that they realized how extraordinary it was to be "taught by a saint."

His Gift of Healing and Peace

Father John was known far beyond the confines of Clongowes. He was a constant friend to the sick, the poor, and to anyone who was in distress or need. His reputation for a gift of healing, of both the body and the spirit, reached out to many seeking his help—and his prayers worked. The accounts of his reputed cures are legion, although he himself would have been appalled at the mere suggestion that he had cured anybody. But his many friends recognized "the power of God working in him." John's deep faith, his prayer, and his determination won results over and over again. There are many families who treasure the records of the past, records of how Father John brought healing and peace to many troubled lives. And it goes on.

The long years in Clongowes are a spiritual testimony. He lived a very rugged and ascetical life. His meals were of the simplest. He lived mainly on a diet of dry bread, porridge, rice, and cold tea. He slept little, spending most of the night in prayer. His room lacked even the very ordinary comforts of the day. The fire in winter was lit only when he was expecting a visitor. His lifestyle reflected the simplicity and hardship of the Desert Fathers. The stylish dress of his earlier years was gone forever. He now wore the worn, patched garments of the poor.

To the time of his death, he was in demand as a preacher of retreats to religious communities of men and of women, which again were an experience of his holiness rather than eloquence. One interest that he maintained from the past was cycling. His old-fashioned bicycle was a familiar sight around the roads of Kildare. He was known to have cycled to Dublin on more than one occasion to visit the sick. Having prayed with the sick person, he then set out immediately on the return journey. His passion for what in his younger days was a new-fangled invention stood him in good stead in later years. When not traveling by bicycle, he usually walked. His stooped, shuffling figure was well known, and it was always presumed, when he was seen along the roads, that he was on his way to attend someone who valued his presence and prayers.

Father John's reputation as a saint grew rapidly during his time in Clongowes. Very few knew of his brilliant family history or of the fashionable well-dressed young man—a past fame that starkly contrasted with the sight of the poor man who was their priest and friend. When he died on February 19, 1933, in Saint Vincent's Nursing Home in Leeson Street, Dublin, a short distance from the Sullivan family home, great crowds gathered in Clongowes for his funeral Mass to bid an earthly farewell to their beloved priest.

Conor Harper, SJ

John Sullivan was declared blessed on May 13, 2017 in Saint Francis Xavier's Church, Dublin. The petition at the ceremony was made by the Roman Catholic archbishop of Dublin and the archbishop of the Church of Ireland, in the name of the two traditions shared by John Sullivan.

Take life in instalments, this day now. At least let this be a good day. Be always beginning. Let the past go. The saints were always beginning. That is how they became saints.

Blessed John Sullivan

Blessed Victor Emilio Moscoso (1846–97)

Optional Memorial on November 23

"Purity of Heart"

Salvador Victor Emilio Moscoso Cárdenas, known simply as Emilio, was born in Cuenca, Ecuador, in 1846. He was the ninth of thirteen children of Juan Manuel Moscoso Benítez and his wife María Antonia Cárdenas y Arcinaga. From his youth, he was distinguished by his virtue and piety.

On April 4, 1864, he entered the Society of Jesus in Cuenca. He completed his novitiate formation in Quito, where he made his first vows on April 27, 1866. In the following years, he practiced teaching in Riobamba (1867), Guayaquil (1868–72), and again in Riobamba (1873–74). He continued his theological studies in Quito (1875–76) and in Pifo, east of Quito (1877). Here he was ordained a priest on November 1, 1877. In 1878, he went to complete his studies in Poyans, France. The year after, he did his tertianship in Manresa, Spain. From the start of his formation, he distinguished himself by his religious fervor, charity, and spirit of service.

He spent his first years as a priest in the Colegio de la Inmaculada in Lima (1879–82), teaching grammar, arithmetic, and history. Here he made his final vows on September 8, 1879. In 1882, he was sent to the Colegio San Luis in Quito (1882–88) as minister of the community, prefect of the church, confessor, spiritual director of the students, and director of the Marian Sodality of the Daughters of Mary. In 1889, he was missioned to the Colegio San Felipe in Riobamba, where he served as minister and spiritual prefect of the community, as well as spiritual director for the students and members of the parish. He was also appointed director of the Apostleship of Prayer.

Emilio won the affection of the people. He was mild, wise, and kind. José María Velasco, dean of the cathedral, said of him: "His friendly appearance,

Symbolic representation of the sacrilege committed by the liberal militia by destroying the tabernacle in the chapel of the college, then by assassinating the blessed Emilio Moscoso (who was actually killed in his room). Mural by Gerardo Astudillo (1944).

his gentle gaze, modest air, and sweet words captivated my soul. His attractive and delicate figure revealed a paternal and discreet heart. With what affability and delicacy did he attend to the student youth! His countenance, all smile and peace, fostered and maintained an atmosphere of joy and love." Another person conveyed: "Father Moscoso was one of those personalities that spread goodness, that won your sympathy through purity of heart."

On September 12, 1892, he was named vice-rector of the school, but he did not feel fit to carry out this assignment. He did not believe he possessed the necessary constitutional character; moreover, the stresses harmed his health considerably. Therefore, on December 17, he petitioned the Jesuit superior general Luis Martín to relieve him from this mission, "which I consider and have always considered disproportionate to my strengths, as I suffer frequently from my head and stomach, and I also do not have sufficient prudence and strength of mind." Father General dismissed his request.

Toward Martyrdom

In Ecuador, the Church was going through a very difficult period. Ecuador had been officially declared a Catholic country in 1862 by President Gabriel García Moreno (1821–75), but in 1875, Moreno was assassinated. A very long period of instability followed. A liberal revolution was breaking through, with a strongly anti-religious spirit. In 1877, the bishop of Quito, José Ignacio Checa y Barba, was assassinated. On January 17, 1895, Father Moscoso informed Rome of all that was happening. On the seventeenth of the following May, Father General answered with these words of praise: "I cannot be but pleased with Your Reverence, because you were found worthy to be the instrument of the divine goodness for the restoration of the discipline and of the religious spirit of this school." But the violence continued to increase. On June 5, 1895, General Eloy Alfaro (1842–1912) led a military uprising of the Liberals. After a few months of battle, on September 4, they took control of power.

Father Lorenzo Sanvicente, superior of the Jesuit mission of Ecuador, made his canonical visit to the community of the Colegio San Felipe from January 10–26, 1896. He had written that he thought the vice-rector "too soft" in leadership, but he did not think it necessary to replace him. For his part, Father Emilio wrote a report to Father General making reference to the visible deterioration of the social situation.

A year later, on January 20, 1897, he again asked to be dispensed from his assignment, "because I lack the strength in body (I suffer not infrequently from my head and my stomach) as well as in mind to fulfill well all the duties of such great importance." The awareness of his weakness makes even more appreciable the spiritual integrity with which Emilio faced his last days before his martyrdom.

On April 27, the bishop of Riobamba, Arsenio Andrade, was detained, and only released on May 1. On May 2, a Sunday, the military presented themselves at the Colegio San Felipe and in a very violent manner detained in a barracks all the Jesuits who were in the residence. Father Moscoso was outside of the house when this occurred, and when he returned, some people pressed him to flee. He answered confidently that he had no reason to fear prison and exile. He went to the capital to ask for the release of his companions, but it was not granted. The people of Riobamba were furious when they heard what had happened and went out to protest. This resulted in the release of most of the detained Jesuits.

Meanwhile, a group of Catholic Ecuadorians organized an uprising against the Liberal government. In the early morning of May 4, 1897, some of these revolutionary leaders arrived at Riobamba and took refuge in the Jesuit college without the fathers noticing it. Shortly after, at six in the morning, Liberal troops began the siege of the Colegio San Felipe. An hour later, the troops violently broke into the school and detained the subversives.

The commander ordered his men to search for the Jesuits and terminate them. Father Emilio locked himself in his room to pray. The military captains Santos Manzanilla and Luis Soto arrived at his room and found him with a rosary in his hand praying before a crucifix. They shot him dead and put in his arms the rifle with which he was killed, to make it seem like there had been a combative confrontation (which was later denied by direct witnesses). Other Liberal troops then arrived and looted his belongings. One soldier wanted to tie his corpse to the halter of a horse to drag Moscoso through the streets, but the people prevented this.

After the death of Father Moscoso, the soldiers sacked the school, profaned the church, and maltreated the other Jesuits, but none of them was killed. The martyr's body was brought to the hospital. Very soon, the expressions of deep pain for his death were transformed into manifestations of joy for his fidelity.

Throughout the country, the Church multiplied acts of Eucharistic reparation. That same year, the Congregation of the Franciscan Missionary Sisters of the Immaculate Conception came into existence, devoted to prayer and Eucharistic reparation; it participated actively in the promotion of the cause for canonization of Father Moscoso. On the fiftieth anniversary of his death, the "Colegio San Felipe" was restored and the remains of the martyr were transferred there.

Jaime Castellón, SJ[56]

Emilio Moscoso was beatified in Riobamba on November 16, 2019, by the cardinal prefect of the Congregation for the Causes of the Saints. The following day in the Vatican, Pope Francis prayed "that his example as a humble religious, apostle of prayer, and educator of youth may sustain our journey of faith and Christian witness."

---

56. Translation by Philip Cooley, SJ.

From a Letter of Superior General Arturo Sosa

The simple life and brave martyrdom of this brother of ours, Emilio Moscoso, teaches us many lessons: the joy and austerity of his dedication; his deep devotion to the Eucharist and to Mary; his witness of poverty and obedience as he faithfully fulfilled his daily obligations; the simple and orderly community life of his day; his bravery in defending the faith and the Church; his steadfast solidarity with the citizens of Riobamba, as he remained with them in the most difficult times; his care for the body of the Society, evident from his visits of his companions in prison and his return to the college to share the fate of his community.

After many years dedicated to teaching and to the apostolate of prayer, Emilio Moscoso came face to face with persecution. A few years ago, General Congregation 36 desired to address a special message to Jesuits working in zones of war and conflict. Calling to mind the martyrdom of Father Moscoso and many other companions of times past and present, the letter read: "The struggle for justice, peace, and reconciliation brings us back to our Jesuit roots in the Formula of the Institute. It has been reiterated in recent general congregations and is as relevant —and as urgent—today as it was when our first companions founded the Society of Jesus. This mission is at the frontier of war and peace, it is a mission that touches us all whether we are Jesuit novices, scholastics, brothers, priests ..."

On the occasion of the beatification of our brother, I desire that all of us, strengthened by the Eucharist as he was, may show ourselves to be in solidarity with those living with conflict, especially with the most vulnerable and disregarded of our society.

Letter of November 8, 2019 on the beatification of Emilio Moscoso

Blessed Miguel Agustín Pro (1891–1927)

"MARTYR OF CHRIST THE KING"

Optional Memorial on November 23

Jesus at the Last Supper said to the disciples who were ready to abandon him during his Passion, "No one has greater love than this, that he lays down his life for his friends." Centuries later in Mexico, Jesus met friends who did indeed lay down their lives for him. One of these was Miguel Agustín Pro, a Mexican Jesuit who died with his arms extended in the form of a cross like his Savior. And like him, too, Pro was shamed and publicly executed by the powerful of this world.

Since his death on November 23, 1927, Miguel Agustín Pro has earned the great admiration of the Catholics of his country and of many countries in the world, especially where the Church does not enjoy freedom. For he was shot during a period of religious persecution, out of hate for the Catholic faith, and for priests.

His Crime: Being a Priest

Miguel Agustín was born in Guadalupe, Zacatecas, in 1891. At twenty, he entered the Society of Jesus at the novitiate in El Llano, Michoacán. In 1914, disguised as a cowboy, he fled his country and went to the United States, to Los Gatos, California, to continue his novitiate. The rest of his priestly studies, outlawed in Mexico, he did in Spain, Nicaragua, and Belgium. He was ordained a priest in Belgium on August, 30, 1925, and then the following July returned to his country, just as churches were closing in protest against the laws of persecution passed by the Mexican government of that time.

Father Pro set himself to comforting persecuted Catholics. He celebrated Mass in homes where he inspired everyone. On his bicycle, he rode around

Mexico City distributing communion to hundreds. He preached to groups of students, to workers, to domestic help, to clerks, and construction workers. He helped them all to persevere in their Christian faith, and with his contagious good humor he invited everyone to believe in Jesus Christ and in his message of love and true liberty. Even though he was working in secret, little by little he became known to the police. Without ever having seen him, they disapproved of his priestly work, which by then was prohibited by law. His crime was to be a priest and to dedicate himself to baptizing, to pardoning in the name of God, and to bringing moral and material help to many poor families. Miguel Agustín asked his friends to pray that Christ the King would give him the grace of martyrdom. "My life. What's it for? Wouldn't I really be gaining it if I gave it for my brothers?" he asked, knowing all the time that his priestly activity was very necessary for Catholics deprived of bishops and priests. For that reason, he never exposed himself to capture. On the contrary, his tremendous ingenuity kept finding ways to evade those who were looking for him. Disguised as a mechanic, as an office worker, or as a beggar, he managed to find his way into every possible quarter of the city.

His One Preference: The Neediest People

Those were years of armed resistance, in the western part of the country, against a tyrannical government. Many Catholics took up arms to defend their right to believe. Miguel Agustín viewed these rebels sympathetically, but he was of the conviction that his priestly state would not permit him either to take up arms or to foster the rebellion, though he considered it legitimate.

He worked for a year and a half in Mexico City. He helped and supported many single mothers in the face of criticism and misunderstanding, bringing them material and moral help at the Good Shepherd Home. He did the same thing for women who were trying to reform their lives. Because his days were completely filled with activity, Father Pro passed long hours of the night in prayer. He kept up, at the same time, an enormous correspondence with people who were asking for his counsel and direction. In the one winter he passed in Mexico City, that of 1926–27, he suffered frequently from the cold because he kept giving away even essential clothing to the poor whom he met. If he had any preference, it was for the neediest people, those who had no food, no clothes, and those who lacked understanding, affection, and human warmth.

The banner bears the famous last words of Blessed Father Miguel Pro: "Long live Christ the King!" Painting by Raúl Berzosa (2017).

Every poor person, everyone in need, was the object of Miguel Agustín's attention; he was the Good Samaritan on a bicycle!

Reading his letters, one finds some filled with humor and sprinkled with Mexican slang, others profound and very personal. In these, he constantly expresses his desire to give his life for Christ the King. "I want to die, repudiated, like Christ ... but I do not deserve this grace." Someone asked him: "What would you do if the government arrested you to kill you?" His response: "I would ask to be able to kneel, have time to make an *Act of Contrition*, and die with my arms stretched out like a cross, crying "Long live Christ the King!"

His Prayer Heard

On November 13, 1927, a group of young men who opposed the anti-religious policies of the government tried to assassinate General Álvaro Obregón, a former president and an important leader who had fought the attempt at blocking a second term and so was seeking re-election as the president of a tyrannical government. The attempt on the general failed, and in its search for those responsible for it the government jailed many innocent people, as often happens. Among those were the three Pro brothers: Roberto, Umberto, and Miguel Agustín.

Even though the police and the government knew from the outset that the three brothers were absolutely innocent, they were not going to bypass the opportunity to take revenge on a rebellious priest. He was rebellious precisely because he was exercising his priesthood, not in church as the government demanded, but clandestinely. This was his crime, to celebrate Mass, hear confessions, distribute communion, and give material help to the poor. Evidently, had he been guilty of the assassination attempt against Obregón, the government would have given him a public trial as a way of lessening respect for the Church and its priests. It could not accuse him of guilt because he was not guilty. But it could teach a lesson by the death of someone innocent.

Precisely in order to prevent his innocence from being recognized, they decided to shoot Father Pro without any trial. Moreover, they moved up the hour of execution in order to avoid any legal maneuver in favor of his innocence.

On November 23, 1927, at about ten in the morning, a police official went down to the cells where he was. "Miguel Agustín Pro," he demanded. "Here I am," the priest answered. "Follow me." Miguel Pro took his bag, and his brother Roberto, ever hopeful, said to him, "Now they're going to let us go." "No, we will see each other in heaven. They're going to shoot me." On the patio of the police headquarters, the government had called journalists, photographers, and a number of others to see how it punished a priest. Between the door of the cells and the wall of execution, the official who had arrested him asked his pardon. "I not only pardon you, I thank you," Miguel answered. He was shaken looking at his executioners, but happy that God would hear his prayer. "Would that I might have the good fortune to be counted among the martyrs!" Miguel had said to his friends. He asked for a minute to recollect himself. He knelt, and then he stood and grasped his crucifix with one hand, holding his rosary in the other. He refused to allow them to blindfold him. He found the strength to shout, "Long live Christ the King!" The fuselage of shots brought him down. An official with a pistol gave him the *coup de grâce*.

The Homage of the Church

One unmistakable characteristic of the saint is that a tremendous number of persons, groups, and communities of various kinds know him. Moreover, people are interested in the smallest details of his life: they want to be on an intimate footing with him. This is one way, often surprisingly, that the deep love for others that moved him during life becomes apparent. Father Pro's tomb in the Temple of Sorrows was always covered with flowers and written messages, in which people of all walks of life sought his intercession with the Lord. When his remains were transferred to the Church of the Holy Family, they continued to attract flowers and supplications.

Moreover, on the twenty-third of each month, the anniversary of his death, numerous needy families have come together, uninterruptedly over the years, to receive a gift of food. That is exactly what Father Pro had done for families who had been impoverished by the religious persecution in that conflictive era of the revolutionary government.

Sixty-one years later, the Catholic Church announced to its members, spread across the five continents, that Miguel Agustín Pro was a martyr of Christ the King. Pope John Paul II affirmed that the young Jesuit is a model for our times, when so many in the world believe in no one and nothing and resist any kind of commitment. He is a priest who is attractive because he models a love of life, sincerity, selfless response to everyone's needs, and love for Jesus Christ and for every human being.

Elías Basila, SJ[57]

On September 25, 1988, in Saint Peter's Square, Miguel Agustín Pro was declared a martyr and blessed by Pope John Paul II.

From a Letter of Blessed Miguel Pro

This something that I find within me and I had never felt before, which makes me view everything differently, is not the fruit of study or our own greater or lesser holiness, or anything personal and hence human. It is the divine mark the Holy Spirit imprints on the soul when he gives us the priestly character. It is a closer participation in the divine life that raises us to divine dignity. It is a superior power that renders easy and accessible the wishes and aspirations we might not have fulfilled before.

I did not notice this change until I found myself in touch with souls ... God our Lord chose to use me as his instrument to do good. How many souls I consoled, how many tears I wiped, how much courage I infused to walk the difficult road of life! Two vocations that were almost lost returned to God; a seminarian who had decided to give up is now following the designs of Providence with new strength. And is it not crystal clear that whatever good I happened to accomplish was all due to the grace of the priesthood, to the Holy Spirit, who was guiding and governing me, to that something that was nothing human and that I had not felt before the day I was ordained?

Liturgy of the Hours, Second Reading on November 23

---

57. Jesuits, *Yearbook of the Society of Jesus* (Rome, 1989), 10–13.

Blessed Rutilio Grande and His Two Companions

(✝1977)

Optional Memorial on November 23

Rutilio Grande was born in El Paisnal (El Salvador) on July 5, 1928. In 1941, he entered the minor seminary of San Salvador and joined the Society of Jesus in Venezuela in 1945. As a Jesuit, he studied the humanities, philosophy, theology, and pastoral ministry at schools in Quito, Oña (Spain), Paris, Córdoba (Spain), and Brussels. He was ordained to the priesthood in Oña on July 30, 1959, and professed final vows on August 15, 1964 in Brussels.

Rutilio experienced intimately the weaknesses of the human condition. He endured two serious nervous breakdowns, likely associated with infantile trauma. The first attack, which was the most severe, limited much of his ability to study and to serve in the apostolate. His desire for perfection and to be in the good graces of all became an obsession. For Rutilio, life was an ultimatum of "all or nothing." On various occasions, he questioned his priestly vocation, the very thing he loved most. According to his own testimony, in times of darkness and uncertainty, he always placed himself in the hands of God.

Formator of the Clergy

In 1951, he began working in the formation of the Salvadoran clergy. His superiors missioned him to the national seminary because they saw in him a hard-working and responsible Jesuit, of right judgment and of great pedagogical ability. In 1971, he became the prefect of the seminary, a position in which he proved to be both a challenging and understanding leader. He did not want seminarians who were overly submissive to authority, but rather those that

"The Great Amen": Saint Óscar Romero (1917–80), Archbishop of San Salvador, raises the consecrated host, assisted by Blessed Rutilio Grande, SJ, who preceded him in martyrdom and here raises the chalice with the Blood of Christ. Painting by Peter Bridgman (2018).

were responsible and mature. He would severely admonish his seminarians, but also tenderly care for them with discreet charity. Thus was born a close, strong, and intimate bond with the diocesan clergy. Later on, many priests would seek him out for assistance.

Rutilio aspired to form priests for the service of the people, not just to be clerical chieftains. For this reason, he made an effort to open the seminary to the reality of El Salvador. The seminarians had to leave the comfort of their residence and the outside reality had to enter their classrooms and corridors so that they could discover the people from whom they came and to whom they were going to serve. With similar determination, he desired to introduce the spirit of Vatican II and its Latin American interpretation, the Conference of Medellín. Rutilio worked earnestly to have the Salvadoran Church accept both of these teaching authorities. The reception of this created a serious ecclesial crisis, which frightened many, especially the episcopate.

Aguilares: The Experiment of Rural Evangelization

Faithfulness to the teachings of Vatican II and of Medellín exacted a high cost. The bishops of El Salvador did not permit Rutilio to reform the seminary, nor did they approve of his candidacy for rector, first proposed by the Society of Jesus in 1970. Since he did not enjoy the confidence of the bishops, Rutilio left the seminary and moved on to a traditional Jesuit high school and also to an intensive pastoral experiment in Ecuador. In September 1972, he arrived at his home parish of Aguilares in El Salvador. Here he dedicated the last four years of his life to proclaiming the Gospel among the rural farmers.

Rutilio's preaching was incisive and opportune. He announced the justice of the reign of God and performed the works of that kingdom in a reality dominated by economic exploitation, social oppression, and state hegemony. He denounced injustice and the oppression of the Salvadoran people. Inspired by Vatican II, Medellín, and the encyclical *Evangelii nuntiandi*, Rutilio labored to construct a Church that would truly meet the conciliar definition of "the people of God."

In Aguilares, Rutilio and his missionary team promoted the creation of small active faith communities, which were in constant dialogue with the local parish. The first task consisted in invigorating popular religiosity. The missionaries relied less on the distribution of sacraments, which highlighted the need for ordained ministers, and instead focused more on the dynamic Word of God that emphasized the Good News of liberation. The Gospel had to become more accessible to all to create community, according to God's plan, without oppressor or oppressed.

These evangelization efforts also took on a prophetic dimension. Rutilio denounced the exploiter and reminded the exploited of their dignity. He called the former to repentance and conversion, and to the latter he preached the Word of God that had long been denied to them. Eventually, the rural farmers discovered that they had something valuable to say and something important to do. Rutilio invited them to assume their Christian responsibility in bringing about a societal transformation. Newly liberated men and women would emerge throughout this process of personal and community rebirth.

From the heart of the Christian communities emerged numerous agents of pastoral ministry. In a short period of time, these people, especially the women, would determine the dynamic of the entire parish. Rutilio dreamed of such a parish where the priest would concentrate on the aspects of ordained ministry with an empowered laity collaborating to meet the remaining needs of the church community. He did not have false illusions concerning the efficacy of his labors, however. Toward the end of his life, Rutilio knew that the majority of the parish was still immersed in magical ritualism, oblivious to reality.

The Relationship between Faith and Politics

The prophetic dimension of Rutilio's preaching heightened political tension. The rural farmers discovered the efficacy of organizing in order to reclaim their labor, social, and political rights. The most invested leaders of the communities, galvanized by their Christian commitment, became even more active in political organizing. The transformation of these agents of pastoral ministry into political leaders perturbed Rutilio immensely. He had foreseen this level of political engagement but expected it in an intermediate timeframe. The harsh context of Aguilares brought about this political crisis almost at the same time as the renewal of the Christian community.

Rutilio strove to maintain the difference between the parish's activities from those of the political activists. However, the latter sought to subordinate pastoral ministry to their own agenda, to which Rutilio responded: "We cannot wed ourselves to political groups of any kind." This difference in perspective provoked confrontations between the leaders of the Christian communities and the activists, the most valued and appreciated people in the parish. Another source of disagreement was the prudence with which Rutilio repeatedly asked the organizers, enthusiastic with their many early successes, to temper their operations due to his fear of military repression. This fear was not without reason. Concerns over the behavior of the political activists manifested themselves weeks after the assassination of Rutilio when the military invaded the parish. In any case, despite the internal differences and the signaling of the military, which considered him a political agitator, Rutilio always defended the rural poor: "We cannot remain indifferent to the politics of the common good and of the great majority of Salvadorans ... We cannot become disinterested in this now or ever."[58] Consequently, from the outside, he was perceived to be the leader of a social movement that threatened to destabilize the country's decade-old oligarchic order.

Rutilio's Martyrdom and Óscar Romero

The complexities of parish work and the growing attacks on "subversive" rural farmers made Rutilio question whether he should continue in his ministry. In 1976, he attempted to resign from his work, but the people would not accept it. Rutilio did not abandon the parish, despite the threats. He remained there with Manuel Solórzano, his inseparable, seventy-two year-old companion. On March 12, 1977, the two of them were driving to El Paisnal to continue the celebration of the novena to Saint Joseph, the patron saint of the village. On the way there, they picked up Nelson Rutilio Lemus, a sixteen year-old youth, another dear collaborator in El Paisnal. The three were assassinated by a military "death squad" encamped along a roadside creek. Upon investigation of the attack, it appeared that Manuel had attempted to shield Rutilio with his body from the gunshots.

Despite the criticisms and accusations against Rutilio, Bishop Óscar Romero explicitly approved of his preaching and pastoral legacy, which he defined as a "glimpse of God, and from looking at God, seeing one's neighbor as a

---

58. Rutilio Grande, *Navidad Campesina*, Aguilares, December 21, 1975. Archivo Centroamericano de la Compañía de Jesús, San Salvador.

brother," and as "constructing a way of life according to the heart of God."[59]

Rutilio and Óscar Romero cultivated a loving friendship, although not free from painful disagreements. It was often said—to the point of becoming a local tradition—that Romero had been converted immediately following Rutilio's assassination. Some voices, although rather few, said that the transformation of Archbishop Romero was a posthumous miracle of Rutilio, but this interpretation was not accepted until Pope Francis affirmed that "the great miracle" of Rutilio is Archbishop Romero. Rutilio did indeed prepare the way that Romero was beginning to travel. He formed various generations of priests, spread and defended the Church teachings of Rome and Latin America and put them into practice. On the first anniversary of his martyrdom, Romero pointed to Rutilio as "the model that must be followed."[60]

Rutilio was a priest and a Jesuit of unsuspected human and religious brilliance. In his weaknesses, he found his greatest strengths. Most of his life was spent in silence. He was not an outstanding student, nor was he noted for his leadership among the Jesuits. At times, Rutilio was even the victim of disparagement among his superiors and companions. However, those who interacted with him found in him a close friend who was service-oriented and full of goodness. The seminarians and clergy that knew him revered him as a formator; a compassionate and amiable counselor who was also firm and challenging. The rural farmers, too, found in him a close, selfless, and loving priest. In the words of Óscar Romero: "We know that in him pulsed the Spirit of the Lord."[61]

Rodolfo Cardenal, SJ[62]

On February 21, 2020, Pope Francis recognized the martyrdom of Rutilio Grande and signed the decree for his beatification. He will be solemnly declared a blessed at a Mass that will be celebrated in El Salvador in 2020.

---

59. Óscar A. Romero, *Homilías* (San Salvador, 2005), 1:31, March 14, 1977.
60. Ibid., 2:322, El Paisnal, March 5, 1978.
61. Ibid., 326, El Paisnal, March 5, 1978.
62. Translation by Philip Cooley, SJ.

Love, the Code of the Kingdom! It is the only key word that sums all the ethical codes of humankind; it elevates them and unites them into Jesus. It is the love of a shared brotherhood that breaks down and destroys all types of barriers, prejudice, and must overcome hatred itself.

Blessed Rutilio Grande

Saint José Maria Rubio (1864–1929)

"THE APOSTLE OF MADRID"

Optional Memorial on May 4

Born at Dalías (Almería, Spain) in 1864, José Maria Rubio entered the seminary while still a boy. He was ordained a priest in 1887 and exercised his ministry at the Madrid parishes of Chinchón and Estremera before being appointed as professor in the Madrid seminary and as diocesan notary. In 1906, he could finally enter the Society of Jesus. In 1911, after finishing his formation, he was appointed as "apostolic worker" to the professed house in Madrid where he would spend the rest of his life, dedicating himself wholeheartedly to the ministry of preaching, spiritual guidance, and hearing confessions. He was the father of the poor and dispossessed and trained a large number of lay apostles so that the needs of the poor could be met more efficaciously. He died in 1929 at Aranjuez, just south of Madrid.

A Paradoxical Saint

Father Rubio escapes the categories that are used to pigeon-hole Jesuits—supposedly erudite and brilliant—and yet for all his simplicity he has more than his share of the paradoxical. Here was someone who was a diocesan priest and also a Jesuit; a man of the provinces and also the apostle of the capital of Spain; timid and famous; weak and strong; devoid of human attraction and capable of drawing large masses; a silent man and at the same time a great preacher; a fun-loving Andalusian by birth and yet an austere Castilian by adoption; someone needing direction from others and yet incredibly daring in his apostolic enterprises; an invalid all his life and a tireless worker until his death; adorned with university titles, yet thought to be an ignoramus; unnoticed and a miracle-worker; both very active, and a great contemplative and mystic; marked by the typical piety and traditional theology of his time and simultaneously a pioneer in his social consciousness and commitment to the poor.

The Tireless Invalid

A tall man, with penetrating, deep-set eyes beneath a broad forehead that gave him a mysterious look; a timid smile on his lips, as if he were constantly apologizing for something, yet in contrast an athletic jaw that seemed out of place with his slightly melancholic, yet very kindly and unpretentious appearance. Probably even today José Maria Rubio would pass unnoticed among us, given the peculiar way in which he could be near and at the same time floating above things: he was centered in his inner being, radiating peace, pointing out the best path, speaking the right word, and seeking at every moment the truth, his truth, the truth that he always called "the will of God."

His face suggests firmness, and yet despite this appearance José Maria was a fragile, weak person, as his health showed. Already, when living in Almería in 1875, he suffered from the cold in the venerable, desolate corridors of the seminary. Curiously enough, this would lead to a deep friendship with the man, Canon Joaquín Torres Asensio, who became his patron: on one occasion, while he was in the seminary of Granada, Canon Joaquín noticed that the young Rubio was spitting blood. This physical weakness would trouble him all his life. He was a man who never looked after himself. On the contrary, he always worked beyond the limits of his strength. He would rise very early in the morning, and retire late at night, to give himself extra time for prayer. Often he forgot to take any breakfast. Canon Joaquín had literally to drag him out of the confessional. He ate little, and in the process of canonization the curious fact emerged that although Father Rubio was fond of fried eggs for a meal, he spent fourteen years without them because the person in charge disliked them. Later, when he became a Jesuit, the brother sacristan would bring a cup of coffee for him, only to find later that it had gone cold or been given to someone in need. Father Rubio, when giving the *Spiritual Exercises*, was happy to pick up the scraps of bread left behind on the table by others for his meals. Moreover, he practiced severe penances, especially as a young priest; in Chinchón and Estremera, they used to wash his blood-stained underwear separately, thinking that he might be suffering from some illness. Later as a Jesuit he came to redirect his penitential inclinations to the love and service of others.

Both his provincial, Father Valera, and his superior, Alfonso Torres, frequently told José Maria's brother, Serafín, that as a Jesuit he overworked himself: "We take away some of his work in one area, and he goes and finds more work in another!" Once when he was seriously ill, some people came to fetch him, so that he could hear the final confession of his friend, the count of Grove. Father Torres said that in his present state he could not go, but Rubio begged to be allowed as the count was his regular penitent. "All right, off you go, and may you both die!" exclaimed Torres. And in the end, that was what happened as eventually Father Rubio died of exhaustion and repeated attacks of angina.

The Strength of the Weak

This physical weakness mirrored the fragility of a delicate inner spirit, which nevertheless had a great depth and tenacious strength. From childhood, this was the inner human support for a life of self-giving and prayer. Psychologically, he comes across as a man who felt lost in the world, and once this is grasped several episodes in his life become more meaningful. For example, he seems to have been enormously dependent on Canon Joaquín Torres, to the point that, while Torres was living, he never broke away from him to follow his vocation as a Jesuit, even though he always felt that to be a Jesuit was where his inclination lay. He mentioned his wish to be a Jesuit to many friends, and he chose to celebrate his first Mass at the altar where Saint Aloysius Gonzaga first felt his vocation to the Society. On two occasions, while his patron was still alive, he felt an overwhelming inclination to enter the Jesuit novitiate, but on both occasions he held back.

However, this very fragility and psychological indecisiveness would become his greatest strength. At the death of Canon Joaquín, in 1906, José Maria was already forty-two years of age, and he experienced a period of doubt and darkness. He looked for support from another friend, Carlos Manuel y Villameriel, who loved him like a brother; he would later die in extreme poverty, but with a reputation of great holiness. Eventually Rubio made up his mind to become a Jesuit, and told his mother, who broke into tears. Another of her sons, Serafín, consoled her with the words, "Don't cry, mother! Let him join the Jesuits; he's always needed somebody to give him orders. Otherwise he'll be eaten alive!"

The secret of Father Rubio's sanctity sprang precisely from his psycholog-

Saint José Maria Rubio stands in front of the statue of the Sacred Heart that adorns the facade of the Church of Saint Francis Borgia in Madrid (Spain), in which he exercised his priestly ministry. The light that radiates from the Heart of Jesus also shines from within Rubio's cassock. Icon of Francisca Leighton Munizaga (between 2000 and 2015).

ical limitations, as these were balanced by a will of iron and an extraordinary inner coherence. First, there was his humility: he thought of himself as so childlike that he recognized throughout his life that the most important thing for him is to do the will of God. "To do what God wants; to want what God does!" All his spiritual evolution would be one of progressive interior emptying of self. This was his advice to others: "Empty yourself, and then God will work wonders in you!" Second, the principle of availability: he always had time for others, and none for himself. The queues at his confessional were endless, and his dedication to those in need was absolute.

There is another facet of Father Rubio's character that is all too little known: he had a wonderful sense of humour. Even as a child and while a boy at the seminary, he had an unusual gift for telling stories and recounting incidents. This led to his being sent, while a seminarian, as a "reporter" to the local bullfights: Canon Joaquín could not go in person, as clerics of his rank were forbidden to attend spectacles, but he was happy to have the young Rubio report in detail all that had happened. On other occasions, his Andalusian sense of fun stood him in good stead. Once, when it was raining, he was offered a lift in a car: "No, thank you," he said, "I prefer to walk: a Jesuit has to 'get wet'" (a word-play in Spanish as *"mojarse"* means "to take a risk" or "to get involved"). To counterbalance the picture of a harsh ascetic, his letters home reveal a man full of affection, who never forgot his family. Again the testimony of those who met him in his pastoral work reveals his flexibility; he was convinced that God had a special path for each individual. A favorite saying of his was: "More are attracted by a drop of honey than by a thousand liters of vinegar!"

"A Man for Others"

A mention of Father Rubio's death cannot be omitted from this brief overview. It is said that a person's death is a summary and the kernel of one's life, and that is how Ignatius considered the death of a Jesuit should be. José Maria Rubio died in the novitiate in Aranjuez in 1929. He was sitting in a wicker chair, he was alert, he had just torn up his spiritual notes and put them in his biretta —out of a sense of humility (so that none would know the kindness that God had shown him), and he had turned his eyes to heaven. He died consciously, as he had himself foretold, after having bade farewell to his friends, putting himself into the hands of God's will, as he had lived all his life, and bowing his head, just as Jesus had done on the cross. He left a message of simplicity and hope. Even in his death, Father Rubio, worn out by becoming "a man for others," took on a shining brightness and put the finishing touches to the true picture of himself: here was finally a mystic who allowed the fire of God to take over his whole being, so that he could live and die, "like a burning lamp."

Pedro Miguel Lamet, SJ[63]

José Maria Rubio was beatified by John Paul II in 1985, and canonized by the same pope on May 4, 2003, in Madrid.

---

63. Jesuits, *Yearbook of the Society of Jesus* (Rome, 2004), 10–18 (abridged). Translation by Joseph Munitiz, SJ.

From a Letter of Superior General Peter-Hans Kolvenbach

Trained in the school of the *Spiritual Exercises*, Father Rubio made use of the sacramental ministry to lead men and women to a genuine conversion and to order their lives according to God. His assiduous and enlightened spiritual direction possessed truly extraordinary characteristics. For him who was a man of prayer as well as a teacher of prayer, to reconcile oneself with God meant genuinely to take on in one's everyday, personal, social, and ecclesial life those attitudes and conduct of a true Christian that bring one to the ultimate demands of faith and love for others, particularly the most needy. In this authentic way, Father Rubio formed committed lay Christians.

Moreover, in his ministry there stood out, forcefully and to an extraordinary degree, that dimension that we today call "the preferential option for the poor," lived and carried out with exemplary zeal. The outlying districts of Madrid were the field of his apostolic and charitable action, where he himself worked and where he brought the people whom he guided and directed for their own apostolic work. There he searched out and helped the most needy: young boys and girls, recently arrived in the city from the countryside, who lacked means of livelihood and were easy prey to exploitation; poor children in need of care and instruction; jobless fathers of families; junk dealers, gypsies ... All were objects of his attention, his solicitude, and his apostolic charity in which he involved those laypersons whom he had formed as Christian for the service of others.

In this manner, this Jesuit of our century presents himself to us, drawing our attention to the needs and tasks that we are called to confront with particular urgency: "to strive, personally and communally, toward an even greater integration of our spiritual life and apostolate" (GC 33, d. 1, 11); the formation of a truly apostolic laity through the communication of our spirituality (ibid., 47); the preferential love for the poor, which spurred and crowned his apostolic action among all kinds of persons (ibid., 48). Rightly has it been said of him that "with his deep interior life, and with his preaching of faith and justice, he anticipated our times."

Letter of September 8, 1985, to the whole Society, on the beatification of José Maria Rubio

Blessed Rupert Mayer (1876–1945)

Optional Memorial on November 3

Historical Context

Rupert Mayer was born in 1876 and died in 1945. What an ominous, tragic period in German history! Although for young people today this period of history may seem to have been a long time ago, in reality it is recent history. There are still people in Munich who remember seeing and hearing Father Mayer when in 1945 he returned to Munich from his forced monastic exile in the Benedictine Abbey of Ettal.

Rupert was born under Bismarck five years after the unification of Germany, followed by Germany's victory over France in the Franco-Prussian War of 1870. In his early years, the fall of Bismarck and the rise of the autocratic regime of Kaiser Wilhelm II occurred. He lived through the First World War, the subsequent financial collapse of the German economy in the early years of the Weimar Republic, the growing power of the Nazi Party under Hitler, and the horrors of the Second World War, which led to the division of Germany and the Russian dictatorship in East Germany. To better understand the meaning of Rupert Mayer's life, it is necessary to have an understanding of the turbulent times in which he lived. Europe, and the world, had never seen upheavals on such a scale.

It should be borne in mind that the seeds of the Second World War were sown during the First World War and that the seeds of the First World War were sown during the Franco-Prussian War of 1870. It should also be remembered that, understandably, France thirsted for retaliation after the humiliation of 1870 and the loss of the two regions of Alsace and Lorraine. Especially during the ten years before the outbreak of World War I in 1914, Europe resembled a powder keg that could explode at any time. The main European states, France, Germany, Russia, and England, were in intense competition militarily and economically. Most modern historians consider the terms of the 1919 Treaty of Versailles to have been overly harsh on Germany and Austria, which viewed the treaty as a humiliation.

The reparations imposed on Germany served only to weaken the German economy, the largest in Europe, a catastrophe that paved the way for Hitler's rise. It was at the start of this turbulent period that Father Mayer began his apostolate in Munich, an apostolate that lasted for thirty-three years, interrupted only by the First and Second World Wars.

So much for the historical context.

Rupert Mayer's Reaction to Hitler's Rise

The German people were confused and disillusioned in 1919. Their emperor had abdicated and fled the country. The parliament in Berlin, not really a democratic one, was "volatile," to put it mildly. There was anarchy on the streets of the big cities, especially in the capital Berlin. The political spectrum ranged from extreme communists and socialists to far-right groups who fought for power. We should also remember that Germany had only been a united state since 1871. It had no democratic tradition or history. From this chaos arose the well-intentioned but weak Weimar Republic. It lasted from 1919 to 1933, when Hitler became Reich Chancellor.

From his room in the Jesuit residence behind Saint Michael's Church, right in the centre of Munich, Rupert Mayer thought a lot about what he saw as his apostolic mission for the people of Munich. He had given everything in the previous four years as a chaplain in the army, risked his life, on the front line and suffered terrible injuries. These injuries led to the loss of his left leg as he tried to provide spiritual assistance to the soldiers in the heat of battle. By a special act of providence, he had survived the war; he would not now let his weakened condition impede his efforts to bring Christ to the people of Munich.

In the face of the political upheaval in Munich, Father Mayer felt obliged to keep an open mind regarding all the new ideas for political development. He made it his practice to listen to as many potential political leaders as possible, including Hitler, because he realized that a political change was coming. He wanted to be in a position to give his parishioners good, reasonable advice on which political group they could join. He sought to find out which groups were pursuing which political program. It will not come as a surprise that, while recognizing Hitler's remarkable talent as a speaker, Father Mayer realized that his ideas were contrary to Christianity. As a result, he began to criticize Nazi policies, and he quickly came under surveillance as the Nazis gained political influence.

What Can We Learn from Rupert Mayer's Life?

First of all, there is a wonderful consistency in his whole life. Even as a young boy, he tackled life with enthusiasm. He loved sports, although he was very small for his age. He trained so hard that he became one of the best athletes in his school. He loved riding and was a remarkably accomplished rider. He also had an excellent way with young people. He loved to share in their joy and could understand their problems and temptations. In fact, the reason he became known as the Apostle of Munich was because of his wonderful ability to appeal to ordinary people at their level. He was never happier than when talking to the less well-educated people from the factories and agriculture. They saw him as one of their own and they trusted him. They gathered in droves to hear him whenever he spoke. They queued to go to confession to him. Mayer never pretended to be a profound theologian or a great, learned preacher. He met the people and talked to them where they were.

One gets the clear impression that people who knew him and sought his help and advice said to themselves: "Father Rupert Mayer is one of us! He speaks our language; he knows our way of thinking. When so many of our sons fought in the trenches of the First World War, Father Mayer was there, right next to them; he shared the dangers and also their wounds. He is the type of priest I can trust when I seek help and guidance."

The Climax of Rupert Mayer's Path to Holiness

Before Father Mayer was sent to Ettal Abbey in 1940—under obedience to protect him from further persecution by the Nazis ("We don't need a martyr")—he was already a holy man. He was very close to God. But it was during these frustrating years of imposed silence and inactivity from the apostolic

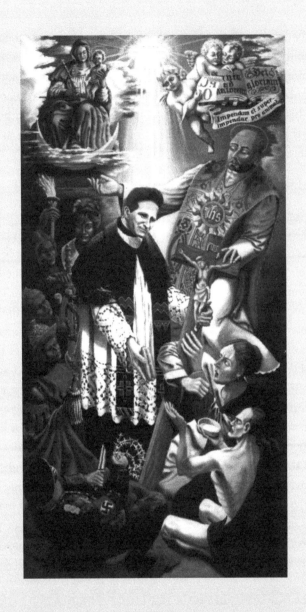

Encouraged by Saint Ignatius, Blessed Rupert Mayer offers, under the protection of the Mother of God, bread and the crucifix to the suffering people of Munich. Silhouettes symbolizing war prowl behind him and a Nazi officer threatens him with his knife and the barbed wire of the prison. In the top right corner, angels carry the Jesuit Constitutions and a banner proclaiming the words of Saint Paul: "I will be very happy to spend and to spend all of myself for you" (2 Cor. 12:15). Painting by Helmut Schwarz (1991).

front that he became a saint. He was prepared to give his life for Christian values, but God demanded of him an even harder, more subtle sacrifice. He was not allowed to preach, not allowed to hear confession, and not even allowed to speak to visitors. He retreated to prayer, deepening his relationship with God to a stage of true holiness.

Suffering is part of Christian life. God seems to have an uncanny way of asking us to accept this, but not the form of suffering that we ourselves would choose. In Mayer's case, it was not actual martyrdom but a much more difficult form of suffering, much more subtle: the sacrifice of his particular vocation as an apostle. Imagine him, the priest who continues his work as an apostle with a burning zeal, knowing how fruitful this work is, and who then is forced to withdraw from his apostolic activity in obedience. That was Father Mayer's great sacrifice.

He returned to Munich in May 1945 immediately after the end of the war to find that some people believed he had surrendered to the Nazis. His motives for obeying his superiors could be misunderstood, and during all these frustrating years in Ettal, he knew that some people were saying, "Oh, Father Mayer left Munich. He ran away to seek security in the countryside, away from the bombings. He no longer speaks against the Nazis. They scared him." Mayer became a saint, because of the way he accepted his special cross that God asked him to carry. In this context, his favorite prayer comes to mind: "Lord, let happen whatever you will; and as you will, so will I walk ..."

Peter Linster, SJ[64]

Rupert Mayer was beatified on May 3, 1987 at the Olympic Stadium in Munich by Pope John Paul II, who then visited the tomb.

---

64. Translation by Patrick Burns, SJ.

Prayer of Blessed Rupert Mayer

Lord, let happen whatever you will;
and as you will, so will I walk;
help me only to know your will!
Lord, whenever you will, then is the time;
today and always

Lord, whatever you will, I wish to accept,
and whatever you will for me is gain;
enough that I belong to you.
Lord, because you will it, it is right;
and because you will it, I have courage.
My heart rests safely in your hands!

From a Homily of Pope John Paul II

Dear brothers and sisters! The blessed and saints of the Church are God's living and lived message to us. Therefore she presents them to us *for veneration and imitation.* So let us open ourselves today to that message, which the new Blessed Rupert Mayer so vividly proclaims to us through his word and work. Like him, let us seek in God the center and source of our life. He relied on God in unshakable, childlike trust. "Lord, let happen whatever you will; and as you will, so I will walk. Help me only to know your will," is the first line of his favorite prayer. The Lord God was the source from which he drew the strength for his amazing life's work, in long hours of prayer, at Holy Mass, and in the daily faithful fulfillment of his duties.

Let us seek to shape our lives and our environment from that same source of strength. Blessed Rupert Mayer is an example and *a call for us all to live a holy life.* Holiness is not a matter for a few chosen souls: we are all called to holiness, all without exception. And he himself also tells us what belongs to a holy life: "No extraordinary work, no extraordinary religious experiences, no apparitions. Only: heroic virtue." This means: to do God's will faithfully and unwaveringly day after day and to live from his presence; each one of us personally and also in our family. We know how our Blessed was especially concerned about the *Christian family* and how, to promote it, he even founded with two other priests his own community of sisters. The high number of divorces and the low number of children show what great burdens and threats the family faces in today's society. Yet in your families the future of your people is decided, and in your people the future of the Church. Stick together, that the families may be strengthened. Keep marriage holy and let conjugal love be fruitful in the children God wants to give you.

But sanctifying one's life also means feeling *co-responsible for public life* and helping to shape it from the Spirit of Christ. No Christian can be indifferent to the way the world is going. Men, women, and my young friends, I call upon all of you: Like Rupert Mayer, stand up for God's rights and God's glory also in public. Do not let the de-Christianization continue to spread. Be salt of the earth and carry the light of God's truth into all areas of life. This is the service we owe to the world. We cannot do it without God! Following the example of our Blessed, you must above all have *a heart for the poor*. You live in a country that is one of the most prosperous in the world. Do not let your possessions blunt your heart for the needs of the needy and the forgotten on the margins of your society and throughout the world. Through your goodness, you, too, make God's love visible and tangible among your fellow men.

Homily of May 3, 1987, in Munich, at the beatification of Rupert Mayer[65]

---

65. Translation by Marc Lindeijer, SJ.

Martyrs of the Spanish Civil War

BLESSED TOMÁS SITJAR AND HIS ELEVEN COMPANIONS

(†1936)

Optional Memorial on September 2

The 233 "Martyrs of Valencia," beatified in 2001, were a small segment of the over ten thousand priests, brothers, nuns, and Catholic laypersons who suffered persecution for the faith and were killed in the Spanish Civil War (1936–39), as leftist forces attempted to wipe out what they saw as the Catholic resistance. Among those beatified were eleven Jesuits—seven priests and four brothers—who belonged to the then Aragon province of the Society of Jesus, and an important lay collaborator in the Marian sodalities. They were martyred in Gandía and Valencia between August 19 and December 29, 1936.

"We Belong to the Party of God"

The Society of Jesus was legally dissolved in Spain in 1932. The novices and those in formation, along with their professors and formators, found asylum in various European Jesuit provinces. An appreciable number of fathers and brothers continued to live dispersed and in hiding, in small apartments, carrying out their pastoral ministries under very adverse circumstances. Father Tomás Sitjar was the superior of this dispersed community.

Born in 1866, Sitjar had joined the Society at the age of fourteen in Veruela. His intellectual gifts were soon recognized: in 1890, he was sent to teach metaphysics at the seminary college of Montevideo in Uruguay after completing his course in philosophy. Health issues forced him to return to Spain in 1897 and complete his course in theology before he was ordained a priest in 1900. He was professor of metaphysics to young Jesuits for twenty-three years, till he was appointed superior at Tarragona, and then, in 1929, in Gandía.

Following the dissolution of the order in Spain in 1932, he moved to a small apartment in the city, having refused to take refuge with friends, saying: "If they kill us, then it will be God's will." His companion was Brother Pedro Gelabert (b. 1887), from Mallorca, who had served as gardener as well as electrician and carpenter.

On July 25, 1936, a group of militiamen arrested Father Sitjar in the apartment. Brother Gelabert was able to escape through a window but was eventually caught, too. They were joined in prison by Father Constantino Carbonell (b. 1886), formerly rector and minister in Jesuit institutions in Alicante, Almería, and Gandía, much appreciated for his managerial skills and his patience and kindness as a confessor and spiritual director, and by Brother Ramón Grimaltos (b. 1861), a humble and hardworking son of farmers, who had recently served in Gandía as gardener and other domestic duties.

During an interrogation, their captors asked them which party they were affiliated with. Father Sitjar replied, "We belong to the Party of God." The Jesuits were tortured, and they recognized that their fate was inevitable. At midnight on August 19, Sitjar was taken out on the pretext of being released, but about seven kilometers down the road he was executed under an olive tree. He was holding a rosary in his hand as the bullet pierced his heart. Carbonell, Grimaltos, and Gelabert were executed four days later. The two brothers fell on their knees and asked Carbonell for absolution just before they were shot.

The September Murders

After the dissolution of the order, three elderly Jesuits—a priest and two brothers—were living in retirement in a residence adjacent to a nursing home run by the Little Sisters in Valencia, where several old Jesuits were living in retirement. On August 24, 1936, a month after the Civil War erupted, the home was taken over by the communists, who brought their own staff in. They converted the chapel into a dining hall.

Brother José Tarrats (b. 1878), who had joined the Society in 1895, had worked with great dedication as a tailor in Tortosa and as infirmarian in Valencia. Brother Vicente Sales (b. 1881), from Valencia, was thirty-four when he entered the novitiate in 1915. He had spent his entire Jesuit life as a porter in Gandía. The two brothers helped the sisters in their chores. Father Pablo

On July 28, 1936, Red militiamen shot the statue of the Sacred Heart of Jesus, erected in 1919 on the Hill of Angels outside Madrid to symbolize Spain's consecration to the Sacred Heart. The Sacred Heart was the only place not hit by the bullets. Anonymous drawing from the iconic photograph taken by the militiamen (1950s).

Bori (b. 1864) had joined the Society in 1891 already ordained a priest. He had been involved with the religious instruction of Jesuit brothers. When the home's chaplain had to leave at the outbreak of the Civil War, Bori assumed his duties until the communists took over. Unable to celebrate Mass, he went on comforting the sick and hearing confessions. Most importantly, he served as the spiritual director of the Jesuits in dispersion.

These three Jesuits managed to go about their work without the communists knowing who they were until September 28, when Tarrats's identity was denounced. He and three other infirmary staff were taken to Rambleta, on the outskirts of Valencia, and executed. Bori and Sales were arrested the following day and executed near a secluded cemetery called Picadero de Paterna. Bori asked the soldiers: "Which of you are going to kill me?" When they indicated the men, he said: "In the name of that God for whom you are about to kill me and in whom you do not believe, I forgive you." He then gave his blessing before they shot him.

Father Dario Hernández (b. 1880) was martyred on the same day. He had joined the Society at the age of sixteen and after his ordination in 1912 had taught rhetoric at the college in Zaragoza, before being missioned to do parish work in Valencia and Barcelona. From 1928, he had been superior of the Jesuit residence in Valencia, where he was much sought after as confessor. After the dissolution of the Society, he continued his ministry under false identities and by changing residence frequently. In mid-September, he was finally arrested and put in prison, where he remained until September 29, when he was taken to the outskirts of Valencia and executed.

Spiritual Leaders—Lay and Ordained

Four other martyrs of Valencia were incarcerated under different circumstances. Father Narciso Basté (b. 1866) had graduated in law and philosophy from the University of Barcelona and simultaneously completed two years of theological studies at the seminary before he joined the Society in 1890. Ordained a priest in 1899, he was appointed director of the Marian sodality of the Workers' Youth Board in Valencia. During the Civil War, he moved to a small apartment, where he and other Jesuits were able to celebrate Mass daily. Initially he was respected by the communists because of what he had done over the years in promoting workers' causes. They arrested and released him twice, until the fatal day of October 15, when he was apprehended again and shot.

Six weeks later, the young widower Luis Campos Górriz (b. 1905) was executed on the same spot, Picadero de Paterna. A former pupil of the Jesuits, he had studied law and philosophy at the Universities of Valencia and Madrid. During those years, he was engaged in the Catholic Students Federation at Valencia, the National Confederation of Catholic Students, the Marian sodality at Valencia (where he collaborated with Father Basté), and the town's Catholic Action. In 1933, he was appointed general secretary of Catholic Action in Madrid. The Civil War caught him at Torrent near Valencia, where his father was living. After a few relatively quiet months, the militia discovered this important Catholic lay apostle. Campos was arrested on November 28 and killed as he held a rosary in his hand.

Father Alfredo Simón (b. 1877), a native from Valencia, had joined the Society of Jesus in 1895. After his ordination in 1909, he was dean at the college in Valencia and then appointed rector of other institutions before returning to Valencia in 1931 as rector of the college. At the end of November 1936, after several arrests and imprisonments, Simón ended up as one of twelve priests in the San Miguel Prison of Valencia, in a room so crowded that they could hardly sleep on the floor. He led his fellow prisoners in the recitation of the rosary and heard their confessions until his execution at Picadero de Paterna on November 29.

Like Luis Campos, Father Juan Bautista Ferreres (b. 1861) was arrested at his hometown near Valencia. He had been a diocesan priest before joining the Society. As an expert in canon law, he had worked at the Jesuit curia in Rome in 1918; he also taught moral theology at the Gregorian University. In 1924, he returned to Spain, to Sarrià, where he continued teaching and writing. Arrested in August 1936, he was imprisoned at San Miguel Prison, too, but his frail health necessitated his transferal to the prison infirmary. There, he counselled the sick and led them in the rosary, as Father Simón had done. When he suffered a stroke and was paralyzed, one of the priests arranged for Holy Communion to be smuggled in on December 8, feast of the Immaculate Conception. After the Jesuit received the sacrament, he said: "I'm so happy, now I can die." On Christmas Day, he was brought communion again, and four days later he passed away peacefully. Ferreres was recognized by the

Church as a true martyr for the faith, even though he was not directly killed by persecutors.

Hedwig Lewis, SJ

The ten Jesuit martyrs of Valencia and their lay collaborator were beatified on March 11, 2001 by Pope John Paul II.

Blessed Giovanni Fausti (1899–1946)

Gaining the Martyr's Palm

"I came to India solely with the hope of saving many souls and to gain a martyr's palm," wrote Saint Mother Teresa of Kolkata in her letter to Ferdinand Périer, SJ, who was at the time archbishop of Kolkata, reflecting on her "call within a call" that she had received on September 10, 1946 to leave the Loreto Sisters and establish a new religious order. In the early Church, martyrs were both witnesses to Christ and sufferers for his sake. Saint Cyprian, bishop of Carthage (200–58 CE), speaks of two types of martyrdom, which were equally rewarded by God—white and crimson: "To those victorious in time of peace, He will give a white crown for their corporal works of mercy; to those victorious in time of persecution, He will give a second crown, crimson for their sufferings" (*De opere et eleemosynis*, 26). If the white/crimson dichotomy of martyrdom is followed, Mother Teresa's martyrdom was a white or spiritual martyrdom. She earned the palm of a martyr's victory, the white crown, satiating Jesus's thirst for souls by giving "herself in absolute poverty to Christ in His suffering poor,"[66] and for her "mercifulness of cherishing the poor, obtain[ed] the retribution of a heavenly treasure," to quote Saint Cyprian again (*De zelo et livore*, 16).

Unlike the white martyrdom of Mother Teresa, the martyrdom of Blessed Giovanni Fausti was the martyrdom of blood, giving witness to Christ by shedding blood as Christ did. His martyrdom was an imitation of that of Christ, who "came into the world, to testify to the truth" (John 18:37), an ul-

---

66. *Mother Teresa: Come Be My Light*, Kindle ed. (New York, 2007), 92.

Blessed Giovanni Fausti (center), Daniel Dajani (left), and their companions are arrested by communist militiamen at the Pontifical Seminary in Shkodër. The painting by P. Sheloka (2014) is exhibited here in Shkodër on the occasion of the 2016 beatification of the Albanian martyrs, flanked by the flags of the Vatican and Albania.

timate witnessing "to the ends of the earth" (Acts 1:8). Fausti, a second-millennium martyr was like the martyrs, of the early Church: he was Christ's imitator, sufferer, and sower, and for this he gained the crimson crown of martyrdom. Moreover, his martyrdom proves that the history of Christian persecution is current history. Pope John Paul II, in the apostolic letter *tertio millennio adveniente*, affirmed that the Church of the first millennium was born of the blood of the martyrs, as Tertullian wrote in 197 CE: *Sanguis martyrum— semen christianorum* (The blood of martyrs is the seed of Christians). If it were not for martyrs like Father Fausti, the seeds they sowed and their ultimate sacrifice, the Church of the first and second millennia would not have survived. As John Paul II reminds the faithful: "The Church has once again become a Church of martyrs. The persecutions of believers— priests, Religious and laity—has caused a great sowing of martyrdom in different parts of the world. The witness to Christ borne even to the shedding of blood has become a common inheritance of Catholics" (*Tertio millennio adveniente*, 37).

Who Was Blessed Giovanni Fausti?

Giovanni Fausti was a man of great faith, an intellectual, a philosopher, an academic, a missionary, and a pioneer of Christian-Muslim dialogue. He was born on October 9, 1899 in Brozzo, Val Trompia in Brescia, Italy, the first of twelve children of Antonio Fausti and Maria Sigolini. At the age of ten, he was accepted at the seminary of Brescia, where he befriended Giovanni Battista Montini, the future Saint Pope Paul VI. At the age of eighteen, Fausti was drafted into the army, and in 1920, after attending a course at the Military Academy of Modena, he was sent into service in Rome. Discharged from the armed forces with the rank of lieutenant, he resumed his studies at the Pontifical Lombard Seminary in Rome. Fausti was ordained a priest at the age of twenty-three, on July 9, 1922, and he earned degrees in sacred theology from the Pontifical Gregorian University and philosophy from the Pontifical University of Saint Thomas Aquinas.

On October 30, 1924, Giovanni entered the Society of Jesus's novitiate in Gorizia. After five years of formation, he was sent to Albania, where he served as a professor of philosophy at the Pontifical Albanian Seminary of Shkodër, which was founded and run by the Society of Jesus. In three years, he was able to learn Albanian and made significant progress in his studies of Sunni Islam and ascetic or mystic Islamic brotherhoods, including the Bektashis, Khalwatis, and Rufais, who were active in Albania. In 1928, when Fausti began his first period of apostolate in Albania, he combined his teaching at the seminary with hands-on apostolic experience as a director of the Marian congregation. He was "a missionary-professor," as he described himself, willing to imitate the prototype: Jesus's infinite patience.

In a letter from Shkodër on October 5, 1931, to the Jesuit provincial in Rome,[67] Father Fausti explained his missionary focus in Albania: "to initiate a fraternal dialogue with Albanian Muslims, who seemed to have been—at least some—well-disposed towards us [the Jesuits], clarify some doctrinal points, and prepare the road for further discussion and rapprochements." With the genius of what would later be called an inter-religious dialoguer, Fausti wanted to build on common ground and common doctrine—"this will start a pacific dialogue between the two"—and then proceed to difficult topics. He realized early in his inter-religious apostolate the difficulty "of looking for some light through many existent prejudices on both camps which had been fighting for many centuries." Based on what he learned through his extensive conversations with Albanian Muslims, he was convinced that while entering a profound theological dialogue with Islam, he had "to leave out all hostility, sincerely recognizing the good that is in Islam, usually misunderstood in our polemics." His research and firsthand experience with the Sufi orders living in Albania resulted in a series of articles published in the Jesuit magazine *La Civiltà Cattolica* from 1931 to 1933.

In 1932, Fausti returned to Italy (Mantu) as a professor of cosmology, still suffering from the tuberculosis he detected when serving in Albania. He underwent treatment before resuming his teaching at the Jesuit Institute of Philosophy Aloisianum in Gallarate (Milan), where, on February 2, 1936, he took his final vows. In July 1942, Father Fausti returned to Albania, serving as rector of the Albanian Pontifical Seminary in Shkodër, and then moved to the capital, Tirana, to serve the population devastated by war, misery, displacement, and famine. Despite being wounded by a German bullet that hit his healthy lung and broke his collarbone, he continued his works of mercy,

---

67. Archives of the Venetian province (Gallarate-Varese), 30–32.

serving the people of Albania. After the war, in 1944, the communists took over, and the persecution of Albanian religions started. Intellectuals like Fausti became the Communist Party's targets.

Martyrdom Gains Father Fausti a Crimson Crown in Heaven

Fausti was arrested on December 31, 1945, together with another Jesuit, Father Daniel Dajani, born in 1906 and rector of the Pontifical Seminary. They were accused of organizing "United Albania—an organization to overthrow the regime"; secret contact with the Anglo-Americans for a military intervention in Albania, and other false accusations that were leveled against every clergy member brought to trial. In the early morning of March 4, 1946, the road to martyrdom, which he called the "road to eternity,"[68] started for Giovanni Fausti and seven other clergy, who, before dawn, were brought to the infamous place called Zalli in Kirit on the periphery of Shkodër. At six o'clock, the order was given to the execution squad to execute the prisoners. Father Fausti was given a chance to pronounce his last wishes, and the martyr spoke with the language of the Master, imitating the suffering Christ on the Cross: "I am happy to die fulfilling my responsibility. Give my best to my Jesuit brothers, deacons, priests and the Archbishop."[69] As soon as his last wishes were pronounced, a chorus of strong voices of those who were going to be executed joined in: "Long live Christ the King! Long Live Albania. We forgive those who kill us."[70]

Albania and its people lived to witness martyrs including Giovanni Fausti beatified. Genuine faith, unlike gold (1 Peter 1:7), is not perishable, and the martyrs are witnesses, sufferers, and sowers for excellence. The seed of Father Fausti's martyrdom fell on rich soil (Matthew 13:8). Only six months after his martyrdom, Mother Teresa received the call to establish the Missionaries of Charity and satiate Christ's thirst for souls. In gaining the martyr's palm—white and crimson, respectively—Blessed Father Fausti and Saint

---

68. Armando Guidetti, *Padre Fausti un precursore del dialogo islamico-cristiano: Martire in Albania* (Rome, 1974), 104.
69. Ines A. Murzaku, "Ad maiorem Dei gloriam: The Jesuits in Albania," *Occasional Papers on Religion in Eastern Europe* 37, no. 6 (2017): 121.
70. Ibid.

Mother Teresa, Albania's adopted son and Albania's most celebrated daughter, will be everlasting sowers of seeds for the Church.

Ines Angeli Murzaku

Giovanni Fausti was beatified in Shkodër on November 5, 2016, together with thirty-seven other martyrs of Albania, including Daniel Dajani and Jesuit Brother Gjon Pantalia (1887–1947), nicknamed the "cornerstone" of the Shkodër Jesuit college.

Blessed Jan Beyzym (1850–1912)

Optional Memorial on October 12

Jan Beyzym was born on May 15, 1850 in Beyzymy Wielkie (now in Ukraine) as the oldest child of Count Jan Beyzym and Countess Olga Beyzym née Stadnicka. When his father was sentenced in absentia to death for taking part in the January Uprising of 1863, the count fled to Galicia, under Austrian rule. Their mansion in Onackowce was burnt down by Cossacks, and the countess and her children took refuge with relatives. Then the older sons went to study in Kyiv, where Jan earned a living for his younger brothers by giving private lessons. After passing his final exams in 1871, he entered the Society of Jesus on December 10, 1872, and after the usual studies he was ordained a priest in 1881. For the next seventeen years, Father Beyzym worked as an educator in Jesuit colleges, first at Ternopil and then at Khyriv, where he taught French and Russian, and nursed the sick boys.

Something Greater

Much as he loved the work with young people, Jan Beyzym felt a growing desire for something greater: he wanted to sacrifice himself to God by serving the most miserable, the least privileged—the lepers in Madagascar. Having obtained permission from the superior general, he wrote to him in 1897: "I know very well what leprosy is and what I must expect, but all this does not frighten me; on the contrary, it attracts me."

On October 17, 1898, Father Beyzym left Poland for good and headed for France to take the boat to Madagascar. He arrived at Antananarivo two months later and was assigned to the leper asylum in Ambahivoraka, which was founded in the desert near Antananarivo in 1872. The lepers, some 150 of them, lived in crumbling shacks divided into small windowless rooms, without flooring or furniture. They received no medication and lived, day by day, without any help. They often died of hunger rather than of sickness. With the permission of his superiors, Jan built a small house with a chapel near the shacks. He was the first priest in the history of the Madagascar mission who lived with the lepers permanently.

After two weeks, Beyzym wrote a letter to the French provincial about the situation, admitting that he wept in private at the sufferings of these unhappy people and that he asked the Good Lord to help him bring relief to this misery. He devoted all his strength, his talents as an organizer, and, above all, his heart to the sick. He lived among them to bear witness to the fact that they were human beings and that they must be saved. He even asked Our Lady "to infect him with leprosy," so as to obtain graces for the wellbeing and salvation of as many sufferers as possible. He collected money and tried helping them in any way he could. At the time, there was no effective medication for leprosy, but Beyzym noticed that healthy food and adequate hygiene limited the contagion. So he called on the charity of his Polish compatriots and soon was able to increase his children's ration of rice. "It reduced the number of burials from fifty-seven a week to five a year," said an eyewitness.

Miracles of Providence

The greatest wish of Father Beyzym, however, was to build a hospital where the lepers would be taken care of and protected from the moral permissiveness that prevailed in the state-run hospices. In September 1902, he left Ambahivoraka for Fianarantsoa, located about 395 kilometers from the capital city. He went there on foot in tropical heat and rain. Again with the invaluable support from the Polish people and, despite mounting problems of all kinds, he built his hospital at Marana, near Fianarantsoa, and could receive the first lepers on August 16, 1911.

The main means for his fundraising activities was the Jesuit periodical *The Catholic Missions*. His letters brought attention to the fate of the lepers and the misery they lived in. Thanks to his persuasive writing skills and to the intercession of Our Lady, who never let him down, people responded generously. The lists of donations for the years 1899–1912 show the names of people of different professions and social status, from cities and from villages; most of the donations were small and anonymous, evidently coming from the poor. At the inauguration of the hospital, a medical doctor said: "The construction

Piotr Ostrowski, S. G. Żeleński workshop, Kraków (Poland), Blessed Jan Beyzym is surrounded by children from the Ambahivoraka leper colony. Stained glass made from a photograph of around 1900 (2010).

and equipping of this vast hospital in a country where everything is lacking was a colossal undertaking, but Father Beyzym completed the task. Arriving there penniless, he found ways of collecting thousands of francs in Europe (principally in Poland, Austria, and Germany) for such a vast project, his trust in God's help was unshakeable. Providence has almost worked miracles for him."

Soon after that, Father Beyzym started to fail in health himself. He was very much in pain. He got bedsores and was moaning at night, but when asked how much it hurt he used to say, "It is nothing compared to Christ's pain." Near the end, he asked his companion who was keeping a vigil at his bedside, to go on his behalf to the lepers and beg forgiveness for any grievances he might have caused them. On hearing that, the lepers burst out in tears. On October 2, 1912, exhausted from hard work and a harsh way of life, Jan Beyzym died.

His had been a life marked by a profound bond with Christ, with the Eucharist, and with Our Lady, to whom he attributed his successes. Prayer played an essential role; it was the source of his strength. Not having much time for quiet prayer, Jan prayed everywhere all the time. He often repeated that his prayer was not worth much and that he had trouble praying. This was why he asked the Carmelite nuns to pray for him. "One must be in constant union with God and pray without respite," he had written to his provincial in 1901, when asked about the working conditions among the sick. "One must get used little by little to the stench, for here we don't breathe the scent of flowers but the putrefaction of bodies, caused by leprosy."

Czeslaw H. Tomaszewski, SJ

On August 18, 2002, in Kraków, Pope John Paul II included Jan Beyzym, the Apostle of the Lepers of Madagascar, among the blessed of the Catholic Church.

When I first received a piece of cloth and began to bandage the wound of one of the lepers, everyone surrounded me as if it were an extraordinary sight. However, this service requires heroic self-denial. You have to remain constantly united to God and be able to pray always. Now I look at the wounds of my unfortunate patients, I touch them while treating them or giving them Extreme Unction with holy oil, without being impressed. To tell the truth, I do feel something in my heart when I attend to their wounds, but only because I would prefer to have them all on me, rather than to see them on these poor wretches.

Blessed Jan Beyzym, Letter from Madagascar

Blessed Tiburcio Arnaiz (1865–1926)

Optional Memorial on July 2

Tiburcio Arnaiz Muñoz was born in Valladolid (Spain) on August 11, 1865, into a modest family of weavers. He was a lively, joyful, and good-hearted youth when he entered the seminary at age thirteen. He took to his studies with great profit and brilliance because of his extraordinary talent, so much so that one of his former companions attested that "he was a brainiac, in the best sense of the word. He never took a textbook home; if anything, I would find him hidden away in the cloisters of the seminary before class."

Tiburcio Arnaiz was ordained a priest on April 20, 1890. He was first entrusted, for three years, with the parish of Villanueva de Duero in Valladolid, and after, for nine years, the parish of Poyales del Hoyo, in Ávila. He always attended to his parishioners with loving care. When he had to leave Poyales to enter the Society of Jesus, he said, moved with emotion: "I love my people so much that I would not exchange them for a miter; only the voice of God has the power to tear me away from my parish."

"Until We Meet Again in Heaven"

As a parish priest, Father Arnaiz would spend his days and years laboring in the vineyard of the Lord and providing for his family. However, God was spurring him on to a greater summons, and on one occasion he confessed: "I lived very well and was enjoying a great life, but I feared condemning myself." His thoughts flew to joining religious life, but he was met with an insurmountable obstacle in his elderly mother, whom he loved and venerated, for he was the only support for her in her old age. Eventually, the day came when God drew her soul to heaven; the separation caused Father Arnaiz devastating pain: "I suffered so much that I told myself: now no one will cause me to die again, because I am going to die to everything that is not God."

One night after reading Año Cristiano, Arnaiz's sister, Gregoria, exclaimed with uncontrollable tears: "Oh Tiburcio, how many wonderful things have the saints done for our Lord, and we, how little have we done? Are we going to live all our lives doing nothing for him? Each one of us should go to a convent and there serve God with perfection for the remainder of our lives." Thus unfolded the path that each one was to follow in their particular vocation. Gregoria entered the Dominican Convent of San Felipe, and Father Arnaiz, after making sure that she would be content there, bid her farewell: "Well then, sister, until we meet again in heaven!" Then with much joy, he set out to ask for admission to the Society of Jesus.

It was the year 1902 when Father Arnaiz entered the Jesuit novitiate in Granada; he was thirty-seven years old. From the beginning, he disposed himself to the practice of all virtue. He made two promises to himself during this time, which he fulfilled with the utmost integrity: "Never to ask for anything and to content myself with whatever is given to me," and: "I will never refuse any task, under any pretext." The desire to make up for lost time and his advanced age spurred him on to eagerly seek perfection.

Father Arnaiz professed first vows on April 3, 1904. During this time, he wonderfully integrated the tenets of Ignatian spirituality and began directing a series of retreats on the *Spiritual Exercises*; further, he embarked on the difficult ministry of rural missionary work.

Before leaving for Loyola in 1911 to complete tertianship, Father Arnaiz was missioned to Murcia, where he lived for two years laboring for the good of souls and directing them with admirable success. Many who interacted with him would say: "This priest is a saint and makes saints of others." There he discovered the need to care for the young women of the small towns and countryside who were coming into the city to serve and were exposed to a thousand dangers. He sought out a house where the women could have, besides a place of shelter and refuge, someone to teach them to know and love God.

After completing tertianship in Loyola and several brief ministry assignments during Lent in the Canary Islands and Cádiz, he left for Málaga where his final incorporation into the Society of Jesus would take place, pronouncing his final vows on August 15, 1912.

Blessed Tiburcio Arnaiz. In the background, we can make out the landscape of his beloved Andalusia, where he preached his popular missions. Altarpiece above his tomb, from a photograph from around 1910.

"He Likes Everything, Everything Suits Him"

His tireless apostolate as a rural missionary, director of the *Spiritual Exercises*, confessor, and spiritual director, although extended throughout various parts of Spain, were abundant in Andalusa, and principally throughout all the diocese of Málaga. Upon finishing his mission work, Father Arnaiz would return to his home in Málaga and sometimes, without even going up to his room, would leave his briefcase at the doorway and fly to visit the sick. He would visit hospital wards but also private homes, and in these personal encounters Father Arnaiz's charity overflowed.

His creativity in alleviating ignorance or human suffering knew no limits. On Cañaveral Street in Málaga, he advocated for the construction of a house to provide shelter for women of slender means, with more than thirty individual rooms. He promoted the opening of the Catholic Library of Málaga and attended with the utmost concern to many small schools and workshops of the working class. The prisons were another object of his indefatigable efforts; there, through his preaching and charity, the Lord touched many anguished hearts.

His efforts were multiplied thanks to a company of unconditional collaborators who labored in the diverse apostolates that he established, some in the city and others even preparing his missions in local villages. In his visits to marginalized neighborhoods, he became thoroughly acquainted with the hostile spirit toward religion that reigned there (even to the point of having a rat thrown at him). Faithful to the Gospel and full of compassion for such ignorance that he saw to be the cause of so much animosity, he resolved to remedy it.

The famous "compounds" were neighboring houses where each family had for their privacy only one or two rooms around a large patio. Father Arnaiz would rent, or request, some of these residences and send some of his brigade there to improvise schools. They taught the people there how to read and write, aspects of general culture, and the most fundamental elements of the faith: that there is a God and that he loves us to the point of giving his life for us, that we have a soul, and the promise of eternal life. Father Arnaiz would arrive at these schools after one or two months and give a preached retreat to all gathered there; afterward, he would usually appoint a pious woman to lead that particular school, so that she could continue teaching the children and sustain the good fruit being achieved there. During his lifetime Father Arnaiz would work to establish twenty such schools.

This form of evangelization, developed by young women temporarily stationed in small towns and farms, was the most original work of Father Arnaiz and continues to this day in the missionaries of the rural parishes.

The preaching of the rural missions was one of Father Arnaiz's principal ministries. His close friend, Mr. Antonio Membibre, accompanied him on one mission and related his impressions to Father Arnaiz's sister, herself now a religious: "I had the pleasure of spending ten days with your brother and he is a holy missionary indeed, mortified and penitent, he does not usually even sleep on the bed, but lies down on the ground in peace ... You would not recognize your brother: he is rejuvenated, he likes everything, everything suits him, he does not have comforts, nor idleness, nor necessities, but a great voice, powerful, tireless, preaching all day and all night, a life of penances, sacrifices and humiliations, truly all of this attracts the torrent of graces that God rains down upon him as he performs his ministry."

Reading the list of all of his concurrent ministries, it seemed impossible that he would ever be able to accomplish them all. In Chiclana, for example, a town of Cádiz, he preached a mission in two parishes while giving a retreat to a religious order at the same time; he also visited the prison and had meetings with various religious groups.

In the towns through which he passed giving missions, he recognized the need for and founded associations to maintain the life of faith like Marian sodalities, Saint Vincent de Paul communities, the Apostleship of Prayer, or Eucharistic Adoration vigils, and he was always able to find a gap so that he could minister to female religious. Behind the construction or arrangement of various churches and schools, there was also the initiative of Father Arnaiz and his tireless collaboration.

In early July 1926, Father Arnaiz was in Algodonales (Cádiz), preaching a mission, when he suddenly found himself extraordinarily disoriented. The doctor diagnosed him with bronchitis and pleuritis. He was transferred to Málaga, and when it was known that Father Arnaiz had arrived in this condition, the city mobilized itself, and it was necessary to place him in a visible area every day so the people could see him. On July 10, they administered the last sacraments to him while he remained joyful and anxious to depart for heaven; he was not able to speak of anything else. "How exceedingly beautiful is the Sacred Heart of Jesus! ... I will see it soon ... and I will be satisfied! How good it is! How much he loves us! ... And the Virgin, how kind she is! How she loves me!" At 10 o'clock on July 18, 1926, Father Arnaiz surrendered his soul to God.

Patronato del P. Arnaiz[71]

Tiburcio Arnaiz was beatified by Pope Francis on October 20, 2018.

---

71. Cf. the biography on www.padrearnaiz.es (abbreviated). Translation by Philip Cooley, SJ.

Saint Alberto Hurtado (1901–52)

Father Alberto Hurtado was an apostle who carried out vast and fruitful pastoral activity that was a reflection of his own interior life in love with Christ Jesus. He sought to live every moment in accord with his will.

He was born in Viña del Mar, Chile, on January 22, 1901. His father died when Alberto was only four. With his mother and younger brother, he lived the following years in great economic difficulty. He attended the Colegio de San Ignacio in Santiago. Even when quite young, he did apostolic work in the most wretched quarters of Santiago. The sufferings of the poor marked his life and his spirituality. Upon completion of secondary school, Alberto had already decided to become a priest, but his family situation did not allow it. Instead, he studied law at the Catholic University, graduating in 1923.

His family's problems were finally resolved, and on August 14, 1923, he entered the novitiate of the Society of Jesus. He received the rest of his Jesuit formation outside Chile. In 1925, he finished his novitiate and went to do his juniorate studies in Córdoba, Argentina. Two years later, he left to study philosophy and theology in Sarria, Spain. In 1931, the Jesuits were expelled from Spain; after a short stay in Ireland, Alberto went to Louvain, where he completed his theological studies. He was ordained a priest on August 24, 1933. Two years later, he received a doctorate in education and psychology.

It was here, in Louvain, that he attained his spiritual maturity. Father John Baptiste Janssens, future superior general of the Society of Jesus, who was his superior at the time, declared that he had never known anyone with greater apostolic radiance than Father Hurtado.

Apostle of Youth

In 1936, Alberto returned to Chile. He soon began to stand out as an apostle of youth. He was a religion teacher and a spiritual director for the studies in the Colegio de San Ignacio. One of the college's students recalls that Father Hurtado formed a very close relation with them, "for rather than a classroom of apologetics he ran a classroom of spirituality, of knowledge of the Lord, and of a call to Christian commitment by the students to the Lord to his Church, and to the poor."

It was Father Hurtado's goal to awaken in young men this personal contact with God. To this end, he promoted retreats, spiritual direction, and the sacrament of confession. He urged frequent, even daily, communion. He presented the filial love of Mary as a short path to the Lord. He insisted on the importance of constantly seeking God's will, of asking oneself what Christ would do today in my place. Once God's will has been found, one could face life with joy: "I am happy, Lord, happy!"

With young people, he himself practiced what he demanded of good educators: "He must have a warm and open heart, ready to listen to all the sorrows and needs of young people, even their material troubles. A teacher teaches less by what he says and by what he knows than by what he is."

His work expanded when he was assigned to be national moderator of the youth wing of Catholic Action. One of his main concerns was that Catholics should live their faith integrally. In 1941, he published a book entitled *Is Chile a Catholic Country?* In it, he denounced the scandal of Chile's moral and material poverty as a contradiction of the Catholic faith, which most of the country's inhabitants professed but hardly knew. Toward the end of 1944, painful differences with the auxiliary bishop of Santiago led to Father Hurtado leaving the work of Catholic Action. Many young people wanted to follow him but he stopped them, reminding them of the need to love the church and obey its hierarchy.

Apostle of Vocations

Hurtado was an apostle of priestly vocations. He preached urgently about the need for them and pointed out to young men the possibility of this path. Many Jesuit, diocesan, and other religious priests experienced God's call to them through Father Hurtado's words.

In his *Educational Topics*, he describes this vocation: "The priest spends much of his day giving consolation, dispelling useless pessimism, sowing happiness in souls—often at the cost of his own satisfaction—and renouncing all power in order to serve more generously. His life is an extension of Christ's life. His basic aspirations are to stand nearer to God every day, to resemble Jesus more closely, so as to devote himself more fully and effectively to the good of his brothers and sisters."

Social Apostle

Father Hurtado was a social apostle. Towards the end of 1944, he founded a residence for homeless children, a place to shelter Christ in his poor. He called it *"Hogar de Christo"* (Christ's Home). He himself walked the streets on cold nights to invite children to come in. He put laypersons in charge of the home, himself acting as chaplain. Today it is one of Latin America's most important charitable institutions.

But this did not content him. Society as a whole is sick when it produces so many people suffering want. Hurtado undertook to do something to change social structures in accord with the Church's teaching. In 1947, with this in view, he founded the Chilean Workers Association. His intention was to provide Christian leadership formation for workers so that, through labor unions, they could help the working class become an active force for social change. Silence in the face of today's social injustice "is not a virtue but cowardice. Resignation in the face of suffering that one can and should remedy is a tremendous betrayal of God's plan of human dignity, of the family, of society."

In 1951, Hurtado founded *Mensaje* (Message), a magazine with a religious, social, and philosophical orientation. In his first editorial, he explained that the title referred to "the message that the Son of God brought from heaven to earth, and whose resonance our periodical desires to extend and apply to our Chilean fatherland and our tormented times." The magazine remains a prestigious publication to this day.

Apostle of the Family

Father Hurtado was an apostle of the family. In his *Educational Topics*, he defines the family as "the basic cell of society, the first school, and the highest university." The family is where one learns to love and respect the neighbor, "to be an image of God—sometimes very disfigured, but in any case an image of the Creator, a son of God, and a brother of Christ."

Saint Albert Hurtado poses with one of the boys he cared for in front of the Hogar de Cristo in Santiago (Chile). Behind him is the green truck he used to pick up destitute children on the banks of the Mapocho River. He is carrying the book entitled Is Chile Catholic? Above him, angels hold a banner with his words: "Glad, Lord, glad." Painting by Raúl Berzosa (2019).

He states that the family is in crisis because "young people today are largely being formed by an environment that says that pleasure is obligatory, life is short, and there is no point in making useless sacrifices." That is why so many marriages fail: "There is no courage for accepting a hard life in which there are misunderstandings and difficulties ... People choose the easy way of breaking up, in search of an easy solution that will let them 'remake their lives.'"

Marked by Love

Love for the Church marked the activity of Alberto Hurtado. For him, "the Church is not a mere official body; it is Christ prolonged and living among us." He also had a deep love for the Society of Jesus. He wrote to his provincial: "I believe that if I gave the *Exercises* to our men, I would include a talk on 'feeling ourselves members of the Society'; that is, not looking on the Society as something outside of ourselves, which we can criticize or approve, but as something of which we are an intimate part, a kind of smaller Mystical Body. I believe in this idea and live it fully."

Hurtado died of pancreatic cancer on August 18, 1952. His agony was followed by the whole country. When informed of his illness, he rejoiced that his meeting with the Father was near and thanked God for giving him time to prepare. His last words, addressed to his superior, were: "Believe me, Father, I am happy, profoundly happy."

Jaime Castellón, SJ[72]

John Paul II beatified Alberto Hurtado in 1994. The Chilean Congress decreed on that occasion that his death anniversary, August 18, be Solidarity Day. Hurtado was canonized by Pope Benedict XVI on October 23, 2005. On that occasion, the president of Chile called Father Hurtado a "new Father of the Nation."

---

72. Jesuits, *Yearbook of the Society of Jesus* (Rome, 1995), 74–77 (abridged). Translation by Martin Palmer, SJ.

From the Spiritual Writings of Saint Alberto Hurtado

You ask me how I manage to put some balance into my life. This is a question I ask myself, as each day I am more swallowed up by my work —letters, telephone calls, articles, visits: the wearing routine of business —congresses, study sessions, conferences agreed to out of weakness, because I could not say no, or because I did not want to miss an opportunity to do good; bills to be paid, decisions to be made in the stress of unforeseen circumstances. Then there is some pressing apostolate, the urgency to arrive before materialism gains a complete victory. So often I feel I am on a rock, battered from all sides by the rising waves. The only escape route is heavenward. For an hour, or a day, I let the waves beat upon the rock; I stop looking out to the horizon and only look upwards toward God.

How blessed is the active life, a life completely consecrated to God and completely given over to those around me! Its very demands lead me to rediscover myself and direct myself to God. God is the only possible way out. In all my worries, he alone is my refuge.

There are also dark times. There comes a moment when my mind is being pulled in so many directions that I cannot stand it any longer; the body cannot go along with the will; it has obeyed so often, but now it gives in. My head is an aching void. Ideas fail to come. My imagination ceases to function, and my memory is blank. We have all had moments like this!

The only remedy seems to be to resign oneself for a few days, or for a few months, or perhaps even for a few years. To be obstinate would be no help: one simply has to give in. And then, as in all the difficulties, I escape to God. I hand over to him all my being and all my desires, everything to his fatherly Providence, even if I lack the strength to speak to him. What understanding God has shown me in his goodness even in those moments!

In God, I feel a hope that is almost boundless. My worries disappear. I let them go, and I let myself go completely into his hands ... I belong to him, and he takes care of all and of me myself. At long last, my soul can surface once more, tranquil and serene. Yesterday's worries, the thousand and one preoccupations about "Thy Kingdom come," and even the dreadful torment I felt just now fearing the triumph of his enemies ...

everything gives way to calmness in God, held ineffably in the very depth of my soul. God, the rock against which all waves break in vain, God the perfect radiance marred by no shadow, God, the all-conquering victor, dwells within me. I can reach him fully, as the highest aim of my love. My whole soul is within him. And then, sweetly and surely, it is as if all life's trials, all the insecurities and uncertainties, had left me completely. I am bathed in light. He fills me with his strength. He loves me.

Liturgy of the Hours, Second Reading on August 18

Part 6

THE CELESTIAL SOCIETY

Servant of God Pedro Arrupe (1907–91)

General of the Post-Conciliar Society

Deceased on February 5

Pedro Arrupe was born in Bilbao, Spain, on November 14, 1907. He studied medicine in Madrid from 1923 to 1927, the year in which he entered the novitiate in Loyola. After his studies in the humanities and philosophy, he earned a degree in theology and was ordained a priest in 1936. He asked his superiors to allow him to go as a missionary to Japan, to which he was missioned in 1938. He was the master of novices when, on August 6, 1945, he was a witness to the atomic explosion at Hiroshima. In 1958, he was named provincial of the recently founded Jesuit province of Japan.

He was a member of the Thirty-First General Congregation, which elected him superior general on May 22, 1965. He was struck by cerebral thrombosis on August 7, 1981, and on September 3, 1983, the Thirty-Third General Congregation accepted his resignation from the position of superior general. He died in Rome, at the general curia, on February 5, 1991, after almost ten years of illness. On November 14, 1997, his mortal remains were transferred from the Campo Verano Cemetery, where he had been buried, to the Church of the Gesù.

A Man of God, a Man of the Spirit

All his biographers observe that Arrupe slept very little and prayed much. Despite his busy agenda, he always found time to pray at length in his private chapel, the "little-big cathedral," as he liked to call it. He was a "man of God" not only because he prayed a lot but also because he reasoned and decided according to divine categories. He thought, spoke, and acted according to these perspectives; he had interiorized the preparatory prayer of the *Spiritual Exer-*

cises: "That all my intentions, actions and operations may be ordered purely to the service and praise of the Divine Majesty" (*Spir. Ex.*, 46).

As a good disciple of Ignatius, he acknowledged the Lord as the one absolute dimension of his life; all the rest was relative. He had united in himself an identity as "a man of God and a man of the Spirit," that is, a man who lets himself be guided by God, attentive to not setting limits on God and not confining God within narrow human categories. He truly believed that the Spirit rules the Church, and within it, the Society of Jesus. He understood very well how to make himself an available "instrument" in the hands of the Lord (*Constitutions*, no. 638).

Here is found the deep roots of his contagious optimism, which some interpreted as naiveté and even as a lack of the gifts of governance. He himself admitted to being an optimist and explained the reasons for this: "I am an optimist because I believe in God and in people." His faith was in the Lord in whom "alone hope must be placed" (*Constitutions,* no. 812). This was also the source of his apostolic enthusiasm, his audacity and resoluteness in seeking answers to the problems of evangelization of his time and in the prophetic intuition of the future.

Jesus Christ, the "Everything" of His Life

When I was a Jesuit student in Rome, I heard on the radio an interview with Father Arrupe. One of the interviewer's questions was: "For you, who is Jesus Christ?" Arrupe remained silent for some time, as if looking into the depths of his own soul, and answered with just one word: "Everything." Then he added: "If you take Jesus from my life, it will collapse like a house of cards." And, in fact, if any passion is evident in the life of Pedro Arrupe, that passion is Jesus Christ. The "everything" and the "more"—a typical Ignatian unity— summarize his interior biography, that of a person in love with Jesus Christ, who therefore lives "only desiring and choosing that which is more conducive to the end for which we are created" (*Spir. Ex.*, 23). Only from this experience of faith can one understand the personality and the work of Father Arrupe. It is here that his Ignatian identity is grounded: availability to the will of God, mystic in mission. He looked for nothing else.

This is the content of the "sphere that is hidden, or half-hidden, even from ourselves" that Father Arrupe defines as "truly interesting" and that is found

One of the most emblematic photos of the Servant of God Pedro Arrupe, praying in his private chapel at the Jesuit general curia in Rome (Italy).

in intimate terms within an exceptional text from his spiritual notes on the *Exercises* of August 1965: "The thanksgiving [for being elected superior general] obliges me to be very faithful to the Lord, so much so that I cannot deny him even the smallest thing that I see that he is asking of me ... It follows that, even if already it normally is the case, now the vow of perfection becomes especially real. Now I must observe it with extreme diligence, given that such diligence will consist of my preparation for listening, seeing and being an instrument in the hands of the Lord: which is equivalent to doing his will in everything."

On the occasion of his golden jubilee as a Jesuit, Arrupe reaffirmed the same point and summarized his own life as a constant gaze on the face of the One with whom he felt in love: "Reviewing the course of my seventy years, of which fifty have been in the Society, I cannot help but recognize that the decisive stages, the radical turning points in my life's path have always been unexpected, I might even say irrational. But sooner or later, in every instance, I have had to recognize the hand of God that gave the helm a bold twist."

One of these "surprises of the mystery of God," a new "twist of the helm," the last and the most unexpected, was without doubt that of the night between August 6 and 7, 1981. Father Arrupe experienced a cerebral thrombosis that forced him to resign as general of the Society and led him to the end of his life in a "pilgrimage" of almost ten years in the mysterious silence of God, where existed only the prayer "Not my will but yours be done."

On September 3, 1983, he presented his resignation to the Thirty-Third General Congregation. He could not read out the message, nor was the form written by him, but the content and the explicit approval were his. And again we find that flow of the Spirit that marked his entire life: being in the hands of God, wanting to live immersed in the mystery of God, and accomplishing his will. In his renunciation, he affirmed: "More than ever, I now find myself in the hands of God. This is what I have wanted all my life, from my youth. And this is still the one thing I want. But now there is a difference: the initiative is entirely with God. It is indeed a profound spiritual experience to know and feel myself so totally in his hands."

Love for Our Holy Mother, the Hierarchical Church

From the love for Jesus Christ, from his passion for Jesus Christ flows in Arrupe—as in Saint Ignatius—love for "our Holy Mother, the hierarchical

Church" and his service of "the Church his spouse, under the Roman pontiff, vicar of Christ on earth." From his first love, from the passion that pervades his entire life, is nurtured his love for the Church.

Father Arrupe wrote and spoke on numerous occasions of the fidelity of the Society and of every Jesuit to the person of the Roman pontiff, expressing his own conviction that in such fidelity is contained something essential to the charism of the Society. He loved with "effective and affective" devotion the vicar of Christ, and he showed it with gestures that some judged naïve, such as standing every Sunday at the door of the curia to see the pope pass by on the way to visit a Roman parish. For him, this was neither naiveté nor formalism. He went down to greet the vicar of Christ. It was an authentic "Ignatian devotion."

Father Arrupe lived intensely the application of the council, but "thanks to prayerful discernment, practiced in the Church, with the Church and for the Church, behind the letter of the conciliar documents he recognized always the revelation of the Spirit that makes all things new," as Father Peter-Hans Kolvenbach remembered.

From August 7, 1981, he resided in the infirmary of the Jesuit curia, where he would remain for ten years, until his death on February 5, 1991. On October 5, 1981, John Paul II made the decision to nominate Father Paolo Dezza his delegate for the Society, and Father Giuseppe Pittau as his coadjutor. The letter was read to Father Arrupe, in the infirmary, by the secretary of state, Cardinal Agostino Casaroli. Arrupe followed the letter attentively, understood the contents perfectly, and cried softly. A new and definitive "twist of the helm."

On February 27, 1982, Father Dezza called to Rome all the provincials of the Society. In the Eucharist celebrated at the beginning of the meeting, Father Pittau read the homily that Father Arrupe had dictated to him. In it, among other things, he said: "In the Roman pontiff we recognize and love the vicar of Christ on earth, under whom we serve only the Lord and the Church his spouse ... The links that bind us to him, for love and in service are 'our principle and foundation.'" And further: "I feel a great joy in seeing and contemplating all this, because through human mediation I see the will of God, source of grace for our sanctification and that of our neighbors. And I desire that the entire Society live with the same joy and gladness this moment of concrete manifestation of the divine will."

To conclude, we can affirm that Pedro Arrupe, whether in his full lucidity or in his sickness, with his attitude and with his sufferings, has pointed out to the Society the road to live out its own charism: "Serving the Lord and the Church under the Roman pontiff." On February 5, 2019, the twenty-eighth anniversary of his death, in the Basilica of Saint John Lateran, the cause of his beatification was opened.

Elías Royón, SJ[73]

---

73. *La Civiltà Cattolica*, 2019, I, 478–91 (abridged).

Prayer Attributed to Pedro Arrupe

Nothing is more practical than
finding God, than
falling in Love
in a quite absolute, final way.
What you are in love with,
what seizes your imagination, will affect everything.
It will decide
what will get you out of bed in the morning,
what you do with your evenings,
how you spend your weekends,
what you read, whom you know,
what breaks your heart,
and what amazes you with joy and gratitude.
Fall in Love, stay in love,
and it will decide everything.

Mary, Mother of the Society of Jesus

Feast on April 22

"The Mother of God is my mother": this expression of Saint Stanislaus Kostka represents the conviction and the experience of every member of the Society of Jesus. "All members of our Society have rightly had an outstanding devotion to Mary our mother ... No mother ever had more sons, none was ever more blessed or showed such fidelity ... For none was ever so holy, beautiful, and fair, none so honored or endowed with the gifts of the Holy Spirit. No mother ever had more love for her Son ... Mother of the living, who found grace and bore Life itself, Mother of God, our mother, who therefore loves us and out of love prays to God on our behalf and begs for us."[74] Mary is indeed the Mother of the Society.

The Blessed Virgin Mary and Saint Ignatius

Mary played her part in the conversion and training of Saint Ignatius: "One night, while he lay awake, he saw clearly the likeness of Our Lady with the Holy Child Jesus, at the sight of which he received most abundant consolation for a considerable period of time. He felt so great a disgust with his past life, especially his sins of the flesh, that he thought all such images which had formerly occupied his mind were wiped out."[75] She also had a role in the composition of the *Spiritual Exercises*[76] and the *Constitutions*.[77] The young Society

74. Peter Canisius, *De cultu Beatae Virginis, exhortationes domesticae*, ed. G. Schlosser (Rure-mundae, 1876), 230, 234, 235–36.

75. Ignatius of Loyola, *Autobiography*, no. 10.

76. Arturo Codina, *Los Orígenes de los ejercicios espirituales de San Ignacio de Loyola* (Barce-lona, 1926) 85–93. Pablo Dudon, *San Ignacio de Loyola* (Mexico, 1945), 73–75.

77. Ignatius of Loyola, *Autobiography*, no. 100.

saw Mary as "the Virgin Mother of God, who has undertaken the patronage of the entire Society."[78]

Ignatius's devotion, which was "not according to knowledge"[79] at the beginning, was gradually purified, from the time when he wanted "to avenge the honor of the motherhood of Mary with a dagger" directed against the Moor who had insulted her,[80] and then left his dagger and his sword on Our Lady's altar and gave his clothes to a poor man "on the eve of the Feast of Our Lady in March [the Annunciation], by night,[81] until he attained the heights of mystical prayer, when "the Mother interceded for him before her Son and the Father."[82] His entire life was marked by her presence "whom he saw with his inner eye."[83]

Ignatius's constant petition "to the Mother" was "that she would place him with her Son." This grace was granted, and "he felt such a change in his soul that he saw clearly that the Father placed him with his Son in such a way that he could not doubt it."[84]

In Ignatius's writing, Mary always appears together with her Son, in the offering at the end of the Exercise of the Kingdom, as well as in the first companions' final vows at Saint Paul's Outside the Walls. While Ignatius was deliberating about the poverty of professed houses, on February 15, 1544, he said the Mass of Our Lady, offering her Son to the Father. On the following day, he notes in his *Spiritual Diary* that "at the consecration I could not help feeling or seeing her, as though she were a part, or the gateway of all the grace that I felt within my soul. (At the consecration she showed that her flesh was in that of her Son.)"[85]

The figure of Mary was always prominent in Ignatius's life, especially while

---

78. Jerónimo Nadal, *Scholia in constitutiones et declarationes S. P. Ignatii* (Prati in Etruria, 1883), 79.

79. Letter, June 16, 1547, in *Fontes Narrativi de S. Ignatio de Loyola et de Societatis Iesu initiis*, Monumenta Historica Societatis Iesu 66 (Rome 1943), 1:76, no. 5.

80. Ignatius of Loyola, *Autobiography*, no. 15.

81. Ibid., nos. 17–18.

82. Ignatius of Loyola, *Spiritual Diary*, no. 7.

83. Ignatius of Loyola, *Autobiography*, no. 29.

84. Ibid., no. 96.

85. Ignatius of Loyola, *Spiritual Diary*, no. 14.

he was writing the *Exercises* and the *Constitutions*, appearing to him repeatedly both at Manresa and in Rome. Those documents form the basis of the Society of Jesus, and Mary played her part in their development.

The Presence of Mary in the Society's History and in the Life of Every Jesuit

Mary always appears in the light of her Son's work.[86] Mother and Son belong alike to the mystery of our redemption, into which we were born as sons of God. Between Mary's immaculate conception and her glory comes the sacrifice of the cross. It was for the cross that Mary had been given her Son, and for the cross that she had to give him up again to God. "This maternity of Mary in the order of grace began with the consent which she gave in faith at the Annunciation and which she sustained without wavering beneath the cross."[87] The Virgin Mary is seen as indissolubly linked to the work for which Christ desired to be born of her. And so Mary is mother also to the "Companions of Jesus"; she brings them forth as sons of Christ, and places them under his standard.

Throughout its history, the Society has been linked to Mary in this way, in its individual members and as a body. The Jesuit's vows are made to the Son of Mary, Jesus who is God Almighty, and "Eternal Lord of all things," in the presence of his Mother.[88] She has always been regarded by Jesuits as mediatrix of all graces, and the Society has loved her at different times as Lady, Queen, and Mother. It can be said of every Jesuit that "he is most tenderly attached to Our Blessed Lady, regarding her as his mother,"[89] but, like Ignatius, without being excessively emotional about it. There is not a saint or blessed of the Society of whom it cannot be said that he cultivated Mary's love with the affection of a son. "I shall never be at peace, until I have achieved a tender love for our most sweet Mother Mary."[90]

---

86. Vatican II, Dogmatic Constitution *Lumen gentium*, no. 61.

87. Ibid., no. 62.

88. *Constitutions*, part 5, c. 3, no. 6 (532).

89. "E. Villaret, Marie et la Compagnie de Jésus", in: Maria. Études sur la Sainte Vierge, II, Paris: Hubert du Manoir, 1952, p. 940, note 11..

90. *Virgilio Cepari, Vita di S. Giovanni Berchmans della Compagnia di Gesù*, nuova edizione corredata di brevi note e appendice (Rome, 1921), 211.

The Society has always defended the glories of Mary in a number of different ways, by theological study, preaching, and teaching the faith, in art and architecture, in its missions and its Marian sodalities, but above all in its daily life. In all these ways, the Society's apostolic activity has been such that the Jansenists said that, under the influence of the Jesuits, Christianity had degenerated into "Marianity."[91] This was a false interpretation of the maxim "To Jesus through Mary" that the Society has made its own. It is true, however, that we have always regarded Mary as Mother, as the way (*Strada*), and as "Advocate, Help, Succor, and Mediatrix," but always in such a way as to draw attention to Christ, as Ignatius would insist.[92]

Marks of the Society's Devotion to Mary

One pre-eminent feature of the Society's devotion to Mary is a remarkable trust,[93] as of a son for his mother, a mother who showed complete submission in order to give a mother's "service" to her son,[94] becoming "the handmaid of the Lord," which for Ignatius was always the expression of man's ultimate end.[95]

The theologians—Francisco Suárez, Robert Bellarmine, Peter Canisius—present Mary to us as the immaculate one, the fairest of creatures, who is exalted above all the angels and saints put together, since Jesus Christ is the only man who was able not merely to choose his own Mother, but actually to create her, in his omniscience and omnipotence, as the most perfect creature, "raised up by the Lord as Queen of the Universe."[96]

Mary was the fruit of God's omnipotence and was placed at the service of his infinite love, and therefore as daughter of the Father, mother of the Son,

---

91. "Litterae a nonnullis protestantibus theologis Groninganis ad S. Patrem Pium IX datae," d.d. December 1, 1868, in *Acta et decreta Sacrosancti Oecumenici Concilii Vaticani: Cum permultis aliis documentis ad concilium ejusque historiam spectantibus*, Acta et decreta Sacrorum Conciliorum recentiorum (Freiburg im Breisgau: 1982), c. 1127, no. 7.

92. "P. Hieronymi Nadal adhortatio in Collegio Romani die 4 ianuarii 1557 habita," in *Fontes Narrativi de San Ignatio de Loyola et de Societatis Iesu initiis*, 2 (Monumenta Historica Societatis Iesu 73 Rome, 1951), 9–10.

93. Ignatius of Loyola, *Spiritual Diary*, no. 1, 3, 4.

94. Ignatius of Loyola, *Spiritual Exercises*, no. 108.

95. Ibid., no. 23.

96. Vatican II, Dogmatic Constitution *Lumen gentium*, no. 59.

Andrea Sacchi, The Virgin and Child, surrounded by Saints Ignatius of Loyola, Francis Xavier, Cosmas and Damian. On the feast day of the latter two, September 27, 1540, the Society of Jesus was approved by Pope Paul III (1629).

and spouse of the Holy Spirit "after her Son, was exalted above all the angels and above all mankind"[97] and is closest to the Trinity, so that we can use of her the words of Leo XIII, quoting Saint John Damascene, that "she carries in her hands the treasures of the Lord's mercies."[98]

Scripture complements this picture, telling us that Mary was the creature who was closest to the mystery of Christ, since she alone gave him his humanity and shared most fully in his Cross. Mary is the Mother of Sorrows, who suffered as no one else in the world suffered, and thus became "our mother in the order of grace,"[99] inspiring compassion in us and at the same time encouraging us to be what we really are. When we see her suffer so much "with no wavering at the foot of the Cross,"[100] and realize that Jesus gives her to us: "Woman, behold your son. Son, behold your mother;"[101] when we consider "the loneliness of Our Lady with so much suffering and weariness," we can be sure that the Queen of Heaven, perfect and powerful as she is, knows our sufferings, since she brought us forth in pain, with a love inferior only to the love of God. She is the Virgin "who gave an example of that maternal love"[102] with which she is willing and able to come to our aid. "She cares with a mother's love for the brothers of her Son who are still on their pilgrimage, surrounded by dangers and difficulties."[103] For that reason, she is a sign of hope and consolation, and so in our difficulties the cry that is forced from us is, "Show thyself our mother."[104]

This spirit of sonship, like that of a child with its mother, is a characteristic of Ignatius. It was this same spirit that made him see himself as "an unworthy little servant" of Mary in Bethlehem, that made him feel, when he failed in something, "a certain shame or something like it before the Mother of God," as he says several times in his *Spiritual Diary*: "I imagined being in the presence of Our Lady, and realized how serious had been my fault of the other

---

97. Ibid., no. 66.

98. Leo XIII, *Diuturni temporis*, in *Acta Apostolicae Sedis* 31 (1898–99), 146–47.

99. Vatican II, Dogmatic Constitution *Lumen gentium*, no. 61.

100. Ibid., no.62.

101. John 19:26–27.

102. Ignatius of Loyola, *Spiritual Exercises*, no. 208

103. Vatican II, Dogmatic Constitution *Lumen gentium*, no. 65.

104. Hymn *Ave Maris Stella*.

day, not without some interior distress and tears, since it seemed that I was in disgrace with Our Lady who prayed for me so often, after my many failings, so much so that she hid herself from me, and I found no devotion either in her or from on high." "As I was praying to the Son to help me with the Father in company with his Mother, I felt within me an impulse to go before the Father, and in this motion I felt my hair stand on end, and also a very noticeable burning in my whole body, and following upon this tears and devotion at Mass."[105]

The Jesuit continues to look for help and protection from Mary as mother, just as Ignatius himself hoped and desired: "May it please Our Lady to intercede between us sinners and her Son and Lord, and obtain for us that with the co-operation of our own toil and effort she may change our weak and sorry spirits and make them strong and joyful to praise God."[106]

Pedro Arrupe, SJ
Superior General of the Society of Jesus

---

105. Ignatius of Loyola, *Spiritual Diary*, nos. 14 and 7.
106. Letter, December 6, 1524, in *San Ignatii de Loyola epistolae et instructiones*, Monumenta Ignatiana, series prima, 1(Madrid, 1903), 72.

Saint Joseph, Spouse of the Blessed Virgin Mary

PATRON SAINT OF THE SOCIETY OF JESUS

Solemnity on March 19

Saint Joseph has given rise to a prodigious hagiography. The conditions are ideal: the written account of him is sparse, and there are no other historical data. At the same time, he could hardly have been closer to Our Lord and his Blessed Mother, and as a man he gives a very particular profile to the universal figures of husband, father, and worker. All of which explains his emergence as an inspiring and instructive model, in addition to being a reliable intercessor.

The Jesuits in particular rejoice to have Saint Joseph as their patron. He is the servant of Christ's mission *par excellence*, playing an indispensable supportive role in the history of salvation, with his great faith and love "shown more in deeds than in words." Vowed to obedience, the Jesuits find guidance in Saint Joseph's total acceptance of the difficult mission asked of him by God. And with his fundamental virtues, he inspires the whole Ignatian family across its myriad specific apostolates, ministries, and tasks.

"Dreams Take Us Further"

We can imagine Joseph as a good, upright man leading a laudable, if unremarkable life, just prior to the moment when he enters the Gospel story. What would be the ordinary dreams of this ordinary man who just happened to be of the house and family of David (Lk. 2:4)? He would have aspired to religious fidelity and to human fulfillment by being of good character, competent in his trade, and matched with a good spouse. He would have hoped to have a family that enjoyed good health, avoided accidents and political turmoil, and was valued by the community. For his old age, he would have hoped to leave his earthly life without great suffering and confident that his widow would be cared for and his children's children would prosper. Such are the dreams of an "ordinary Joe," so to speak.

But life took an extraordinary turn for this Joseph who proved sufficiently sensitive to apprehend difficult visions and dreams and obey them.

We first meet Joseph as a disappointed fiancé who hears from an angel of the Lord in a dream: "Joseph, son of David, do not be afraid to take Mary your wife into your home. For it is through the Holy Spirit that this child has been conceived in her. She will bear a son, and you are to name him Jesus, because he will save his people from their sins" (Mt. 1:20–21). What faith, humility, and courage it must have taken to obey. We can imagine him thinking, like Mary, "May it be done to me according to your word" (Lk. 1:38). In his Apostolic Exhortation *Redemptoris custos*, Pope Saint John Paul II affirms "that Joseph is the first to share in the faith of the Mother of God."

Thus originates the portrait of Joseph as a protector. First, he protected the young woman who would otherwise be subject to great shame, condemnation, and even stoning by her community. Then of course, as protector of his little family, he abandoned his established life and instead of returning to his hometown and resuming his livelihood after the birth of our Savior, he fled with Jesus and Mary to Egypt. Again, it is an angel of the Lord who warns in a dream: "Rise, take the child and his mother, flee to Egypt, and stay there until I tell you. Herod is going to search for the child to destroy him" (Mt. 2:13–14). This harrowing episode was reflected in Pope Francis's chosen theme for the 2020 World Day of Migrants and Refugees: "Forced like Jesus Christ to flee."

After that, more dreams: first with the message that it was safe to return from Egypt because Herod had died (Mt. 2:20); then, more perplexingly, that rather than re-establish in Bethlehem—there might still be danger because Judea was ruled by Archelaus, the violent son of Herod—he must make their home in Galilee (Mt. 2:22).

Joseph is a man of dreams! As Pope Francis explained to young people in Rome on August 11, 2018, "dreams are important. They keep our eyes wide open, they help us to embrace the horizon, to cultivate hope in all daily action ... Dreams awaken us, take us further, they are the most luminous stars, the ones that indicate a different path for humanity ..."

So it was by paying attention to his dreams that Joseph managed to keep Jesus out of harm's way, to make it so that he was known as a Nazarene (Mt.

Pietro Annigoni, Saint Joseph the carpenter teaches the trade to Jesus (1964).

2:23), growing up not near or in the glorious ghetto of Jerusalem but rather in Galilee of the nations (Is. 9:1, Mt. 4:15).

Teaching Jesus the Basics

Saint Joseph as protector is central to the thoughts of Pope Francis. When in 1992 Jorge Mario Bergoglio became an auxiliary bishop, he included the spikenard, the emblem of Saint Joseph, on his coat of arms. Then, in 2013, one of his first pontifical acts was to have Joseph's name follow that of Mary in all the Eucharistic prayers of the Latin rite.

On March 19, 2013, when Francis took up the Petrine ministry, he spoke about Joseph exercising his role as head of the Holy Family "discreetly, humbly, and silently, but with an unfailing presence and utter fidelity, even when he finds it hard to understand." His ability "to hear God's voice and be guided by his will" makes him "all the more sensitive to the persons entrusted to his safekeeping. From the time of his betrothal to Mary until the finding of the twelve-year-old Jesus in the Temple of Jerusalem, he is there at every moment with loving care. As the spouse of Mary, he is at her side in good times and bad, on the journey to Bethlehem for the census and in the anxious and joyful hours when she gave birth; amid the drama of the flight into Egypt and during the frantic search for their child in the Temple; and later in the day-to-day life of the home of Nazareth, in the workshop where he taught his trade to Jesus."

Notice that Pope Francis has added "teacher" to the role of Joseph. We can imagine Jesus learning the basics—proper use and care of tools, respect for materials, and "Measure twice, cut once"—in the workshop. And Joseph would have taught Jesus to do his chores properly, willingly and punctually, because this would create a more pleasant "common home" for the whole family.

Moreover, there was more to be learned outside the home and workshop. It is quite possible that Joseph settled in Nazareth because, six kilometers to the north west, Herod Antipas was rebuilding Diocaesarea (Sepphoris or Zippori) as the new capital of Galilee. Joseph would have gotten good work there, and Jesus, soon after the finding in the Temple (Lk. 2:51), would have begun accompanying Joseph, first as his helper, then as apprentice builder, and finally as his anticipated successor.

This could be how Jesus absorbed the practices and expectations of the world of work; lessons that would later bear fruit in parables about bosses and workers, fair payment, stewards, and shepherds. He would have learned that a house must be sited on firm ground, not sand. He would have witnessed people of different backgrounds working together, and the mingling of cultures themselves—Sepphoris was a place where Hellenistic culture and society were mingling with the Jewish. This may have led Jesus to make an outsider, a Samaritan, the exemplar of "neighbor" in his singular teaching about active goodness. For all of this exposure, we can credit Joseph as the faithful, protective earthly father to Jesus. And we can also observe that Jesus was acculturated not only as a Jew, but also as a very young child among Egyptians and later, as an adolescent and young adult, in a cosmopolitan crossroads of cultures.

"Protect One Another, Keep Watch Over Ourselves"

Later in his inaugural homily, Pope Francis lists other forms of protection: "The vocation of being a protector ... means protecting all creation, the beauty of the created world ... It means respecting each of God's creatures and respecting the environment in which we live. It means protecting people, showing loving concern for each and every person, especially children, the elderly, those in need, who are often the last we think about. It means caring for one another in our families: husbands and wives first protect one another, and then, as parents, they care for their children, and children themselves, in time, protect their parents. It means building sincere friendships in which we protect one another in trust, respect, and goodness." And finally, "We also have to keep watch over ourselves! Let us not forget that hatred, envy, and pride defile our lives! Being protectors, then, also means keeping watch over our emotions, over our hearts, because they are the seat of good and evil intentions: intentions that build up and tear down! We must not be afraid of goodness or even tenderness!"

Saint Joseph is the patron saint and protector of the universal Church, and the patron saint of workers. He is venerated in the Catholic and Orthodox Churches of East and West, as well as in the Anglican and Lutheran Churches.

With the feasts of January 3, the Most Holy Name of Jesus, and of April 22, Mary as Mother of the Society of Jesus, the patronal feast of Saint Joseph on

March 19 combine to ensure that the entire Holy Family is actively implicated in this "least Society" and quietly invite the Jesuits and their collaborators to reciprocate.

Cardinal Michael Czerny, SJ and Mr. Robert Czerny

All Saints' Day of the Society of Jesus

Feast on November 5

"Abide in me as I abide in you. Those who abide in me and I in them bear much fruit" (Jn. 15:4a,5b). This Gospel call expresses the central purpose of the feast of All Saints of the Society of Jesus: to help us to have a deeper bond with the Lord, so that our lives may bear fruit. Looking at the lives of holy women and men should help us see more clearly how much the witness of faith and spiritual fruitfulness depend on a lived relationship with Jesus Christ. Their lives should encourage us to follow the example of their faith and entrust us with their intercession.

God Calls, We Answer

The feast first of all reminds us in general terms of our baptism and the universal call to holiness—a holiness that consists in perfect union with Christ. However, we cannot do this on our own, but it is rather a product of God's grace at work in us human beings. God wants to give this to us and make us "new people," but it depends on us, whether we are open to it and respond to his call. God created us as his "image" and called us to follow his Son, so that through our relationship with him we can gain a deeper inner knowledge of Christ, experience his love, and be transformed and sanctified by him through him.

God, who has appointed us to "participate in the nature and form of his Son" (Rom. 8:29), comes to our aid in the saints and shows us in their lives "in a living way his presence and face. In them he himself speaks to us and gives us a sign of his kingdom, to which we are mightily drawn, surrounded by such a great cloud of witnesses, and in the face of such testimony of the truth of the Gospel" (*Lumen gentium, 50*).

The saints are people who not only imitated Christ superficially and followed him, but who truly took up residence with him and were entirely with him. They have made themselves his disciples and learned from him. This inner connection with Jesus Christ made them more and more like him and made them a sign of God's presence among men.

Our answer, therefore, can only be to thank the Lord again and again for these sisters and brothers, friends and co-heirs of Christ filled with the Spirit of God (cf. Rom. 8:12–17), to look at their example, "to call them for help, and to take refuge in their prayers, for their mighty help, to implore benefits from God through his Son Jesus Christ, who alone is our Redeemer and Savior" (*LG*, 50).

Examples

In addition to this general invitation to worship the saints, this proper feast invites the Society of Jesus to look at the saints, above all with Ignatius and in the spirit of his retreat, in order to challenge us while we are at the same time encouraged by God's actions in them. It is precisely being attentive to the gradual change in Ignatius's relationship with the saints that can help us to better understand the distinctive and deeper meaning of this feast of the "All Saints of the Society of Jesus."

Ignatius professed his devotion to the saints from a young age, and he "always had a special devotion to Saint Peter" (*Autobiography*, 3). For him, the saints were role models that he wanted to imitate or even surpass. As a "man of action" (cf. *Autobiography*, 1), in the sick room of Loyola he was initially only interested in the "doing" of the saints, but he hardly saw the work of God behind it. The saints remained "human role models" and "leading figures" for Ignatius but were not yet perceived by him as "signs" and "witnesses" of God's act of grace.

The comparison with the saints led him gradually to the realization that he could only imitate them with the "grace of God," but it was only the crisis in Manresa that called into question the false trust in his own actions and gave him a "feeling for God's work" (*Autobiography*, 14). The spiritual experiences made there ushered in a significant change in his devotion to the saints: he was no longer moved so much by their being "human models" but above all by God's actions in them. For Ignatius, the saints became "examples of divine action" and thus also an orientation for his own life, but the real "model" for his behavior became more and more Jesus Christ.

This increased focus on Jesus Christ as his "teacher and master" (*Autobiography*, 75) meant that Ignatius no longer looked so much at the apostles' actions, but rather at their "being sent by Christ," which became an example for him. With this in mind, he invites us in the *Spiritual Exercises* to "consider how the Lord of the whole world chooses so many persons, apostles, disciples, etc. and sends them out throughout the world, so that they may spread his sacred doctrine to all the persons of all conditions and circumstances" (*Spir. Ex.*, 145); he wants us all to be sent by the Lord as witnesses of his Good News.

Advocates

The growing sensitivity to God's ministry not only changed Ignatius's way of seeing the saints as a "model" but through the more deeply recognized connection with God, they also became more and more for him his "intercessors" with God, whose intercession he recommended. In order to learn more about the love of God, he invites us in retreat to "see how I stand before God our Lord, before the angels, before the saints who intercede for me" (*Spir. Ex.*, 232).

The request for intercession had particular weight for Ignatius when it came to decisions and important choices for life—as in the vows he made before "the whole heavenly court" (*Constitutions*, 527). The offer of one's own life in the contemplation of the king's call "in the presence of your glorious mother and all the holy men and women of the heavenly court" (*Spir. Ex.*, 98) does not come solely from wanting to have the saints as witnesses of this promise, but above all is a request for their help and intercession.

Ignatius's plea for their intercession, however, not only expresses trust in the saints, but also his trust in God, who uses the saints as his "tools" and helpers to build his kingdom. In this way, however, they also become a "model" for the vocation Ignatius owned: to be unreservedly available to God and to become a "tool in his hand." Thus Ignatius learned that it is not the "external imitation" of the saints that leads to the goal, but the trust in God. It is precisely in this that the saints are "models" for him that must be "imitated"—in faith and in devotion. And because Ignatius had realized that he was not able to do so on his own, he increasingly confided in the saints' "intercession."

"Let us praise the glorious men and our fathers of their generation. Ignatius, Stanislaus Kostka, Aloysius Gonzaga, and Francis Xavier adore Christ on the cross, who says to them: "I am the true vine, and you are the branches" (Jn. 15:5). Engraving by Hieronymus Wierix (circa 1610).

Connectedness

With the feast of "All Saints of the Society of Jesus" the change of Ignatius in his relationship with the saints reflected that we stand not before individual canonized saints but rather before "the entire heavenly court." We are invited to look gratefully at our calling as a graceful affiliation with this "community with Christ in heaven. For in him God chose us before the creation of the world, that we may live holy and blameless before him" (cf. Eph 1:3–4). It is precisely through the often unnoticed "saints of everyday life" that God shows us his closeness. He shows us that he also wants to "make his home" among us (cf. *Spir. Ex.*, 235) and to "sanctify" us in the same way through his love.

The feast invites us to remember in particular the people through whom God led us on the path of our vocation, thus helping us to truly live out the spirit of the Exercises and to constantly seek to re-invigorate our relationship with Jesus Christ, as Paul exclaims: "I want to know Christ and the power of his resurrection and communion with his sufferings; his death is supposed to shape me. Thus I hope to come also to the resurrection from the dead" (Phil. 3:10–11; cf. *Spir. Ex.*, 104).

We are on our way to this goal: we have not yet achieved it but can only "strive to seize it" (Phil. 3:12). The grateful memory of the people, women and men, who have accompanied us on our journey as role models should help us to remember the lasting closeness of God and to continue to strive with confidence in the Lord to deepen our vocation. Knowing our limitations and weaknesses, we call on these saints at the same time to intercede for us, that we do not lose sight of the goal of our "heavenly vocation which God gives us in Christ Jesus" (cf. Phil. 3:14).

At their intercession, we can hope that, like the many "saints of the Society of Jesus," a deep attachment to Christ will give us that inner freedom that enables us to give our lives and, like the grain of wheat, to fall into the earth and die and to bear rich fruit (cf. Jn. 12:24).

Toni Witwer, SJ[107]

---

107. Translation by Patrick Burns, SJ.

A Re-reading by Way of Conclusion

We have come to the end of a five-century overview of the history of the Society of Jesus, as seen through the lives of more than two hundred of its members, canonized or beatified by the Church. Only about fifty of them could be presented here; they represent the others, too.

HISTORICAL RE-READING

Why a Progressive Rarefaction of Jesuit Saints?

A statistically minded observer will note that most of the "confessors" or non-martyrs (thirteen out of twenty) lived in the first century of the Society's existence: the second half of the sixteenth century and the first half of the seventeenth. The next fifty years added its share of saints and blessed. But the eighteenth and the first half of the nineteenth centuries, which includes the forty years of the order's suppression, are characterized by a kind of void of non-martyr saints and blessed, with only two confessors, namely Bernardo de Hoyos and Joseph Pignatelli. A minor reprisal can be noted in the twentieth century. Does this mean that the original Jesuit charism, so fertile in the beginning, gradually lost its force? Or that the Society, after the experience of the suppression, had become more modest and less prone to propose its saintly members for canonization? The two reasons are not mutually exclusive.

If we look at the martyrs, who constitute the vast majority of the saints and blessed, we note again a near absence during the eighteenth and most of the nineteenth centuries, with one notable exception during the period of the suppression: the twenty-five former Jesuits who gave their lives during the French Revolution (in Paris in 1792 and near Rochefort in 1794) out of fidelity to the Church and the pope. This fidelity was all the more remarkable, given that their order had been suppressed by the pope some twenty years earlier.

Why So Many Martyrs?

The martyrs of the old Society came from two different contexts. The first, European, was that of the divisions between Christians, especially in Great Britain, but also in France, the present Slovakia, and Poland. The other context was that of the foreign missions, from Asia to the Americas and Oceania, where missionaries fell victim to the violent rejection of the Christian faith by the indigenous people anxious to defend their cultural and religious traditions.

We have seen that the political and the religious domain are often intertwined. The missionaries were driven by a passionate desire to proclaim Jesus Christ, but they arrived on ships of Portuguese, Spanish, or French merchants, and were often perceived by the indigenous people as collaborators of their oppressors. Thus, the martyrs of Salcete, India, were massacred by the inhabitants of a village when they set up a cross on the site of the village temple that had been destroyed by Portuguese soldiers a few years earlier. In Japan, the emperors saw how Manila, converted to Christianity, fell under Spanish rule from 1571; they, too, became ever more hostile toward the foreign faith. In the decree with which he expelled the Christians, Emperor Hideyoshi wrote: "The *Kirishitan* [Christians] came to Japan not only sending merchant ships to exchange goods, but also desirous to disseminate an evil law, to overthrow the true doctrine, so that they can change the country's government and take over the land."

Another striking case of mixed motivations, this time in the context of divisions between Christians, is that of the martyrdom of Ignatius de Azevedo. On his way to Brazil with thirty-nine companions, they were killed and thrown into the sea by the Calvinist privateer Jacques de Sores. The latter took revenge for the destruction of a Calvinist outpost in North America, carried out five years earlier in a rather brutal fashion by the Spanish military. French missionaries in Canada were also caught up in complex conflicts, becoming enemies of the Iroquois (allied with the English and the Dutch) while making friends with the Hurons. It was amidst these troubled dynamics of colonization that the Jesuits (along with many other religious, notably the Franciscans) gave their lives for the faith in Christ and his Church. They died "in hatred of the faith," even if it was also in hatred of many other things ...

Martyrdom Always New

The greater part of Jesuit martyrs lived and died in the second half of the sixteenth and seventeenth centuries. But as we saw, "modern" times also had their martyrs—witnesses of Christ who courageously confronted totalitarian regimes based on ideologies that were profoundly alien to Christianity. Today, in the twenty-first century, with religious tolerance becoming the norm in most of the world, is the age of martyrdom over? It is not, as we all know. Whoever chooses to be present where there is poverty, hatred, and violence, to be a worker of justice and peace on the side of the victims, runs the risk of being persecuted and murdered. Several Jesuit companions gave their lives defending the oppressed, remaining with the poor whom they served in zones of conflict. One of the most recent examples is Frans van der Lugt, a Dutch Jesuit who chose to stay with the people he served in Homs, Syria, and who was killed on April 7, 2014. In 2019, the process to canonize him has been initiated. His was an option of solidarity, even to the point of bloodshed. To understand this, another point of view is necessary, which can be described as mystical.

A MYSTICAL RE-READING

The Society of Jesus was founded at a time when Europe was opening to humanity spread across the newly discovered world. Ignatius sent Francis Xavier on mission to India when the Church had not yet recognized the order. From then on, many Jesuits burned with the desire to go to India, and later to Japan or New France, if possible to die there as a martyr. This was the case with John Francis Regis and many others. Thus, in the second half of the sixteenth and the first half of the seventeenth centuries, a mystical bond was created between those who remained in Europe and their companions who had gone far away, a bond similar to that between the martyrs of England and Wales and their Jesuit brethren on the continent. Upon learning that he had been sent on a dangerous mission to Aubenas in central France, the French Jesuit Jacques Salès kissed the relic of the English martyr Edmund Campion, which he always carried with him. The Jesuits of the time of the Reformation, in fact, often stood over against the Protestants, and many times they shed their blood in these conflicts, these wars of religion. But mark that in Germany or Switzerland, where the Society was very much active, none of its members suffered martyrdom. On the other hand, in England, Canada, Japan, and elsewhere, this inter-Christian antagonism would be a serious obstacle to their apostolate.

In England and in Japan, we find the same courage of these apostles of Christ. They wanted to remain with or return to the Catholic faithful at the risk of their lives, even though civil authorities had prohibited their presence under pain of death. Like the Good Shepherd, they could not resign themselves to abandon their sheep at the moment of danger. In return, in England as well as in Japan, a strange thing happened: lay collaborators and even diocesan priests asked their Jesuit fellow-prisoners to be allowed to join the Society of Jesus a few days before their death. This request speaks eloquently about how strongly united with the Jesuits they felt themselves to be.

Today's Christians are sometimes a bit embarrassed by the aspiration to martyrdom, so strong in not a few of these missionaries from the past. There is a mystical dimension in this imitation of Christ, in this wanting to share in his Passion so as to share in his glory, too, which has become, if not foreign to us, then at least "strange." Imagine the mother of John de Brito, who put on a festive dress when she learned of her son's martyrdom in India; or Isaac Jogues, who, faced with the chance to escape from his executioners, took a day of reflection to discern whether this was the will of God or not. Think of Ignatius de Azevedo facing the danger of the privateers and preferring the riskiest solution: "If the French take us, what harm can they do us? The most they can do is to send us to paradise quickly." These words seem suicidal to us ... Ours is a different mindset, but let us for a moment acknowledge theirs and feel its appeal. The aspiration of these martyrs is not different from that of the early second-century martyr Saint Ignatius of Antioch, a "folly" indeed, but a response to the love of "God's fool" Jesus Christ, who gave his life for us.

Men with a Passion for Christ

Confessors or martyrs, all these our elder brothers in Christ have a trait in common, a family trait one could say, namely the mark of the *Spiritual Exercises*. It is a personal and unconditional attachment to Christ, lived in a passionate service to his Church. Many of them, by word and deed, have rendered an eminent service, some as theologians, like Robert Bellarmine; others as apostles consolidating the Catholic faith in peril, like Peter Canisius in Germany; yet others as bearers of the Good News in distant lands, like Francis Xavier in Asia, José de Anchieta in Brazil, John de Brébeuf in Canada, John de Brito in India. Others again announced the Gospel to inhabitants of neglected villages and poor town districts in Europe, like Bernardine Realino in Italy, Julian Maunoir in France, Philipp Jeningen in Germany, and in our time Tiburcio Arnaiz in Spain. Others became true social apostles, like Rupert Mayer in Munich or Alberto Hurtado in Chile—a new form of apostolate in the Society of Jesus, yet in line with the creative and liberating dynamics of the Exercises. Some, like Alphonsus Rodríguez or John Sullivan, dedicated their entire lives to the colleges, which from the Society's start was one of the main loci of Jesuit ministry. Almost all our saints and blessed spent at least a few years in them during their formation period. Yet whatever their field of work, they all shared a sense of closeness to the poor and needy, which has intensified among Jesuits since the Thirty-Second General Congregation, with its option for "the service of faith, of which the promotion of justice is an absolute requirement."

Far from Any Form of Triumphalism

The pope's suppression of the Society of Jesus was and remains a great humiliation, inviting us to humbleness even more, given that apparently it did not arouse much protest from other religious orders. The constant decrease in number of members over the last sixty years, from thirty-six thousand to fewer than sixteen thousand, is another reason for the Society to be modest. Certainly, the history of the Jesuit missions is still something to admire and marvel about, with the epic travels of Francis Xavier, the reductions in South America made famous again by the movie *The Mission* (1986), the heroic evangelization of the Hurons in Canada, or the extraordinary cultural dialogue of the Servant of God Matteo Ricci and his companions in China. But history aside, what remains today of these impressive ventures? What has become of the indigenous people in the Americas? Did the vast majority of Asians not remain impervious to Christianity? As for Europe, the Jesuits moved from fighting Protestantism to engaging in ecumenical dialogue.

Our re-reading is conscious of the context of violence in which the evangelization of the "new world" took place from the sixteenth century onward, of the failures, the missed opportunities, the disputes with deplorable effects.

Yet one cannot help but recognize the power of grace at work in the lives of these saints and blessed of the Society of Jesus. In the midst of complex and ambiguous situations, with their personal limits and weaknesses, these men proclaimed Jesus Christ in their words and deeds, in a way that the Church has judged to be exemplary and that touches us profoundly.

A PERSONAL RE-READING

At the end, the reader is invited to make an exercise dear to Saint Ignatius, namely a personal re-reading, the most important one. What fruit have I gained from this journey? Which saint attracted me more? By what trait of his personality, of his way of proceeding? What desires did reading these profiles awaken in me? How would I myself now like to become more engaged in God's service, after the example of these elder brothers in Christ, to respond to the call of this time and age? Taking a moment to answer these questions is worthwhile. In each of these men, God has something to say to us.

The saints and blessed are our brothers and "friends in the Lord." They pray for us, so that we may safely get through today's uncertainties; we entrust ourselves to their intercession. The history of the Jesuits is that of a fire communicated from one person to another: from Ignatius to Francis Xavier, from Peter Faber to Peter Canisius and Francis Borgia, from Robert Bellarmine to Aloysius Gonzaga, from Alphonsus Rodríguez to Peter Claver, but also from Rutilio Grande to Monsignor Óscar Romero. May this book contribute to the spreading of this fire.

Saints and blessed of the Society of Jesus, pray for us!

Jacques Fedry, SJ[108]

---

108. Translation by Marc Lindeijer, SJ.

Society of Jesus Proper Calendar

JANUARY

3   THE MOST HOLY NAME OF JESUS
    Titular Feast of the Society *SOLEMNITY*
19 Saint John Ogilvie, Priest
    Saints Stephen Pongrácz, Melchior Grodziecki, Priests,
    and Mark of Križevci, Canon of Esztergom
    Blessed Ignatius de Azevedo, Priest, and Companions
    Blessed James Salès, Priest, and Guillaume Saultemouche, Religious,
      Martyrs

FEBRUARY

4   Saint John de Brito, Priest
    Blessed Rudolph Acquaviva, Priest, and Companions, Martyrs
6   Saint Paul Miki, Religious, and Companions
    Blessed Charles Spinola, Sebastian Kimura, Priests, and
    Companions, Martyrs *MEMORIAL*
15 Saint Claude La Colombière, Priest *MEMORIAL*

MARCH

19 SAINT JOSEPH, SPOUSE OF THE BLESSED VIRGIN MARY,
    Patron Saint of the Society of Jesus *SOLEMNITY*

APRIL

22 THE BLESSED VIRGIN MARY, MOTHER OF THE SOCIETY OF JESUS *FEAST*
27 Saint Peter Canisius, Priest and Doctor of the Church *MEMORIAL*

MAY

4   Saint José Maria Rubio, Priest
8   Blessed John Sullivan, Priest
16 Saint Andrew Bobola, Priest and Martyr
24 Our Lady of the Way

JUNE

8   Saint James Berthieu, Priest and Martyr *MEMORIAL*
9   Saint Joseph de Anchieta, Priest
21 Saint Aloysius Gonzaga, Religious *MEMORIAL*

JULY

2   Saint Bernardine Realino
    Saint John Francis Regis
    Saint Francis Jerome
    Blessed Julian Maunoir
    Blessed Anthony Baldinucci
    Blessed Tiburcio Arnáiz, Priests
    Blessed Philipp Jeningen
9   Saints Leo Ignatius Mangin, Priest, Mary Zhu-Wu, and Companions, Martyrs *MEMORIAL*
31 SAINT IGNATIUS OF LOYOLA, Priest and Founder of the Society of Jesus
    SOLEMNITY

AUGUST

2   Saint Peter Faber, Priest
18 Saint Alberto Hurtado Cruchaga, Priest *MEMORIAL*

SEPTEMBER

2   Blessed James Bonnaud, Priest, and Companions; Joseph Imbert and John Nicolas Cordier, Priests
    Blessed Thomas Sitjar, Priest, and Companions
    Blessed John Fausti and Companions, Martyrs

9 Saint Peter Claver, Priest MEMORIAL
10 Blessed Francis Gárate, Religious
17 Saint Robert Bellarmine, Bishop and Doctor of the Church MEMORIAL

OCTOBER

3 Saint Francis Borgia, Priest MEMORIAL
12 Blessed Jan Beyzym, Priest
19 Saints John de Brébeuf, Isaac Jogues, Priests, and Companions,
  Martyrs MEMORIAL *(in the United States, celebrated as a FEAST)*
21 Blessed Diego Luis de San Vitores, Priest, and Saint Pedro Calungsod,
  Martyrs
30 Blessed Dominic Collins, Religious and Martyr
31 Saint Alphonsus Rodríguez, Religious MEMORIAL

NOVEMBER

3 Blessed Rupert Mayer, Priest
5 ALL SAINTS OF THE SOCIETY OF JESUS FEAST
6 Commemoration of All the Departed of the Society of Jesus
13 Saint Stanislaus Kostka, Religious MEMORIAL
14 Saint Joseph Pignatelli, Priest MEMORIAL
16 Saints Roch González, Alphonsus Rodríguez, and John del Castillo, Priests
  and Martyrs
23 Blessed Miguel Pro and Emilio Moscoso, Priests and Martyrs
  Blessed Rutilio Grande
26 Saint John Berchmans, Religious MEMORIAL
29 Blessed Bernardo Francis de Hoyos, Priest

DECEMBER

1 Saints Edmund Campion, and Robert Southwell, Priests, and Companions,
  Martyrs MEMORIAL
3 SAINT FRANCIS XAVIER, PRIEST FEAST